# THE GREAT GOD BROWN

*and*

# LAZARUS LAUGHED

# The Great God Brown
## and
# Lazarus Laughed

*by*

# Eugene O'Neill

Jonathan Cape Ltd
Thirty Bedford Square London

*THE GREAT GOD BROWN*

with

*The Fountain*
*The Dreamy Kid*
*Before Breakfast*

FIRST PUBLISHED 1926

★

*LAZARUS LAUGHED*

and

*DYNAMO*

FIRST PUBLISHED 1929

★

THESE PLAYS FIRST ISSUED IN ONE VOLUME
1960

PRINTED IN GREAT BRITAIN BY BUTLER & TANNER LTD
FROME AND LONDON

# Contents

Contents

# The Great God Brown

# Characters

WILLIAM A. BROWN
HIS FATHER, *a contractor*
HIS MOTHER
DION ANTHONY
HIS FATHER, *a builder*
HIS MOTHER
MARGARET
HER THREE SONS
CYBEL
TWO DRAUGHTSMEN ⎫
A STENOGRAPHER ⎭ *in Brown's office*

# Scenes

## PROLOGUE

The Pier of the Casino. Moonlight in middle June.

## ACT ONE

SCENE I: Sitting-room, Margaret Anthony's apartment. Afternoon, seven years later.

SCENE II: Billy Brown's office. The same afternoon.

SCENE III: Cybel's parlour. That night.

## ACT TWO

SCENE I: Cybel's parlour. Seven years later. Dusk.

SCENE II: Drafting-room, William A. Brown's office. That evening.

SCENE III: Library, William A. Brown's home. That night.

## ACT THREE

SCENE I: Brown's office, a month later. Morning.

SCENE II: Library, Brown's home. That evening.

SCENE III: Sitting-room, Margaret's home. That night.

# THE GREAT GOD BROWN
## ACT FOUR

## EPILOGUE

# The Great God Brown

## PROLOGUE

SCENE. *A cross-section of the pier of the Casino. In the rear, built out beyond the edge, is a rectangular space with benches on the three sides. A rail encloses the entire wharf at the back.*

*It is a moonlight night in mid-June. From the Casino comes the sound of the school quartet rendering "Sweet Adeline" with many ultra-sentimental quavers. There is a faint echo of the ensuing hand-clapping — then nothing but the lapping of ripples against the piles and their swishing on the beach — then footsteps on the boards and Billy Brown walks along from right with his mother and father. The mother is a dumpy woman of forty-five, overdressed in black lace and spangles. The father is fifty or more, the type of bustling, genial, successful, provincial business man, stout and hearty in his evening dress.*

*Billy Brown is a handsome, tall and athletic boy of nearly eighteen. He is blond and blue-eyed, with a likeable smile and a frank good-humoured face, its expression already indicating a disciplined restraint. His manner has the easy self-assurance of a normal intelligence. He is in evening dress.*

*They walk arm in arm, the mother between.*

7

MOTHER (*always addressing the father*). This Commencement dance is badly managed. Such singing! Such poor voices! Why doesn't Billy sing?

BILLY (*to her*). Mine is a regular fog horn ! (*He laughs.*)

MOTHER (*to the air*). I had a pretty voice, when I was a girl. (*Then, to the father, caustically.*) Did you see young Anthony strutting around the ball-room in dirty flannel trousers?

FATHER. He's just showing off.

MOTHER. Such impudence! He's as ignorant as his father.

FATHER. The old man's all right. My only kick against him is he's been too damned conservative to let me branch out.

MOTHER (*bitterly*). He has kept you down to his level – out of pure jealousy.

FATHER. But he took me into partnership, don't forget –

MOTHER (*sharply*). Because you were the brains! Because he was afraid of losing you! (*A pause.*)

BILLY (*admiringly*). Dion came in his old clothes for a bet with me. He's a real sport. He wouldn't have been afraid to appear in his pyjamas! (*He grins with appreciation.*)

MOTHER. Isn't the moonlight clear! (*She goes and sits on the centre bench. Billy stands at the left corner, forward, his hand on the rail, like a prisoner at the bar, facing the judge. His father stands in front of the bench on right. The mother announces, with finality.*) After he's through college, Billy must study for a profession of some sort, I'm determined on that! (*She turns to her husband, defiantly, as if expecting opposition.*)

FATHER (*eagerly and placatingly*). Just what I've been thinking, my dear. Architecture! How's that? Billy a first-rate number-one architect! That's my proposition! What I've always wished I could have been myself. Only I never had the opportunity. But Billy — we'll make him a partner in the firm after. Anthony, Brown *and Son, architects* and builders — instead of *contractors* and builders!

MOTHER (*yearning for the realization of a dream*). And we won't lay sidewalks — or dig sewers — ever again?

FATHER (*a bit ruffled*). I and Anthony can build anything your pet can draw — even if it's a church. (*Then, selling his idea.*) It's a great chance for him! He'll design — expand us — make the firm famous.

MOTHER (*to the air — musingly*). When you proposed, I thought your future promised success — my future — (*with a sigh*) — Well, I suppose we've been comfortable. Now, it's his future. How would Billy like to be an architect? (*She does not look at him.*)

9

BILLY (*to her*). All right, Mother. (*Then sheepishly.*) I guess I've never bothered much about what I'd like to do after college — but architecture sounds all right to me, I guess.

MOTHER (*to the air — proudly*). Billy used to draw houses when he was little.

FATHER (*jubilantly.*) Billy's got the stuff in him to win, if he'll only work hard enough.

BILLY (*dutifully*). I'll work hard, Dad.

MOTHER. Billy can do anything!

BILLY (*embarrassed*). I'll try, Mother. (*There is a pause.*)

MOTHER (*with a sudden shiver*). The nights are so much colder than they used to be! Think of it, I once went moonlight bathing in June when I was a girl — but the moonlight was so warm and beautiful in those days, do you remember, Father?

FATHER (*puts his arm around her affectionately*). You bet I do, Mother. (*He kisses her. The orchestra at the Casino strikes up a waltz.*) There's the music. Let's go back and watch the young folks dance. (*They start off, leaving Billy standing there.*)

MOTHER (*suddenly calls back over her shoulder*). I want to watch Billy dance.

BILLY (*dutifully*). Yes, Mother!

(*He follows them. For a moment the faint sound of the music and the lapping of waves is heard. Then footsteps again and the three Anthonys come in. First come the father and mother, who are not masked. The father is a tall lean man of fifty-five or sixty, with a grim, defensive face, obstinate to the point of stupid weakness. The mother is a thin, frail, faded woman, her manner perpetually nervous and distraught, but with a sweet and gentle face that had once been beautiful. The father wears an ill-fitting black suit, like a mourner. The mother wears a cheap, plain, black dress. Following them, as if he were a stranger, walking alone, is their son, Dion. He is about the same height as young Brown, but lean and wiry, without repose, continually in restless nervous movement. His face is masked. The mask is a fixed forcing of his own face — dark, spiritual, poetic, passionately supersensitive, helplessly unprotected in its childlike, religious faith in life — into the expression of a mocking, reckless, defiant, gaily scoffing and sensual young Pan. He is dressed in a grey flannel shirt, open at the neck, rubber-soled shoes over bare feet, and soiled white flannel trousers. The father strides to the centre bench and sits down. The mother, who has been holding to his arm, lets go and stands by the*

> *bench at the right. They both stare at
> Dion, who, with a studied carelessness,
> takes his place at the rail, where
> young Brown had stood. They watch
> him, with queer, puzzled eyes.)*

MOTHER (*suddenly – pleading*). You simply must send him to college.

FATHER. I won't. I don't believe in it. Colleges turn out lazy loafers to sponge on their poor old fathers! Let him slave like I had to! That'll teach him the value of a dollar! College'll only make him a bigger fool than he is already! I never got above grammar school but I've made money and established a sound business. Let him make a man out of himself like I made of myself!

DION (*mockingly – to the air*). This Mr. Anthony is my father, but he only imagines he is God the Father. (*They both stare at him.*)

FATHER (*with angry bewilderment*). What – what – what's that?

MOTHER (*gently remonstrating to her son*). Dion, dear! (*Then to her husband – tauntingly*). Brown takes all the credit! He tells every one the success is all due to his energy – that you're only an old stick-in-the-mud!

FATHER (*stung, harshly*). The damn fool! He knows better'n anyone if I hadn't held him down to common sense, with his crazy wild-cat notions, he'd have had us ruined long ago!

MOTHER. He's sending Billy to college – Mrs. Brown just told me – going to have him study architecture afterwards, too, so's he can help expand your firm!

FATHER (*angrily*). What's that? (*Suddenly turns on Dion furiously.*) Then you can make up your mind to go too! And you'll learn to be a better architect than Brown's boy or I'll turn you out in the gutter without a penny! You hear?

DION (*mockingly – to the air*). It's difficult to choose – but architecture sounds less laborious.

MOTHER (*fondly*). You ought to make a wonderful architect, Dion. You've always painted pictures so well –

DION (*with a start – resentfully*). Why must she lie? Is it my fault? She knows I only try to paint. (*Passionately.*) But I will, some day! (*Then quickly, mocking again.*) On to college! Well, it won't be home, anyway, will it? (*He laughs queerly and approaches them. His father gets up defensively. Dion bows to him.*) I thank Mr. Anthony for this splendid opportunity to create myself – (*He kisses his mother, who bows with a strange humility as if she were a servant being saluted by the young master – then adds lightly*) – in my mother's image, so she may feel her life comfortably concluded.

> (*He sits in his Father's place at centre and his mask stares with a frozen mockery before him. They stand on each side, looking dumbly at him.*)

MOTHER (*at last, with a shiver*). It's cold. June didn't use to be cold. I remember the June when I was carrying you, Dion – three months before you were born. (*She stares up at the sky.*) The moonlight was warm, then. I could feel the night wrapped around me like a grey velvet gown lined with warm sky and trimmed with silver leaves!

FATHER (*gruffly – but with a certain awe*). My mother used to believe the full of the moon was the time to sow. She was terrible old-fashioned. (*With a grunt.*) I can feel it's bringing on my rheumatism. Let's go back indoors.

DION (*with intense bitterness*). Hide! Be ashamed! (*They both start and stare at him.*)

FATHER (*with bitter hopelessness. To his wife – indicating their son*). Who is he? You bore him!

MOTHER (*proudly*). He's my boy! He's Dion!

DION (*bitterly resentful*). What else, indeed! The identical son. (*Then, mockingly.*) Are Mr. Anthony and his wife going in to dance! The nights grow cold! The days are dimmer than they used to be! Let's play hide-and-seek! Seek the monkey in the moon!

> (*He suddenly cuts a grotesque caper, like a harlequin, and darts off, laughing with forced abandon. They stare after him – then slowly follow. Again there is silence except for the sound of the lapping waves. Then Margaret comes in, fol-*

*lowed by the humbly worshipping Billy Brown. She is almost seventeen, pretty and vivacious, blonde, with big romantic eyes, her figure lithe and strong, her facial expression intelligent but youthfully dreamy, especially now in the moonlight. She is in a simple white dress. On her entrance, her face is masked with an exact, almost transparent reproduction of her own features, but giving her the abstract quality of a Girl instead of the individual Margaret.)*

MARGARET *(looking upward at the moon and singing in low tone as they enter).* " Ah, moon of my delight that knowest no wane!"

BILLY *(eagerly).* I've got that record – John McCormack. It's a peach! Sing some more. *(She looks upward in silence. He keeps standing respectfully behind her, glancing embarrassedly toward her averted face. He tries to make conversation.)* I think the *Rubáiyát's* great stuff, don't you? I never could memorize poetry worth a darn. Dion can recite lots of Shelley's poems by heart.

MARGARET *(slowly takes off her mask – to the moon).* Dion! *(A pause.)*

BILLY *(fidgeting).* Margaret!

MARGARET *(to the moon).* Dion is so wonderful!

BILLY *(blunderingly).* I asked you to come out here because I wanted to tell you something.

MARGARET (*to the moon*). Why did Dion look at me like that? It made me feel so crazy!

BILLY. I wanted to ask you something, too.

MARGARET. That one time he kissed me – I can't forget it! He was only joking – but I felt – and he saw and just laughed.

BILLY. Because that's the uncertain part. My end of it is a sure thing, and has been for a long time, and I guess everybody in town knows it – they're always kidding me – so it's a cinch you must know – how I feel about you.

MARGARET. Dion's so different from all the others. He can paint beautifully and write poetry and he plays and sings and dances so marvellously. But he's sad and shy, too, just like a baby sometimes, and he understands what I'm really like inside – and – and I'd love to run my fingers through his hair – and I love him! Yes, I love him! (*She stretches out her arms to the moon*). Oh, Dion, I love you!

BILLY. I love you, Margaret.

MARGARET. I wonder if Dion – I saw him looking at me again to-night – Oh, I wonder . . .!

BILLY (*takes her hand and blurts out*). Can't you love me? Won't you marry me – after college –

MARGARET. Where is Dion, now, I wonder?

BILLY (*shaking her hand in an agony of uncertainty*). Margaret! Please answer me!

MARGARET (*her dream broken, puts on her mask and turns to him — matter-of-factly*). It's getting chilly. Let's go back and dance, Billy.

BILLY (*desperately*). I love you! (*He tries clumsily to kiss her.*)

MARGARET (*with an amused laugh*). Like a brother! You can kiss me if you like. (*She kisses him.*) A big-brother kiss. It doesn't count. (*He steps back crushed, with head bowed. She turns away and takes off her mask — to the moon.*) I wish Dion would kiss me again!

BILLY (*painfully*). I'm a poor boob. I ought to know better. I'll bet I know. You're in love with Dion. I've seen you look at him. Isn't that it?

MARGARET. Dion! I love the sound of it!

BILLY (*huskily*). Well — he's always been my best friend — I'm glad it's him — and I guess I know how to lose — (*He takes her hand and shakes it*) — so here's wishing you all the success and happiness in the world, Margaret — and remember I'll always be your best friend! (*He gives her hand a final shake — swallows hard — then manfully.*) Let's go back in!

MARGARET (*to the moon — faintly annoyed*). What is Billy Brown doing here? I'll go down to the end of the dock and wait. Dion is the moon and I'm the sea. I want to feel the moon kissing the sea. I want Dion to leave the sky to me. I want the tides of my blood to leave my heart and follow

him! (*She whispers like a little girl.*) Dion!
Margaret! Peggy! Peggy is Dion's girl — Peggy
is Dion's little girl — (*She sings laughingly, elfishly.*)
Dion is my Daddy-O! (*She is walking toward the
end of the dock, off left.*)

BILLY (*who has turned away*). I'm going. I
tell Dion you're here.

MARGARET (*more and more strongly and assertively
until at the end she is a wife and a mother*). And I'll
be Mrs. Dion — Dion's wife — and he'll be my
Dion — my own Dion — my little boy — my baby!
The moon is drowned in the tides of my heart, and
peace sinks deep through the sea!

> (*She disappears off left, her upturned un-
> masked face like that of a rapturous
> visionary. There is silence again, in
> which the dance music is heard. Then
> this stops and Dion comes in. He walks
> quickly to the bench at centre, and throws
> himself on it, hiding his masked face in
> his hands. After a moment, he lifts his
> head, peers about, listens huntedly,
> then slowly takes off his mask. His real
> face is revealed in the bright moonlight,
> shrinking, shy and gentle, full of a deep
> sadness.*)

DION (*with a suffering bewilderment.*) Why am I
afraid to dance, I who love music and rhythm and
grace and song and laughter? Why am I afraid to
live, I who love life and the beauty of flesh and the

living colours of earth and sky and sea? Why am I afraid of love, I who love love? Why am I afraid, I who am not afraid? Why must I pretend to scorn in order to pity? Why must I hide myself in self-contempt in order to understand? Why must I be so ashamed of my strength, so proud of my weakness? Why must I live in a cage like a criminal, defying and hating, I who love peace and friendship? (*Clasping his hands above in supplication.*) Why was I born without a skin, O God, that I must wear armour in order to touch or to be touched?

(*A second's pause of waiting silence — then he suddenly claps his mask over his face again, with a gesture of despair, and his voice becomes bitter and sardonic.*) Or rather, Old Graybeard, why the devil was I ever born at all?

> (*Steps are heard from the right. Dion stiffens and his mask stares straight ahead. Billy comes in from the right. He is shuffling along disconsolately. When he sees Dion, he stops abruptly and glowers resentfully — but at once the "good loser" in him conquers this.*)

BILLY (*embarrassedly*). Hello, Dion. I've been looking all over for you. (*He sits down on the bench at right, forcing a joking tone.*) What are you sitting here for, you nut — trying to get more moon-struck? (*A pause — awkwardly.*) I just left Margaret —

19

DION (*gives a start — immediately defensively mocking*). Bless you, my children!

BILLY (*gruffly and slangily*). I'm out of it — she gave me the gate. You're the original white-haired boy. Go on in and win! We've been chums ever since we were kids, haven't we? — and — I'm glad it's you, Dion. (*This huskily — he fumbles for Dion's hand and gives it a shake.*)

DION (*letting his hand fall back — bitterly*). Chums? Oh no, Billy Brown would despise me!

BILLY. She's waiting for you now, down at the end of the dock.

DION. For me? Which? Who? Oh no, girls only allow themselves to look at what is seen!

BILLY. She's in love with you.

DION (*moved — a pause — stammers*). Miracle? I'm afraid! (*He chants flippantly.*) I love, thou lovest, he loves, she loves! She loves, she loves — what?

BILLY. And I know damn well, underneath your nuttiness, you're gone on her.

DION (*moved*). Underneath? I love love! I'd love to be loved! But I'm afraid! (*Then aggressively.*) *Was* afraid! Not now! Now I can make love — to anyone! Yes, I love Peggy! Why not? Who is she? Who am I? We love, you love, they love, one loves! No one loves! All the world loves a lover, God loves us all and we love Him! Love is a word — a shameless ragged ghost of a word – begging at all doors for life at any price!

BILLY (*always as if he hadn't listened to what the other said*). Say, let's you and me room together at college –

DION. Billy wants to remain by her side!

BILLY. It's a bet, then! (*Forcing a grin.*) You can tell her I'll see that you behave! (*Turns away.*) So long. Remember she's waiting. (*He goes.*)

DION (*dazedly, to himself*). Waiting – waiting for me! (*He slowly removes his mask. His face is torn and transfigured by joy. He stares at the sky raptly.*) O God in the moon, did you hear? She loves me! I am not afraid! I am strong! I can love! She protects me! Her arms are softly around me! She is warmly around me! She is my skin! She is my armour! Now I am born – I – the I! – one and indivisible – I who love Margaret! (*He glances at his mask triumphantly – in tones of deliverance.*) You are outgrown! I am beyond you! (*He stretches out his arms to the sky.*) O God, now I believe! (*From the end of the wharf, her voice is heard.*)

MARGARET. Dion!

DION (*raptly*). Margaret!

MARGARET (*nearer*). Dion!

DION. Margaret!

MARGARET. Dion! (*She comes running in, her*

*mask in her hands. He springs toward her with out-
stretched arms, but she shrinks away with a frightened
shriek and hastily puts on her mask. Dion starts back.
She speaks coldly and angrily.*) Who are you? Why
are you calling me? I don't know you!

DION (*heart-brokenly*). I love you!

MARGARET (*freezingly*). Is this a joke — or are
you drunk?

DION (*with a final pleading whisper*). Margaret!
(*But she only glares at him contemptuously. Then
with a sudden gesture he claps his mask on and laughs
wildly and bitterly.*) Ha-ha-ha! That's one on you,
Peg!

MARGARET (*with delight, pulling off her mask*).
Dion! How did you ever — Why, I never knew
you!

DION (*puts his arm around her boldly*). How? It's
the moon — the crazy moon — the monkey in the
moon — playing jokes on us! (*He kisses her with his
masked face with a romantic actor's passion again and
again.*) You love me! You know you do! Say it!
Tell me! I want to hear! I want to feel! I want
to know! I want to want! To want you as you
want me!

MARGARET (*in ecstasy*). Oh, Dion, I do! I do
love you!

DION (*with ironic mastery — rhetorically*). And I
love you! Oh, madly! Oh, for ever and ever,
amen! You are my evening star and all my

Pleiades! Your eyes are blue pools in which gold dreams glide, your body is a young white birch leaning backward beneath the lips of spring. So! (*He has bent her back, his arms supporting her, his face above hers.*) So! (*He kisses her.*)

MARGARET (*with overpowering passionate languor*). Oh, Dion! Dion! I love you!

DION (*with more and more mastery in his tone*). I love, you love, we love! Come! Rest! Relax! Let go your clutch on the world! Dim and dimmer! Fading out in the past behind! Gone! Death! Now! Be born! Awake! Live! Dissolve into dew — into silence — into night — into earth — into space — into peace — into meaning — into joy — into God — into the Great God Pan! (*While he has been speaking, the moon has passed gradually behind a black cloud, its light fading out. There is a moment of intense blackness and silence. Then the light gradually comes on again. Dion's voice, at first in a whisper, then increasing in volume with the light, is heard.*) Wake up! Time to get up! Time to exist! Time for school! Time to learn! Learn to pretend! Cover your nakedness! Learn to lie! Learn to keep step! Join the procession! Great Pan is dead! Be ashamed!

MARGARET (*with a sob*). Oh, Dion, I am ashamed!

DION (*mockingly*). Sssshh! Watch the monkey in the moon! See him dance! His tail is a piece of string that was left when he broke loose from

Jehovah and ran away to join Charley Darwin's circus!

MARGARET. I know you must hate me now! (*She throws her arms around him and hides her head on his shoulder.*)

DION (*deeply moved*). Don't cry! Don't — ! (*He suddenly tears off his mask — in a passionate agony.*) Hate you? I love you with all my soul! Love me! Why can't you love me, Margaret?

> (*He tries to kiss her but she jumps to her feet with a frightened cry, holding up her mask before her face protectingly.*)

MARGARET. Don't! Please! I don't know you. You frighten me!

DION (*puts on his mask again — quietly and bitterly*). All's well. I'll never let you see again. (*He puts his arm around her — gently mocking.*) By proxy, I love you. There! Don't cry! Don't be afraid! Dion Anthony will marry you some day. (*He kisses her.*) "I take this woman — " (*Tenderly joking.*) Hello, woman! Do you feel older by æons? Mrs. Dion Anthony, shall we go in and may I have the next dance?

MARGARET (*tenderly*). You crazy child. (*Then, laughing with joy.*) Mrs. Dion Anthony! It sounds wonderful, doesn't it?

(*They go out as*

*The Curtain Falls*)

24

# ACT ONE

## SCENE ONE

SCENE. *Seven years later.*

*The sitting-room of Mrs. Dion Anthony's half of a two-family house in the residential quarter of the town — one of those one-design districts that daze the eye with multiplied ugliness. The four pieces of furniture shown are in keeping — an arm-chair at left, a table with a chair behind it at centre, a sofa at right. The same court-room effect of the arrangement of benches in Act One is held to here. The background is a backdrop on which the rear wall is painted with the intolerable lifeless realistic detail of the stereotyped paintings which usually adorn the sitting-rooms of such houses. It is late afternoon of a grey day in winter.*

*Dion is sitting behind the table, staring before him. The mask hangs on his breast below his neck, giving the effect of two faces. His real face has aged greatly, grown more strained and tortured, but at the same time, in some queer way, more selfless and ascetic, more fixed in its resolute withdrawal from life. The mask, too, has changed. It is older, more defiant and mocking, its sneer more forced and bitter, its Pan quality becoming Mephistophelean. It has already begun to show the ravages of dissipation.*

DION (*suddenly reaches out and takes up a copy of*

*the New Testament which is on the table and, putting
a finger in at random, opens and reads aloud the text
at which it points).* "Come unto me all ye who are
heavy laden and I will give you rest." (*He stares
before him in a sort of trance, his face lighted up from
within but painfully confused — in an uncertain whisper.*) I will come — but where are you, Saviour?
(*The noise of the outer door shutting is heard. Dion
starts and claps the mocking mask on his face again.
He tosses the Testament aside contemptuously.*) Blah!
Fixation on old Mamma Christianity! You infant
blubbering in the dark, you!

> (*He laughs, with a bitter self-contempt. Foot-
> steps approach. He picks up a news-
> paper and hides behind it hurriedly.
> Margaret enters. She is dressed in
> stylish, expensive clothes and a fur coat,
> which look as if they had been re-
> modelled and seen service. She has
> grown mature and maternal, in spite of
> her youth. Her pretty face is still fresh
> and healthy but there is the beginning
> of a permanently worried, apprehensive
> expression about the nose and mouth —
> an uncomprehending hurt in her eyes.
> Dion pretends to be engrossed in his
> paper. She bends down and kisses him.*)

MARGARET (*with a forced gaiety*). Good morning
— at four in the afternoon! You were snoring
when I left!

DION (*puts his arms around her with a negligent, accustomed gesture — mockingly*). The Ideal Husband!

MARGARET (*already preoccupied with another thought — comes and sits in chair on left*). I was afraid the children would disturb you, so I took them over to Mrs. Young's to play. (*A pause. He picks up the paper again. She asks anxiously.*) I suppose they'll be all right over there, don't you? (*He doesn't answer. She is more hurt than offended.*) I wish you'd try to take more interest in the children, Dion.

DION (*mockingly*). Become a father — before breakfast? I'm in too delicate a condition. (*She turns away, hurt. Penitently he pats her hand — vaguely.*) All right. I'll try.

MARGARET (*squeezing his hand — with possessive tenderness*). Play with them. You're a bigger kid than they are — underneath.

DION (*self-mockingly — flipping the Bible*). Underneath — I'm becoming downright infantile! "Suffer these little ones!"

MARGARET (*keeping to her certainty*). You're my oldest.

DION (*with mocking appreciation*). She puts the Kingdom of Heaven in its place!

MARGARET (*withdrawing her hand*). I was serious.

DION. So was I — about something or other.

(*He laughs.*) This domestic diplomacy! We communicate in code – when neither has the other's key!

MARGARET (*frowns confusedly – then forcing a playful tone*). I want to have a serious talk with you, young man! In spite of your promises, you've kept up the hard drinking and gambling you started the last year abroad.

DION. From the time I realized it wasn't in me to be an artist – except in living – and not even in that! (*He laughs bitterly.*)

MARGARET (*with conviction*). But you *can* paint, Dion – beautifully!

DION (*with deep pain*). No! (*He suddenly takes her hand and kisses it gratefully.*) I love Margaret! Her blindness surpasseth all understanding! (*Then bitterly*) – or is it pity?

MARGARET. We've only got about one hundred dollars left in the bank.

DION (*with dazed surprise*). What? Is all the money from the sale of the house gone?

MARGARET (*wearily*). Every day or so you've been cashing cheques. You've been drinking – you haven't counted –

DION (*irritably*). I know! (*A pause – soberly.*) No more estate to fall back on, eh? Well, for five years it kept us living abroad in peace. It bought us a little happiness – of a kind – didn't it? – living and loving and having children – (*A slight pause –*

*bitterly*) – thinking one was creating before one discovered one couldn't!

MARGARET (*this time with forced conviction*). But you *can* paint – beautifully!

DION (*angrily*). Shut up! (*A pause – then jeeringly.*) So my wife thinks it behoves me to settle down and support my family in the meagre style to which they'll have to become accustomed?

MARGARET (*shamefacedly*). I didn't say – still – something's got to be done.

DION (*harshly*). Will Mrs. Anthony helpfully suggest what?

MARGARET. I met Billy Brown on the street. He said you'd have made a good architect, if you'd stuck to it.

DION. Flatterer! Instead of leaving college when my Old Man died? Instead of marrying Peggy and going abroad and being happy?

MARGARET (*as if she hadn't heard*). He spoke of how well you used to draw.

DION. Billy was in love with Margaret at one time.

MARGARET. He wanted to know why you've never been in to see him.

DION. He's bound heaven-bent for success. It's the will of Mammon! Anthony and Brown, contractors and builders – death subtracts Anthony and I sell out – Billy graduates – Brown and Son, architects and builders – old man Brown perishes of paternal pride – and now we have William A. Brown, architect! Why his career itself already has an architectural design! One of God's mud pies!

MARGARET. He particularly told me to ask you to drop in.

DION (*springs to his feet – assertively*). No! Pride! I have been alive!

MARGARET. Why don't you have a talk with him?

DION. Pride in my failure.

MARGARET. You were always such close friends.

DION (*more and more desperately*). The pride which came after man's fall – by which he laughs as a creator at his self-defeats!

MARGARET. Not for my sake – but for your own – and, above all, for the children's!

DION (*with terrible despair*). Pride! Pride without which the Gods are worms!

MARGARET (*after a pause, meekly and humbly*). You don't want to? It would hurt you? All right, dear. Never mind. We'll manage somehow – you mustn't worry – you must start your beautiful painting again – and I can get that position in the library – it would be such fun for me working there! . . . (*She reaches out and takes his hand – tenderly.*) I love you, dear. I understand.

DION (*slumps down into his chair, crushed, his face averted from hers, as hers is from him, although their hands are still clasped — in a trembling, expiring voice*). Pride is dying! (*As if he were suffocating, he pulls the mask from his resigned, pale, suffering face. He prays like a Saint in the desert, exorcizing a demon.*) Pride is dead! Blessed are the meek! Blessed are the poor in spirit!

MARGARET (*without looking at him — in a comforting motherly tone*). My poor boy!

DION (*resentfully — clapping on his mask again and springing to his feet — derisively*). Blessed are the meek for they shall inherit graves! Blessed are the poor in spirit for they are blind! (*Then with tortured bitterness.*) All right! Then I ask my wife to go and ask Billy Brown — that's more deadly than if I went myself! (*With wild mockery.*) Ask him if he can't find an opening for a talented young man who is only honest when he isn't sober — implore him, beg him in the name of old love, old friendship — to be a generous hero and save the woman and her children! (*He laughs with a sort of diabolical, ironical glee now, and starts to go out.*)

MARGARET (*meekly*). Are you going up street, Dion?

DION. Yes.

MARGARET. Will you stop at the butcher's and ask them to send two pounds of pork chops?

DION. Yes.

MARGARET. And stop at Mrs. Young's and tell the children to hurry right home?

DION. Yes.

MARGARET. Will you be back for dinner, Dion?

DION. No. (*He goes, the outer door slams. Margaret sighs with a tired incomprehension and goes to the window and stares out.*)

MARGARET (*worriedly*). I hope they'll be careful, crossing the street.

(*Curtain*)

# ACT ONE

SCENE. *Billy Brown's Office, at five in the afternoon.
At centre, a fine mahogany desk with a swivel
chair behind it. To the left of desk, an office arm-
chair. To the right of desk, an office lounge. The
background is a backdrop of an office wall,
treated similarly to that of Scene One in its over-
meticulous representation of detail.*

*Billy Brown is seated at the desk looking over
a blue print by the light of a desk lamp. He has
grown into a fine-looking, well-dressed, capable,
college-bred American business man, boyish still
and with the same engaging personality.*

*The telephone rings.*

BROWN (*answering it*). Yes? Who? (*This in
surprise — then with eager pleasure.*) Ask her to
come right in.

> (*He gets up and goes to the door, expectant
> and curious. Margaret enters. Her face
> is concealed behind the mask of the
> pretty young matron, still hardly a
> woman, who cultivates a naïvely inno-
> cent and bravely hopeful attitude toward
> things and acknowledges no wound to
> the world. She is dressed as in Scene
> One but with an added touch of effective
> primping here and there.*)

MARGARET (*very gaily*). Hello, Billy Brown!

33

BROWN (*awkward in her presence, shakes her hand*). Come in. Sit down. This is a pleasant surprise, Margaret.

> (*She sits down on the lounge. He sits in his chair behind the desk, as before.*)

MARGARET (*looking around*). What lovely offices! My, but Billy Brown is getting grand!

BROWN (*pleased*). I've just moved in. The old place was too stuffy.

MARGARET. It looks so prosperous — but then, Billy is doing so wonderfully well, every one says.

BROWN (*modestly*). Well, to be frank, it's been mostly luck. Things have come my way without my doing much about it. (*Then, with an abashed pride.*) Still — I have done a little something myself. (*He picks the plan from the desk.*) See this? It's my design for the New Municipal Building. It's just been accepted — provisionally — by the Committee.

MARGARET (*taking it — vaguely*). Oh? (*She looks at it abstractedly. There is a pause. Suddenly.*) You mentioned the other day how well Dion used to draw —

BROWN (*a bit stiffly*). Yes, he certainly did. (*He takes the drawing from her and at once becomes interested and squints at it frowningly.*) Did you notice that anything seemed lacking in this?

MARGARET (*indifferently*). Not at all.

BROWN (*with a cheerful grin*). The Committee

want it made a little more American. It's too much of a conventional Greco-Roman tomb, they say. (*Laughs.*) They want an original touch of modern novelty stuck in to liven it up and make it look different from other town halls. (*Putting the drawing back on his desk.*) And I've been figuring out how to give it to them, but my mind doesn't seem to run that way. Have you any suggestion?

MARGARET (*as if she hadn't heard*). Dion certainly draws well, Billy Brown was saying?

BROWN (*trying not to show his annoyance*). Why, yes — he did — and still can, I expect. (*A pause. He masters what he feels to be an unworthy pique and turns to her generously.*) Dion would have made a cracking good architect.

MARGARET (*proudly*). I know. He could be anything he wanted to.

BROWN (*a pause — embarrassedly*). Is he working at anything these days?

MARGARET (*defensively*). Oh, yes! He's painting wonderfully! But he's just like a child, he's so impractical. He doesn't try to have an exhibition anywhere, or anything.

BROWN (*surprised*). The one time I ran into him, I thought he told me he'd destroyed all his pictures — that he'd got sick of painting and completely given it up.

MARGARET (*quickly*). He always tells people that. He doesn't want anyone even to look at his things, imagine! He keeps saying they're rotten — when they're really too beautiful! He's too modest for his own good, don't you think? But it is true he hasn't done so much lately since we've been back. You see the children take up such a lot of his time. He just worships them! I'm afraid he's becoming a hopeless family man, just the opposite of what anyone would expect who knew him in the old days.

BROWN (*painfully embarrassed by her loyalty and his knowledge of the facts*). Yes, I know. (*He coughs self-consciously.*)

MARGARET (*aroused by something in his manner*). But I suppose the gossips are telling the same silly stories about him they always did. (*She forces a laugh.*) Poor Dion! Give a dog a bad name! (*Her voice breaks a little in spite of herself.*)

BROWN (*hastily*). I haven't heard any stories — (*he stops uncertainly, then decides to plunge in*) — except about money matters.

MARGARET (*forcing a laugh*). Oh, perhaps they're true enough. Dion is such a generous fool with his money, like all artists.

BROWN (*with a certain doggedness*). There's a rumour that you've applied for a position at the Library.

MARGARET (*forcing a gay tone*). Yes, indeed! Won't it be fun! Maybe it'll improve my mind! And one of us has got to be practical, so why not me? (*She forces a gay, girlish laugh.*)

BROWN (*impulsively reaches out and takes her hand – awkwardly*). Listen, Margaret. Let's be perfectly frank, will you? I'm such an old friend, and I want like the deuce to. . . . You know darn well I'd do anything in the world to help you – or Dion.

MARGARET (*withdrawing her hand, coldly*). I'm afraid I – don't understand, Billy Brown.

BROWN (*acutely embarrassed*). Well, I – I just meant – you know, if you needed – (*A pause. He looks questioningly at her averted face – then ventures on another tack, matter-of-factly.*) I've got a proposition to make to Dion – if I could ever get hold of him. It's this way: business has been piling up on me – a run of luck – but I'm short-handed. I need a crack chief draughtsman darn badly – or I'm liable to lose out. Do you think Dion would consider it – as a temporary stop-gap – until he felt in the painting mood again?

MARGARET (*striving to conceal her eagerness and relief – judicially*). Yes – I really do. He's such a good sport and Billy and he were such pals once. I know he'd be only too tickled to help him out.

BROWN (*diffidently*). I thought he might be sensitive about working for – I mean, with me – when, if he hadn't sold out to Dad he'd be my partner now – (*earnestly*) – and, by jingo, I wish he was! (*Then, abruptly.*) Let's try to nail him down right away, Margaret. Is he home now? (*He reaches for the 'phone.*)

MARGARET (*hurriedly*). No, he — he went out for a long walk.

BROWN. Perhaps I can locate him later around town somewhere.

MARGARET (*with a note of pleading*). Please don't trouble. It isn't necessary. I'm sure when I talk to him — he's coming home to dinner — (*Getting up.*) Then it's all settled, isn't it? Dion will be so glad to be able to help an old friend — he's so terribly loyal, and he's always liked Billy Brown so much! (*Holding out her hand.*) I really must go now!

BROWN (*shakes her hand*). Good-bye, Margaret. I hope you'll be dropping in on us a lot when Dion gets here.

MARGARET. Yes. (*She goes.*)

BROWN (*sits at his desk again, looking ahead in a not unsatisfying melancholy reverie. He mutters admiringly but pityingly*). Poor Margaret! She's a game sport, but it's pretty damn tough on her! (*Indignantly.*) By God, I'm going to give Dion a good talking-to one of these days!

(*Curtain*)

# ACT ONE

## SCENE THREE

SCENE. *Cybel's parlour. An automatic, penny-in-the-slot player-piano is at centre, rear. On its right is a dirty gilt second-hand sofa. At the left is a bald-spotted crimson plush chair. The backdrop for the rear wall is cheap wall-paper of a dull yellow-brown, resembling a blurred impression of a fallow field in early spring. There is a cheap alarm clock on top of the piano. Beside it her mask is lying.*

*Dion is sprawled on his back, fast asleep on the sofa. His mask has fallen down on his chest. His pale face is singularly pure, spiritual and sad.*

*The player-piano is groggily banging out a sentimental medley of "Mother — Mammy" tunes.*

*Cybel is seated on the stool in front of the piano. She is a strong, calm, sensual, blonde girl of twenty or so, her complexion fresh and healthy, her figure full-breasted and wide-hipped, her movements slow and solidly languorous like an animal's, her large eyes dreamy with the reflected stirring of profound instincts. She chews gum like a sacred cow forgetting time with an eternal end. Her eyes are fixed, incuriously, on Dion's pale face.*

CYBEL (*as the tune runs out, glances at the clock,*

*which indicates midnight, then goes slowly over to Dion and puts her hand gently on his forehead).* Wake up!

DION (*stirs, sighs and murmurs dreamily*). "And He laid his hands on them and healed them." (*Then with a start he opens his eyes and, half sitting up, stares at her bewilderedly.*) What — where — who are you? (*He reaches for his mask and claps it on defensively.*)

CYBEL (*placidly*). Only another female. You was camping on my steps, sound asleep. I didn't want to run any risk getting into more trouble with the cops pinching you there and blaming me, so I took you in to sleep it off.

DION (*mockingly*). Blessed are the pitiful, Sister! I'm broke — but you will be rewarded in Heaven!

CYBEL (*calmly*). I wasn't wasting my pity. Why should I? You were happy, weren't you?

DION (*approvingly*). Excellent! You're not a moralist, I see.

CYBEL (*going on*). And you look like a good boy, too — when you're asleep. Say, you better beat it home to bed or you'll be locked out.

DION (*mockingly*). Now you're becoming maternal, Miss Earth. Is that the only answer — to pin my soul into every vacant diaper? (*She stares down at his mask, her face growing hard. He laughs.*) But please don't stop stroking my aching brow. Your hand is a cool mud poultice on the sting of thought!

CYBEL (*calmly*). Stop acting. I hate ham fats. (*She looks at him as if waiting for him to remove his mask — then turns her back indifferently and goes to the piano.*) Well, if you simply got to be a regular devil like all the other visiting sports, I s'pose I got to play with you. (*She takes her mask and puts it on — then turns. The mask is the rouged and eye-blackened countenance of the hardened prostitute.  In a coarse, harsh voice.*) Kindly state your dishonourable intentions, if any! I can't sit up all night keeping company! Let's have some music! (*She puts a plug in the machine. The same sentimental medley begins to play. The two masks stare at each other. She laughs.*) Shoot! I'm all set! It's your play, Kid Lucifer!

DION (*slowly removes his mask. She stops the music with a jerk. His face is gentle and sad — humbly*). I'm sorry. It has always been such agony for me to be touched!

CYBEL (*taking off her mask — sympathetically as she comes back and sits down on her stool*). Poor kid! I've never had one, but I can guess. They hug and kiss you and take you on their laps and pinch you and want to see you getting dressed and undressed — as if they owned you — I bet you I'd never let them treat one of mine that way!

DION (*turning to her*). You're lost in blind alleys,

too. (*Suddenly holding out his hand to her.*) But you're strong. Let's be friends.

CYBEL (*with a strange sternness, searches his face*). And never nothing more?

DION (*with a strange smile*). Let's say, never anything less!

> (*She takes his hand. There is a ring at the outside door bell. They stare at each other. There is another ring.*)

CYBEL (*puts on her mask, Dion does likewise. Mockingly*). When you got to love to live it's hard to love living. I better join the A.F. of L. and soap-box for the eight-hour night! Got a nickel, baby? Play a tune. (*She goes out. Dion puts a nickel in. The same sentimental tune starts. Cybel returns, followed by Billy Brown. His face is rigidly composed, but his superior disgust for Dion can be seen. Dion jerks off the music and he and Billy look at each other for a moment, Cybel watching them both – then, bored, she yawns.*) He's hunting for you. Put out the lights when you go. I'm going to sleep. (*She starts to go – then, as if reminded of something – to Dion.*) Life's all right, if you let it alone. (*Then mechanically flashing a trade smile at Billy.*) Now you know the way, Handsome, call again! (*She goes.*)

BROWN (*after an awkward pause*). Hello, Dion! I've been looking all over town for you. This place was the very last chance. . . . (*Another pause – embarrassedly.*) Let's take a walk.

DION (*mockingly*). I've given up exercise. They claim it lengthens your life.

BROWN (*persuasively*). Come on, Dion, be a good fellow. You're certainly not staying here —

DION. Billy would like to think me taken in *flagrante delicto*, eh?

BROWN. Don't be a damn fool! Listen to me! I've been looking you up for purely selfish reasons. I need your help.

DION (*astonished*). What?

BROWN. I've a proposition to make that I hope you'll consider favourably out of old friendship. To be frank, Dion, I need you to lend me a hand down at the office.

DION (*with a harsh laugh*). So it's the job, is it? Then my poor wife did a-begging go!

BROWN (*repelled — sharply*). On the contrary, I had to beg her to beg you to take it! (*More angrily*.) Look here, Dion! I won't listen to you talk that way about Margaret! And you wouldn't if you weren't drunk! (*Suddenly shaking him*.) What in hell has come over you, anyway! You didn't use to be like this! What the devil are you going to do with yourself — sink into the gutter and drag Margaret with you? If you'd heard her defend you, lie about you, tell me how hard you were working, what beautiful things you were painting, how you stayed at home and idolized the children! — when every one knows you've been

out every night sousing and gambling away the
last of your estate. . . . (*He stops, ashamed, controlling himself.*)

DION (*wearily*). She was lying about her husband, not me, you fool! But it's no use explaining.
(*Then, in a sudden, excitable passion.*) What do you
want? I agree to anything – except the humiliation of yelling secrets at the deaf!

BROWN (*trying a bullying tone – roughly*). Bunk!
Don't try to crawl out! There's no excuse and you
know it. (*Then as Dion doesn't reply – penitently.*)
But I know I shouldn't talk this way, old man!
It's only because we're such old pals – and I hate
to see you wasting yourself – you who had more
brains than any of us! But, damn it, I suppose
you're too much of a rotten cynic to believe I
mean what I've just said!

DION (*touched*). I know Billy was always Dion
Anthony's friend.

BROWN. You're damn right, I am – and I'd
have proved it long ago if you'd only given me
half a chance! After all, I couldn't keep chasing
after you and be snubbed every time. A man
has some pride!

DION (*bitterly mocking*). Dead wrong! Never
more! None whatever! It's unmoral! Blessed are
the poor in spirit, Brother! When shall I report?

BROWN (*eagerly*). Then you'll take the – you'll
help me?

DION (*wearily bitter*). I'll take the job. One must do something to pass away the time, while one is waiting – for one's next incarnation.

BROWN (*jokingly*). I'd say it was a bit early to be worrying about that. (*Trying to get Dion started.*) Come along, now. It's pretty late.

DION (*shakes his hand off his shoulder and walks away from him – after a pause*). Is my father's chair still there?

BROWN (*turns away – embarrassed*). I – I don't really remember, Dion – I'll look it up.

DION (*taking off his mask – slowly*). I'd like to sit where he spun what I have spent. What aliens we were to each other! When he lay dead, his face looked so familiar that I wondered where I had met that man before. Only at the second of my conception. After that, we grew hostile with concealed shame. And my mother? I remember a sweet, strange girl, with affectionate, bewildered eyes as if God had locked her in a dark closet without any explanation. I was the sole doll our ogre, her husband, allowed her and she played mother and child with me for many years in that house until at last through two tears I watched her die with the shy pride of one who has lengthened her dress and put up her hair. And I felt like a forsaken toy and cried to be buried with her, because her hands alone had caressed without clawing. She lived long and aged greatly in the two days before they closed her coffin. The last time I looked, her purity had forgotten me, she was stainless and imperishable, and I knew my sobs were ugly and meaningless to her virginity; so I shrank away, back into life, with naked nerves jumping like fleas, and in due course of nature another girl called me her boy in the moon and married me and became three mothers in one person, while I got paint on my paws in an endeavour to see God! (*He laughs wildly – claps on his mask.*) But that Ancient Humorist had given me weak eyes, so now I'll have to foreswear my quest for Him and go in for the Omnipresent Successful Serious One, the Great God Mr. Brown, instead! (*He makes him a sweeping, mocking bow.*)

BROWN (*repelled but cajolingly*). Shut up, you nut! You're still drunk. Come on! Let's start! (*He grabs Dion by the arm and switches off the light.*)

DION (*from the darkness – mockingly*). I am thy shorn, bald, nude sheep! Lead on, Almighty Brown, thou Kindly Light!


(*Curtain*)

# ACT TWO

SCENE. *Cybel's parlour – about sunset in spring seven years later. The arrangement of furniture is the same but the chair and sofa are new, bright-coloured, costly pieces. The old automatic piano at centre looks exactly the same. The cheap alarm clock is still on top of it. On either side of the clock, the masks of Dion and Cybel are lying. The background backdrop is brilliant, stunning wall-paper, on which crimson and purple flowers and fruits tumble over one another in a riotously profane lack of any apparent design.*

*Dion sits in the chair on left, Cybel on the sofa. A card-table is between them. Both are playing solitaire. Dion is now prematurely grey. His face is that of an ascetic, a martyr, furrowed by pain and self-torture, yet lighted from within by a spiritual calm and human kindliness.*

*Cybel has grown stouter and more voluptuous, but her face is still unmarked and fresh, her calm more profound. She is like an unmoved idol of Mother Earth.*

*The piano is whining out its same old senti-mental medley. They play their cards intently and contentedly. The music stops.*

CYBEL (*musingly*). I love those rotten old sob tunes. They make me wise to pcople. That's

47

what's inside them – what makes them love and murder their neighbour – crying jags set to music!

DION (*compassionately*). Every song is a hymn. They keep trying to find the Word in the Beginning.

CYBEL. They try to know too much. It makes them weak. I never puzzled over them myself. I gave them a Tart. They understood her and knew their parts and acted naturally. And on both sides we were able to keep our real virtue, if you get me. (*She plays her last card – indifferently.*) I've made it again.

DION (*smiling*). Your luck is uncanny. It never comes out for me.

CYBEL. You keep getting closer, but it knows you still want to win – a little bit – and it's wise all I care about is playing. (*She lays out another game.*) Speaking of my canned music, our Mr. Brown hates that old box. (*At the mention of Brown, Dion trembles as if suddenly possessed, has a terrible struggle with himself, then while she continues to speak, gets up like an automaton and puts on his mask. The mask is now terribly ravaged. All of its Pan quality has changed into a diabolical Mephistophelean cruelty and irony.*) He doesn't mind the music inside. That gets him somehow. But he thinks the case looks shabby and he wants it junked. But I told him that just because he's been keeping me so long, he needn't start bossing like a husband or I'll – (*She looks up and sees the masked Dion standing by the piano – calmly.*) Hello! Getting jealous again?

DION (*jeeringly*). Are you falling in love with your keeper, old Sacred Cow?

CYBEL (*without taking offence*). Cut it! You've been asking me that for years. Be yourself! He's healthy and handsome – but he's too guilty. What makes you pretend you think love is so important, anyway? It's just one of a lot of things you do to keep life living.

DION (*in same tone*). Then you've lied when you've said you loved me, have you, Old Filth?

CYBEL (*affectionately*). You'll never grow up! We've been friends, haven't we, for seven years? I've never let myself want you nor you me. Yes, I love you. It takes all kinds of love to make a world! Ours is the living cream, I say, living rich and high! (*A pause. Coaxingly.*) Stop hiding. I know you.

DION (*taking off his mask, wearily comes and sits down at her feet and lays his head in her lap – with a grateful smile*). You're strong. You always give. You've given my weakness strength to live.

CYBEL (*tenderly, stroking his hair maternally.*) You're not weak. You were born with ghosts in your eyes and you were brave enough to go looking into your own dark – and you got afraid. (*After a pause.*) I don't blame your being jealous of Mr. Brown sometimes. I'm jealous of your wife, even though I know you do love her.

DION (*slowly*). I love Margaret. I don't know who my wife is.

CYBEL (*after a pause – with a queer broken laugh*). Oh, God, sometimes the truth hits me such a sock between the eyes I can see the stars! – and then I'm so damn sorry for the lot of you, every damn mother's son-of-a-gun of you, that I'd like to run out naked into the street and love the whole mob to death like I was bringing you all a new brand of dope that'd make you forget everything that ever was for good! (*Then, with a twisted smile.*) But they wouldn't see me, any more than they see each other. And they keep right on moving along and dying without my help anyway.

DION (*sadly*). You've given me strength to die.

CYBEL. You may be important but your life's not. There's millions of it born every second. Life can cost too much even for a sucker to afford it – like everything else. And it's not sacred – only the you inside is. The rest is earth.

DION (*gets to his knees and with clasped hands looks up raptly and prays with an ascetic fervour*). "Into thy hands, O Lord," . . . (*Then suddenly, with a look of horror.*) Nothing! To feel one's life blown out like the flame of a cheap match . . .! (*He claps on his mask and laughs harshly.*) To fall asleep and know you'll never, never be called to get on the job of existence again! "Swift be thine approaching flight! Come soon – soon!" (*He quotes this last with a mocking longing.*)

CYBEL (*pats his head maternally*). There, don't
be scared. It's born in the blood. When the time
comes, you'll find it's easy.

DION (*jumps to his feet and walks about excitedly*).
It won't be long. My wife dragged in a doctor the
day before yesterday. He says my heart is gone –
booze – He warned me, never another drop or –
(*Mockingly.*) What say? Shall we have a drink ?

CYBEL (*like an idol*). Suit yourself. It's in the
pantry. (*Then, as he hesitates.*) What set you off
on this bat? You were raving on about some
cathedral plans. . . .

DION (*wildly mocking*). They've been accepted –
Mr. Brown's designs! My designs really! You
don't need to be told that. He hands me one
mathematically correct barn after another and I
doctor them up with cute allurements so that fools
will desire to buy, sell, breed, sleep, love, hate,
curse and pray in them! I do this with devilish
cleverness to their entire delight! Once I dreamed
of painting wind on the sea and the skimming
flight of cloud shadows over the tops of trees!
Now . . . (*He laughs.*) But pride is a sin – even
in a memory of the long deceased! Blessed are the
poor in spirit! (*He subsides weakly on his chair, his
hand pressed to his heart.*)

CYBEL (*like an idol*). Go home and sleep. Your
wife'll be worried.

DION. She knows – but she'll never admit to
herself that her husband ever entered your door.

# THE GREAT GOD BROWN

(*Mocking.*) Aren't women loyal – to their vanity and their other things!

CYBEL. Brown is coming soon, don't forget.

DION. He knows too and can't admit. Perhaps he needs me here – unknown. What first aroused his passion to possess you exclusively, do you think? Because he knew you loved me and he felt himself cheated. He wanted what he thought was my love of the flesh! He feels I have no right to love. He'd like to steal it as he steals my ideas – complacently – righteously. Oh, the good Brown!

CYBEL. But you like him, too! You're brothers, I guess, somehow. Well, remember he's paying, he'll pay – in some way or other.

DION (*raises his head as if starting to remove the mask*). I know. Poor Billy! God forgive me the evil I've done him!

CYBEL (*reaches out and takes his hand*). Poor boy!

DION (*presses her convulsively – then with forced harshness*). Well, homeward Christian Soldier! I'm off! By-bye, Mother Earth. (*He starts to go off right. She seems about to let him go.*)

CYBEL (*suddenly starts and calls with deep grief*). Dion! (*He looks at her. A pause. He comes slowly back. She speaks strangely in a deep, far-off voice – and yet like a mother talking to her little son.*) You mustn't forget to kiss me before you go, Dion. (*She removes his mask.*) Haven't I told you to take off your mask in the house? Look at me, Dion.

I've – just – seen – something. I'm afraid you're going away a long, long way. I'm afraid I won't see you again for a long, long time. So it's good-bye, dear. (*She kisses him gently. He begins to sob. She hands him back his mask.*) Here you are. Don't get hurt. Remember, it's all a game, and after you're asleep I'll tuck you in.

DION (*in a choking, heart-broken cry*). Mother! (*Then he claps on his mask with a terrible effort of will – mockingly.*) Go to the devil, you sentimental old pig! See you to-morrow! (*He goes, whistling, slamming the door.*)

CYBEL (*like an idol again*). What's the good of bearing children? What's the use of giving birth to death? (*She sighs wearily, turns, puts a plug in the piano, which starts up its old sentimental tune. At the same moment Brown enters quietly from the left. He is the ideal of the still youthful, good-looking, well-groomed, successful provincial American of forty. Just now, he is plainly perturbed. He is not able to see either Cybel's face or her mask.*)

BROWN. Cybel! (*She starts, jams off the music and reaches for her mask, but has no time to put it on.*) Wasn't that Dion I just saw going out – after all your promises never to see him ! (*She turns like an idol, holding the mask behind her. He stares, bewildered – stammers.*) I – I beg your pardon – I thought –

CYBEL (*in her strange voice*). Cybel's gone out to dig in the earth and pray.

BROWN (*with more assurance*). But—aren't those her clothes?

CYBEL. Cybel doesn't want people to see me naked. I'm her sister. Dion came to see me.

BROWN (*relieved*). So that's what he's up to, is it? (*Then with a pitying sigh.*) Poor Margaret! (*Then with playful reproof.*) You really shouldn't encourage him. He's married and got three big sons.

CYBEL. And you haven't.

BROWN (*stung*). No, I'm not married.

CYBEL. He and I were friends.

BROWN (*with a playful wink*). Yes, I can imagine how the platonic must appeal to Dion's pure, innocent type! It's no good your kidding me about Dion. We've been friends since we were kids. I know him in and out. I've always stood up for him whatever he's done—so you can be perfectly frank. I only spoke as I did on account of Margaret—his wife—it's pretty tough on her.

CYBEL. You love his wife.

BROWN (*scandalized*). What? What are you talking about? (*Then uncertainly.*) Don't be a fool! (*A pause—then as if impelled by an intense curiosity.*) So Dion is your lover, eh? That's very interesting. (*He pulls his chair closer to hers.*) Sit down. Let's talk. (*She continues to stand, the mask held behind her.*) Tell me—I've always been curious —what is it that makes Dion so attractive to women

– especially certain types of women, if you'll pardon me? He always has been and yet I never could see exactly what they saw in him. Is it his looks – or because he's such a violent sensualist – or because he poses as artistic and temperamental – or because he's so wild – or just what is it?

CYBEL. He's alive!

BROWN (*suddenly takes one of her hands and kisses it – insinuatingly*). Well, don't you think I'm alive, too? (*Eagerly.*) Listen. Would you consider giving up Dion – and letting me take care of you under a similar arrangement to the one I've made with Cybel? I like you, you can see that. I won't bother you much – I'm much too busy – you can do what you like – lead your own life – except for seeing him. (*He stops. A pause. She stares ahead unmoved as if she hadn't heard. He pleads.*) Well – what do you say? Please do!

CYBEL (*her voice very weary*). Cybel asked me to tell you she'd be back next week, Mr. Brown.

BROWN (*with queer agony*). You mean you won't? Don't be so cruel! I love you! (*She walks away. He clutches at her, pleadingly.*) At least – I'll give you anything you ask! – please promise me you won't see Dion Anthony again!

CYBEL (*with deep grief*). He will never see me again, I promise you. Good-bye!

BROWN (*jubilantly, kissing her hand – politely*). Thank you! Thank you! I'm exceedingly grateful. (*Tactfully.*) I won't disturb you any further. Please forgive my intrusion, and remember me to Cybel when you write. (*He bows, turns, and goes off left.*)

**(Curtain)**

# ACT TWO

## SCENE TWO

SCENE. *The draughting-room in Brown's office. Dion's draughting table with a high stool in front is at centre. Another stool is to the left of it. At the right is a bench. It is in the evening of the same day. The black wall drop has windows painted on it with a dim, street-lighted view of black houses across the way.*

*Dion is sitting on the stool behind the table, reading aloud from the "Imitation of Christ" by Thomas à Kempis to his mask, which is on the table before him. His own face is gentler, more spiritual, more saintlike and ascetic than ever before.*

DION (*like a priest, offering up prayers for the dying*). "Quickly must thou be gone from hence, see then how matters stand with thee. Ah, fool — learn now to die to the world that thou mayst begin to live with Christ! Do now, beloved, do now all thou canst because thou knowest not when thou shalt die; nor dost thou know what shall befall thee after death. Keep thyself as a pilgrim, and a stranger upon earth, to whom the affairs of this world do not — belong! Keep thy heart free and raised upwards to God because thou hast not here a lasting abode. 'Because at what hour you know not the Son of Man will come!'" Amen. (*He raises his hand over the mask as if he were bless-*

*ing it, closes the book and puts it back in his pocket. He raises the mask in his hands and stares at it with a pitying tenderness.*) Peace, poor tortured one, brave pitiful pride of man, the hour of our deliverance comes. To-morrow we may be with Him in Paradise! (*He kisses it on the lips and sets it down again. There is the noise of footsteps climbing the stairs in the hallway. He grabs up the mask in a sudden panic and, as a knock comes on the door, he claps it on and calls mockingly.*) Come in, Mrs. Anthony, come in!

> (*Margaret enters. In one hand behind her, hidden from him, is the mask of the brave face she puts on before the world to hide her suffering and disillusionment, and which she has just taken off. Her own face is still sweet and pretty, but lined, drawn and careworn for its years, sad, resigned, but a bit querulous.*)

MARGARET (*wearily reproving*). Thank goodness I've found you! Why haven't you been home the last two days? It's bad enough your drinking again without your staying away and worrying us to death!

DION (*bitterly*). My ears knew her footsteps. One gets to recognize everything – and to see nothing!

MARGARET. I finally sent the boys out looking for you and came myself. (*With tired solicitude.*)

I suppose you haven't eaten a thing, as usual. Won't you come home and let me fry you a chop?

DION (*wonderingly*). Can Margaret still love Dion Anthony? Is it possible she does?

MARGARET (*forcing a tired smile*). I suppose so, Dion. I certainly oughtn't to, ought I?

DION (*in same tone*). And I love Margaret! What haunted, haunting ghosts we are! We dimly remember so much it will take us so many million years to forget! (*He comes forward, putting one arm around her bowed shoulders, and they kiss.*)

MARGARET (*patting his hand affectionately*). No, you certainly don't deserve it. When I stop to think of all you've made me go through in the years since we settled down here . . . ! I really don't believe I could ever have stood it if it weren't for the boys! (*Forcing a smile.*) But perhaps I would, I've always been such a big fool about you.

DION (*a bit mockingly*). The boys! Three strong sons! Margaret can afford to be magnanimous!

MARGARET. If they didn't find you, they were coming to meet me here.

DION (*with sudden wildness — torturedly, sinking on his knees beside her*). Margaret! Margaret! I'm lonely! I'm frightened! I'm going away! I've got to say good-bye!

MARGARET (*patting his hair*). Poor boy! Poor Dion! Come home and sleep.

DION (*springs up frantically*). No! I'm a man.

I'm a lonely man! I can't go back! I have conceived myself! (*Then with desperate mockery.*) Look at me, Mrs. Anthony! It's the last chance! To-morrow I'll have moved on to the next hell! Behold your man – the snivelling, cringing, life-denying Christian slave you have so nobly ignored in the father of your sons! Look! (*He tears the mask from his face, which is radiant with a great pure love for her and a great sympathy and tenderness.*) O woman – my love – that I have sinned against in my sick pride and cruelty – forgive my sins – forgive my solitude – forgive my sickness – forgive me! (*He kneels and kisses the hem of her dress.*)

MARGARET (*who has been staring at him with terror, raising her mask to ward off his face*). Dion! Don't! I can't bear it! You're like a ghost. You're dead! Oh, my God! Help! Help! (*She falls back fainting on the bench. He looks at her – then takes her hand which holds her mask and looks at that face – gently.*) And now I am permitted to understand and love you, too! (*He kisses the mask first – then kisses her face, murmuring.*) And you, sweetheart! Blessed, thrice blessed are the meek!

> (*There is a sound of heavy, hurrying footsteps on the stairs. He puts on his mask in haste. The three sons rush into the room. The Eldest is about fourteen, the two others thirteen and twelve. They look healthy, normal, likeable boys, with*

*much the same quality as Billy Brown's in Act One, Scene One. They stop short and stiffen all in a row, staring from the woman on the bench to their father, accusingly.)*

ELDEST. We heard some one yell. It sounded like Mother.

DION (*defensively*). No. It was this lady – my wife.

ELDEST. But hasn't Mother come yet?

DION (*going to Margaret*). Yes. Your Mother is here. (*He stands between them and puts her mask over Margaret's face – then steps back.*) She has fainted. You'd better bring her to.

BOYS. Mother! (*They run to her side, kneel and rub her wrists. The Eldest smooths back her hair.*)

DION (*watching them*). At least I am leaving her well provided for. (*He addresses them directly.*) Tell your mother she'll get word from Mr. Brown's house. I must pay him a farewell call. I am going. Good-bye. (*They stop, staring at him fixedly, with eyes a mixture of bewilderment, distrust and hurt.*)

ELDEST (*awkwardly and shamefacedly*). Honest, I think you ought to have . . .

SECOND. Yes, honest you ought . . .

YOUNGEST. Yes, honest . . .

DION (*in a friendly tone*). I know. But I couldn't.

That's for you who can. You must inherit the earth for her. Don't forget now, boys. Good-bye.

BOYS (*in the same awkward, self-conscious tone, one after another*). Good-bye – good-bye – good-bye. (*Dion goes.*)

(*Curtain*)

# ACT TWO

### SCENE THREE

SCENE. *The library of William Brown's home — night of the same day. A backdrop of carefully painted, prosperous, bourgeois culture, bookcases filled with sets, etc. The heavy table at centre is expensive. The leather arm-chair at left of it and the couch at right are opulently comfortable. The reading lamp on the table is the only light.*

*Brown sits in the chair at left reading an architectural periodical. His expression is composed and gravely receptive. In outline, his face suggests a Roman consul on an old coin. There is an incongruous distinction about it, the quality of unquestioning faith in the finality of its achievement.*

*There is a sudden loud thumping on the front door and the ringing of the bell. Brown frowns and listens as a servant answers. Dion's voice can be heard, raised mockingly.*

DION. Tell him it's the devil come to conclude a bargain.

BROWN (*suppressing annoyance, calls out with forced good nature*). Come on in, Dion. (*Dion enters. He is in a wild state. His clothes are dishevelled, his masked face has a terrible deathlike intensity, its mocking irony becomes so cruelly malignant*

63

*as to give him the appearance of a real demon, tortured into torturing others.*) Sit down.

DION (*stands and sings*). William Brown's soul lies mouldering in the crib, but his body goes marching on!

BROWN (*maintaining the same indulgent, bigbrotherly tone, which he tries to hold throughout the scene.*) Not so loud, for Pete's sake! I don't mind – but I've got neighbours.

DION. Hate them! Fear thy neighbour as thyself! That's the leaden rule for the safe and sane. (*Then advancing to the table with a sort of deadly calm.*) Listen! One day when I was four years old, a boy sneaked up behind when I was drawing a picture in the sand he couldn't draw and hit me on the head with a stick and kicked out my picture and laughed when I cried. It wasn't what he'd done that made me cry, but him! I had loved and trusted him and suddenly the good God was disproved in his person and the evil and injustice of Man was born! Every one called me cry-baby, so I became silent for life and designed a mask of the Bad Boy Pan in which to live and rebel against that other boy's God and protect myself from His cruelty. And that other boy, secretly he felt ashamed but he couldn't acknowledge it; so from that day he instinctively developed into the good boy, the good friend, the good man, William Brown!

BROWN (*shamefacedly*). I remember now. It

was a dirty trick. (*Then with a trace of resentment.*) Sit down. You know where the booze is. Have a drink, if you like. But I guess you've had enough already.

DION (*looks at him fixedly for a moment — then strangely*). Thanks be to Brown for reminding me. I must drink. (*He goes and gets a bottle of whisky and a glass.*)

BROWN (*with a good-humoured shrug*). All right. It's your funeral.

DION (*returning and pouring out a big drink in the tumbler*). And William Brown's! When I die, he goes to hell! Shöal! (*He drinks and stares male-volently. In spite of himself, Brown is uneasy. A pause.*)

BROWN (*with forced casualness*). You've been on this toot for a week now.

DION (*tauntingly*). I've been celebrating the acceptance of *my* design for the cathedral.

BROWN (*humorously*). You certainly helped me a lot on it.

DION (*with a harsh laugh*). O perfect Brown! Never mind! I'll make him look in my mirror yet — and drown in it! (*He pours out another big drink.*)

BROWN (*rather tauntingly*). Go easy. I don't want your corpse on my hands.

DION. But I do. (*He drinks.*) Brown will still need me — to reassure him he's alive! I've loved, lusted, won and lost, sung and wept! I've been life's lover! I've fulfilled her will and if she's through with me now it's only because I was too weak to dominate her in turn. It isn't enough to be her creature, you've got to create her or she requests you to destroy yourself.

BROWN (*good-naturedly*). Nonsense. Go home and get some sleep.

DION (*as if he hadn't heard – bitingly*). But to be neither creature nor creator! To exist only in her indifference! To be unloved by life! (*Brown stirs uneasily.*) To be merely a successful freak, the result of some snide neutralizing of life forces – a spineless cactus – a wild boar of the mountains altered into a packer's hog eating to become food – a Don Juan inspired to romance by a monkey's glands – and to have Life not even think you funny enough to see!

BROWN (*stung – angrily*). Bosh!

DION. Consider Mr. Brown. His parents bore him on earth as if they were thereby entering him in a baby parade with prizes for the fattest – and he's still being wheeled along in the procession, too fat now to learn to walk, let alone to dance or run, and he'll never live until his liberated dust quickens into earth!

BROWN (*gruffly*). Rave on! (*Then with forced good-nature.*) Well, Dion, at any rate, I'm satisfied.

DION (*quickly and malevolently*). No! Brown isn't satisfied! He's piled on layers of protective fat, but vaguely, deeply he feels at his heart the gnawing of a doubt! And I'm interested in that germ which wriggles like a question mark of insecurity in his blood, because it's part of the creative life Brown's stolen from me!

BROWN (*forcing a sour grin*). Steal germs? I thought you caught them.

DION (*as if he hadn't heard*). It's mine — and I'm interested in seeing it thrive and breed and become multitudes and eat until Brown is consumed!

BROWN (*cannot restrain a shudder*). Sometimes when you're drunk, you're positively evil; do you know it?

DION (*sombrely*). When Pan was forbidden the light and warmth of the sun he grew sensitive and self-conscious and proud and revengeful — and became Prince of Darkness.

BROWN (*jocularly*). You don't fit the rôle of Pan, Dion. It sounds to me like Bacchus, alias the Demon Rum, doing the talking. (*Dion recovers from his spasm with a start and stares at Brown with terrible hatred. There is a pause. In spite of himself, Brown squirms and adopts a placating tone.*) Go home. It's all well enough celebrating our design being accepted, but —

DION (*in a steely voice*). I've been the brains! I've been the design! I've designed even his success — drunk and laughing at him — laughing at his career! Not proud! Sick! Sick of myself and him! Designing and getting drunk? Saving

67

my woman and children! (*He laughs.*) Ha! And this cathedral is my masterpiece! It will make Brown the most eminent architect in this state of God's Country. I put a lot into it — what was left of my life! It's one vivid blasphemy from pavement to the tips of its spires! — but so concealed that the fools will never know. They'll kneel and worship the ironic Silenus who tells them the best good is never to be born! (*He laughs triumphantly.*) Well, blasphemy is faith, isn't it? In self-preservation the devil must believe! But Mr. Brown, the Great Brown, has no faith! He couldn't design a cathedral without it looking like the First Supernatural Bank! He only believes in the immortality of the moral belly! (*He laughs wildly — then sinks down in his chair, gasping, his hands pressed to his heart. Then suddenly becomes deadly calm and pronounces like a cruel malignant condemnation.*) From now on, Brown will never design anything. He will devote his life to renovating the house of my Cybel into a home for my Margaret!

BROWN (*springing to his feet, his face convulsed with strange agony*). I've stood enough! How dare you . . . !

DION (*his voice like a probe*). Why has no woman ever loved him? Why has he always been the Big Brother, the Friend? Isn't their trust — a contempt?

BROWN. You lie!

DION. Why has he never been able to love —

since my Margaret? Why has he never married? Why has he tried to steal Cybel, as he once tried to steal Margaret? Isn't it out of revenge – and envy?

BROWN (*violently*). Rot! I wanted Cybel, and I bought her!

DION. Brown bought her for me! She has loved me more than he will ever know!

BROWN. You lie! (*Then furiously.*) I'll throw her back on the street!

DION. To me! To her fellow-creature! Why hasn't Brown had children – he who loves children – he who loves *my* children – he who envies me *my* children?

BROWN (*brokenly*). I'm not ashamed to envy you them!

DION. They like Brown, too – as a friend – as an equal – as Margaret has always liked him –

BROWN (*brokenly*). And as I've liked her!

DION. How many million times Brown has thought how much better for her it would have been if she'd chosen him instead!

BROWN (*torturedly*). You lie! (*Then with sudden frenzied defiance.*) All right! If you force me to say it, I do love Margaret! I always have loved her and you've always known I did!

DION (*with a terrible composure*). No! That is merely the appearance, not the truth! Brown loves me! He loves me because I have always possessed the power he needed for love, because I am love!

BROWN (*frenziedly*). You drunken fool! (*He leaps on Dion and grabs him by the throat.*)

DION (*triumphantly, staring into his eyes*). Ah! Now he looks into the mirror! Now he sees his face!

(*Brown lets go of him and staggers back to his chair, pale and trembling.*)

BROWN (*humbly*). Stop, for God's sake! You're mad!

DION (*sinking in his chair, more and more weakly*). I'm done. My heart, not Brown — (*Mockingly.*) My last will and testament! I leave Dion Anthony to William Brown — for him to love and obey — for him to become me — then my Margaret will love me — my children will love me — Mr. and Mrs. Brown and sons, happily ever after! (*Staggering to his full height and looking upward defiantly.*) Nothing more — but Man's last gesture — by which he conquers — to laugh! Ha — (*He begins, stops as if paralysed, and drops on his knees by Brown's chair, his mask falling off, his Christian Martyr's face at the point of death.*) Forgive me, Billy. Bury me, hide me, forget me for your own happiness! May Margaret love you! May you design the Temple of Man's Soul! Blessed are the meek and the poor in spirit! (*He kisses Brown's feet — then more and more weakly and childishly.*)

70

What was the prayer, Billy? I'm getting so sleepy. . . .

BROWN (*in a trancelike tone*). "Our Father who art in Heaven."

DION (*drowsily*). "Our Father." . . .

> (*He dies. A pause. Brown remains in a stupor for a moment — then stirs himself, puts his hand on Dion's breast.*)

BROWN (*dully*). He's dead — at last. (*He says this mechanically, but the last two words awaken him — wonderingly.*) At last? (*Then with triumph.*) At last! (*He stares at Dion's real face contemptuously.*) So that's the poor weakling you really were! No wonder you hid! And I've always been afraid of you — yes, I'll confess it now, in awe of you! Paugh! (*He picks up the mask from the floor.*) No, not of you! Of this! Say what you like, it's strong if it is bad! And this is what Margaret loved, not you! Not you! This man! — this man who willed himself to me! (*Struck by an idea, he jumps to his feet.*) By God! (*He slowly starts to put the mask on. A knocking comes on the street door. He starts guiltily, laying the mask on the table. Then he picks it up again quickly, takes the dead body and carries it off left. He reappears immediately and goes to the front door as the knocking recommences — gruffly.*) Hello! Who's there?

MARGARET. It's Margaret, Billy. I'm looking for Dion.

71

BROWN (*uncertainly*). Oh – all right – (*Unfastening door.*) Come in. Hello, Margaret. Hello, Boys! He's here. He's asleep. I – I was just dozing off too.

> (*Margaret enters. She is wearing her mask. The three sons are with her.*)

MARGARET (*seeing the bottle, forcing a laugh*). Has he been celebrating?

BROWN (*with strange glibness now*). No. I was. He wasn't. He said he'd sworn off to-night – for ever – for your sake – and the kids!

MARGARET (*with amazed joy*). Dion said that? (*Then hastily defensive.*) But of course he never does drink much. Where is he?

BROWN. Upstairs. I'll wake him. He felt bad. He took off his clothes to take a bath before he lay down. You just wait here.

> (*She sits in the chair where Dion had sat and stares straight before her. The Sons group around her, as if for a family photo. Brown hurries out left.*)

MARGARET. It's late to keep you boys up. Aren't you sleepy?

BOYS. No, Mother.

MARGARET (*proudly*). I'm glad to have three such strong boys to protect me.

ELDEST (*boastingly*). We'd kill anyone that touched you, wouldn't we?

NEXT. You bet! We'd make him wish he hadn't!

YOUNGEST. You bet!

MARGARET. You're Mother's brave boys! (*She laughs fondly – then curiously.*) Do you like Mr. Brown?

ELDEST. Sure thing! He's a regular fellow.

NEXT. He's all right!

YOUNGEST. Sure thing!

MARGARET (*half to herself*). Your father claims he steals his ideas.

ELDEST (*with a sheepish grin*). I'll bet father said that when he was – just talking.

NEXT. Mr. Brown doesn't have to steal, does he?

YOUNGEST. I should say not! He's awful rich.

MARGARET. Do you love your father?

ELDEST (*scuffling – embarrassed*). Why – of course –

NEXT (*ditto*). Sure thing!

YOUNGEST. Sure I do.

MARGARET (*with a sigh*). I think you'd better start on before – right now – before your father comes – He'll be very sick and nervous and he'll want to be quiet. So run along!

BOYS. All right.

> (*They file out and close the front door as Brown, dressed in Dion's clothes and wearing his mask, appears at left.*)

73

MARGARET (*taking off her mask, gladly*). Dion!
(*She stares wonderingly at him and he at her; goes
to him and puts an arm around him.*) Poor dear, do
you feel sick? (*He nods.*) But you look — (*squeezing his arms*) — why, you actually feel stronger and
better already! Is it true what Billy told me —
about your swearing off for ever? (*He nods. She
exclaims intensely.*) Oh, if you'll only — and get
well — we can still be so happy! Give Mother a
kiss. (*They kiss. A shudder passes through both of
them. She breaks away laughing with aroused
desire.*) Why, Dion? Aren't you ashamed? You
haven't kissed me like that for ages!

BROWN (*his voice imitating Dion's and muffled by
the mask*). I've wanted to, Margaret!

MARGARET (*gaily and coquettishly now*). Were
you afraid I'd spurn you? Why, Dion, something
has happened. It's like a miracle! Even your
voice is changed! It actually sounds younger; do
you know it? (*Then, solicitously.*) But you must
be worn out. Let's go home. (*With an impulsive
movement she flings her arms wide open, throwing her
mask away from her as if suddenly no longer needing
it.*) Oh, I'm beginning to feel so happy, Dion —
so happy!

BROWN (*stifledly*). Let's go home. (*She puts her
arm around him. They walk to the door.*)

(*Curtain*)

# ACT THREE

## SCENE ONE

SCENE. *The draughting-room and private office of Brown are both shown. The former is on the left, the latter on the right of a dividing wall at the centre. The arrangement of furniture in each room is the same as in previous scenes. It is ten in the morning of a day about a month later. The backdrop for both rooms is of plain wall with a few tacked-up designs and blue prints painted on it.*

*Two Draughtsmen, a middle-aged and a young man, both stoop-shouldered, are sitting on stools behind what was formerly Dion's table. They are tracing plans. They talk as they work.*

OLDER DRAUGHTSMAN. W. B. is late again.

YOUNGER DRAUGHTSMAN. Wonder what's got into him the last month? (*A pause. They work silently.*)

OLDER DRAUGHTSMAN. Yes, ever since he fired Dion. . . .

YOUNGER DRAUGHTSMAN. Funny his firing him all of a sudden like that. (*A pause. They work.*)

OLDER DRAUGHTSMAN. I haven't seen Dion around town since then. Have you?

YOUNGER DRAUGHTSMAN. No, not since Brown told us he'd sacked him. I suppose he's off drowning his sorrow!

OLDER DRAUGHTSMAN. I heard some one had seen him at home and he was sober and looking fine. (*A pause. They work.*)

YOUNGER DRAUGHTSMAN. What got into Brown? They say he fired all his old servants that same day and only uses his house to sleep in.

OLDER DRAUGHTSMAN (*with a sneer*). Artistic temperament, maybe — the real name of which is swelled head! (*There is a noise of footsteps from the hall. Warningly.*) Ssstt!

> (*They bend over their table. Margaret enters. She does not need to wear a mask now. Her face has regained the self-confident spirit of its youth, her eyes shine with happiness.*)

MARGARET (*heartily*). Good morning! What a lovely day!

BOTH (*perfunctorily*). Good morning, Mrs. Anthony.

MARGARET (*looking around*). You've been changing around in here, haven't you? Where is Dion? (*They stare at her.*) I forgot to tell him something important this morning and our phone's out of order. So if you'll tell him I'm here — (*They don't move. A pause. Margaret says stiffly.*) Oh, I realize Mr. Brown has given strict orders Dion is not to be disturbed, but surely. . . . (*Sharply.*) Where is my husband, please?

OLDER DRAUGHTSMAN. We don't know.

MARGARET. You don't know?

YOUNGER DRAUGHTSMAN. We haven't seen him.

MARGARET. Why, he left home at eight-thirty!

OLDER DRAUGHTSMAN. To come here?

YOUNGER DRAUGHTSMAN. This morning?

MARGARET (*provoked*). Why, of course, to come here – as he does every day! (*They stare at her. A pause.*)

OLDER DRAUGHTSMAN (*evasively*). We haven't seen him.

MARGARET (*with asperity*). Where is Mr. Brown?

YOUNGER DRAUGHTSMAN (*at a noise of footsteps from the hall – sulkily.*) Coming now.

> (*Brown enters. He is now wearing a mask which is an exact likeness of his face as it was in the last scene – the self-assured success. When he sees Margaret, he starts back apprehensively.*)

BROWN (*immediately controlling himself – breezily*). Hello, Margaret! This is a pleasant surprise! (*He holds out his hand.*)

MARGARET (*hardly taking it – reservedly*). Good morning.

BROWN (*turning quickly to the Draughtsmen*). I hope you explained to Mrs. Anthony how busy Dion . . .

MARGARET (*interrupting him – stiffly*). I certainly can't understand –

BROWN (*hastily*). I'll explain. Come in here and be comfortable. (*He throws open the door and ushers her into his private office.*)

OLDER DRAUGHTSMAN. Dion must be putting over some bluff on her.

YOUNGER DRAUGHTSMAN. Pretending he's still here – and Brown's helping him. . . .

OLDER DRAUGHTSMAN. But why should Brown, after he . . .?

YOUNGER DRAUGHTSMAN. Well, I suppose — Search me. (*They work.*)

BROWN. Have a chair, Margaret. (*She sits on the chair stiffly. He sits behind the desk.*)

MARGARET (*coldly*). I'd like some explanation. . . .

BROWN (*coaxingly*). Now, don't get angry, Margaret! Dion is hard at work on his design for the new State Capitol, and I don't want him disturbed, not even by you! So be a good sport! It's for his own good, remember! I asked him to explain to you.

MARGARET (*relenting*). He told me you'd agreed to ask me and the boys not to come here – but then, we hardly ever did.

BROWN. But you might! (*Then with confidential friendliness.*) This is for his sake, Margaret. I know Dion. He's got to be able to work without distractions. He's not the ordinary man; you appreciate that. And this design means his whole future! He's to get full credit for it, and as soon as it's accepted, I take him into partnership. It's all agreed. And after that I'm going to take a long vacation – go to Europe for a couple of years – and leave everything here in Dion's hands! Hasn't he told you all this?

MARGARET (*jubilant now*). Yes – but I could hardly believe . . . (*Proudly.*) I'm sure he can do it. He's been like a new man lately, so full of ambition and energy! It's made me so happy! (*She stops in confusion.*)

BROWN (*deeply moved, takes her hand impulsively*). And it has made me happy, too!

MARGARET (*confused – with an amused laugh*). Why, Billy Brown! For a moment, I thought it was Dion, your voice sounded so much . . .!

BROWN (*with sudden desperation*). Margaret, I've got to tell you! I can't go on like this any longer! I've got to confess. . . .! There's something. . .!

MARGARET (*alarmed*). Not – not about Dion?

BROWN (*harshly*). To hell with Dion! To hell with Billy Brown! (*He tears off his mask and reveals a suffering face that is ravaged and haggard, his own face tortured and distorted by the demon of Dion's mask.*) Think of me! I love you, Margaret! Leave him! I've always loved you! Come away with me! I'll sell out here! We'll go abroad and be happy!

MARGARET (*amazed*). Billy Brown, do you realize what you're saying? (*With a shudder.*) Are you crazy? Your face – is terrible. You're sick! Shall I phone for a doctor?

BROWN (*turning away slowly and putting on his mask – dully.*) No. I've been on the verge – of a breakdown – for some time. I get spells. . . . I'm better now. (*He turns back to her.*) Forgive me! Forget what I said! But, for all our sakes, don't come here again.

MARGARET (*coldly*). After this – I assure you . . . ! (*Then looking at him with pained incredulity.*) Why, Billy – I simply won't believe – after all these years. . . .!

BROWN. It will never happen again. Good-bye.

MARGARET. Good-bye. (*Then, wishing to leave on a pleasant change of subject – forcing a smile.*) Don't work Dion to death! He's never home for dinner any more.

> (*She goes out past the Draughtsmen and off right, rear. Brown sits down at his desk, taking off the mask again. He stares at it with bitter, cynical amusement.*)

BROWN. You're dead, William Brown, dead beyond hope of resurrection! It's the Dion you buried in your garden who killed you, not you him! It's Margaret's husband who ... (*He laughs harshly.*) Paradise by proxy! Love by mistaken identity! God! (*This is almost a prayer – then fiercely defiant.*) But it *is* paradise! I *do* love!

> (*As he is speaking, a well-dressed, important, stout man enters the draughting-room. He is carrying a rolled-up plan in his hand. He nods condescendingly and goes directly to Brown's door, on which he raps sharply, and, without waiting for an answer, turns the knob. Brown has just time to turn his head and get his mask on*).

MAN (*briskly*). Ah, good morning! I came right in. Hope I didn't disturb ...?

BROWN (*the successful architect now – urbanely*). Not at all, sir. How are you? (*They shake hands.*) Sit down. Have a cigar. And now what can I do for you this morning?

MAN (*unrolling his plan*). It's your plan. My wife and I have been going over it again. We like it – and we don't – and when a man plans to lay out half a million, why he wants everything exactly right, eh? (*Brown nods.*) It's too cold, too spare, too like a tomb, if you'll pardon me, for a liveable home. Can't you liven it up, put in some decorations, make it fancier and warmer – you know what I mean. (*Looks at him a bit doubtfully.*) People tell me you had an assistant, Anthony, who was a real shark on these details but that you've fired him —

BROWN (*suavely*). Gossip! He's still with me but, for reasons of his own, doesn't wish it known. Yes, I trained him and he's very ingenious. I'll turn this right over to him and instruct him to carry out your wishes.

(*Curtain*)

# ACT THREE

SCENE. *The same as Act Two, Scene Three — the library of Brown's home about eight the same night. He can be heard feeling his way in through the dark. He switches on the reading lamp on the table. Directly under it on a sort of stand is the mask of Dion, its empty eyes staring front.*

*Brown takes off his own mask and lays it on the table before Dion's. He flings himself down in the chair and stares without moving into the eyes of Dion's mask. Finally, he begins to talk to it in a bitter, mocking tone.)*

BROWN. Listen! To-day was a narrow escape — for us! We can't avoid discovery much longer. We must get our plot to working! We've already made William Brown's will, leaving you his money and business. We must hustle off to Europe now — and murder him there! (*A bit tauntingly.*) Then you — the I in you — *I* will live with Margaret happily ever after. (*More tauntingly.*) She will have children by me! (*He seems to hear some mocking denial from the mask. He bends toward it.*) What? (*Then with a sneer.*) Anyway, that doesn't matter! Your children already love me more than they ever loved you! And Margaret loves me more! You think you've won, do you — that I've got to vanish into you in order to live? Not yet, my friend! Never! Wait! Gradually Margaret will love what is beneath — me! Little by little I'll teach her to know me, and then finally I'll reveal myself to her, and confess that I stole your place out of love for her, and she'll understand and forgive and love me! And you'll be forgotten! Ha! (*Again he bends down to the mask as if listening — torturedly.*) What's that? She'll never believe? She'll never see? She'll never understand? You lie, devil! (*He reaches out his hands as if to take the mask by the throat, then shrinks back with a shudder of hopeless despair.*) God have mercy! Let me believe! Blessed are the merciful! Let me obtain mercy! (*He waits, his face upturned — pleadingly.*) Not yet? (*Despairingly.*) Never? (*A pause. Then, in a sudden panic of dread, he reaches out for the mask of Dion like a dope fiend after a drug. As soon as he holds it, he seems to gain strength and is able to force a sad laugh.*) Now I am drinking your strength, Dion — strength to love in this world and die and sleep and become fertile earth, as you are becoming now in my garden — your weakness the strength of my flowers, your failure as an artist painting their petals with life! (*Then, with bravado.*) Come with me while Margaret's bridegroom dresses in your clothes, Mr. Anthony! I need the devil when I'm in the dark! (*He goes off left, but can be heard talking.*) Your clothes begin to fit me better than my own! Hurry, Brother! It's time we were home. Our wife is waiting! (*He reappears, having changed his*

# THE GREAT GOD BROWN

*coat and trousers.*) Come with me and tell her again I love her! Come and hear her tell me how she loves you! (*He suddenly cannot help kissing the mask.*) I love you because she loves you! My kisses on your lips are for her! (*He puts the mask over his face and stands for a moment, seeming to grow tall and proud — then with a laugh of bold self-assurance.*) Out by the back way! I mustn't forget I'm a desperate criminal, pursued by God, and by myself! (*He goes out right, laughing with amused satisfaction.*)

## (*Curtain*)

# ACT THREE

## SCENE THREE

SCENE. *Is the same as Scene One of Act One – the sitting-room of Margaret's home. It is about half an hour after the last scene. Margaret sits on the sofa, waiting with the anxious, impatient expectancy of one deeply in love. She is dressed with a careful, subtle extra touch to attract the eye. She looks young and happy. She is trying to read a book. The front door is heard opening and closing. She leaps up and runs back to throw her arms around Brown as he enters from right, rear. She kisses him passionately.*

MARGARET *(as he recoils with a sort of guilt – laughingly).* Why, you hateful old thing, you! I really believe you were trying to avoid kissing me! Well, just for that, I'll never . . .

BROWN *(with fierce, defiant passion, kisses her again and again).* Margaret!

MARGARET. Call me Peggy again. You used to when you really loved me. *(Softly.)* Remember the school commencement dance – you and I on the dock in the moonlight?

BROWN *(with pain).* No. *(He takes his arms from around her.)*

MARGARET *(still holding him – with a laugh).* Well, I like that! You old bear, you! Why not?

BROWN *(sadly).* It was so long ago.

86

MARGARET (*a bit melancholy*). You mean you don't want to be reminded that we're getting old?

BROWN. Yes. (*He kisses her gently.*) I'm tired. Let's sit down. (*They sit on the sofa, his arm about her, her head on his shoulder.*)

MARGARET (*with a happy sigh*). I don't mind remembering — now I'm happy. It's only when I'm unhappy that it hurts — and I've been so happy lately, dear — and so grateful to you! (*He stirs uneasily. She goes on joyfully.*) Everything's changed! I'd got pretty resigned to — and sad and hopeless, too — and then all at once you turn right around and everything is the same as when we were first married — much better even, for I was never sure of you then. You were always so strange and aloof and alone, it seemed I was never really touching you. But now I feel you've become quite human — like me — and I'm so happy, dear! (*She kisses him.*)

BROWN (*his voice trembling*). Then I have made you happy — happier than ever before — no matter what happens? (*She nods.*) Then — that justifies everything! (*He forces a laugh.*)

MARGARET. Of course it does! I've always known that. But you — you wouldn't be — or you couldn't be — and I could never help you — and all the time I knew you were so lonely! I could always hear you calling to me that you were lost, but I couldn't find the path to you because I was lost, too! That's an awful way for a wife to feel!

(*She laughs – joyfully.*) But now you're here! You're mine! You're my long-lost lover, and my husband, and my big boy, too!

BROWN (*with a trace of jealousy*). Where are your other big boys to-night?

MARGARET. Out to a dance. They've all acquired girls, I'll have you know.

BROWN (*mockingly*). Aren't you jealous?

MARGARET (*gaily*). Of course! Terribly! But I'm diplomatic. I don't let them see. (*Changing the subject.*) Believe me, they've noticed the change in you! The eldest was saying to me to-day: "It's great not to have Father so nervous, any more. Why, he's a regular sport when he gets started!" And the other two said very solemnly: "You bet!" (*She laughs.*)

BROWN (*brokenly*). I – I'm glad.

MARGARET. Dion! You're crying!

BROWN (*stung by the name, gets up – harshly*). Nonsense! Did you ever know Dion to cry about anyone?

MARGARET (*sadly*). You couldn't – then. You were too lonely. You had no one to cry to.

BROWN (*goes and takes a rolled-up plan from the table drawer – dully*). I've got to do some work.

MARGARET (*disappointedly*). What, has that old Billy Brown got you to work at home again, too?

BROWN (*ironically*). It's for Dion's good, you know – and yours.

MARGARET (*making the best of it – cheerfully*). All right, I won't be selfish. It really makes me proud for you to be so ambitious. Let me help.

(*She brings his drawing-board, which he puts on the table and pins his plan upon. She sits on sofa and picks up her book.*)

BROWN (*carefully casual*). I hear you were in to see me to-day?

MARGARET. Yes, and Billy wouldn't hear of it! I was quite furious until he convinced me it was all for the best. When is he going to take you into partnership?

BROWN. Very soon now.

MARGARET. And will he really give you full charge when he goes abroad?

BROWN. Yes.

MARGARET (*practically*). I'd pin him down if I could. Promises are all right, but – (*she hesitates*) I don't trust him.

BROWN (*with a start, sharply*). What makes you say that?

MARGARET. Oh, something that happened to-day.

BROWN. What?

MARGARET. I don't mean I blame him, but – to be frank, I think the Great God Brown, as you call him, is getting a bit queer and it's time he took a vacation. Don't you?

D

BROWN (*his voice a bit excited – but guardedly*). But why? What did he do?

MARGARET (*hesitatingly*). Well – it's really too silly – he suddenly got awfully strange. His face scared me. It was like a corpse. Then he raved on some nonsense about he'd always loved me. He went on like a perfect fool! (*She looks at Brown, who is staring at her. She becomes uneasy.*) Maybe I shouldn't tell you this. He simply wasn't responsible. Then he came to himself and was all right and begged my pardon and seemed dreadfully sorry, and I felt sorry for him. (*Then with a shudder.*) But honestly, Dion, it was just too disgusting for words to hear him! (*With kind, devastating contempt.*) Poor Billy!

BROWN (*with a show of tortured derision*). Poor Billy! Poor Billy the Goat! (*With mocking frenzy.*) I'll kill him for you! I'll serve you his heart for breakfast!

MARGARET (*jumping up – frightenedly*). Dion!

BROWN (*waving his pencil knife with grotesque flourishes*). I tell you I'll murder this God-damned disgusting Great God Brown who stands like a fatted calf in the way of our health and wealth and happiness!

MARGARET (*bewilderedly, not knowing how much is pretending, puts an arm about him*). Don't, dear! You're being horrid and strange again. It makes me afraid you haven't really changed, after all.

BROWN (*unheeding*). And then my wife can be

happy! Ha! (*He laughs. She begins to cry. He controls himself — pats her head — gently.*) All right, dear. Mr. Brown is now safely in hell. Forget him!

MARGARET (*stops crying — but still worriedly*). I should never have told you — but I never imagined you'd take it seriously. I've never thought of Billy Brown except as a friend, and lately not even that! He's just a stupid old fool!

BROWN. Ha-ha! Didn't I say he was in hell? They're torturing him! (*Then controlling himself again — exhaustedly.*) Please leave me alone now. I've got to work.

MARGARET. All right, dear. I'll go into the next room and anything you want, just call. (*She pats his face — cajolingly.*) Is it all forgotten?

BROWN. Will you be happy?

MARGARET. Yes.

BROWN. Then it's dead, I promise! (*She kisses him and goes out. He stares ahead, then shakes off his thoughts and concentrates on his work — mockingly.*) Our beautiful new Capitol calls you, Mr. Dion! To work! We'll adroitly hide old Silenus on the cupola! Let him dance over their law-making with his eternal leer! (*He bends over his work.*)

(*Curtain*)

# ACT FOUR

## SCENE ONE

SCENE. *Same as Scene One of Act Three — the draughting-room and Brown's office. It is dusk of a day about a month later.*

*The two draughtsmen are bent over their table, working.*

*Brown, at his desk, is working feverishly over a plan. He is wearing the mask of Dion. The mask of William Brown rests on the desk beside him. As he works, he chuckles with malicious glee — finally flings down his pencil with a flourish.*

BROWN. Done! In the name of the Almighty Brown, amen, amen! Here's a wondrous fair capitol! The design would do just as well for a Home for Criminal Imbeciles! Yet to them, such is my art, it will appear to possess a pure common-sense, a fat-bellied finality, as dignified as the suspenders of an assemblyman! Only to me will that pompous façade reveal itself as the wearily ironic grin of Pan as, his ears drowsy with the crumbling hum of past and future civilizations, he half-listens to the laws passed by his fleas to enslave him! Ha-ha-ha! (*He leaps grotesquely from behind his desk and cuts a few goatish capers, laughing with lustful merriment.*) Long live Chief of Police Brown! District Attorney Brown! Alderman Brown! Assemblyman Brown! Mayor Brown!

Congressman Brown! Governor Brown! Senator Brown! President Brown! (*He chants.*) Oh, how many persons in one God make up the good God Brown? Hahahaha! (*The two Draughtsmen in the next room have stopped work and are listening.*)

YOUNGER DRAUGHTSMAN. Drunk as a fool!

OLDER DRAUGHTSMAN. At least Dion used to have the decency to stay away from the office —

YOUNGER DRAUGHTSMAN. Funny how it's got hold of Brown so quick!

OLDER DRAUGHTSMAN. He was probably hitting it up on the Q.T. all the time.

BROWN (*has come back to his desk, laughing to himself and out of breath*). Time to become respectable again! (*He takes off the Dion mask and reaches out for the William Brown one — then stops, with a hand on each, staring down on the plan with fascinated loathing. His real face is now sick, ghastly, tortured, hollow-cheeked and feverish-eyed.*) Ugly! Hideous! Despicable! Why must the demon in me pander to cheapness — then punish me with self-loathing and life-hatred? Why am I not strong enough to perish — or blind enough to be content? (*To heaven, bitterly but pleadingly.*) Give me the strength to destroy this! — and myself! — and him! — and I will believe in Thee! (*While he has been speaking there has been a noise from the stairs. The two Draughtsmen have bent over their work. Margaret enters, closing the door behind her. At this sound, Brown starts. He immediately senses who it is*

94

*— with alarm.*) *Margaret!* (*He grabs up both masks and goes into room off right.*)

MARGARET (*she looks healthy and happy, but her face wears a worried, solicitous expression — pleasantly to the staring Draughtsmen.*) Good morning. Oh, you needn't look worried, it's Mr. Brown I want to see, not my husband.

YOUNGER DRAUGHTSMAN (*hesitatingly*). He's locked himself in — but maybe if you'll knock —

MARGARET (*knocks — somewhat embarrassedly*). Mr. Brown!

(*Brown enters his office, wearing the William Brown mask. He comes quickly to the other door and unlocks it.*)

BROWN (*with a hectic cordiality*). Come on, Margaret! Enter! This is delightful! Sit down! What can I do for you?

MARGARET (*taken aback — a bit stiffly*). Nothing much.

BROWN. Something about Dion, of course. Well, your darling pet is all right — never better!

MARGARET (*coldly*). That's a matter of opinion. I think you're working him to death.

BROWN. Oh, no, not him. It's Brown who is to die. We've agreed on that.

MARGARET (*giving him a queer look*). I'm serious.

BROWN. So am I. Deadly serious! Hahaha!

MARGARET (*checking her indignation*). That's

what I came to see you about. Really, Dion has acted so hectic and on edge lately I'm sure he's on the verge of a breakdown.

BROWN. Well, it certainly isn't drink. He hasn't had a drop. He doesn't need it! Haha! And I haven't either, although the gossips are beginning to say I'm soused all the time! It's because I've started to laugh! Hahaha! They can't believe in joy in this town except by the bottle! What funny little people! Hahaha! When you're the Great God Brown, eh, Margaret? Hahaha!

MARGARET (*getting up – uneasily*). I'm afraid I –

BROWN. Don't be afraid, my dear! I won't make love to you again! Honour bright! I'm too near the grave for such folly! But it must have been funny for you when you came here the last time – watching a disgusting old fool like me, eh? – too funny for words! Hahaha! (*Then with a sudden movement he flourishes the design before her.*) Look! We've finished it! Dion has finished it! His fame is made!

MARGARET (*tartly*). Really, Billy, I believe you are drunk!

BROWN. Nobody kisses me – so you can all believe the worst! Hahaha!

MARGARET (*chillingly*). Then if Dion is through, why can't I see him?

BROWN (*crazily*). See Dion? See Dion? Well,

why not? It's an age of miracles. The streets are full of Lazaruses. Pray! I mean – wait a moment, if you please.

> (*Brown disappears into the room off right. A moment later he reappears in the mask of Dion. He holds out his arms and Margaret rushes into them. They kiss passionately. Finally he sits with her on the lounge.*)

MARGARET. So you've finished it.

BROWN. Yes. The Committee is coming to see it soon. I've made all the changes they'll like, the fools!

MARGARET (*lovingly*). And can we go on that second honeymoon, right away now?

BROWN. In a week or so, I hope – as soon as I've got Brown off to Europe.

MARGARET. Tell me – isn't he drinking hard?

BROWN (*laughing as Brown did*). Haha! Soused to the ears all the time! Soused on life! He can't stand it! It's burning his insides out!

MARGARET (*alarmed*). Dear! I'm worried about you. You sound as crazy as he did – when you laugh! You must rest!

BROWN (*controlling himself*). I'll rest in peace – when he's gone!

MARGARET (*with a queer look*). Why, Dion, that isn't your suit. It's just like –

BROWN. It's his! We're getting to be like twins. I'm inheriting his clothes already! (*Then calming himself as he sees how frightened she is.*) Don't be worried, dear. I'm just a trifle elated, now the job's done. I guess I'm a bit soused on life, too!

> (*The Committee, three important-looking, average personages, come into the draughting-room.*)

MARGARET (*forcing a smile.*) Well, don't let it burn *your* insides out!

BROWN. No danger! Mine were tempered in hell! Hahaha!

MARGARET (*kissing him, coaxingly*). Come home, dear — please!

OLDER DRAUGHTSMAN (*knocks on the door*). The Committee is here, Mr. Brown.

BROWN (*hurriedly to Margaret*). You receive them. Hand them the design. I'll get Brown. (*He raises his voice.*) Come right in, gentlemen.

> (*He goes off right, as the Committee enter the office. When they see Margaret, they stop in surprise.*)

MARGARET (*embarrassedly*). Good afternoon. Mr. Brown will be right with you. (*They bow. Margaret holds out the design to them.*) This is my husband's design. He finished it to-day.

COMMITTEE. Ah! (*They crowd around to look at it*

*— with enthusiasm.*) Perfect! Splendid! Couldn't be better! Exactly what we suggested.

MARGARET (*joyfully*). Then you accept it? Mr. Anthony will be so pleased!

MEMBER. Mr. Anthony?

ANOTHER. Is he working here again?

THIRD. Did I understand you to say this was your husband's design?

MARGARET (*excitedly*). Yes! Entirely his! He's worked like a dog — (*Appalled.*) You don't mean to say — Mr. Brown never told you? (*They shake their heads in solemn surprise.*) Oh, the contemptible cad! I hate him!

BROWN (*appearing at right — mockingly*). Hate me, Margaret? Hate Brown? How superfluous! (*Oratorically.*) Gentlemen, I have been keeping a secret from you in order that you might be the more impressed when I revealed it. That design is entirely the inspiration of Mr. Dion Anthony's genius. I had nothing to do with it.

MARGARET (*contritely*). Oh, Billy! I'm sorry! Forgive me!

BROWN (*ignoring her, takes the plan from the Committee and begins unpinning it from the board — mockingly*). I can see by your faces you have approved this. You are delighted, aren't you? And why not, my dear sirs? Look at it, and look at you! Hahaha! It'll immortalize you, my good men! You'll be as death-defying a joke as any in

Joe Miller! (*Then with a sudden complete change of tone – angrily.*) You damn fools! Can't you see this is an insult – a terrible, blasphemous insult! – that this embittered failure Anthony is hurling in the teeth of our success – an insult to you, to me, to you, Margaret – and to Almighty God! (*In a frenzy of fury.*) And if you are weak and cowardly enough to stand for it, I'm not!

> (*He tears the plan into four pieces. The Committee stand aghast. Margaret runs forward.*)

MARGARET (*in a scream*). You coward! Dion! Dion! (*She picks up the plan and hugs it to her bosom.*)

BROWN (*with a sudden goatish caper*). I'll tell him you're here. (*He disappears, but reappears almost immediately in the mask of Dion. He is imposing a terrible discipline on himself to avoid dancing and laughing. He speaks suavely.*) Everything is all right – all for the best – you mustn't get excited! A little paste, Margaret! A little paste, gentlemen! And all will be well. Life is imperfect, Brothers! Men have their faults, Sister! But with a few drops of glue much may be done! A little dab of pasty resignation here and there – and even broken hearts may be repaired to do yeoman service! (*He has edged toward the door. They are all staring at him with petrified bewilderment. He puts his finger to his lips.*) Ssssh! This is Daddy's bedtime secret for to-day: Man is born broken. He lives by mending. The grace of God is glue! (*With a quick prancing movement, he has opened the door, gone through, and closed it after him silently, shaking with suppressed laughter. He springs lightly to the side of the petrified Draughtsmen – in a whisper.*) They will find him in the little room. Mr. William Brown is dead!

> (*With light leaps he vanishes, his head thrown back, shaking with silent laughter. The sound of his feet leaping down the stairs, five at a time, can be heard. Then a pause of silence. The people in the two rooms stare. The Younger Draughtsman is the first to recover.*)

YOUNGER DRAUGHTSMAN (*rushing into the next room, shouts in terrified tones*). Mr. Brown is dead!

COMMITTEE. He murdered him!

> *They all run into the little room off right. Margaret remains, stunned with horror. They return in a moment, carrying the mask of William Brown, two on each side, as if they were carrying a body by the legs and shoulders. They solemnly lay him down on the couch and stand looking down at him.*)

FIRST COMMITTEEMAN (*with a frightened awe*). I can't believe he's gone.

SECOND COMMITTEEMAN (*in same tone*). I can

almost hear him talking. (*As if impelled, he clears his throat and addresses the mask importantly.*) Mr. Brown — (*then stops short.*)

THIRD COMMITTEEMAN (*shrinking back*). No. Dead, all right! (*Then suddenly, hysterically angry and terrified.*) We must take steps at once to run Anthony to earth!

MARGARET (*with a heart-broken cry*). Dion's innocent!

YOUNGER DRAUGHTSMAN. I'll phone for the police, sir! (*He rushes to the phone.*)

(*Curtain*)

# ACT FOUR

## SCENE TWO

SCENE. *The same as Scene Two of Act Three — the library of William Brown's home. The mask of Dion stands on the table beneath the light, facing front.*

*On his knees beside the table, facing front, stripped naked except for a white cloth around his loins, is Brown. The clothes he has torn off in his agony are scattered on the floor. His eyes, his arms, his whole body strain upward, his muscles writhe with his lips as they pray silently in their agonized supplication. Finally a voice seems torn out of him.*

BROWN. Mercy, Compassionate Saviour of Man! Out of my depths I cry to you! Mercy on thy poor clod, thy clot of unhallowed earth, thy clay, the Great God Brown! Mercy, Saviour! (*He seems to wait for an answer — then leaping to his feet he puts out one hand to touch the mask like a frightened child reaching out for its nurse's hand — then with immediate mocking despair.*) Bah! I am sorry, little children, but your kingdom is empty. God has become disgusted and moved away to some far ecstatic star where life is a dancing flame! We must die without him. (*Then — addressing the mask — harshly.*) Together, my friend! You, too! Let Margaret suffer! Let the whole world suffer as I am suffering!

(*There is a sound of a door being pushed violently open, padding feet in slippers, and Cybel, wearing her mask, runs into the room. She stops short on seeing Brown and the mask, and stares from one to the other for a second in confusion. She is dressed in a black kimono robe and wears slippers over her bear feet. Her yellow hair hangs down in a great mane over her shoulders. She has grown stouter, has more of the deep objective calm of an idol.*)

BROWN (*staring at her – fascinated – with great peace as if her presence comforted him*). Cybel! I was coming to you! How did you know?

CYBEL (*takes off her mask and looks from Brown to the Dion mask, now with a great understanding*). So that's why you never came to me again! You are Dion Brown!

BROWN (*bitterly*). I am the remains of William Brown! (*He points to the mask of Dion.*) I am his murderer and his murdered!

CYBEL (*with a laugh of exasperated pity*). Oh, why can't you ever learn to leave yourselves alone and leave me alone.

BROWN (*boyishly and naïvely*). I am Billy.

CYBEL (*immediately, with a motherly solicitude*). Then run, Billy, run! They are hunting for some one! They came to my place, hunting for a murderer, Dion! They must find a victim! They've got to quiet their fears, to cast out their devils, or they'll never sleep soundly again! They've got to absolve themselves by finding a guilty one! They've got to kill some one now, to live! You're naked! You must be Satan! Run, Billy, run! They'll come here! I ran here to warn — some one! So run away if you want to live!

BROWN (*like a sulky child*). I'm too tired. I don't want to.

CYBEL (*with motherly calm*). All right, you needn't, Billy. Don't sulk. (*As a noise comes from outside.*) Anyway, it's too late. I hear them in the garden now.

BROWN (*listening, puts out his hand and takes the mask of Dion — as he gains strength, mockingly*). Thanks for this one last favour, Dion! Listen! Your avengers! Standing on your grave in the garden! Hahaha! (*He puts on the mask and springs to the left and makes a gesture as if flinging French windows open. Gaily mocking.*) Welcome, dumb worshippers! I am your great God Brown! I have been advised to run from you but it is my almighty whim to dance into escape over your prostrate souls!

> (*Shouts from the garden and a volley of shots. Brown staggers back and falls on the floor by the couch, mortally wounded.*)

CYBEL (*runs to his side, lifts him on to the couch and*

*takes off the mask of Dion).* You can't take this to bed with you. You've got to go to sleep alone.

> (*She places the mask of Dion back on its stand under the light and puts on her own, just as, after a banging of doors, crashing of glass, trampling of feet, a Squad of Police with drawn revolvers, led by a grizzly, brutal-faced Captain, run into the room. They are followed by Margaret, still distractedly clutching the pieces of the plan to her breast.*)

CAPTAIN (*pointing to the mask of Dion — triumphantly*). Got him! He's dead!

MARGARET (*throws herself on her knees, takes the mask and kisses it — heart-brokenly*). Dion! Dion!

> (*Her face hidden in her arms, the mask in her hands above her bowed head, she remains, sobbing with deep, silent grief.*)

CAPTAIN (*noticing Cybel and Brown — startled*). Hey! Look at this! What're you doin' here? Who's he?

CYBEL. You ought to know. You croaked him!

CAPTAIN (*with a defensive snarl — hastily*). It was Anthony! I saw his mug! This feller's an accomplice, I bet yuh! Serves him right! Who is he? Friend o' yours! Crook! What's his name? Tell me or I'll fix yuh!

CYBEL. Billy.

CAPTAIN. Billy what?

CYBEL. I don't know. He's dying. (*Then suddenly.*) Leave me alone with him and maybe I'll get him to squeal it.

CAPTAIN. Yuh better! I got to have a clean report. I'll give yuh a couple o' minutes.

> (*He motions to the Policemen, who follow him off left. Cybel takes off her mask and sits down by Brown's head. He makes an effort to raise himself toward her and she helps him, throwing her kimono over his bare body, drawing his head on to her shoulder.*)

BROWN (*snuggling against her – gratefully*). The earth is warm.

CYBEL (*soothingly, looking before her like an idol*). Ssshh! Go to sleep, Billy.

BROWN. Yes, Mother. (*Then explainingly.*) It was dark and I couldn't see where I was going and they all picked on me.

CYBEL. I know. You're tired.

BROWN. And when I wake up . . .?

CYBEL. The sun will be rising again.

BROWN. To judge the living and the dead! (*Frightenedly.*) I don't want justice. I want love.

CYBEL. There is only love.

BROWN. Thank you, Mother. (*Then feebly.*)

I'm getting sleepy. What's the prayer you taught me — Our Father — ?

CYBEL (*with calm exultance*). Our Father Who Art!

BROWN (*taking her tone — exultantly*). Who art! Who art! (*Suddenly — with ecstasy.*) I know! I have found Him! I hear Him speak! "Blessed are they that weep, for they shall laugh!" Only he that has wept can laugh! The laughter of Heaven sows earth with a rain of tears, and out of Earth's transfigured birth-pain the laughter of Man returns to bless and play again in innumerable dancing gales of flame upon the knees of God! (*He dies.*)

CYBEL (*gets up and arranges his body on the couch. She bends down and kisses him gently — she straightens up and looks into space — with a profound pain*). Always spring comes again bearing life! Always again! Always, always for ever again! — Spring again! — life again! — summer and autumn and death and peace again! — (*with agonized sorrow*) — but always, always, love and conception and birth and pain again — spring bearing the intolerable chalice of life again! — (*then with agonized exultance*) — bearing the glorious, blazing crown of life again! (*She stands like an idol of Earth, her eyes staring out over the world.*)

MARGARET (*lifting her head adoringly to the mask — triumphant tenderness mingled with her grief*). My lover! My husband! My boy! (*She kisses the*

108

*mask.*) Good-bye. Thank you for happiness! And you're not dead, sweetheart! You can never die till my heart dies! You will live for ever! You will sleep under my heart! I will feel you stirring in your sleep, for ever under my heart! (*She kisses the mask again. There is a pause.*)

CAPTAIN (*comes just into sight at left and speaks front without looking at them — gruffly*). Well, what's his name?

CYBEL. Man!

CAPTAIN (*taking a grimy notebook and an inch-long pencil from his pocket*). How d'yuh spell it?

(*Curtain*)

# EPILOGUE

SCENE. *Four years later.*

> *The same spot on the same pier as in Prologue on another moonlight night in June. The sound of the waves and of distant dance music.*

> *Margaret and her three sons appear from the right. The eldest is now eighteen. All are dressed in the height of correct school elegance. They are all tall, athletic, strong and handsome-looking. They loom up around the slight figure of their mother like protecting giants, giving her a strange aspect of lonely, detached, small femininity. She wears her mask of the proud, indulgent Mother. She has grown appreciably older. Her hair is now a beautiful grey. There is about her manner and voice the sad but contented feeling of one who knows her life-purpose well accomplished but is at the same time a bit empty and comfortless with the finality of it. She is wrapped in a grey cloak.*

ELDEST. Doesn't Bee look beautiful to-night, Mother?

NEXT. Don't you think Mabel's the best dancer in there, Mother?

YOUNGEST. Aw, Alice has them both beat, hasn't she, Mother?

MARGARET (*with a sad little laugh*). Each of you is right. (*Then, with strange finality.*) Good-bye, boys.

BOYS (*surprised*). Good-bye.

MARGARET. It was here on a night just like this your father first — proposed to me. Did you ever know that?

BOYS (*embarrassedly*). No.

MARGARET (*yearningly*). But the nights now are so much colder than they used to be. Think of it, I went in for moonlight-bathing in June when I was a girl. It was so warm and beautiful in those days. I remember the Junes when I was carrying you boys — (*A pause. They fidget uneasily. She asks pleadingly.*) Promise me faithfully never to forget your father!

BOYS (*uncomfortably*). Yes, Mother.

MARGARET (*forcing a joking tone*). But you mustn't waste June on an old woman like me! Go in and dance. (*As they hesitate dutifully.*) Go on. I really want to be alone — with my Junes.

BOYS (*unable to conceal their eagerness*). Yes, Mother. (*They go away.*)

MARGARET (*slowly removes her mask, laying it on the bench, and stares up at the moon with a wistful, resigned sweetness*). So long ago! And yet I'm still the same Margaret. It's only our lives that grow old. We *are* where centuries only count as seconds and after a thousand lives our eyes begin to open — (*she looks around her with a rapt smile*) — and the moon rests in the sea! I want to feel the moon at peace in the sea! I want Dion to leave the sky for me! I want him to sleep in the tides of my heart! (*She slowly takes from under her cloak, from her bosom, as if from her heart, the mask of Dion as it was at the last and holds it before her face.*) My lover! My husband! My boy! You can never die till my heart dies! You will live for ever! You are sleeping under my heart! I feel you stirring in your sleep, for ever under my heart. (*She kisses him on the lips with a timeless kiss.*)

**(Curtain)**

# The Fountain

# Characters

IBNU ASWAD, *a Moorish chieftain*

JUAN PONCE DE LEON

PEDRO, *his servant*

MARIA DE CORDOVA

LUIS DE ALVAREDO

YUSEF, *a Moorish minstrel*

DIEGO MENENDEZ, *a Franciscan*

VICENTE DE CORDOVA, *Maria's husband*

ALONZO DE OVIEDO

MANUEL DE CASTILLO  } *nobles*

CRISTOVAL DE MENDOZA

A SOLDIER

FRIAR QUESADA, *a Franciscan*

BEATRIZ DE CORDOVA, *daughter of Maria and Vicente*

NANO, *an Indian chief*

A CHIEF OF THE INDIANS IN FLORIDA

A MEDICINE MAN

A FIGURE

A POET OF CATHAY

AN OLD INDIAN WOMAN OF THE BAHAMAS

A DOMINICAN MONK

FATHER SUPERIOR OF THE DOMINICANS IN CUBA

JUAN, *nephew of Juan Ponce de Leon*

*Nobles, Monks, Soldiers, Sailors, Captive Indians of Porto Rico, Indians in Florida.*

TIME: Late Fifteenth and early Sixteenth Centuries.

3

# Scenes

## PART ONE

5

# The Fountain

## SCENE ONE

SCENE. *Courtyard of Ibnu Aswad's palace in Granada.*

The section forms a right triangle, its apex at the rear, right. In the left, centre, a massive porte-cochère opens on the street. On the right, a door leading into the house itself. In the centre of the courtyard, a large splendid fountain of green marble with human and animal figures in gilt bronze. The peristyle of the gallery running around the court is supported by slender columns of polished marble, partly gilded. The interspaces above the horseshoe arches springing from the columns are filled with arabesques, texts from the Koran, red, blue and gold in colour. Above are the latticed windows of the women's apartments. Over the house-top a sky with stars can be seen. It is early night.

As the curtain rises, the court is empty and there is silence except for the splash of the fountain. Then a loud, imperious knocking, as of someone pounding with the hilt of a sword, is heard from the porte-cochère. Ibnu Aswad enters from the right. He is an elderly, noble-looking Moor, the lower part of his face covered by a long, white beard. His expression is one of great pride borne down by sorrow and humiliation. He goes out through the porte-cochère,

7

*and returns ushering in Juan Ponce de Leon and his servant, Pedro. Juan is a tall, handsome Spanish noble of thirty-one, dressed in full uniform. His countenance is haughty, full of a romantic adventurousness and courage; yet he gives the impression of disciplined ability, of a confident self-mastery — a romantic dreamer governed by the ambitious thinker in him. Pedro is a dull-looking young fellow.*

JUAN (*as they enter*) (*to Aswad*). Your pardon, Sir Moor.

ASWAD (*haughtily*). You are quartered here? (*Juan bows in affirmation.*) Welcome then, since it is the will of Allah that you should conquer.

JUAN (*graciously*). I am no conqueror here. I am a stranger grateful for hospitality.

ASWAD (*unbending a bit*). You are kind. I have seen you in action on the field. You are brave. Defeat loses its bitterness when the foe is noble. (*Moodily and bitterly — staring at the fountain.*) The waters of the fountain fall — but ever they rise again, Sir Spaniard. Such is the decree of destiny. (*With fervour.*) Blessed be Allah who exalteth and debaseth the kings of the earth, according to his divine will, in whose fulfilment consists eternal justice. (*Fiercely and defiantly.*) Whosoever the victor, there is no conqueror but Allah!

JUAN (*stiffening — coldly*). Your fortitude does you honour. (*By way of dismissing the subject —*
8

*abruptly*.) I am expecting friends. Will that disturb your household? If so —

ASWAD (*coldly*). My house is your house. It is decreed. (*He bows with stately grace and goes out, right*.)

JUAN (*makes a movement as if to detain him — then shrugs his shoulders*). What can I do for him? (*Ironically repeating Ibnu's inflexion*.) It is decreed by Spain if not by Allah. (*Seeing Pedro lolling against the wall, drowsily staring at the fountain — amused*.) Lazy lout! Does the fountain cause you, too, to dream? (*In a tone of command*.) Bring the wine. They will be here soon.

PEDRO. Yes, sir. (*He goes. Juan paces back and forth, humming to himself. Pedro returns and approaches his master cautiously — in a mysterious whisper*.) A lady, sir.

JUAN (*frowning*). Is she alone? (*Pedro nods, Juan smiles cynically*.) Surely you have mistaken her calling. Tell her I am not here.

> (*As Pedro turns to go, Maria de Cordova appears in the arch of the porte-cochère. A heavy black veil is thrown over her face*.)

MARIA (*her voice forced and trembling*). Juan!

JUAN (*immediately the gallant cavalier, makes a motion for Pedro to leave, and bows low — mockery in his voice*). Beautiful lady, you do me an unmerited honour.

MARIA (*wearily*). Spare me your mockery, Juan.

> (*She throws back her veil. She is a striking-looking woman of thirty-eight or forty, but discontent and sorrow have marked her age clearly on her face.*)

JUAN (*astonished*). Maria! (*Then with genuine alarm.*) In God's name!

MARIA (*her voice breaking*). Juan, I had to come.

JUAN (*sternly*). Your husband is my brother in arms. To-night — here — he is to be among my guests. I feel that every word we speak now degrades me in my honour.

MARIA (*in a tone of great grief*). You are cruel! I had to speak with you alone. This is my one chance. I leave the Court to-morrow.

JUAN (*with evident relief*). Ah.

MARIA (*stares at him with a pitiful appeal. He avoids her eyes*). Oh, what a fool I am — (*with a half-sob, as if the confession were wrung from her*) — to love you, Juan!

> (*She makes a movement toward him, but he steps back, aloof and cold.*)

JUAN (*frowning*). That word — we have never uttered it before. You have always been — my friend. (*After a pause, with deep earnestness.*) Why must you ruin our rare friendship for a word that every minstrel mouths? (*Then with irritation.*)

Love, love, love we chatter everlastingly. We pretend love alone is why we live! Bah! Life is nobler than the weak lies of poets — or it's nothing!

MARIA (*wounded and indignant*). If you had had to fight for love as you have fought for glory! —

JUAN (*struck by the pain in her tone, kneels and kisses her hand — remorsefully*). Forgive me! I would die rather than bring sorrow to a heart as kind as yours. Keep me for ever in that heart, I beg — but as a friend — as it has always been.

MARIA (*with a gasp of pain*). Ah! (*Taking her hand from his — with a deep sigh.*) God give you knowledge of the heart!

JUAN (*rises — plainly endeavouring to change the subject*). You are leaving the Court?

MARIA. The Queen has granted my wish to retire to Cordova. (*Passionately.*) I'm sick of the Court! I long for simple things! I pray to become worthy again of that pure love of God I knew as a girl. I must seek peace in Him! (*After a pause.*) Granada is ours. The Moors are driven from Spain. The wars are over. What will you do now, Juan?

JUAN. Peace means stagnation — a slack ease of cavaliers and songs and faded roses. I must go on.

MARIA. Where will you go?

JUAN (*smiles half-whimsically at an idea*). Perhaps with the Genoese, Christopher Columbus, when he sails to find the western passage to Cathay.

MARIA (*disturbed*). But they say he is mad.

JUAN (*seriously now*). Mad or not, he dreams of glory. I have heard he plans to conquer for Spain that immense realm of the Great Khan which Marco Polo saw.

MARIA. What! Abandon your career at Court now when your exploits have brought you in such favour? No one would ruin himself so senselessly save in despair! (*Jealously.*) It must be from love you are fleeing! (*Fiercely mocking.*) Is a woman avenging women? Tell me her name!

JUAN (*with a mocking laugh*). Love, love, and always love! Can no other motive exist for you? God pity women!

MARIA (*after a pause — sadly*). God pity me — because pity is what you offer me. (*As Juan seems about to protest wearily.*) Don't deny it, Juan. It sneers at me in your pretended scorn of love — You wish to comfort my humiliation! Am I a fool? Have you not loved others? I could name ten —

JUAN. Maria!

MARIA. Do you imagine I haven't guessed the truth? Those others had youth — while I — And my love seems to you — pitiable!

JUAN (*kneeling and taking her hand — with passionate earnestness*). No, dear friend, no!

swear to you! (*After a pause.*) What you call loves – they were merely moods – dreams of a night or two – lustful adventures – gestures of vanity, perhaps – but I have never loved. Spain is the mistress to whom I give my heart, Spain and my own ambitions, which are Spain's. Now do you understand?

MARIA (*sadly*). No, Juan. (*He rises.*) I understand that I am growing old – that love has passed for me – and that I suffer in my loneliness. Perhaps if God had granted me a child – But His justice punishes. He has seen my secret sin. I have loved you, Juan, for years. But it was only in the last year when my heart, feeling youth die, grew desperate that I dared let you see. And now, farewell, until God's will be done in death. We must not meet again.

JUAN (*sternly*). No. (*Passionately.*) I wish to God you had not told me this!

MARIA (*gently*). If you are still my friend you will not wish it. It was my final penance – that you should know. And, having told you, I am free, for my heart is dead. There is only my soul left that knows the love of God which blesses and does not torture. Farewell once more, Juan. (*He kneels and kisses her hand. She puts the other on his head as if blessing him.*) You are noble, the soul of courage, a man of men. You will go far, soldier of iron – and dreamer. God pity you if those two selves should ever clash! You shall have all my prayers for your success – but I shall add, Dear Saviour, let him know tenderness to recompense him when his hard youth dies! (*She turns quickly and goes out.*)

JUAN (*looks after her in melancholy thought for a while – then sighs deeply and shrugs his shoulders*). Time tarnishes even the pure, difficult things with common weakness.

> (*Luis de Alvaredo enters through the porte-cochère. He is a dissipated-looking noble, a few years older than Juan. His face is homely but extremely fetching in its nobility, its expression of mocking fun and raillery. He is dressed carelessly, is slightly drunk.*)

LUIS (*mockingly*). Lover of glory, beloved of women, hail! (*He comes to the startled Juan as voices are heard from the porte-cochère – in a hurried, cautioning whisper.*) The devil, Juan! Have you lost your wits – or has she? I recognized her – and Vicente was only ten paces behind. (*Then again mockingly.*) Discretion, my stainless knight, discretion!

JUAN (*sternly*). Stop! You wrong her and me. (*Sounds of a loud, angry dispute are heard from without.*) What is that brawling?

LUIS. My Moor. (*Explaining hurriedly to Juan.*) A fellow poet – a minstrel of their common folk. We found him running amuck about the streets

14

declaiming to the stars that their king, Abdallah, had sold his soul to hell when he surrendered. (*With admiration.*) By God, Juan, how he cursed! Oh, he's a precious songster, and as poet to poet I collared him and dragged him with us. Our friend, Diego, would have cut his throat for the Church's glory had I not interfered.

JUAN (*smiling*). As madman for madman, eh? But why bring him here to howl?

LUIS. He has a lute. It is my whim he should sing some verses (*With an amused grin.*) The dog speaks only Arabic. If he is wily, he will chant such curses on our heads as will blight that fountain dry — and no one of us but me will understand. (*With great glee.*) It will be sport, Juan! (*The clamour from outside grows more violent.*) By God, Diego will murder my minstrel — after all my pains. (*Starts to hurry out — stops in the entrance.*) Remember, Juan. Vicente may have recognized — the lady.

JUAN (*nods, frowning*). The devil take all women! (*Luis goes out. Pedro enters, carrying two large baskets full of bottles and sets them down, rear.*) Drink and forget sad nonsense. Bring out cushions. We will sit beside the fountain.

> (*Pedro goes into the house, right. Luis reenters, holding Yusef by the arm — a wizened old Moor dressed in the clothes of the common people, but wearing the turban signifying that he has made the pilgrimage to Mecca. His*

*deep-set eyes smoulder with hatred, but physically he is so exhausted as to seem resigned to his fate. They are followed by Diego Menendez, a Franciscan monk, about the same age as Juan and Luis. He has a pale, long face, the thin, cruel mouth, the cold, self-obsessed eyes of the fanatic. Just now he is full of helpless fury and indignation. Accompanying him is Vicente de Cordova, a grey-haired, stern, soldierly noble of forty-five. Following them are the three nobles, Oviedo, Castillo and Mendoza. They are the type of adventurous cavaliers of the day — cruel, courageous to recklessness, practically uneducated — knights of the true Cross, ignorant of and despising every first principle of real Christianity — yet carrying the whole off with a picturesque air.)*

MENENDEZ (*angrily*). I protest to you, Juan. It is heresy to suffer this dog's presence when we offer thanks to God for victory.

JUAN (*stares at the Moor interestedly for a moment — then carelessly*). I see no desecration, Diego — if he will sing, not howl. (*Turning to Vicente, scrutinizing his face keenly — carelessly.*) What do you say, Vicente?

VICENTE (*gives him a dark look of suspicion — coldly and meaningly*). I say nothing — now.

JUAN. Ah! (*He and Luis exchange a look.*)

OVIEDO. Well, I say let him remain. We may have sport with him.

CASTILLO (*with a cruel smile*). Perhaps with a sword-point we can persuade him to sing where the townsfolk hid their gold.

MENDOZA. Your words are inspired, Manuel!

LUIS (*scornfully*). Materialists! You would sack heaven and melt the moon for silver. Juan, where is your wine?

> (*Pedro appears, bringing cushions and goblets for each. He uncorks the bottles and pours their goblets full. Scorning a goblet, Luis snatches a bottle from him and drinks from that.*)

JUAN (*keeping a wary eye on Vicente*). Let us drink. (*Takes a goblet from Pedro.*) To our most Gracious Sovereigns and to Spain! (*He drinks.*)

MENENDEZ. And to the Church! (*Angrily.*) But I will not drink until that infidel is moved apart!

VICENTE. I agree.

JUAN (*impatiently*). Let the Moor go, Luis — since Diego takes himself so seriously.

VICENTE (*coldly resentful*). And I? (*Juan is about to reply irritably when Luis breaks in hurriedly.*)

LUIS. Shhh! I'll sing a song for you. (*Releasing the Moor and pointing to the rear.*) Go, brother bard, and take your ease.

# THE FOUNTAIN

*(The Moor goes to the right, rear, and squats down in the shadow by the wall. Luis sings.)*

Love is a flower
For ever blooming.
Life is a fountain
For ever leaping
Upward to catch the golden sunlight,
Striving to reach the azure heaven;
Failing, falling,
Ever returning
To kiss the earth that the flower may live.

*(They all applaud as he finishes.)*

JUAN. Charming, Sir Poet — but a lie. *(Mockingly.)* Love, and love, and always love! The devil seize your flower! Do fountains flow only to nourish flowers that bloom a day and die?

LUIS. Roar, lion! You will not wake my dream that life is love!

JUAN. Listen to him, Diego! We know his only love is his old mother; and yet, to judge from his songs, you would think him a greater philanderer than — than —

VICENTE *(interrupting sneeringly)*. Than you, Don Juan?

JUAN *(turning on him — coldly)*. Gossip gives many a false name — but gossip only deludes old women.

18

VICENTE (*growing pale*). Do you intend that insult?

> (*Their hands go to the hilt of their swords. The three nobles quicken to excited interest. Luis leaps between them.*)

LUIS. For God's sake! Is either of you a Moor? (*Raises his bottle.*) Let us drink again to Spain!

OVIEDO. And to the next war!

CASTILLO. May it be soon!

MENDOZA. With a world to sack! Sing us a song of that, Luis!

LUIS. I am too thirsty. But come, I was forgetting our infidel. Let me use persuasion –

> (*He goes back to the Moor, and can be heard talking to him in Arabic.*)

JUAN. We were speaking of wars to come. With whom?

OVIEDO. With anyone!

JUAN. But guess. I think it will be in lands beyond strange seas – Cipango and Cathay – the cities of gold that Marco Polo saw.

OVIEDO. But who will lead us there?

JUAN. Why, Christopher Columbus. (*They all laugh.*)

CASTILLO. That Genoese mongrel! – to lead Spaniards!

MENDOZA. He's mad. He claims the earth is round – like an egg! (*They all laugh.*)

JUAN (*impressively*). I saw him to-day. He was riding his flea-bitten mule as if he were a Cæsar in a triumph. His eyes were full of golden cities.

CASTILLO. Bah, Juan, you romance! The man's an idiot!

LUIS (*coming back*). The more fool you to think so! He will yet find for Spain the Western Passage to the East.

CASTILLO. Or fall off the world's edge! I will wager you would not go with him for all the gold in Indies!

LUIS. You would lose!

JUAN. I'm planning to go. (*All are astonished.*) But not on his first voyage. Before I pledge my sword I must have proof that it can serve Spain's glory. There is no profit in staking life for dreams.

LUIS. There is no profit in anything but that! You're from the East, Moor. Tell us of the Great Khan, of Cipango and Cathay and Cambuluc, of golden roofs and emerald-studded lintels to the doors. Your people must have heard these wonders.

MENDOZA. Yes, let him sing of treasure. (*But the Moor remains silent.*)

LUIS. Wait, I'll talk to him. (*He goes back and speaks to the Moor in Arabic. The latter replies.*)

MENENDEZ (*furiously*). This is all treasonable. The dog had broken the peace. The punishment is death.

JUAN (*mockingly*). Let him sing of treasure, Diego. Even the Church loves gold.

LUIS (*coming back – exultantly*). He consents, Juan – because I am a colleague. He will sing of treasure in the East – a tale told to his father by some wandering poet who came from Cathay with a caravan. (*All except the outraged Diego and the sullen, preoccupied Vicente quicken to interested attention. The Moor strikes a few notes on his lute.*) Hush!

> (*The Moor begins a crooning chant of verses, accompanying himself on the lute. At first they are all held by its strange rhythm, then they begin to betray impatience.*)

OVIEDO. By God, our wolf turns into a sick shepherd.

LUIS. Hush!

CASTILLO (*impatiently*). What does he sing?

LUIS (*enrapt – vaguely*). Hush, hush.

MENENDEZ (*rising to his feet as the Moor's recitative abruptly ends – harshly*). This is the service in a devil's mass!

LUIS (*passes his hand across his eyes, then stares into the fountain dreamily*). He sang of treasure –

but strange to your longing. There is in some far country of the East – Cathay, Cipango, who knows – a spot that Nature has set apart from men and blessed with peace. It is a sacred grove where all things live in the old harmony they knew before man came. Beauty resides there and is articulate. Each sound is music, and every sight a vision. The trees bear golden fruit. And in the centre of the grove, there is a fountain – beautiful beyond human dreams, in whose rainbows all of life is mirrored. In that fountain's waters, young maidens play and sing and tend it everlastingly, for very joy in being one with it. This is the Fountain of Youth, he said. The wise men of that far-off land have known it many ages. They make it their last pilgrimage when sick with years and weary of their lives. Here they drink, and the years drop from them like a worn-out robe. Body and mind know youth again, and these young men, who had been old, leap up and join the handmaids' dance. Then they go back to life, but with hearts purified, and the old discords trouble them no more, but they are holy and the folk revere them. (*With a sigh.*) That's his tale, my friends – but he added it is hard to find that fountain. Only to the chosen does it reveal itself.

MENENDEZ (*furiously*). Idolatry!

OVIEDO. Is this his treasure! By God, he mocks us!

LUIS. Fools! Beauty is lost on you. Your souls

clink like coppers. (*Menendez slinks back step by step toward the Moor. Luis grabs a bottle.*) Come, let us drink! We'll all to Cathay with Don Christopher. You can burrow for dung there – but I will search for this fountain.

JUAN (*drinking – a bit tipsily*). Drink and forget sad nonsense! The devil! His song beguiled me until you tricked it into that old woman's mumble. Youth! Is youth a treasure? Then are we all – except Vicente – priceless rich; and yet, God's blood, one has but to look to see how poor we are!

LUIS. Poor in spirit! I understand you, Juan.

JUAN. Fountain of youth, God help us, with love to boot! I wish he'd sung instead of the armies and power of the Great Khan! (*Then half-aside to Luis.*) The tale is always told to the wrong person. There was one here not long ago who would have given pearls for drops from that same fountain!

VICENTE (*who has crept vengefully toward Juan in time to hear these last words – with cold fury*). A moment ago you taunted me with age – and now you dare – (*He slaps Juan across the face. They draw their swords.*)

LUIS (*trying to intervene*). For God's sake, friends!

OVIEDO (*with excited interest*). A duel!

(*The others echo this. Suddenly there is a harsh shriek from the rear. Menendez*

23

*appears from the shadow, dagger in hand, a look of fanatical triumph on his face. Forgetting the duel, the others stand appalled.)*

MENENDEZ (*sheathing the dagger*). I have slain the dog. It was high time.

LUIS. Miserable bigot!

> (*Raging, he tries to throw himself at the monk, but Juan grasps him and forces him down on a cushion. He breaks down, weeping.*)

MENENDEZ (*coldly scornful*). What! A soldier of Christ weep for an infidel!

JUAN (*sternly*). Be still, Diego! (*Then frowning – curtly, in a tone of dismissal which silences all protest.*) Our revelling is under an ill star. There is blood upon it. Good-night. (*Turning to Vicente.*) Until to-morrow.

> (*Vicente bows and goes, accompanied by Menendez. The young nobles troop out behind, disputing noisily about the coming duel.*)

JUAN (*comes over and puts his hand on Luis' shoulder – in a mocking, but comforting tone*). Come, Luis. Your brother romancer is dead. Tears will not help him. Perhaps even now he drinks of that Fountain of Youth in Dreamland – if he is not in hell.

LUIS (*raising his head*). Juan, why do you always sneer at beauty — while your heart calls you liar?

JUAN (*frowning*). I have Spain in my heart — and my ambition. All else is weakness. (*Changing his tone — carelessly.*) Well, you were right. Vicente recognized — and so, a duel. I'll prick him in the thigh and send him home to bed. She will nurse and love him then — and hate me for a murderer. Thus, all works out for the best in this fair world! But — a rare thing dies — and I'm sad, Luis. (*Shaking himself and taking a goblet of wine.*) Come, forget sad nonsense. We will drink to voyaging with Don Christopher — and to the battles before those golden cities of Cathay!

LUIS (*recovering his spirits — grabbing a bottle*). Lucifer fire your cities! I drink to my fountain!

JUAN. Your health, Sir Lying Poet!

LUIS. And yours, Sir Glory-Glutton!

(*They laugh, clink goblet and bottle, and drink as*

*The Curtain Falls*)

# SCENE TWO

SCENE. *About a year later — Columbus's flagship on the last day of his second voyage. The section of the vessel shown reveals the main deck amidships, the mainmast, the mainsail with its Maltese Cross, the two higher decks of the poop, the lateen sail on the mizzenmast, etc. Wooden stairs on the starboard, near the bulwark, are the means of getting from one deck to another.*

*It is the time just preceding the dawn. The ship is sailing steadily on a calm sea. There is a large lantern at the centre of the main deck, another low down in the rigging on the port side, another over the cross which hangs over the stern from the high poop. The ship is crowded with people. On the main deck are the nobles. They are dressed in rich uniforms, in armour. Most of them are asleep, lying sprawled on the deck, wrapped in their cloaks — or huddled in hunched attitudes, their backs propped against the mast or the bulwarks. But one small group has apparently been awake all night. They are sitting cross-legged, throwing dice by the light of the lantern. The faces of the gamesters are haggard and drawn, their eyes feverish. Prominent among them are Oviedo, Castillo, Mendoza and Luis.*

*On the first deck of the poop, the monks, all Franciscans, are lying asleep. Here, also, are*

*four of the converted Indians Columbus is bring-*
*ing back. They are dressed in incongruous cos-*
*tumes, half savage and half civilized. They are*
*huddled in the right corner, not asleep, but*
*frozen in a helpless apathy.*

*On the highest deck Juan is seen standing by*
*the pilot who tends the helm.*

LUIS (*excitedly*). Double or quits!

OVIEDO. Done. (*They play. Luis loses.*)

LUIS. I am ruined again! (*With a comical groan*
*of despair.*) Fortune is a damned mercenary
wench. She scorns the poor. (*Takes up the dice to*
*throw.*) Once more!

OVIEDO (*grumblingly*). No. You owe me more
than you can pay.

LUIS. I will soon be rich as Crœsus. Don
Columbus says we will sight land to-day – the
Indies, Isles of Spice, Cipango, Cathay, who
knows what? I will stake my future wealth against
yours. Come! One more cast for anything you
wish.

OVIEDO (*dryly*). For gold – gold I can see and
touch.

LUIS (*disgustedly*). The devil! I must borrow
from Juan then. (*He gets to his feet.*)

OVIEDO. He will not thank you to wake him on
a beggar's errand.

LUIS. Do you imagine he sleeps with his Pro-

mised Land so near? He is astern on the
Admiral's poop keeping a watch of his own – for
fear the lookout will miss Cathay!

CASTILLO. Juan is over-eager. He will make
the Genoese jealous.

MENDOZA. Has already. It is plain Columbus
slights him.

OVIEDO. From policy. He knows Juan is in
disgrace at Court since the duel. Our admiral
trims his sails to the wind.

CASTILLO. Juan paid dearly for Vicente's wound
– a pin-prick that hardly drew blood.

MENDOZA. It was the scandal.

LUIS (*indignantly*). All false – the malice of
envious tongues! Vicente himself apologized to
Juan. As for the lady, when I was home in Cordova I saw her with Vicente. You could not find a
more married pair. It was even rumoured they
were to have a child – (*Juan has come down from
the Admiral's poop, passed through the sleeping
monks and now appears by the light of the lamp in the
rigging at the head of the stairs to the main deck.
Luis breaks off suddenly.*) Is that you, Juan?
Come, be a brother. This son of luck (*he indicates
Oviedo*) has won everything but my skin.

JUAN (*with a laugh*). Then stake the Fountain
of Youth which you will find – to-morrow! Sold
by the cask it should make you the richest man in
Spain. (*The nobles laugh.*)

LUIS (*with real aversion*). What trader's scheming – from you! (*Then jokingly.*) Take care! When the pox of old age is on you will come begging to me! (*Then rattling the dice.*) But come, loan me gold for a last cast of revenge. (*Then with a sudden idea.*) And you throw for me. My star is behind a cloud.

OVIEDO. Not fair. Juan always wins.

JUAN (*frowning*). This is no time for gaming.

LUIS (*insistently*). Just once, Juan.

JUAN (*consenting unwillingly*). Only once. The stakes are yours. Let the cast be an augury for me.

> (*He takes gold from his purse. He and Oviedo play. Oviedo wins and there is a murmur of astonishment.*)

OVIEDO (*exultantly*). I win. The first time I have ever beat you, Juan.

JUAN (*getting up*). A poor omen. (*Then mockingly.*) But here on the under side of earth these signs must run by opposites.

MENDOZA (*half frightenedly*). Can we be hanging head down and not know it?

CASTILLO. Bah! The Genoese made his first voyage safely. We cannot fall off, it seems.

OVIEDO. Columbus may be a liar.

MENDOZA (*savagely*). A low-born braggart! He displayed his origin in the hoggish demands he made on the crown. What could the Sovereigns be thinking of – to make this foreign upstart an Admiral and a Viceroy?

JUAN (*sternly rebuking*). It is not for us to question. (*He pauses – then adds.*) His enterprise has served Spain well. He is our commander. That is enough to know.

> (*He turns his back on them and walks to the port side where he stands by the rigging looking out to sea. The nobles look after him for a moment in an abashed silence.*)

CASTILLO (*mockingly*). You are a perfect Christian, Juan – to love your enemy.

OVIEDO (*yawns*). Put out the lantern. Let us sleep. The dawn will wake us.

> (*Mendoza puts out the lantern. All except Luis wrap themselves in their robes and lie down on the deck. Luis comes over to Juan.*)

LUIS (*scornfully*). Look at those clods. They would snore through the Last Judgment. (*Then as Juan is silent.*) What are you dreaming of – Cathay and glory?

JUAN. No. (*Then suddenly.*) When I came down I heard Vicente's name – and mention of a child. What were you saying?

LUIS. Gossip of Cordova. My mother told me

30

Maria was having masses said that she might bear an heir – and the rumour was her prayers were answered.

JUAN (*with deep sincerity*). God grant it. She will be happy then. (*With an ironical laugh.*) Did I not tell you that night our duel would reconcile them? (*Soberly.*) But I pay. Well, what matter the cost if Maria wins happiness?

LUIS (*reassuringly*). One exploit and the Court will be at your feet again.

JUAN (*shaking his head*). We will be far from Spain – out of sight and mind. Columbus will be king here, and he and I are by nature antagonistic.

> (*There is a noise from the higher deck of the poop. A tall figure can be made out coming up on deck there from the companionway. He moves back until the light from the lantern above the cross reveals him. It is Columbus. He is in full uniform but wears no hat on his long, white hair. A commanding figure of noble presence, the face full of the ardent, fixed enthusiasm of the religious devotee.*)

LUIS (*pulling Juan back into the shadow*). Speak the devil's name! (*They stand, watching and listening, but hidden from the poop.*)

COLUMBUS (*to the helmsman*). Have you held the course?

HELMSMAN. South-west by west, sir.

COLUMBUS (*peering about him*). Will the dawn never come? (*He comes to the edge of the deck and calls down where the monks are — in a low voice.*) Father Menendez. Are you awake?

MENENDEZ (*gets up quickly from among the sleeping monks*). I am here, your Excellency. (*He mounts to the deck above and stands waiting respectfully.*)

COLUMBUS (*begins in a blunt, perfunctory tone*). Toscanelli's map must be in error. We should have sighted land before. (*A pause. He paces back and forth.*) The sun will soon be up. It leaps from the darkness in these parts. (*A pause, then with evident irritation.*) A weary voyage, Father! The spirit of these nobles is perverse. They look on this voyage as an escapade in search of easy riches, not as a crusade for the glory of God.

MENENDEZ (*curtly*). They are brave. Many of them have proven their ability in war — Juan Ponce de Leon, for one.

COLUMBUS (*resentfully*). A bravo! A duellist!

LUIS (*in an indignant whisper*). The devil seize him!

JUAN (*grimly*). Another aftermath of that cursed duel!

MENENDEZ (*shortly*). You are unjust, Excellency.

COLUMBUS. Oh, I admit he possesses all the attributes but the one which alone gives them virtue — an humble piety. On this great quest there is no place for egotists who seek only selfish ends. We must all feel ourselves unworthy servants of God's Holy Will. (*Then breaking off – abruptly.*) But I did not call you to speak of him. (*After a pause – despondently.*) My soul is overburdened, Father.

MENENDEZ (*dryly*). You wish to confess?

COLUMBUS (*surprised*). Confess? (*Then in a loud, ringing tone.*) Yes, to all men! Their mouths are full of lies against me. They say the demands I made for my share of discovery prove my lowminded avarice. Knaves! What can they know of my heart? Is it for myself I desire wealth? No! But as a chosen instrument of God, Who led me to His Indies, I need the power that wealth can give. I need it for God's glory, not my own! (*More and more exaltedly.*) I have a dream, Father! Listen! From my earliest youth I have hated the infidel. I fought on the ships of Genoa against their corsairs and as I saw my city's commerce with the East cut off by their ruthlessness, I prayed for one glorious last Crusade that would reclaim the Mediterranean for Christendom and, most fervent prayer of all, regain from profanation the Holy Sepulchre of our Lord Jesus! (*He crosses himself. Menendez also. Then he hurries on exultantly.*) And now an answer is granted! With my share of the wealth from Indies, from Cipango and Cathay, I will fit out an army – the Last Crusade! I have promised it to His Holiness, the Pope –

fifty thousand men, four thousand horse, with a like force to follow after five years. I shall reconquer the Blessed Tomb of Christ for the True Faith! And to that sacred end I devote my life and all my wealth and power! (*He stands looking up to heaven with the rapt gaze of a devotee.*)

MENENDEZ (*dryly*). Such a pious ambition does you honour.

JUAN (*unable to restrain himself, calls mockingly*). The Crusades are dead — and the wealth of the East is still unwon.

COLUMBUS (*stung — indignantly*). Who dares — ?

JUAN (*proudly*). A noble of Spain who thinks of her greatness while you dream of Genoa and Rome; a soldier of the present, not the ghost of a Crusader! (*Then with exasperated mockery.*) God's blood, have all our leaders become half monk? There was a time for that when we fought the Moor, but now a new era of world empire dawns for Spain. By living in the past you will consecrate her future to fanaticism!

COLUMBUS (*angrily*). Insolent!

JUAN (*vehemently*). No. I respect you, Columbus — but I have my vision, too. Spain can become the mistress of the world, greater than ancient Rome, if she can find leaders who will weld conquest to her, who will dare to govern with tolerance. (*He laughs a bitter, mocking laugh.*) But what a time to speak! Look at the men of this fleet —

now when the East dawns for them! I agree with you, Don Christopher — a weary voyage! Adventurers lusting for loot to be had by a murder or two; nobles of Spain dreaming greedy visions of wealth to be theirs by birthright; monks itching for the rack to torture useful subjects of the Crown into slaves of the Church! And for leader to have you, Don Christopher — you who will pillage to resurrect the Crusades! Looters of the land, one and all! There is not one who will see it as an end to build upon! We will loot and loot and, weakened by looting, be easy prey for stronger looters. God pity this land until all looters perish from the earth! (*While he is speaking it has grown perceptibly lighter.*)

COLUMBUS (*furiously*). Who are you? Stand forth! You dare not!

JUAN (*jumps up to the lower level of the poop and advances to the ladder to the Admiral's poop — proudly*). It is I — Juan Ponce de Leon! Why should I not dare? Do you want men under your command — or lackeys?

COLUMBUS (*striving to control his rage*). Silence!

(*A wailing cry of "Land Ho" comes from the mainmast head. Immediately the same cry can be heard coming over the water from the other vessels of the fleet. Instantly all is confusion. Every one jumps to their feet, half awake, peering about bewilderedly. The four Indians*

35

*sense what has happened and hang over
the bulwark, staring over the seas with
intense longing. A crowd of half-
dressed sailors and rabble pour up from
below decks. There is a babble of
excited shouts. Columbus looks upward
to see where the lookout is pointing, then
turns to the horizon off the starboard
bow. Juan leaps to the ratlines.)*

THE CROWD. Land! Land! Where? I heard
the call. He shouted land! Is it Cathay? Where
is he pointing? Look where the Admiral looks.
When the sun comes — (*Suddenly the ship is
flooded by shafts of golden crimson light. They all
cry.*) The sun!

JUAN (*pointing*). There! I see! In a haze of
gold and purple — Greater Spain!

ALL (*crowd to the starboard side and to the front.
The Indians are pushed away, jostled, thrown aside
contemptuously with imprecations until they are
hunched disconsolately in the background in dumb
terror and bewilderment*). Where? I see! Where?
There! There! Cathay. Cipango. Is it Cathay?
Where are the golden cities? Where are the
golden roofs? Is it Cipango? The Indies! The
Isles of Spice! Marco Polo's land!

(*They all crowd, pushing and elbowing each
other, craning their necks, the eyes of
all, rabble, soldiers, nobles, priests,*

*straining with the same greedy longing, the lust to loot.*)

JUAN (*exultantly*). Cathay or Cipango or the Isles of Spice, what difference? It shall be Greater Spain! (*The crowd cheers vociferously.*)

COLUMBUS (*trying to quell the tumult*). Silence, I say! (*Fixing his eyes sternly on Juan with undisguised hostility — rebukingly.*) The earth is God's! Give thanks to Him! Kneel, I command you! Raise the cross!

(*The monks raise their cross. They kneel, but the nobles and soldiers hesitate waiting for Juan as if they saw in him their true commander.*)

JUAN (*leaps down from the rigging, drawing his sword — with fierce exultance*). This is a cross too, a soldier's cross — the cross of Spain!

(*He sticks his sword-point into the deck before him. He kneels before it. All the nobles and soldiers do likewise with a great flourish of gestures and excited shouts. They are all kneeling with their quivering cross swords, hilts rising above their heads.*)

COLUMBUS (*from his knees — looking up to heaven devoutly*). Te Deum!

(*The monks begin to chant. All join in, their*

*pent-up excitement giving to the hymn a
hectic, nervous quality. Juan does not
sing but stares at the land on the distant
horizon.)*

**(The Curtain Falls)**

# SCENE THREE

SCENE. *Twenty years or so later — the courtyard of the Governor's palace, Porto Rico. Flowers, shrubs, a coco-palm, orange and banana trees. A large, handsome fountain closely resembling that of Scene One, is at centre. Two marble benches are at front and rear of fountain. A narrow paved walk encircles the fountain basin, with other walks leading from it to the different entrances. Doors to the interior of the house are at left and right. The main entrance to the courtyard, opening on the road, is at rear centre.*

*It is in the late, languid hours of a torrid afternoon. The courtyard bakes in the heat, the fountain shimmering in the heat-waves.*

*Juan is seated on the stone bench in front of the basin. He is dressed in the full uniform of his authority as Governor. His face is aged, lined, drawn. His hair and beard are grey. His expression and attitude are full of great weariness. His eyes stare straight before him blankly in a disillusioned dream. The lines about his compressed lips are bitter.*

*Luis enters from the left, rear. He is dressed in the robe of a Dominican monk. His face shows the years but it has achieved a calm, peaceful expression as if he were at last in harmony with himself. He comes down to Juan and puts a hand on his shoulder.*

39

JUAN (*starts — then greets his friend with a smile*). Ah, it's you, reverend Father. (*He accents this last mockingly.*)

LUIS (*good-naturedly*). Yes, illustrious Governor. (*He sits beside Juan — with a laugh.*) You are like a sulky child, Juan. Come, is it not time, after five years, you forgave me for being a Dominican?

JUAN (*bitterly*). My friend deserting to my enemy!

LUIS (*protestingly*). Come, come! (*Then after a pause, with a sigh.*) You have always had the dream of Cathay. What had I? What had I done with life? — an aimless, posing rake, neither poet nor soldier, without place nor peace! I had no meaning even to myself until God awakened me to His Holy Will. Now I live in truth. You must renounce in order to possess.

JUAN. The world would be stale indeed if that were true! (*After a pause — irritably.*) I fight the battles; you monks steal the spoils! I seek to construct; you bind my hands and destroy!

LUIS (*remonstrating*). You speak of Diego and his kind.

JUAN (*frowning*). Whether you convert by clemency or he by cruelty, the result is the same. All this baptizing of Indians, this cramming the cross down their throats has proved a ruinous error. It crushes their spirits and weakens their bodies. They become burdens for Spain instead of valuable servitors.

# THE FOUNTAIN

LUIS. Your army crushed them first —

JUAN. They had to be conquered, but there I would have stopped. (*Then irritably.*) God's blood, here we are arguing about this same issue — for the thousandth time! It is too late. Talk is useless. (*With a weary sigh.*) We do what we must — and sand covers our bodies and our deeds. (*With a smile.*) And the afternoon is too hot, besides. Tell me some news. Will the fleet from Spain make port to-day?

LUIS. Just now I saw them rounding the point under full sail. They should anchor soon.

> (*They are interrupted by the noise of several people approaching from outside. Oviedo and Friar Quesada, a Franciscan, enter, followed by the Indian chief, Nano, who is guarded by two soldiers with drawn swords. Quesada is a thin young monk with the sallow, gaunt face and burning eyes of a fanatic. Oviedo is aged but gives no evidence of having changed in character. Nano is a tall, powerfully built Indian of fifty or so. Although loaded down with chains, he carries himself erect with an air of aloof, stoical dignity. He wears a head-dress of feathers. His face and body are painted, ornaments are about his neck. He is naked except for a loin-cloth and moccasins.*)

41

QUESADA (*fiercely and arrogantly*). I demand justice on this dog!

JUAN (*freezing – proudly*). Demand?

QUESADA (*with ill-concealed hatred but awed by Juan's manner*). Pardon my zeal in the service of God, Your Excellency. I ask justice. (*Then defiantly.*) But it is not the Church's custom to be a suppliant.

JUAN. So much the worse – (*Sternly.*) What is this Indian's crime?

QUESADA. His tribe will not pay the tithes – and he himself has dared to refuse baptism!

JUAN (*coldly*). I'll question him. (*Then as Quesada hesitates, raging inwardly – sternly.*) You may go.

QUESADA (*controlling his rage, bows*). Yes, Your Excellency. (*He goes.*)

JUAN (*to Oviedo with a certain contempt*). You also have a charge against this Indian?

OVIEDO (*angrily*). A plea for justice! These dogs will not pay their taxes. And we who own estates cannot get them to work except by force, which you have arbitrarily curtailed. Then why not punish them by leasing their labour to us until their debt's wiped out? Thus the Government will be paid, and we will have workers for our mines and fields.

JUAN (*disgustedly*). Your brain is not inventive,

Oviedo! You are well aware that is the same blunder which failed on Espaniola. It means slavery. It defeats its purpose. The Indians die under the lash – and your labour dies with them. (*Contemptuously.*) Do you think I am Columbus that you ask this folly of me?

OVIEDO (*haughtily*). You refuse? (*He goes to the rear where he turns – threateningly.*) Take care, Juan! There will come a day of reckoning – when Diego returns from Spain. (*He goes out.*)

JUAN (*frowning*). Diego? What do you mean?

OVIEDO (*with a revengeful smile*). Nothing. Adios, Don Juan. (*He goes out.*)

JUAN (*with a bitter laugh*). There you have it! Bah! What use – ? (*He suddenly seems to see Nano for the first time. They stare at each other.*) I was forgetting you. Are you not Nano, chief of the last tribe I conquered? (*As the Indian is silent – imperiously.*) Speak!

NANO. The devils were with you. Our villages were burned. Women and children were killed – my wives, my children!

JUAN (*frowning*). Contrary to my command. But, again, what use? The dead are dead. It is too late. (*After a pause – with a sort of weary self-mockery.*) Have you ever heard of Cathay – Cipango? Do you know of vast countries to the west – many peoples – great villages with high walls – much gold?

NANO. I have heard.

JUAN (*surprised – eagerly*). Ah! Where are they? (*Nano points west.*)

LUIS (*amusedly*). Where the fountain of youth of my drunken days is located – in dreamland!

JUAN (*with a certain seriousness*). Do you know, they say there is a similar fountain legend among these tribes. (*Then to Nano with a mocking smile.*) My friend here is growing impatient waiting for immortality in heaven and would rather gain it here on earth –

LUIS. Juan!

JUAN. So tell him, O Mighty Chief, if there is not over there – a fountain – a spring – in which old men bathe or drink and become young warriors again?

NANO (*to both their surprise*). The tale is told. Not here. In my home – a land that never ends. Our priests told the tale. I was young then. I was captured in war and brought here. I was adopted. I have never returned.

JUAN (*lost in thought*). So? Where is this land, your home? (*Nano points as before.*) Where Cathay is? And the fountain – the spring – is there?

NANO (*after a moment's hesitation*). Yes. My people call it the Spring of Life.

LUIS (*whimsically*). A pretty title, indeed. (*Sceptically.*) But none can find it, I suppose?

NANO. Those the Gods love can find it.

JUAN (*scornfully*). Aha, that old trick of poets – evasion of facts! (*Turning to Luis.*) Do you remember the Moor that night in Granada? "Only to the chosen." Here is the echo! Bah! What jugglery! (*Then thoughtfully.*) But it is strange. Where there is so much smoke, there must be a spark of fire. The Moor traced his myth back to the East – Cathay – and now we discover it again – still in Cathay – circling the world – (*Then, as if ashamed of himself for taking it so seriously – carelessly.*) At all events, it is added evidence that Cathay is near. (*The boom of a cannon comes from the harbour.*)

LUIS. The fleet has anchored. Diego will soon be here. If you can give this Indian into my keeping I will attempt his conversion.

JUAN (*impatiently*). Until his case is investigated, he must go to prison. You may see him there. (*To Nano, sternly.*) If it is proven you have encouraged rebellion against Spain, you will be hung. Against any other charge I will try to save you. (*Summoning the soldiers.*) Guard. (*They salute and lead Nano out, left. Juan paces up and down in frowning thought.*) Diego! Did you hear Oviedo threaten me with him? What mischief will he bring from Spain this time, I wonder? The cursed spider! His intriguing will destroy all my work here – (*With impotent anger.*) And the fight is hopeless. His weapons are whispers. A man of honour stands disarmed. (*Intensely.*)

Would to God this fleet brought me the King's patent to discover new lands! I would sail to-morrow for Cathay — or for the moon!

LUIS (*firmly*). Fight your battle here! This is your land. You conquered it.

JUAN. Columbus discovered it; and I still feel his influence, like a black fog, stifling me!

LUIS (*mollifyingly*). He is dead. Forgive. He suffered too much injustice to be just.

JUAN. How can my pride forgive? For years I held his solitary outposts; I suffered wounds and fevers; I fought the Indians for him while he went sailing for the Garden of Eden, the mines of Solomon, his Bible-crazed chimeras! He knew my honour would not permit my conspiring against him as others did. So he ignored my services and deliberately condemned me to obscurity! Never one mention of my name in his reports to Spain! It is only since his downfall — (*Breaking off.*) But this, too, is an old story. (*Then with sudden exasperation.*) Why should I not sail to find Cathay? He failed in that — but I would succeed! I am no visionary chasing rainbows. (*Desperately.*) I tell you I loathe this place! I loathe my petty authority! By God, I could sink all Porto Rico under the sea for one glimpse of Cathay!

LUIS (*alarmed*). Juan!

JUAN (*after a pause — ironically*). Well, do not

fear that I will leave your precious island. The patent will never come — and if it did, there is a flaw — (*Despondently, with a great weariness.*) It is too late. Cathay is too far. I am too weary. I have fought small things so long that I am small. My spirit has rusted in chains for twenty years. Now it tends to accept them — to gain peace. (*With passionate yearning.*) If I could only feel again my old fire, my energy of heart and mind — ! If I could be once more the man who fought before Granada — ! But the fire smoulders. It merely warms my will to dream of the past. It no longer catches flame in deeds. (*With a desolate smile of self-pity.*) I begin to dread — another failure. I am too old to find Cathay.

(*Menendez appears in rear in time to hear this last. He is dressed in a Bishop's robes. He looks his years, but his expression of rabid fanaticism has changed to one, not less cruel, of the crafty schemer made complacent by a successful career, the oily intriguer of Church politics. He hesitates with a suspicious, inquisitive glance from one to the other — then advances with a forced air of joviality.*) What is this I hear? Too old? Tut-tut! This is heresy, Juan. (*The two turn, startled. Juan stares at him resentfully. Menendez exchanges a cold bow of condescension with Luis, then comes to Juan with outstretched hands, smiling oilily.*) Have you no greeting for me, old friend?

JUAN (*takes his hands perfunctorily — then sar-*

*castically*). Who would expect you unattended –
like any eavesdropping monk?

MENENDEZ (*unruffled*). My eagerness to see you.
I have great news. I often spoke to the King
about you. He now holds you in the highest
esteem, and as a proof of his favour I bring you –
(*Then with a sly smile.*) But, on second thought, I
should not say, I bring you. That is reserved for a
worthier hand!

JUAN (*impatiently*). I dislike mysteries.

MENENDEZ (*provokingly*). I will give you this
hint out of respect for the old age you were lamenting! Prepare to welcome youth – and a prize
you have sought for all your life in the Indies – a
gift more welcome to you than wine was to Luis
before he repented! (*With this parting gibe, he
turns away.*) Pardon me if I leave you. I must
make preparations – for this event. (*He bows
mockingly and goes off right.*)

JUAN (*angrily*). Schemer! (*He paces up and
down.*)

LUIS (*after pondering a moment – suddenly*). I
have it! It must be your patent to explore! He
has obtained it from the King – because he wishes
to get rid of you here! You stand in his way –
your policy of clemency. He wants to be dictator
to introduce torture and slavery! Yet he is afraid
to fight you openly, so what craftier scheme than
to send you away contented, grateful for a gift,
bribed without knowing it?

JUAN (*resentfully*). Then I will fool the fox! There is no compulsion in such a patent. (*Then confused.*) But – it would be my highest hope come true – too late! Too late! I am too old. (*With an attempt at a railing tone.*) God's blood, I need to find Cathay – if your Fountain of Youth is there!

LUIS. I hear a crowd coming. I must go. It adds to their spleen to find us together. (*He presses Juan's hand.*) Whatever comes, be firm, old friend.

> (*He goes out left. The murmur of the crowd increases. Juan sinks on the bench before the fountain, oblivious to it, lost in gloomy thought. Beatriz de Cordova appears, attended by her duenna and a crowd of richly dressed nobles. She is a beautiful young girl of eighteen or so, the personification of youthful vitality, charm and grace. The nobles point out Juan to her. She dismisses them, motioning for them to be quiet – then comes in and approaches Juan, keeping the fountain between them. She holds a sealed document in her hand. Finally she calls in a trembling, eager voice.*)

BEATRIZ. Don Juan!

> (*Juan whirls on his bench and stares through the fountain at her. He utters a stunned exclamation as if he saw a ghost. His*

*eyes are held fascinated by her beauty. Then suddenly she laughs — a gay, liquid, clear note — and coming quickly around confronts him.*) It is I, Don Juan.

JUAN (*stares at her still fascinated — then, reminded, springs to his feet and bows low with his old mocking gallantry*). Pardon! I am bewitched! I thought you were the spirit of the fountain. (*Then more mockingly.*) Beautiful lady, you do me unmerited honour!

BEATRIZ (*hurt and confused by his tone*). You don't know me? Why, I'm Beatriz. (*As he bows but shows no recognition.*) Has Bishop Menendez not told you — ?

JUAN (*suspiciously*). Nothing of you, my lady.

BEATRIZ. I am Beatriz de Cordova —

JUAN (*guessing — amazed, stares at her — a pause, slowly*). Maria's child! — you!

BEATRIZ (*letting it all pour forth regardless*). She died a year ago — and — I am your ward now. It was her last wish. My father was dead. There was no near relative whom she would trust. I asked the King to send me here to you. He bade me wait until the Bishop could escort me. He made me the bearer of this gift for you — your dearest wish, he said. (*She gives him the document.*)

JUAN (*unrolls it — a pause as he stares at it dully, then bitterly*). The patent — to find Cathay!

BEATRIZ. Yes! And you can find it where the others failed, I know! You were my dear mother's ideal of Spanish chivalry, of a true knight of the Cross! That was her prophecy, that you would be the first to reach Cathay!

JUAN. She spoke of the man she knew. (*Staring at her fascinatedly – eagerly.*) She sends me you – and you are youth! Is it in mockery?

BEATRIZ (*suddenly*). Oh, Don Juan, I recall something she said I must remember when we should meet. "Bring him tenderness," she said. "That will repay the debt I owe him for saving me for you." She said these words were secrets to tell you alone. What did she mean, Don Juan?

JUAN (*deeply moved*). Tenderness? Do you bring me that, Beatriz? (*Then as if recalling himself.*) No, do not – for it means weakness. Bring me the past instead. Give me back – the man your mother knew.

BEATRIZ (*who has been scrutinizing him without paying attention to his words*). You are older than I dreamed, Don Juan.

JUAN (*wounded – with harsh violence*). No tenderness there! Youth! A cuirass of shining steel! A glittering sword! Laughter above the battle! (*Then seeing her look of frightened astonishment at his wild words, he controls himself and adds with a melancholy bitterness.*) It was so long ago, Beatriz – that night in Granada – a dimly-remembered dream — (*Then with a sudden return of his mockingly gallant manner.*) Forgive me. I have become a savage lost to manners. (*He kneels and kisses her hand with all his old-time gallantry.*) Welcome, dear ward, to Porto Rico!

(*She looks down at his bowed head, blushing with pleasure and naïve embarrassment, as*

*The Curtain Falls*)

# SCENE FOUR

SCENE. *Three months later — Menendez' official study in the palace — a large, high-ceilinged, bare room with a heavy table at centre. The colour scheme is dark and gloomy, the atmosphere that of a rigid, narrow ecclesiasticism. In one corner is an altar with high candles burning before it. Heavy hangings shut out the light from the lofty, arched windows. An enormous crucifix hangs on the wall in rear. The room is like an exaggerated monk's cell, but it possesses a sombre power over the imagination by the force of its concentration. There is a main entrance at rear, centre, and a smaller side door at left, hidden by curtains.*

*It is early evening. Menendez is seated at the table. He is frowningly impatient, listening and waiting for some one. There is the sound of approaching footsteps. Menendez turns eagerly in his chair. Quesada enters through the hangings on the left. His face is ominous and set. He wears a sword and pistols over his robe which is tucked up over high riding boots and spurs. He is covered with dust, and has evidently been riding hard. He bows respectfully to Menendez.*

MENENDEZ. I had begun to think you would never come. (*Then with anxiety.*) What news?

QUESADA. The meeting is being held. They have gathered in the fort outside the town.

53

MENENDEZ. Good! It is moving according to my plan, then.

QUESADA. They all agree that Don Juan must resign his patent.

MENENDEZ. Unless he sails to find Cathay at once?

QUESADA. Yes. They are all mad for the gold (*with a sneer*) over there, the report of which I have had rumoured about, as you directed.

MENENDEZ. Good. Then we shall be rid of Juan and all the discontented spirits on the island at one stroke!

QUESADA (*excitedly*). But they also demand that first the Indian, Nano, must be burned at the stake. They believe he has bewitched the Governor. They know of Don Juan's secret interviews with him.

MENENDEZ (*angrily*). Who told them?

QUESADA (*after a moment's hesitation – defiantly*)· I did.

MENENDEZ (*angrily*). Fool!

QUESADA (*alarmed – humbly*). But the dog still refuses baptism.

MENENDEZ (*sternly*). Is this a time to consider one Indian? Idiot! You know as well as I that my intention has been to attack Juan on one issue, and only one – his failure to sail for Cathay now that he has the King's patent. What have all the Nanos, hung or unhung, to do with that?

QUESADA. Much! If Don Juan were not bewitched by Nano's spells, he would have sailed
long since.

MENENDEZ. And you told the rabble that? God
pardon you! Was it any part of my orders that
you should play upon the mob's lust for blood? I
have worked for a peaceable revolt that would
awaken Juan to his weakness and shame him into
leaving. You have dared to evoke a madness
which might easily sweep away all recognized
authority. Quick! What was the rabble's mood
when you left? (*Quesada avoids his eyes. Menendez
pounds the table.*) Answer me!

QUESADA (*evasively*). They had been drinking –

MENENDEZ (*furiously, a note of alarm creeping in*).
Ah!

QUESADA (*now thoroughly cowed*). They were
clamouring to march on the palace. Don Oviedo
was trying to restrain them –

MENENDEZ (*fiercely – with bitter scorn*). You
cursed blunderer! No, I am the dolt for having
trusted you!

QUESADA (*kneeling – cowed*). Forgive me, Your
Grace!

MENENDEZ. Your action was treachery to me!
And I shall punish you! When this expedition
sails for that golden fable, Cathay, you shall go

with it. Then blunder all you like! (*He rises and strides to the window at rear.*)

QUESADA (*humbly*). I humbly accept my penance.

MENENDEZ (*bitterly*). Behold the first fruits of your excessive piety! (*He points.*) The southern horizon is aflame!

QUESADA (*rising*). They must have set fire to the Indian villages.

MENENDEZ. Blood and fire! Your merry dance begins well! (*He lets the curtains fall back.*) Only Juan can control them now – if he would only promise them to sail at once – but no, he is too proud. He will fight armed rebellion to the last – and we will all go down in the same ruin!

QUESADA (*scornfully*). He is not the man he was – since Nano bewitched him.

MENENDEZ (*disgustedly*). Bah! You fool! (*Then intently.*) Yet there is truth in what you say. He has grown weak – between Luis' influence and the girl's meddling – (*Abruptly.*) Come! There is still a chance. Summon Don Juan to me at once! (*This last in a shout of impatience.*)

JUAN (*from outside, rear, mockingly*). There is no need for messengers.

> (*He enters. In the three months he has aged greatly. His hair and beard have grown perceptibly white. Beneath the bitter, mocking mask there is an expres-*

*sion of deep, hidden conflict and suffer-
ing on his face as if he were at war with
himself.*)

MENENDEZ (*startled, afraid of what Juan may
have overheard*). You heard — ?

JUAN (*scornfully*). Only what you shouted. Am
I a monk to listen at keyholes? (*This with a glance
at Quesada.*) But I know your intrigues. This
meeting of yapping curs — you see, I have heard
the rumour — you would have me sail at their bid-
ding, and thus you would be free to rule this
island in God's Holy Name! Is it not so?

MENENDEZ (*controlling his anger*). You have lost
your senses. You will not realize that things have
reached a crisis! The government has slipped
through your fingers while you played at being a
loving father —

JUAN (*stung — fiercely*). It's a lie! (*Controlling
himself.*) I tell you again, Diego, I will sail at my
pleasure, not yours.

MENENDEZ (*persuasively*). You have kept repeating that — and meanwhile your apathy has ruined
us. Your soldiers and sailors are in open mutiny.
The mob has risen. (*Urgently.*) Juan, do you want
rebellion to overwhelm us? You promised them
Cathay —

JUAN (*proudly*). It was you who promised them
in my name, you mean, to make certain you would
be rid of me!

MENENDEZ (*tauntingly – noting Juan's reactions craftily*). I promised because I thought you were still Juan Ponce de Leon. But you are not. You have become merely a slave to a girl's sentimental whims! You are too feeble to govern here and too weak for Cathay. (*Juan's hand goes to his sword. Menendez continues cuttingly.*) Then for the sake of Spain, resign your office and surrender your patent for discovery to some one with the youth and courage to dare!

JUAN (*infuriated, half drawing his sword*). Take care, Diego! Your cloth cannot condone such insults!

MENENDEZ (*in a softened, oily tone*). Forgive me, Juan. I insult you for your own sake! Push on to your greatest victory! Do not wait here in a stupor for inglorious defeat!

JUAN (*shaken*). I shall sail – but first I must know – know for a certainty, beyond all doubt – exactly where – (*He stops abruptly.*)

MENENDEZ (*inquisitively*). What?

JUAN (*suspiciously*). Nothing.

QUESADA (*who has been listening with feverish interest – points to Juan accusingly*). He has gone to Nano every day. Look at his eyes! He is bewitched! (*Juan starts guiltily but tries to ignore him contemptuously.*)

MENENDEZ. Be still, Quesada! (*He looks at Juan.*) These interviews *are* mysterious, Juan.

JUAN (*quickly – half turning away and averting his eyes – with forced carelessness*). I need accurate information for my voyage that only Nano can give me. That is why I have delayed.

MENENDEZ (*looking at him sharply*). So? I had thought it might be affection for Beatriz that held you.

JUAN (*vehemently*). No!

MENENDEZ (*keenly*). Why are you so vehement? It would be natural enough. You have lived alone. To find a daughter in your declining years –

JUAN (*pale with rage and agony*). Daughter? How could she look upon me – ?

MENENDEZ (*soothingly but with a taunting intent*). She used to regard you as her hero, her great commander. She must wonder now at this old man's weakness in you.

JUAN (*frenziedly*). Do you dare taunt me in her name? I *will* sail, I say! I will sail the very first day after I discover – (*Then distractedly, shaken.*) Enough, Diego! I shall do what I wish and when it pleases me!

> (*He rushes out rear as if furies were hounding him. Menendez looks after him, a sneering smile of satisfaction gradually coming over his face as if something were proven to him.*)

MENENDEZ (*half to himself, half to Quesada*). I should have guessed it before. Yet, who would have thought – He is bewitched, certainly.

QUESADA (*eagerly*). Yes!

MENENDEZ (*dryly*). But you are blaming the wrong witch. The guilty one is sinless. (*Quesada puzzles over this paradox with open eyes. Menendez ponders for a moment, then he turns to Quesada.*) Bring the Lady Beatriz.

QUESADA. Yes, Your Grace. (*He bows and hurries out, left. Menendez sits thoughtfully, evidently planning out his campaign. A moment later Beatriz enters. She bows respectfully.*)

BEATRIZ (*reservedly*). You wish to see me, Your Grace?

MENENDEZ (*nods and motions her to a chair. He scrutinizes her face carefully for a moment, then begins in a playful, ironical tone*). Beauty did not leave a stone on stone of ancient Troy. Are you another Helen, Beatriz?

BEATRIZ (*confused*). I – don't understand.

MENENDEZ (*coldly and brusquely*). Not understand that rebellion is seething in Porto Rico? – a rebellion that will deal destruction to us all!

BEATRIZ (*bewildered*). Rebellion? (*Then spiritedly.*) Who would dare rebel against Don Juan?

MENENDEZ (*belittlingly*). Juan is powerless. His own soldiers have taken the lead against him. He is facing ruin! Do you understand? I wish I had

words of fire to brand it on your brain! For I tell
you on my conscience, as God's minister, you are
the one responsible!

BEATRIZ (*stunned*). I? I? You are jesting!
(*Then with haughty resentment.*) I harm Don Juan,
who is my second father!

MENENDEZ (*seeming to grow more icy under her
anger*). Who has done most in influencing him to
softness and lax discipline –

BEATRIZ (*indignantly*). You mean because I have
pitied the suffering of the Indians – ?

MENENDEZ (*dryly*). Let us judge your pity by
its results. These heathen no longer fear. They
defy our Holy Faith. They sneer at baptism.
These Indians shirk their labour. And because
Don Juan spends his time with you, he has forgotten not only his duty to govern but his oath to
seek Cathay. The soldiers and sailors have waited
too long in idleness. Now they revere him no
longer as a daring general who will lead them to
glory but despise him for a dissembler, delaying
because he has lost the courage for action! And
so they have conspired. Those are the facts. Will
you deny your influence is deep at the root of
them? (*Beatriz is too overwhelmed by the ruthlessness of his attack to reply. He pushes his advantage.*)
And can you deny that a great change has come
over Don Juan since your arrival? You cannot
have helped but notice this!

BEATRIZ. He has seemed — to become despondent at times.

MENENDEZ (*vehemently*). Spiritless! Infirm! His thoughts wander like a senile old man's! I believe his mind is failing him!

BEATRIZ (*horrified*). No! No!

MENENDEZ. You must face the truth! (*Sternly.*) When you take a life's ambition from a man like Juan, the man withers away. You have made him forget Cathay. Why? Why have you not urged him to go — for his own sake? When you brought out the patent, you dreamed of him as he dreams of himself — a conqueror and hero!

BEATRIZ (*hesitatingly*). Father Luis told me we must keep him here — or else his good work would be undone —

MENENDEZ. This uprising will undo it in an hour! (*Then soothingly.*) Father Luis is a good man — but blind. You are a girl — and inexperienced — Come. (*He pauses, watching her keenly, then takes her hand, and leading her to the window, pulls back the curtain.*) Look!

BEATRIZ (*with a shudder of horror*). Ah!

MENENDEZ. Now do you believe in the rebellion — in Juan's danger?

BEATRIZ (*horrified*). Fire!

MENENDEZ. And murder! In the Indian villages. See what your pity for them has done! And it will not stop there. That is only the first spark of revolution. They'll march here! (*Impressively*.) Beatriz, you can save Don Juan. He loves you — as his daughter. Urge him to sail at once! Rouse the hero in him! Give him back his sanity! He is my old friend. I implore you for his sake, Beatriz!

BEATRIZ (*bewilderedly*). Yes — yes — but give me time to think — to pray for guidance —

(*She kneels before the altar.*)

MENENDEZ (*impatiently*). There is no time!

(*There is a noise of hurrying steps and Oviedo enters. He is booted, spurred, covered with dust, his face betraying anxiety and alarm.*)

OVIEDO (*without stopping to see who is there, bursts forth*). Diego! I tried to check them, but they have gone mad! They are marching on the town! Juan will be lost!

MENENDEZ (*to Beatriz who has turned around in terror*). You hear!

OVIEDO. The time has come to abandon that sick fool! We must openly lead this rebellion!

BEATRIZ (*springs to her feet and faces him — her eyes flashing*). Coward! (*He falls back, his hand on his sword, glaring at her.*)

MENENDEZ (*urgently*). Go, Beatriz!

(*She passes Oviedo with a scathing glance,*

# THE FOUNTAIN

*and goes out rear. Menendez turns to Oviedo with an ironical but worried smile.*)

MENENDEZ. If she will but speak to Juan as she did to you, we may still win, my friend!

*(The Curtain Falls)*

# SCENE FIVE

SCENE. *Nano's dungeon — a circular cavern, hollowed out by Nature and cut out by man in the solid rock under the Government house. The enclosed space is narrow but lofty, cylindrical in form. A cut-in flight of steps leads from the floor in rear to a trap-door above. The high wall glistens with moisture. A small bench is at right. A lantern stands on one of the lower steps. In the middle of the floor stands a soldier, thick-set, brutal-looking, his sleeves rolled up over his muscular arms. He is blowing with a bellows on a charcoal brazier, glowing red-hot, in which are thrust several irons. On the wall in the rear, his toes barely touching the floor, Nano hangs with his arms outstretched over his head, the wrists bound by chains to iron sockets in the rock. His head hangs on one side as if he were in a state of semi-consciousness. His body is thin and wasted.*

*The trap-door is opened and a circular patch of grey light falls on the stairs. This is obscured as some one descends. It is Juan. He shuts the trap-door behind him and comes down. He stops when he is opposite Nano's head, and, leaning over, stares at the savage's face. The latter opens his eyes. His head stiffens proudly erect on his shoulders. He and Juan stare into each other's eyes. Juan drops his guiltily, turns away and descends to the floor, where the soldier is standing at attention.*

65

JUAN (*harshly*). Has he spoken?

SOLDIER. Not one word, sir.

JUAN. Then you have not obeyed —

SOLDIER (*indicates the irons in the fire*). I have tried every trick I know — but he's made of iron.

JUAN (*looks up at Nano with intense hatred*). Dog! (*Then he turns to the soldier.*) Go and keep guard above.

SOLDIER. Yes, sir. (*He bends down to pick up the brazier.*)

JUAN (*harshly*). No.

SOLDIER (*with a glance at him — understandingly*). Yes, sir.

> (*He goes up the stairs, opens the trap-door and disappears, letting it fall shut behind him. Juan sinks on the stone bench at right and stares up at Nano, who looks back at him with unflinching defiance. A pause.*)

JUAN (*his eyes now fixed dully on the floor — half-aloud to himself*). Diego did not lie. The storm is gathering. (*With bitter hopelessness.*) What matter? I could pray that it might be a deluge annihilating mankind — but for Beatriz. (*He groans, then raises his eyes again to Nano.*) Why do you look at me? I can never read your eyes. They see in another world. What are you? Flesh, but not our flesh. Earth. I come after — or before — but lost, blind in a world where my eyes deflect on surfaces. What values give you your loan of life? Answer! I must know the terms in which to make appeal! (*The savage is silent, motionless. A pause. Then Juan, as if suddenly reminded, jumps to his feet in a frenzy of impatience.*) Answer me, dog! I must find the will to act – or be dishonoured!

NANO (*solemnly – in a faint voice*). The Gods are angry.

JUAN (*with wild joy*). You speak! At last! Nano, why have you kept dumb while I implored – ?

NANO. The Gods have stopped your ears.

JUAN (*going on obsessed, regardless*). Juan Ponce de Leon – to torture a helpless captive! Why did you bring me to such shame? Why would you not answer my question?

NANO (*with contempt*). My tongue grew weary. For a moon I answered every day.

JUAN (*fiercely*). But you lied! Tell me the truth now! Where is the fountain?

NANO (*indifferently, shutting his eyes*). Only the Gods know.

JUAN. The same lie! You told me at first that men of your former tribe knew! You must know! This is your revenge – for the death of your wives and children! Must I swear to you again they were killed in spite of my strict orders? Come! Forget them! I will give you your choice of all your women on the island – your freedom – I will petition the King to honour you – give you back your lands — anything if you will answer me! (*Nano remains silent. Juan utters a furious cry and, rushing to the brazier, takes a red-hot coal with the tongs and holds it before the Indian's eyes.*) Dog! I will burn that scorn from your eyes! (*The Indian stares at the hot iron immovably. Juan lets it fall to the floor with a desperate groan of misery.*) Pardon! Forgiveness in Christ's name! It is you who torture me! Nano, I burn to hell! I love! (*He suddenly stops, chilled to despair by the implacable isolation in the savage's face. He throws himself down on the bench in an apathy. Finally he slowly draws his sword and speaks in a dead voice.*) Either you speak or you die. I swear it.

NANO (*with aloof contempt*). What is death?

JUAN (*dully*). I will die, too. Perhaps in the grave there is oblivion and peace. (*After a pause.*) You are a fool, Nano. If you would help me I could make you pilot of the fleet to guide us to your land. The fountain once found, you would be free. No harm should come to your people. Do you never long for your old home?

NANO (*who has been listening with quickened interest*). Home? To the land of flowers. My home of many warriors. (*After a pause.*) You will let me guide the great winged canoes — to my home?

JUAN (*eagerly*). Yes. (*In great suspense.*) Will you help me? Tell me! (*He has sprung to his feet.*)

NANO. Only the Gods — (*He checks himself abruptly.*)

JUAN (*frenziedly*). Ah! (*He raises his sword as if to run the savage through.*)

NANO (*looking into Juan's eyes without noticing the threat*). The tongues of the white devils are false. How can I trust your word?

JUAN. I take my sacred oath! (*He raises his hand.*)

NANO. Your God is a God of lies.

JUAN (*wildly*). By your God then – since mine has forsaken me!

NANO (*lifts his head and murmurs some supplication, as if begging forgiveness – then looks at Juan with savage triumph*). I will guide you – but remember the way is long!

JUAN (*triumphantly*). At last! What does it matter how long or difficult! (*Raising his arms.*) Ah, God's blood, I already feel new life, the will to live! I can conquer now! (*A pounding of a sword-butt on the trap-door. Then it is flung open.*)

SOLDIER. Pardon, Excellency –

BEATRIZ' VOICE (*calls down*). Don Juan! Don Juan!

JUAN (*exultantly*). Her voice! A happy omen! (*He hurries up the stairs.*)

NANO (*again lifting his eyes to heaven – with religious fervour*). Great Spirit, forgive my lie. His blood shall atone!

(*The Curtain Falls*)

# SCENE SIX

SCENE. *Same as Scene Three — Courtyard of the Governor's house — a stifling twilight. The sky is darkening with clouds.*

*Beatriz' voice — from the left — calls down as at the end of preceding scene.*

BEATRIZ. Don Juan! Don Juan!

> (*His voice is heard, "Beatriz." She enters, pale and agitated, runs to rear and looks for signs of the insurrection — then hurries back just in time to meet Juan, who enters, left. He is in a tense state of hectic excitement, his face ghastly pale, his obsessed eyes burning feverishly, his drawn sword still in his hand. She starts back from him, frightened by his appearance.*)

JUAN (*in a strained, high-pitched tone*). Was it the fountain called — or you, Beatriz? You, for you are the fountain! (*He takes her hand impetuously and kisses it.*)

BEATRIZ (*flurriedly*). I came to warn you —

JUAN (*with a sharp glance*). Warn? Then you have seen Diego? Bah! (*He makes a gesture of contempt with his sword as if brushing all revolutions aside.*) When the hour comes, I shall be strong. The will breathes in me again. Forget all else, Beatriz. Give me your thoughts! Have you been happy here with me?

70

BEATRIZ (*not knowing what to say or do*). Yes — yes. (*Trying to return to her mission.*) But —

JUAN. You came as a benediction — that cursed me. (*Abruptly.*) Have you not noticed how much older I have grown?

BEATRIZ (*convinced he is out of his head — resolved to humour him — frightened but pityingly*). You can become young again.

JUAN (*exultantly*). I will! (*Then mysteriously.*) This is a strange world with many wonders still undiscovered.

BEATRIZ (*seeing a chance to bring in her point — quickly*). Then discover them. The search will make you young.

JUAN (*deeply and superstitiously impressed*). From your own lips! It is another blessed augury! (*Eagerly.*) But pretend I am young. What then?

BEATRIZ. Why then you would be happy.

JUAN (*intensely*). You promise — ? Have you never loved?

BEATRIZ (*bewildered*). Loved?

JUAN. Since you speak of happiness.

BEATRIZ. I loved my mother — my father — I love you, Don Juan.

JUAN (*avidly*). Ah, say that again! Those words are blood to my heart!

BEATRIZ (*earnestly*). I love you as I loved my father —

JUAN (*brusquely — wounded to the quick*). Has love never stolen into your dreams? You are no nun. Come, tell me the image of the one you dream of as a lover.

BEATRIZ (*resolved to pass this off jestingly*). It is a great secret. You insist? Well then, it is your double — (*Juan utters a cry of joy, bending toward her. She adds hastily.*) You as my mother described you in the wars before Granada.

JUAN (*bitterly*). When I had youth. But I loved only glory then. Did she not tell you that?

BEATRIZ. Why then — that is why she said, bring him tenderness.

JUAN (*sombrely*). You have fulfilled her wish — or was it her revenge? (*Then abruptly.*) And what if I should myself become that double? — the knight of Granada with your gift of tenderness — what then?

BEATRIZ (*frightened by his strangeness*). Ah, now, you are jesting, Don Juan. (*She forces a laugh.*)

JUAN (*passionately*). No, Beatriz! (*She instinctively shrinks away from him. He calms himself.*) No more now. I fear your laughter. First let the consummation — Then you will not laugh. You — (*Trying to read her mystified eyes — miserably uncertain.*) What will you do?

BEATRIZ (*controlling her timidity — softly persuasive*). You are ill, Don Juan. Will you listen to my cure for you?

JUAN. Yes.

BEATRIZ (*with energy*). Sail and find Cathay!

JUAN (*with a start, tormentedly*). You, too, condemn me! But I swear to you I have longed to go! I have hated my own cowardice! I have played the traitor to every dream, every great hope – But, Beatriz, when I go, I will leave my life behind with you. So – until I knew – I was afraid of losing what I have – (*Then with a quick change to something approaching triumphant decision.*) But that is past! My will has risen from the dead. It is decreed by your own lips. I shall sail at once!

BEATRIZ. Oh, I am glad!

JUAN (*sadly*). Glad I am leaving you?

BEATRIZ. No, I shall be sad and lonely. It is for your own welfare –

JUAN. But promise me one boon –

BEATRIZ (*eagerly*). Anything!

JUAN. Promise you will not marry until I return – or you hear I am dead?

BEATRIZ (*confused*). I have never even thought of marrying.

JUAN (*in deadly earnest in spite of his pitiful pretence at a joking tone*). Until I present my double to you – ?

BEATRIZ (*relieved and laughing easily*). Why, I might change my mind then, Don Juan.

JUAN. Will you seal that pledge with a kiss? (*He forces a smile to conceal his longing.*)

BEATRIZ (*uncertainly – forcing a laugh*). Yes, Don Juan. (*She lifts her face to him. He starts to kiss her on the lips, but something in her face stops him and he ends by kissing her reverentially on the forehead – forcing a smile.*)

JUAN. There – upon your forehead – for remembrance. The other – for tenderness – is still a promise of my dream.

> (*There is a sound of hurrying steps and Juan moves away from Beatriz guiltily. Luis enters from the rear. His face is agitated, full of alarm and anxiety.*)

BEATRIZ (*greeting him eagerly, glad of the interruption*). Father Luis.

LUIS. Juan! I bring you terrible news. (*He sees Juan's drawn sword.*) Ah, you know! It is time you drew your sword.

JUAN (*scornfully*). You mean the scum rises? When I tell them the fleet sails to-morrow –

LUIS. Will you give them Nano to burn at the stake? That is their first demand. (*Beatriz gives a horrified cry.*)

JUAN (*stunned – unbelievingly*). Surrender Nano? No, it is impossible. You have heard rumours –

LUIS. Quesada has roused their cruelty to frenzy. (*He points to where a red glow is mounting up in the sky.*) See! They are burning the Indian quarter. May God have mercy!

JUAN (*in a rage*). Kill Nano? The curs! I shall order a company of my guard —

LUIS (*looking at him pityingly*). Your guard is leading the mob! (*Reproachfully.*) Juan, Juan, why have you lived in a dream! I warned you time after time. If you had been governor in anything but name —

JUAN (*sinking on the bench — stupidly*). Call the guard. I must order them to disperse.

BEATRIZ (*pityingly*). His mind is sick —

LUIS (*rather peremptorily*). Will you leave us, Beatriz?

BEATRIZ (*obediently*). Yes, Father. (*Then excitedly.*) I must see Bishop Menendez — (*She hurries out, right.*)

LUIS (*comes and slaps Juan on the back — sternly*). Juan! Awake, in God's name!

JUAN (*startled to action, springs to his feet*). I shall protect his life with my own!

LUIS. In order to torture him yourself?

JUAN (*vehemently but guiltily*). A lie! (*Suspicious — resentfully.*) Have you seen him? I gave orders —

LUIS. It is weeks since I was permitted to see him; and you have avoided meeting me. Why?

JUAN (*harshly*). I have no patience with your converting. I need Nano as he is.

LUIS. Because you prefer his heathen myths —

JUAN (*controlling an outburst of rage*). Myths? Why myths? Cathay is there. (*He points.*)

LUIS. I was not speaking of Cathay. You are sailing to-morrow? Does this mean you have finally wrung from this poor Indian's agonies a faith in magic fountains — ?

JUAN (*losing control of himself — raging*). Fool! You are like those dullards who, when Columbus said the earth was round, brayed at him for blaspheming! Listen to me! I do not believe Nano, I believe in Nature. Nature is part of God. She can perform miracles. Since this land was discovered have we not found wonders undreamed of before? The points in Nano's story hold true to the facts we know. His home is a beautiful mainland — "A land of flowers," in his own words. Is not Cathay also known as the "Flowery Land"? There are great walled cities with roofs of gold inland to the West. Is not that Marco Polo's land beyond all doubt? And the fountain is in Cathay. All the evidence from around the world proves that! And I shall find it!

LUIS (*pityingly*). But this evidence is merely fable, legend, the dreams of poets!

JUAN (*furiously*). Have praying and fasting made you an imbecile? What evidence had Columbus? And you — you believe Christ lived and died. Well, have you talked with men who saw Him in the manger, or on the cross?

LUIS. Juan, this is blasphemy!

JUAN (*with bitter despair*). Then let it be! I have prayed to Him in vain.

LUIS. Juan!

JUAN (*with all the power of his will in the words*). Let me be damned for ever if Nature will only grant me youth upon this earth again!

LUIS (*horrified*). Juan! You defy your God!

JUAN. There is no God but Love — no heaven but youth!

LUIS (*looks at his tortured face intently — suddenly realizes — in a tone of great pity*). So that is it — I have been blind. I thought your love saw in her — a child, a daughter!

JUAN (*intensely*). A child — yes — for a time — but one morning standing by the fountain she was a woman. More than a woman! She was the Spirit of Youth, Hope, Ambition, Power to dream and dare! She was all that I had lost. She was Love and the Beauty of Love! So I loved her, loved her with all the intensity of Youth's first love — when youth was dead! Oh, it was monstrous folly, I admit. I called myself a senile fool! I suffered with the damned. I lived in hell without the recompense of being dead! And I loved her more — and more! (*His head sinks down on his hands. A great sob racks his whole body.*)

LUIS (*overcome by compassion, his voice trembling*). Old friend — God in His Mercy have pity on you! (*He is interrupted by the hurried entrance of Beatriz from the right.*)

BEATRIZ (*indignantly*). Bishop Menendez says he can do nothing – that you must give Nano up! (*The angry tumult of a mob marching is heard from the distance. Frightenedly.*) Listen! Oh, Don Juan, you will save him, will you not?

JUAN (*starting up – in a voice in which rage and apprehension are blended*). I must! (*He listens to the rising murmur of the mob. As he does so his whole body stiffens into defiant determination. He becomes in an instant the commander again.*) Cowardly rabble! (*He springs to the entrance on the left and shouts to the soldier on guard.*) Bring Nano! (*He comes back to where Beatriz and Luis are standing and looks around the courtyard as if measuring his position.*) I shall face them here. Take Beatriz away, Luis.

BEATRIZ. I wish to stay with you!

MENENDEZ (*enters from the right*). Juan! (*Seeing his drawn sword – apprehensively.*) What? You will defy them? Then you are lost! Yield to them, I advise you. Give Nano to justice. (*While he is speaking Nano is half carried in by the soldiers. He is limp and exhausted.*)

JUAN (*with wild scorn*). Ah, High Priest! Deliver him up, eh?

MENENDEZ. Juan! You are impious! (*Angrily.*) It is sacrilege – to compare this Indian dog – you mock our Blessed Saviour! You are cursed – I wash my hands – His will be done! (*He turns and strides back into the house, right.*)

LUIS (*at a nearer roar from the mob*). Juan! Escape! There is still time –

JUAN. Run from jackals! Is my honour dead?

LUIS (*as a smashing battering sounds from outside*). They are at the outer gate! Come, Beatriz, in God's name!

> (*She struggles, but he succeeds in getting her as far as the entrance, right. A last crashing smash is heard as the outer gate gives way. A moment later the advance guard of the mob pour in – all of the lower rabble, these. Some wave torches above their heads. All are armed with pikes, knives, and various crude weapons that they have picked up or stolen.*)

JUAN (*in a roar of command*). Back!

> (*They hesitate for a moment. Then they see Nano and with yells of fury rush for him around the fountain. Juan springs to meet them. With quick thrusts and cuts of his sword he kills or wounds four of the foremost, who drop to the ground. The rest fall back frightened and awed for the moment. In this lull the remainder of the mob pour in from the rear, crowding and jostling each other. They are a nondescript crowd, ranging from nobles, richly dressed, soldiers, sailors,*)

*to the riff-raff of the criminal element
in bright-coloured rags. There are a
number of monks among them, Franciscans who urge them on, a few Dominicans who plead for restraint.)*

THE MOB. Don Juan! It's the Governor — push
back there! — To the flames with the Indian
dog! Seize him! Stand aside, Don Juan! Here-
tic! He's bewitched! The dog refused baptism!
Torture!

JUAN (*sternly*). I will kill the man who touches
this Indian! (*He walks up and down before them,
his sword ready to thrust, looking from eye to eye —
scathingly.*) Scoundrels! Where is your valour
now? Prick up your courage! (*Mockingly.*)
Come! Who wishes to die?

A NOBLE. We demand justice!

> (*Yells of approval from the crowd. They
> push in closer. Juan levels his sword
> at the breast of the nearest who springs
> back with a frightened cry. The mob
> sways and surges, close packed and in-
> decisive, cowed by Juan's eyes.*)

QUESADA (*suddenly pushing his way to the front of
the crowd — pointing at Nano, frantically*). Give him
up! You are bewitched!

> (*The mob are again aroused. There are cries
> of "To the stake! Torture!" etc.*)

# THE FOUNTAIN

JUAN. No! (*Yells of rage. The mob surges forward. Juan raises his sword.*) I will kill the first one who — (*They recoil again, all but Quesada. With his free hand Juan sweeps him to one side contemptuously — then fiercely threatening the crowd.*) Will you rebel against the Governor of your King? Then you are traitors to Spain! And, by God's blood, I will hang one of you on every tree!

> (*The crowd gives way by inches, sullenly, their yells reduced for the moment to a rebellious muttering:* "The King will remove you! Hang the Indians! Hang them! Hang Nano!" *etc.*)

A SOLDIER. We mean no harm to you, Don Juan. Keep your word to us. Order the fleet to sail. (*A yell of acclamation from the soldiers and sailors.*)

QUESADA. And give over that dog! The Inquisition shall know you protect infidels!

JUAN. I am Spain's soldier, not the Inquisition's! Soldiers and sailors! I tell you it is in Spain's service this Indian's life is spared. The fleet sails to-morrow — and we need Nano to pilot our voyage! (*A tumult from the bewildered crowd. Shouts of various nature:* "The fleet sails! To-morrow! Hurrah! He jokes! He mocks us! Spare him? No luck with a heathen on board! What does he mean? Guide us? No! The curse of the Church!" *But the mob is puzzled, blundering, and Juan con-*

81

*tinues with a sort of condescension as if he were speaking to children.*) Silence! Since you are so stupid, I must explain. This Nano was born on the mainland – Cathay! – our goal, do you understand? – and I have put off sailing while I questioned him. We must have his knowledge. He must be our pilot. (*With a fierce glance at Nano as if to let his threat strike home.*) And if he fails in his promise to me, I will gladly give him to you for punishment.

QUESADA (*furiously*). You say this to save him!

JUAN. Soldiers, sailors, I appeal to you! Can this mad monk lead you to conquest? You must decide between us. (*The crowd are all turning his way, becoming greedily enthusiastic. Juan sees the psychological moment to play a trump card.*) But to convince you finally, listen to Nano. Speak, Nano! Tell them what you told me – of the golden cities. Speak! (*Then under cover of the crowd's shouts of "Down with the dog! Torture! Hear! Let him speak! Don Juan says let him!" etc., he adds in a fierce whisper to the Indian.*) If you wish ever to see your home again!

NANO (*mechanically, in a clear monotonous voice, with expressionless face*). A big land – far mighty cities – gold –

JUAN. You hear? The cities of gold! (*The crowd murmurs excitedly.*)

NANO. There is much gold. The houses have gold on them.

A SOLDIER. Cipango! We'll storm their cities for them!

A SAILOR. Loot, my bullies!

JUAN. Glory and gold for all of you! And now go! (*The crowd are jubilant. Shouts of "Up anchor! Ahoy Cathay! At last! We sail! Sack! Riches! Gold!" etc. Juan shouts above the tumult.*) Go! Disperse! To-morrow we sail! (*A voice cries, "Long live Don Juan!" The whole mob takes it up. Juan begins to give way under the strain — wearily.*) Go. Go.

THE MOB (*led by a sailor, takes up a sort of chanty song in mighty chorus, dancing wildly, waving their torches, crowding out, rear*).

> The Cities of Gold
>     In far Cathay —
> Their great Khan is old,
> And his wealth untold
> In prize for our bold
>     Who sail away.
>         Aye!

His gold for our bold who sail away! !

BEATRIZ (*as the last of the mob disappear — rushing up to Juan with great admiration*). You have saved him! What they have said of you is true indeed — lion by nature as well as name!

JUAN (*bitterly*). Lion? No! Tricky politician! If I had been the Juan of long ago, I would not have pleaded or bargained with such curs. I would have —

> (*He raises his sword threateningly — then lets his arm sink limply. The sword slips from his fingers and falls to the ground.*)

BEATRIZ (*kneels quickly and presents its hilt to him*). I give you back your sword — to bring good fortune. Now you must find the golden cities!

JUAN (*taking it — longingly*). I care only for the one, Beatriz — the golden city of Youth, where you are queen.

> (*She looks into his face smilingly, mystified as —*

> *The Curtain Falls*)

# SCENE SEVEN

SCENE. *Four months later — a strip of beach on the Florida coast — a bright, moonlight night. The forest runs diagonally from right, front, to left, rear — a wall of black shadow. The sand gleams a pallid white in the moonlight. The rhythmic ebb and flow of waves is heard — their voice on a windless night of calm.*

*As the curtain rises, an Indian is discovered, standing in the moonlight, just out of the shadow of the forest. He is old, but still erect and war-rior-like, a chief by his demeanour. His body, naked save for a piece of deerskin at his waist, is elaborately painted, as is his face. A knot of feathers is in his hair. A tomahawk and flint knife are at his waist. He is motionless and silent as a statue, one hand clasping his unslung bow as if it were a staff, but he peers intently at some object in the ocean before him. Finally, he gives an ejaculation of surprise and makes a motion of summons to the forest behind him. The Medicine Man glides out of the darkness to his side. This latter is incredibly old and shrunken, daubed with many insignia in paint, wearing many ornaments of bone and shell. They confer together in low tones with much pantomime. A man is evidently swimming to-ward them from some strange object out at sea. Other Indians steal from the forest, form a group in the shadow behind the two, point out*

85

*to sea, gesticulate. At a sharp command from the Chief, they unsling their bows, fit arrows to strings, crouch in an ambush in the shadow. The Chief does likewise and stands waiting, prepared for what may come. Nano walks up the beach from front, left. His naked body glistens with drops of water. He sees the Chief and stops, raising his right hand above his head. The Chief makes a sign. The other Indians dart from their ambush and surround Nano.*

CHIEF. Bind him.

NANO (*calmly*). Is a brother an enemy? (*They all start with surprise at hearing their own langauge. Nano goes on.*) This is the land of my fathers. I am Nano, a son of Boanu, who was a chief. (*They all stare at him. The Chief makes a sign to the Medicine Man, who comes forward and examines Nano's face intently.*)

MEDICINE MAN. His words are truth. He is Nano — or an evil spirit in his body. (*He shakes a charm at him.*) Are you from the Land of the Dead?

NANO. I am of the living. They did not chain me. They think I fear the sea. I come to warn you. I swam from the great canoes. They are the warships of the Spaniards.

CHIEF (*mystified*). What are Spaniards? Their winged canoes are like the boats of Gods.

NANO. These are no Gods. They are men who

die from wounds. Their faces are white, but they are evil. They wear shirts that arrows cannot pierce. They have strange sticks that spit fire and kill. Their devils make them strong. But they are not true warriors. They are thieves and rapers of women.

CHIEF. Have they no God?

NANO (*with scorn*). Their God is a thing of earth! It is this! (*He touches a gold ornament that the Chief wears.*)

MEDICINE MAN (*mystified*). Gold? Gold is sacred to the Sun. It can be no God itself.

NANO (*contemptuously*). They see only things, not the spirit behind things. Their hearts are muddy as a pool in which deer have trampled. Listen. Their Medicine Men tell of a God who came to them long ago in the form of a man. He taught them to scorn things. He taught them to look for the spirit behind things. In revenge, they killed him. They tortured him as a sacrifice to their Gold Devil. They crossed two big sticks. They drove little sticks through his hands and feet and pinned him on the others – thus.

(*He illustrates. A murmur of horror and indignation goes up among them.*)

MEDICINE MAN. To torture a God! How did they dare?

NANO. Their devils protected them. And now each place they go, they carry that figure of a dying God. They do this to strike fear. They command you to submit when you see how even a God who fought their evil was tortured. (*Proudly.*) But I would not.

MEDICINE MAN (*suspiciously*). If you defied them, how are you alive?

NANO. I am craftier than they. They have an old chief who is cursed with madness. Him I told of the Spring of Life. I said I would find it for him.

MEDICINE MAN. Only the Gods can reveal it. Why have you told this lie?

NANO (*fiercely*). Revenge! I have made a plan. Is there a spring near?

CHIEF (*mystified*). Yes. In the forest.

NANO (*with satisfaction*). Good! Listen. This mad chief is the mightiest among them. Without him they would turn cowards. To-morrow night I will lead him to the spring. You must lie hidden. We will kill him there. Is this clear?

CHIEF. Yes.

NANO. I will swim back now. I escaped to tell you of my plan and warn you. They would lay waste your land as they did mine. They killed my wives and children. They burned. They tortured. They chained warriors neck to neck. They beat them with a whip to dig in the fields like squaws. This old chief led them. My heart is fire. Until he dies, it will know no peace.

CHIEF. I begin to feel your hatred.

NANO. Then remember to hide by the spring.

CHIEF. We will not forget.

NANO. It is well.

> (*He turns and strides down to the sea. They stand watching him in silence.*)

MEDICINE MAN (*uneasily, thoughtful*). Only devils could build great canoes that fly with wings. My brothers, they are evil spirits. Nano has made war with them. They have beaten him. Can we trust his plan?

CHIEF. What is your counsel?

MEDICINE MAN. I have heard the voice of the Great Spirit speaking in the night. Let us first try to propitiate their devils.

CHIEF. I do not know how to war with devils. That is your duty. Let us summon the council.

> (*He makes a sign at which his followers disappear silently into the wood. He and the Medicine Man follow as —*

> *The Curtain Falls*)

# SCENE EIGHT

SCENE. *The same. High noon of the following day —
glaring sunlight on the beach, an atmosphere of
oppressive heat and languor. The earth seems
dead, preserved in some colourless, molten fluid.
The forest is a matted green wall. The sound of
the sea has the quality of immense exhaustion.*

*On the beach, a sort of makeshift altar is
being erected — two round boulders supporting
a flat slab of rock. On top of the slab is placed a
shallow bowl made of bark. A group of Indians, under the direction of the Medicine Man,
are hurriedly putting on the finishing touches to
this shrine. They keep casting awed apprehensive glances seaward. The Medicine Man is
binding two branches of a tree together in the
form of a cross. All the Indians are feathered
and painted as for an unusual solemn occasion.*

THE INDIANS (*their eyes on the sea as they work —
frightenedly*). The small canoes leave the great
winged ones. They are coming! The sun gleams
on their shirts that arrows cannot pierce. Their
fire-sticks glitter in the sun. Their faces are
turned. Their faces are pale! They are watching
us!

MEDICINE MAN (*finishing his work*). Keep your
hearts brave! (*Giving the cross to two Indians.*)
Here. This is their totem pole. Stand it there.
(*They dig a hole in the sand before the altar and set*

*the cross there; but they make the mistake of setting it
head down. The Medicine Man grunts with satisfaction.*) They will think we adore the same devil.
They will leave us in peace.

INDIAN (*his eyes on the sea*). The last canoe has
left the great ships. (*He gives a cry of fear echoed
by the others.*) Aie! Fire and smoke!

> (*They cower. The hollow boom of a cannon
> fired in salute reverberates over the sea.
> They all shrink with terror, bowing
> their heads.*)

INDIAN (*awestruck*). The Thunder fights with
them!

INDIAN. They are white Gods!

MEDICINE MAN (*frightened himself, but rallying
his followers sternly*). You have the hearts of
squaws. Quick! Where is the gold?

> (*An Indian comes to him with an earthen-
> ware vessel. He empties it out on the
> bowl on the top of the altar. It is full of
> gold nuggets of different sizes. They
> form a heap glowing in the sun.*)

INDIANS. They come! They come!

MEDICINE MAN (*sternly*). Pretend to worship
their gold devil but pray to our Great Father, the
Sun. He can defeat all devils. Pray to him! (*An
Indian starts to beat rhythmically on the small drum.
The Medicine Man lifts his shrill voice in the first*

*strains of the chant. Immediately the others all join in as if hypnotized.*) Great Father, Mighty One, Ruler of Earth. Maker of Days. Ripener of the Corn. Creator of Life. Look down upon us out of your Sky-Tent. Let our song rise to you. Let it enter your heart. Mighty One, hear us. Hide not your face in clouds. Bless us at the dawn. And at the day's end.

> (*They form a circle and dance about the altar, their eyes raised to the sun overhead. Their chant hides the noise of the Spaniards landing. Then the Spaniards appear from the left, front. First comes Juan, his face wild and haggard, his eyes obsessed. He is accompanied by Luis. Following him are a squad of Soldiers, guarding Nano, who is in chains. Then come four Franciscan Monks, led by Quesada, who wears a sword and pistol over his robe. The others carry crosses. Following them is a group of Nobles, richly dressed. Then come ranks of Soldiers. They all stare at this Indian ceremony with contemptuous scorn.*)

JUAN (*irritably*). Make them cease their accursed noise, Luis. Let Nano speak to them.

LUIS (*advancing toward the Indians — in a loud but friendly voice, raising his right hand*). Peace, brothers.

(*The Indians stop, petrified, staring with awe at the white men. The Medicine Man lifts his right hand and advances a step toward Luis. Quesada notices the cross, utters a furious exclamation, strides forward to verify his suspicion. When he sees that it is indeed upside down his face grows livid with fury.*)

QUESADA. The cross head down! The black mass! (*He pulls out his pistol.*) Blaspheming dog!

(*He fires. The Medicine Man falls. The other Indians who have shrunk back toward the woods in terror at his first move, now turn tail in panic and flee.*)

LUIS (*in horror*). Stop, Quesada!

(*Quesada pulls up the cross and is setting it back upright when the Medicine Man, by a last dying effort, draws his knife, and writhing to his feet, plunges it into Quesada's back. They both fall together, the Indian dead. Quesada shudders and is still. A yell of rage goes up from the Spaniards. They rush forward toward the woods as if to pursue the Indians, but Juan shouts a command.*)

JUAN. Halt! Fools! (*They stop prudently but sullenly. Juan turns to Luis, who is kneeling beside Quesada.*) Is he dead?

LUIS. Yes. (*Crossing himself.*) May his soul rest in peace. (*All echo this, crossing themselves.*)

JUAN. An eye for an eye, a tooth for a tooth. (*Mockingly.*) And now it is his eye, his tooth. (*Then with a shudder.*) Take him away. This is a bloody baptism for Cathay. (*Turning to Nano as the Soldiers carry the bodies aside.*) Is this the land, Nano?

NANO (*his eyes smouldering with hate*). Yes.

JUAN. You said it was a wonder land – a land of flowers. I see no flowers.

NANO (*in a sinister tone*). In the forest – flowers grow by a spring –

JUAN (*harshly – with an apprehensive glance about*). Silence!

A NOBLE (*from the group that has been stirring impatiently*). Your Excellency. The banners of Castile and Aragon wait on your pleasure.

JUAN (*making a confused gesture as if wiping cobwebs from his brain*). Yes – yes – I must take possession. Bring the banners. (*He kneels on one knee. They all do likewise.*) In the name of Jesus Christ, Our Lord, and of his most gracious Majesty, the sovereign of Castile and Aragon, I do hereby annex to his dominions this land and all its environs. And I call the land Florida.

> (*He bends and kisses the sand. The banners are planted in the ground, where they hang motionless from their poles. Juan,*

*having made this effort, seems to fall
into a stupor.*)

A NOBLE (*in a mocking whisper*). A pretty name!

A NOBLE. He has grown imbecile. Will he go
spring-hunting here, too? My faith, with all the
water he has drunk in the past four months, he
must be flooded. (*They all snicker at this.*)

A NOBLE (*impatiently*). Will he never get off his
knees and let us rise?

LUIS (*sensing what is going on behind their backs –
to Juan – who seems to be praying with bowed head
– plucking his sleeve*). Juan! Come!

JUAN (*vaguely*). I was praying – to what God
who knows?

> (*He rises to his feet weakly. At this, they all
> rise.*)

A NOBLE (*pointing excitedly*). Look! In that bowl
on the stones. Is it not gold? (*They all rush forward to the altar. The Noble picks up a piece of it –
his voice hoarse with greedy triumph.*) Gold! (*They
all grab at the bowl, upsetting its contents on the sand.
They bend down and clutch for it crying.*) Gold!
This must be a rich land! There must be more!
The Golden Cities are near! Cathay at last!

> (*The Soldiers forget discipline, break ranks,
> form a disorderly, pushing crowd about
> their leaders. Even the Monks edge
> forward inquisitively.*)

LUIS (*urgently*). Juan! Look! This is disgraceful!

JUAN (*coming to himself with a start — in a furious tone of command*). Get back to your ranks! A brave example you set, nobles of Spain! (*His personality is compelling. They all slink to their former order again, muttering rebelliously. Juan seems suddenly seized with a wild exultation.*) Cathay! We have found Cathay! This is the land — the Flowery Land! Our dreams lie hidden here! Sing the Te Deum! Sing!

> (*There is an oppressive silence for a moment, in which the heat, the sun glaring on the beach, the green of the forest, all nature seems to lay upon these men a mysterious spell, a sudden exhausted recognition of their own defeat. Then the Franciscan Monks raise their voices mechanically and spiritlessly in the Te Deum. Other listless voices gradually join theirs as —*

> *The Curtain Falls*)

# SCENE NINE

SCENE. *About midnight — in the forest. Gigantic tree-trunks, entwined with vines in flower, are in the foreground. Festoons of Spanish moss hang clear to the ground from the branches. Through the network one sees a circular clearing, grass-grown, flooded with moonlight. There is the soft murmur of a spring which bubbles from the ground in the centre of this open space. Indians are crouched in ambush among the trees, motionless, their eyes fixed on the clearing.*

*The stillness is broken by the whistled call of a bird. The Indians stir alertly. One of them whistles in answer to the call. An Indian creeps swiftly in from the left. The Chief comes from his place of ambush to meet him.*

CHIEF. He comes?

INDIAN. He has entered the forest.

CHIEF. I will give Nano the signal when we are ready. Go. Hide.

(*The Indian takes a place with the others. The Chief fits an arrow to his bow and crouches in the shadow. There is a pause of silence — then the noise of some one pushing his way through the woods at the rear of the clearing. Nano appears there, followed by Juan.*)

JUAN. Why do you stop?

97

NANO. This is the place.

JUAN (*looking around him disappointedly*). This?

NANO. There is the spring.

JUAN (*stepping forward to look at it — with growing anger*). It looks a common spring like any other. Beware, dog! In these past months you have shown me many springs —

NANO (*quickly*). The voyage was long. There were many islands. You forced me to lead you to a spring on each. But I told you the Spring of Life was here.

JUAN. I feared your revenge might lie. (*Relapsed into a mood of sombre preoccupation — bitterly.*) I drank of every one. I closed my eyes. I felt the stirring of rebirth. Fool! Always the mirror in the spring showed me the same loathsome blighted face — (*He groans — then with a harsh laugh.*) A sacred grove, the legend says! Some of those springs bubbled from sandy water! Beautiful maidens? There were none. At one place I found an old hag filling her bowl, who drank and mumbled at me. (*Then in a harsh tone of command.*) Nano! I command you to tell me if you have lied. (*Distractedly.*) I must have certainty, be it of faith or despair!

NANO. This is the spring.

JUAN (*looking around him*). But where are the trees with golden fruit, the maidens, the fountain — ? (*Bewildered, staring — grasping at hope.*) And yet — this spot has singular beauty. I feel enchantment. But why do I shudder? (*A low whistled signal comes from the Chief hidden on the edge of the clearing. Juan starts.*) Sssh! What was that?

NANO. A bird (*Insistently*). It is a magic spring. Drink!

JUAN (*bending over the spring*). A mirror of moonlight. The dead eyes of a corpse stare back in mine. (*He kneels by the spring as if fascinated.*) I dare not drink. To whom can I pray? Beatriz! Oh, to hear your voice once more, to see your face! And yet I see you everywhere. Your spirit inspires all things wherever there is beauty. I hear you call in the song of the waves, the wind is your breath, the trees reach out with your arms, the dawn and sunset promise with your lips! You are everywhere and nowhere — part of all life but mine! (*He breaks off, turning distrustful, harried eyes on the impatient Nano — bitterly.*) I am a spectacle for laughter, eh? A grotesque old fool!

NANO (*in a fierce tone of command*). Drink!

JUAN (*hectically — goading himself to action*). The test. Spirit of Eternal Youth, I pray to you! Beatriz!

> (*He bends down and drinks. As he does so Nano darts away from him to the woods in front.*)

NANO (*hurriedly*). Kill when he stands again!

# THE FOUNTAIN

(*The Indians can be seen raising their bows, taking aim.*)

JUAN (*having drunk, remains kneeling by the spring — in a trembling tone of hesitating joy*). New life thrills in me! Is it youth? Do I dream? Then let me never wake till the end of time! (*Then harshly.*) Coward! How often have you looked death in the face. Are you afraid of life? Open! Open and see! (*He opens his eyes and stares down into the spring. A terrible groan tears from his breast.*) O God! (*His grief is turned immediately into a frenzy of rage.*) Treacherous dog. You betrayed me.

> (*He leaps to his feet, drawing his sword. There is a twanging of many bows, the whiz of a flight of arrows. Juan falls, clutches at the grass, is still. The Indians pour out into the clearing but keep a cautious distance from Juan.*)

NANO (*with more courage than they, he bends down over the body*). He wore no shining shirt. He is dead. (*He does a wild dance of savage triumph beside the body — then stops as suddenly.*) Quick. To their camp. The great Spirit has made them helpless. Be brave and kill!

> (*He runs swiftly into the woods, followed by the whole band, brandishing their weapons. There is a pause. Then the fierce yells of the savages as they fall*)

*upon the sleeping camp, the howls of*
*terror of the Spaniards, the screams of*
*the dying, a few futile musket-shots.)*

*(The Curtain Falls)*

# SCENE TEN

SCENE. *The same clearing in the woods some hours later. There is no intervening fringe of trees in this scene, the open space is in full view. The Spring is at centre. The wall of forest forms a semicircular background. As the curtain rises, there is a pitch-blackness and silence except for the murmur of the Spring. Then the sound of some one struggling to rise from the ground, falling back again with a groan of pain. Juan's voice comes out of the darkness.*

JUAN (*as if he had just regained consciousness — then with a groan of rage and pain as memory returns*). Fool! Why did I look? I might have died in my dream. (*A pause — weakly.*) Sleep seems humming in my ears. Or is it — death! — death, the Merciful One! (*He stirs and his voice suddenly grows strident.*) No, No! Why have I lived! To die alone like a beast in the wilderness? (*With a bitter mocking despair.*) O Son of God, is this Thy justice? Does not the Saviour of Man know magnanimity? True, I prayed for a miracle which was not Thine. Let me be damned then, but (*passionately*) let me believe in Thy Kingdom! Show me Thy miracle — a sign — a word — a second's vision of what I am that I should have lived and died! A test, Lord God of Hosts! (*He laughs with a scornful bravado.*) Nothing! (*But even as he speaks a strange unearthly light begins to flood down upon a spot on the edge of the clearing on the right. Startled in spite of himself.*) This light — the moon has waned — (*Beneath the growing light a form takes shape — a tall woman's figure, like a piece of ancient sculpture, shrouded in long draperies of a blue that is almost black. The face is a pale mask with features indistinguishable save for the eyes that stare straight ahead with a stony penetration that sees through and beyond things. Her arms are rigid at her sides, the palms of the hands turned outward. Juan stares at her, defiance striving with his awe.*) What are you? (*Forcing a sneer.*) An angel in answer to my prayer? (*He cannot control a shudder — tries to calm himself. He stares at the figure — after a pause, boldly.*) Or are you Death? Why then I have often laughed in your eyes! (*Tauntingly.*) Off with your mask, coward! (*Mockingly but uneasy.*) Delightful Lady, you are enigmatic. One must embrace you with bold arms, tear off your masquerade. That was my pastime once — to play at love as gaming. Were I the Juan of long ago — but you see I am old now and wounded. (*He pauses. The figure is frozen. He asks a bit falteringly.*) Are you — death? Then wait — (*In passionate invocation.*) O Beatriz! Let me hear your voice again in mercy of farewell! (*As if in answer to this the voice of Beatriz sings from the darkness.*)

VOICE. Love is a flower
      For ever blooming
      Life is a fountain
      For ever leaping
      Upward to catch the golden sunlight

Upward to reach the azure heaven
Failing, falling,
Ever returning,
To kiss the earth that the flower may
live.

JUAN (*raptly*). Youth! (*As the song is sung, the same mystical light floods down slowly about the Spring, which is transformed into a gigantic fountain, whose waters, arched with rainbows, seem to join earth and sky, forming a shimmering veil, which hides the background of forest. Juan and the Figure are left at the edge of this, on the outside. The form of Beatriz appears within as if rising from the spring. She dances in ecstasy—the personified spirit of the fountain. Juan cries with a voice trembling with joy.*) The Fountain! Let me drink! (*He tries to drag himself to it but cannot—in anguish.*) Must I die —? (*Making a furious gesture of defiance at the Figure and struggling to rise.*) No! I defy you! (*Exhausted, he sinks back crying beseechingly.*) Beatriz! (*But she seems not to see or hear him. Juan half sobs in despair.*) She will not see! She will not hear! Fountain, cruel as the heart of youth, what mercy have you for the old and wounded? (*He sinks down overcome by weakness. Beatriz vanishes from the fountain. In her place appears the form of a Chinese poet. He is a venerable old man with the mild face of a dreamer and scholar. He carries a block and writes upon it with a brush, absorbed in contemplation. Juan looking up and seeing him— startled.*) What are you? (*Groping at some clue in his memory.*) I know – that night in Granada – the Moor's tale – (*Excitedly.*) Of the poet from the East who told his father the Fountain lie! Are you not that poisoner of life? (*The Poet raises his hand as if in summons. The form of the Moorish minstrel of Scene One appears at his side.*) The Moor! (*Raging.*) Infidel dog! Your lie has cursed me! (*The form of Nano appears at the other side of the Chinese poet. Juan struggles to reach his sword in a fury.*) Murderer! (*Then his eyes are caught by a fourth figure which materializes beside the Moor. It is Luis as he was in Scene One. With a cry of joy.*) Luis – old friend – (*Then as Luis seems neither to see nor hear him, he sinks back helplessly.*) No – another mocking phantom! (*He watches the Chinese poet, who seems to be reading what he has written to all of them.*) See! The dead lie to the living. It passes on – from East to West – round the round world – from old worlds to new – cheating the old and wounded – Ha!

> (*He laughs harshly and wildly. The Chinese poet takes the Indian by one hand, the Moor by the other. These latter stretch out their hands to Luis, who takes them, thus completing the circle. Beatriz' voice can be heard singing.*)

VOICE. Life is a field
For ever growing
Beauty a fountain
For ever flowing

# THE FOUNTAIN

Upward beyond the source of sunshine
Upward beyond the azure heaven,
Born of God but
Ever returning
To merge with earth that the field may
    live.

(*As she sings, the four forms disappear as if they were dissolved in the fountain*).

JUAN (*lost in the ecstasy of her song*). Sing on, Youth! (*With a start as the song stops – stupidly.*) The ghosts are gone. What is the answer to their riddle? I am no poet. I have striven for what the hand can grasp. What is left when Death makes the hand powerless? (*Addresses the Figure pitifully, trying to mock.*) O Mighty Relaxer of hands, have you no vision for the graspers of earth? (*The Figure raises a summoning hand. One by one, within the fountain, solemn figures materialize. First the Chinese poet, now robed as a Buddhist priest; then the Moorish minstrel, dressed as a priest of Islam; and then the Medicine Man as he was in Scene Eight, decked out in all the paint and regalia of his office; lastly, Luis, the Dominican monk of the present. Each one carries the symbol of his religion before him. They appear clearly for a moment, then fade from sight, seeming to dissolve in the fountain. Juan has stared at them with straining eyes – in a bewildered voice.*) All faiths – they vanish – are one and equal – within – (*Awe and reverence creeping into his voice.*) What are you, Fountain? That from which all life springs and to which it must return – God! Are all dreams of you but the one dream? (*Bowing his head miserably.*) I do not know. Come back, Youth. Tell me this secret! (*For a moment the voice of Beatriz is heard from the darkness.*)

> Death is a mist
> Veiling sunrise.

> (*Juan seems to fall into a rapt spell. The form of an old Indian woman appears from the left. She falters forward, a wooden bowl under her arm, as if she were going to fill it at the fountain.*)

JUAN (*recognizing her aghast*). Damned hag! I remember you waited beside a spring to mock me! Begone! (*But the old woman stretches out her hands to him with a mysterious beseeching. Juan shudders – then after a struggle with himself, gets to his feet painfully.*) So be it. Sit here by me. I am old, too – and, poor woman, you cannot fill your bowl there. Come. (*He grasps her hands. In a flash her mask of age disappears. She is Beatriz. Juan gazes at her in an ecstasy – faltering, his mind groping.*) Beatriz! Age – Youth – They are the same rhythm of eternal life! (*Without his noticing it, Beatriz recedes from him and vanishes in the Fountain. He raises his face to the sky – with halting joy.*) Light comes! Light creeps into my soul! (*Then he sees the Figure walk slowly from its place and vanish in the Fountain.*) Death is no more! (*The Figure materializes*

*again within the Fountain but this time there is no
mask, the face is that of Beatriz, her form grown tall,
majestic, vibrant with power. Her arms are raised
above her head. Her whole body soars upward. A
radiant, dancing fire, proceeding from the source of
the Fountain, floods over and envelops her until her
figure is like the heart of its flame. Juan stares at this
vision for a moment, then sinks on his knees — exultantly.)* I see! Fountain Everlasting, time without
end! Soaring flame of the spirit transfiguring
Death! All is within! All things dissolve, flow
on eternally! O aspiring fire of life, sweep the
dark soul of man! Let us burn in thy unity!
*(Beatriz' voice rises triumphantly.)*

VOICE. God is a flower
    For ever blooming
    God is a fountain
    For ever flowing.

> *(The song ceases. The light fades. There is
> darkness. Juan's voice is heard sobbing
> with happiness.)*

JUAN. O God, Fountain of Eternity, Thou art
the All in One, the One in All — the Eternal
Becoming which is Beauty! *(He falls unconscious.
A pause. Then the faint misty light of the dawn floats
over the clearing. Juan is seen lying where he had
fallen. There is the noise of some one approaching
from the woods in the rear, Luis and a brother
Dominican enter from the forest.)*

LUIS *(seeing Juan).* God be praised! *(He rushes*

*forward and kneels by Juan's body. Juan stirs and groans.*) He moves! Juan! It's Luis! Our friends were murdered. A boat from the fleet is waiting —

JUAN (*in a dreaming ecstasy*). God — Thou art all —

DOMINICAN. He prays.

LUIS. Delirium. Let us carry him. We'll sail for the nearest settlement —

JUAN (*as they raise him*). Light! I see and know!

LUIS. It is the dawn, Juan.

JUAN (*exultantly*). The dawn!

(*They carry him out as —*

*The Curtain Falls*)

# SCENE ELEVEN

SCENE. *Some months later. The courtyard of a*
*Dominican monastery in Cuba. A crude little*
*home-made fountain is in centre. This is the*
*only adornment of the quadrangle of bald, sun-*
*baked earth, enclosed on the left and in the rear*
*by a high white wall, on the right by the mon-*
*astery building itself. The entrance to this is an*
*arched doorway surmounted by a crucifix of*
*carved wood. Two niches on either side of this*
*door shelter primitive wooden figures of the*
*Holy Family and Saint Dominic. In the wall,*
*centre, is another arched door with a cross above*
*it. Beyond the wall nature can be seen and felt*
*— vivid, colourful, burgeoning with the mani-*
*fold, compelling life of the tropics. Palm trees*
*lean over the wall casting their graceful sha-*
*dows within. Vines in flower have climbed to*
*the top and are starting to creep down inside.*

*A sunset sky of infinite depth glows with*
*mysterious splendour.*

*As the curtain rises, Juan and the Father*
*Superior are discovered. Juan is asleep, reclin-*
*ing on a sort of improvised invalid's chair, his*
*cloak wrapped around him, facing the fountain.*
*He is pale and emaciated but his wasted coun-*
*tenance has gained an entirely new quality, the*
*calm of a deep spiritual serenity. The Father*
*Superior is a portly monk with a simple round*
*face, grey hair and beard. His large eyes have*

*the opaque calm of a ruminating cow's. The
door in the rear is opened and Luis enters. He
closes the door carefully and tiptoes forward.*

LUIS (*in a whisper*). He is sleeping?

FATHER SUPERIOR. As you see, Father.

LUIS (*looking down at Juan*). How calm his face
is – as if he saw a vision of peace.

FATHER SUPERIOR. It is a blessed miracle he has
lived so long.

LUIS. He has been waiting. (*Sadly.*) And now,
I am afraid his desire is fulfilled – but not as he
dreamed. Rather the cup of gall and wormwood –

FATHER SUPERIOR (*mystified*). You mean the
caravel brings him bad tidings?

LUIS. Yes; and I must wake him to prepare his
mind.

FATHER SUPERIOR. I will leave you with him.
It is near vesper time. (*He turns and goes into the
monastery.*)

LUIS (*touching Juan on the arm – gently*). Juan,
awake. (*Juan opens his eyes.*) The caravel has
anchored.

JUAN. From Porto Rico?

LUIS. Yes.

JUAN (*with an air of certainty – with exultant
joy*). Then Beatriz is here!

LUIS (*disturbed – evasively*). There has been a
frightful insurrection of the Indians. Diego was

III

killed. (*Hastily.*) But I will not trouble you with that. (*Then slowly.*) Beatriz comes to nurse you – (*With warning emphasis*) – her second father, those were her words.

JUAN (*smiling*). You need not emphasize. I know her heart. (*Then earnestly.*) But I must tell her my truth. (*Then with a sort of pleading for assurance.*) It is for that I have waited, to tell her of the love I bore her – now – as farewell – when she cannot misunderstand. (*Proudly.*) My love was no common thing. It was the one time Beauty touched my life. I wish to live in her memory as what she was to me. (*Sinking back – with a flickering smile, weakly.*) Come, old friend, are you grown so ascetic you deny my right to lay this Golden City – the only one I ever conquered – at the feet of Beauty?

LUIS (*kindly persuasive*). Silence is better, Juan. You should renounce –

JUAN (*gently*). All is renounced. But do you begrudge a traveller if he begs a flower from this earth, a last token of the world's grace, to lend farewell the solace of regret?

LUIS (*more and more troubled*). Juan – I – I speak because – you have suffered – and now – I would not have you suffer more, dear friend. (*Then blurting out most brusquely.*) The caravel brings you a surprise. Your nephew, Juan, has arrived from Spain and comes from Porto Rico to greet you.

JUAN (*vaguely*). My nephew? (*The sound of voices comes from inside the monastery.*) Beatriz!

> (*The Father Superior appears in the doorway ushering in Beatriz and Juan's nephew. They are followed by the Duenna and the Nephew's Servant, who carries his master's cloak and a lute. During the following scene these two remain standing respectfully by the doorway for a time, then go back into the monastery, the Servant leaving the cloak and lute on the ground beside the doorway. The Father Superior retires immediately. Luis, after a clasp of Juan's hand, also withdraws, exchanging greetings as he passes the Nephew and Beatriz. Beatriz glows with fulfilment, is very apparently deeply in love. The Nephew is a slender, graceful young cavalier. He is dressed richly.*)

BEATRIZ (*halting a moment with a shocked exclamation as she sees Juan's wasted face — then rushing forward and flinging herself on her knees beside his chair. Hastily*). Don Juan! Oh, this is happiness — to find you still — recovered from your wounds! Oh, I'll say prayers of thanksgiving! (*Impulsively she kisses him.*)

JUAN (*thrilled — choked — unable to say but one word*). Beatriz! Beatriz!

NEPHEW (*kneels and kisses Juan's hand. Startled, Juan's eyes search his face keenly, apprehensive of what he, too, plainly sees there*). I greet you, sir. God grant you may soon be strong again.

JUAN (*weakly*). Soon — I shall be strong — against all wounds. (*After a pause.*) And so your name is Juan, too?

NEPHEW. In your honour. Though I can add no honour to it, I hope to bear it worthily.

JUAN (*hostility creeping into his tone*). You come out here adventuring?

NEPHEW. I come to serve Spain!

JUAN (*harshly*). A heart as steeled as your sword. Have you that?

BEATRIZ (*eagerly — somewhat hurt by Juan's reception*). Oh, he is brave! When the mob tried to storm the palace it was Juan who led the defenders.

JUAN (*more and more agitated — trying to hide his growing resentment under effusive amiability*). Bravely done! But you have doubtless heard great tales of mountains of jewels — Golden Cities of Cathay — you hope to grow rich.

NEPHEW (*proudly*). I do not care for riches; and as for Golden Cities, I only wish to plant Spain's banner on their citadels!

JUAN (*inspired by respect in spite of himself*). Brave dreams! Echoes blown down the wind of years.

BEATRIZ (*looking at the Nephew with great pride as Juan searches her face*). He is as you were in my mother's tales. (*She and the Nephew are held by each other's eyes.*)

JUAN (*after a conquering struggle with his bitterness — fatalistically*). So — thus old heart — in silence. (*Then rousing himself — intensely.*) But with joy! with joy! (*They look at him in puzzled alarm. He smiles gently at Beatriz.*) Then you have found him at last — my double?

BEATRIZ (*blushing, confusedly*). I — I do not know, Don Juan.

JUAN. Then I know. (*Musing a bit sadly.*) You have stolen my last gesture. An old man had a tale to tell you — oh, so brave a tale! — but now he sees that if youth cannot, age must keep its secrets! A sad old ghost to haunt your memory, that would be a poor wedding gift. (*They again look from him to each other, mystified and apprehensive. Juan suddenly looks up at them — with a startling directness.*) You love each other! (*He hurries on with feverish gaiety.*) Forgive — I'm a rough soldier — and there is need for haste. Quick. Do you not ask my blessing?

BEATRIZ (*falling on her knees beside him — happily*). Oh, yes, good Don Juan. (*The Nephew kneels beside her.*)

JUAN (*he raises his hands over their heads*). Youth of this earth — love — hail — and farewell! May you be blessed for ever!

*(He touches their heads with his hands — then sinks back, closing his eyes. They rise and stand looking down at him uncertainly.)*

NEPHEW *(after a pause — in a whisper)*. He wishes to sleep.

BEATRIZ *(as they walk apart, in a whisper, the tears in her eyes)*. Oh, Juan, I'm afraid — and yet — I am not sad.

NEPHEW *(takes her in his arms passionately)*. My life! My soul! *(He kisses her.)*

BEATRIZ. My love!

NEPHEW. Life is beautiful! The earth sings for us! Let us sing, too!

*(He strides over to where the lute is and picks it up.)*

BEATRIZ *(happily)*. Yes — *(Then reminded.)* Ssshh! *(She points at Juan.)*

NEPHEW *(urgingly)*. He is asleep. We can go out beyond the walls.

*(He puts his arms around her and leads her out through the door in rear.)*

JUAN *(opening his eyes and looking after them, a tender smile on his lips)*. Yes! Go where Beauty is! Sing!

*(From outside the voices of Beatriz and his Nephew are heard mingling in their version of the fountain song)*

# THE FOUNTAIN

Love is a flower
For ever blooming
Beauty a fountain
For ever flowing
Upward into the source of sunshine,
Upward into the azure heaven;
One with God but
Ever returning
To kiss the earth that the flower may
live.

*(Juan listens in an ecstasy, bows his head,
weeps. Then he sinks back with closed
eyes exhaustedly. Luis enters from the
monastery.)*

LUIS *(hurries forward in alarm)*. Juan! *(He
hears the song and is indignant.)* Have they lost all
feeling? I will soon stop – *(He starts for the door
in rear.)*

JUAN *(in a ringing voice)*. No! I am that song!
One must accept, absorb, give back, become one-
self a symbol! Juan Ponce de Leon is past! He is
resolved into the thousand moods of beauty that
make up happiness – colour of the sunset, of to-
morrow's dawn, breath of the great Trade wind –
sunlight on grass, an insect's song, the rustle of
leaves, an ant's ambitions. *(In an ecstasy.)* Oh,
Luis, I begin to know eternal youth! I have found
my Fountain! O Fountain of Eternity, take back
this drop, my soul!

*(He dies. Luis bows his head and weeps.)*

# THE FOUNTAIN

FATHER SUPERIOR (*enters from the right*). Vespers. (*Then in a voice of awe as he stares at Juan.*) Is he — dead?

LUIS (*aroused — exaltedly*). No! He lives in God! Let us pray.

> (*Luis sinks on his knees beside Juan's body, the Father Superior beside him. He lifts his eyes and clasped hands to heaven and prays fervently. The voices of Beatriz and the Nephew in the fountain song seem to rise to an exultant pitch. Then the chant of the monks swells out, deep and vibrant. For a moment the two strains blend into harmony, fill the air in an all-comprehending hymn of the mystery of life as*
>
> *The Curtain Falls*)

# The Dreamy Kid

## A Play in One Act

# Characters

MAMMY SAUNDERS
ABE, *her grandson*, *"The Dreamy Kid"*
CEELY ANN
IRENE

# The Dreamy Kid

SCENE. *Mammy Saunders' bedroom in a house just off Carmine Street, New York City. The left of the room, forward, is taken up by a heavy, old-fashioned wooden bedstead with a feather mattress. A gaudy red-and-yellow quilt covers the other bedclothes. Behind the bed, a chest of drawers placed against the left wall. On top of the chest, a small lamp. A rocking-chair stands beside the head of the bed on the right. In the rear wall, toward the right, a low window with ragged white curtains. In the right corner, a washstand with bowl and pitcher. Bottles of medicine, a spoon, a glass, etc., are also on the stand. Farther forward, a door opening on the passage and staircase.*

*It is soon after nightfall of a day in early winter. The room is in shadowy half darkness, the only light being a pale glow that seeps through the window from the arc lamp on the street corner, and by which the objects in the room can be dimly discerned. The vague outlines of Mammy Saunders' figure lying in the bed can be seen, and her black face stands out in sharp contrast from the pillows that support her head.*

MAMMY (*weakly*). Ceely Ann! (*With faint querulousness.*) Light de lamp, will you? Hit's

5

mighty dark in yere. (*After a slight pause.*) Ain't you dar, Ceely Ann?

> (*Receiving no reply she sighs deeply and her limbs move uneasily under the bed-clothes. The door is opened and shut and the stooping form of another coloured woman appears in the semi-darkness. She goes to the foot of the bed sobbing softly, and stands there evidently making an effort to control her emotion.*)

MAMMY. Dat you, Ceely Ann?

CEELY (*huskily*). Hit ain't no yuther, Mammy.

MAMMY. Light de lamp, den. I can't see nowhars.

CEELY. Des one second till I finds a match. (*She wipes her eyes with her handkerchief – then goes to the chest of drawers and feels around on the top of it – pretending to grumble.*) Hit beat all how dem pesky little sticks done hide umse'fs. Shoo! Yere dey is. (*She fumbles with the lamp.*)

MAMMY (*suspiciously*). You ain't been cryin', is you?

CEELY (*with feigned astonishment*). Cryin'? I clar' ter goodness you does git de mos' fool notions lyin' dar.

MAMMY (*in a tone of relief*). I mos' thought I yeard you.

CEELY (*lighting the lamp*). 'Deed you ain't.

6

# THE DREAMY KID

(*The two women are revealed by the light.
Mammy Saunders is an old, white-
haired negress about ninety with a
wizened face furrowed by wrinkles and
withered by old age and sickness. Ceely
is a stout woman of fifty or so with grey
hair and a round fat face. She wears
a loose-fitting gingham dress and a
shawl thrown over her head.*)

CEELY (*with attempted cheeriness*). Bless yo' soul,
I ain't got nothin' to cry 'bout. Yere. Lemme fix
you so you'll rest mo' easy. (*She lifts the old woman
gently and fixes the pillows.*) Dere. Now, ain't you
feelin' better?

MAMMY (*dully*). My strenk don' all went. I
can't lift a hand.

CEELY (*hurriedly*). Dat'll all come back ter you
de doctor tole me des now when I goes down to
de door with him. (*Glibly.*) He say you is de mos'
strongest 'oman fo' yo' years ever he sees in de
worl'; and he tell me you gwine ter be up and
walkin' agin fo' de week's out. (*As she finds the old
woman's eyes fixed on her she turns away confusedly
and abruptly changes the subject.*) Hit ain't too
wa'm in dis room, dat's a fac'.

MAMMY (*shaking her head — in a half whisper*).
No, Ceely Ann. Hit ain't no use'n you tellin' me
nothin' but de trufe. I feels mighty poo'ly. En I
knows hit's on'y wid de blessin' er God I kin las'
de night out.

7

CEELY (*distractedly*). Ain't no sich a thing! Hush yo' noise, Mammy!

MAMMY (*as if she hadn't heard – in a crooning sing-song*). I'se gwine soon fum dis wicked yearth – and may de Lawd have mercy on dis po' ole sinner. (*After a pause – anxiously.*) All I'se prayin' fer is dat God don' take me befo' I sees Dreamy agin. Whar's Dreamy, Ceely Ann? Why ain't he come yere? Ain't you done sent him word I'se sick like I tole you?

CEELY. I tole dem boys ter tell him speshul, and dey swar dey would soon's dey find him. I s'pose dey ain't kotch him yit. Don' you pester yo'se'f worryin'. Dreamy 'ull come fo' ve'y long.

MAMMY (*after a pause – weakly*). Dere's a feelin' in my haid like I was a-floatin' yander whar I can't see nothin', or 'member nothin', or know de sight er any pusson I knows; en I wants ter see Dreamy agin befo' –

CEELY (*quickly*). Don' waste yo' strenk talkin'. You git a wink er sleep en I wake you when he comes, you heah me?

MAMMY (*faintly*). I does feel mighty drowsy.

> (*She closes her eyes. Ceely goes over to the window and pulling the curtains aside stands looking down into the street as if she were watching for some one coming. A moment later there is a noise of foot-falls from the stairs in the hall, followed by a sharp rap on the door.*)

CEELY (*turning quickly from the window*). Ssshh!
Ssshh!

> (*She hurries to the door, glancing anxiously
> toward Mammy. The old woman ap-
> pears to have fallen asleep. Ceely
> cautiously opens the door a bare inch
> or so and peeps out. When she sees
> who it is she immediately tries to
> slam it shut again, but a vigorous
> shove from the outside forces her back
> and Irene pushes her way defiantly into
> the room. She is a young, good-looking
> negress, highly rouged and powdered,
> dressed in gaudy, cheap finery.*)

IRENE (*in a harsh voice — evidently worked up to a
great state of nervous excitement*). No you don't,
Ceely Ann! I said I was comin' here and it'll take
mo'n you to stop me!

CEELY (*almost speechless with horrified indignation
— breathing heavily*). Yo' bad 'oman! Git back ter
yo' bad-house whar yo' b'longs!

IRENE (*raising her clenched hand — furiously*).
Stop dat talkin' to me, nigger, or I'll split yo' fool
head! (*As Ceely shrinks away Irene lowers her hand
and glances quickly around the room.*) Whar's
Dreamy?

CEELY (*scornfully*). Yo' ax me dat! Whar's
Dreamy? Ax yo'se'f. Yo's de one ought ter know
whar he is.

IRENE. Den he ain't come here?

CEELY. I ain't tellin' de likes er you wedder he is or not.

IRENE (*pleadingly*). Tell me, Ceely Ann, ain't he been here? He'd be sure to come here 'count of Mammy dyin', dey said.

CEELY (*pointing to Mammy — apprehensively*). Ssshh! (*Then lowering her voice to a whisper — suspiciously.*) Dey said? Who said?

IRENE (*equally suspicious*). None o' your business who said. (*Then pleading again.*) Ceely Ann, I jest got ter see him dis minute, dis secon'! He's in bad, Dreamy is, and I knows somep'n I gotter tell him, somep'n I jest heard —

CEELY (*uncomprehendingly*). In bad? What you jest heah?

IRENE. I ain't tellin' no one but him. (*Desperately.*) For Gawd's sake, tell me whar he is, Ceely!

CEELY. I don' know no mo'n you.

IRENE (*fiercely*). You's lyin', Ceely! You's lyin' ter me jest 'cause I'se bad.

CEELY. De good Lawd bar witness I'se tellin' you de trufe!

IRENE (*hopelessly*). Den I gotter go find him, high and low, somewheres. (*Proudly.*) You ain't got de right not ter trust me, Ceely, where de Dreamy's mixed in it. I'd go ter hell for Dreamy!

CEELY (*indignantly*). Hush yo' wicked cussin'! (*Then anxiously.*) Is Dreamy in trouble?

IRENE (*with a scornful laugh*). Trouble? Good Lawd, it's worser'n dat! (*Then in surprise.*) Ain't you heerd what de Dreamy done last night, Ceely?

CEELY (*apprehensively*). What de Dreamy do? Tell me, gal. Somep'n bad?

IRENE (*with the same scornful laugh*). Bad? Worser'n bad, what he done!

CEELY (*lamenting querulously*). Oh good Lawd, I knowed it! I knowed with all his carryin's-on wid dat passel er tough young niggers — him so uppity 'cause he's de boss er de gang — sleepin' all de day 'stead er workin' an' Lawd knows what he does in de nights — fightin' wid white folks, an' totin' a pistol in his pocket — (*with a glance of angry resentment at Irene*) — an' as fo' de udder company he's been keepin' —

IRENE (*fiercely*). Shut your mouth, Ceely! Dat ain't your business.

CEELY. Oh, I knowed Dreamy'd be gittin' in trouble fo' long! De lowflung young trash! An' here's his ole Mammy don' know no dif'frunt but he's de mos' innercent young lamb in de worl'. (*In a strained whisper.*) What he do? Is he been stealin' somep'n?

IRENE (*angrily*). You go ter hell, Ceely Ann! You ain't no fren' of de Dreamy's, you talk dat way, and I ain't got no time ter waste argyin' wid your fool notions. (*She goes to the door.*) Dreamy'll go ter his death sho's yo' born, if I don't find him an' tell him quick!

CEELY (*terrified*). Oh Lawd!

IRENE (*anxiously*). He'll sho'ly try ter come here and see his ole Mammy befo' she dies, don't you think, Ceely?

CEELY. Fo' Gawd I hopes so! She's been a-prayin' all de day —

IRENE (*opening the door*). You hopes so, you fool nigger! I tells you it's good-bye to de Dreamy, he come here! I knows! I gotter find an' stop him. If he come here, Ceely, you tell him git out quick and hide, he don't wanter git pinched. You hear? You tell him dat, Ceely, for Gawd's sake! I'se got ter go — find him — high an' low.

(*She goes out leaving Ceely staring at her in speechless indignation.*)

CEELY (*drawing a deep breath*). Yo' street gal! I don' b'lieve one word you says — stuffin' me wid yo' bad lies so's you kin keep de Dreamy frum leavin' you! (*Mammy Saunders awakes and groans faintly. Ceely hurries over to her bedside.*) Is de pain hurtin' agin, Mammy?

MAMMY (*vaguely*). Dat you, Dreamy?

CEELY. No, Mammy, dis is Ceely. Dreamy's comin' soon. Is you restin' easy?

MAMMY (*as if she hadn't heard*). Dat you, Dreamy?

# THE DREAMY KID

CEELY (*sitting down in the rocker by the bed and taking one of the old woman's hands in hers*). No. Dreamy's comin'.

MAMMY (*after a pause – suddenly*). Does you 'member yo' dead Mammy, chile?

CEELY (*mystified*). My dead Mammy?

MAMMY. Didn' I heah yo' talkin' jest now, Dreamy?

CEELY (*very worried*). I clar ter goodness, she don' know me ary bit. Dis is Ceely Ann talkin' ter yo', Mammy.

MAMMY. Who was yo' talkin' wid, Dreamy?

CEELY (*shaking her head – in a trembling voice*). Hit can't be long befo' de en'. (*In a louder tone.*) Hit was me talkin' wid a pusson fum ovah de way. She say tell you Dreamy comin' heah ter see yo' right away. You heah dat, Mammy? (*The old woman sighs but does not answer. There is a pause.*)

MAMMY (*suddenly*). Does yo' 'member yo' dead Mammy, chile? (*Then with a burst of religious exaltation.*) De Lawd have mercy!

CEELY (*like an echo*). Bless de Lawd! (*Then in a frightened half-whisper to herself.*) Po' thing! Her min's done leavin' her jest like de doctor said.

(*She looks down at the old woman helplessly. The door on the right is opened stealthily and the Dreamy Kid slinks in on tiptoe.*)

13

CEELY (*hearing a board creak, turns quickly toward the door and gives a frightened start*). Dreamy!

DREAMY (*puts his fingers to his lips — commandingly*). Ssshh!

(*He bends down to a crouching position and holding the door about an inch open, peers out into the passage in an attitude of tense waiting, one hand evidently clutching some weapon in the side pocket of his coat. After a moment he is satisfied of not being followed, and, after closing the door carefully and locking it, he stands up and walks to the centre of the room casting a look of awed curiosity at the figure in the bed. He is a well-built, good-looking young negro, light in colour. His eyes are shifty and hard, their expression one of tough, scornful defiance. His mouth is cruel and perpetually drawn back at the corners into a snarl. He is dressed in well-fitting clothes of a flashy pattern. A light cap is pulled down on the side of his head.*)

CEELY (*coming from the bed to meet him*). Bless de Lawd, here you is at las'!

DREAMY (*with a warning gesture*). Nix on de loud talk! Talk low, can't yuh! (*He glances back at the door furtively — then continues with a sneer.*) Yuh're a fine nut, Ceely Ann! What for you send-

in' out all ober de town for me like you was crazy!
D'yuh want ter git me in de cooler? Don' you
know dey're after me for what I done last night?

CEELY (*fearfully*). I heerd somep'n – but – what
you done, Dreamy?

DREAMY (*with an attempt at a careless bravado*).
I croaked a guy, dat's what! A white man.

CEELY (*in a frightened whisper*). What you mean
– croaked?

DREAMY (*boastfully*). I shot him dead, dat's
what! (*As Ceely shrinks away from him in horror –
resentfully.*) Aw say, don' gimme none o' dem
looks o' yourn. 'T'warn't my doin' nohow. He
was de one lookin' for trouble. I wasn't seekin'
for no mess wid him dat I could help. But he told
folks he was gwine ter git me for a fac', and dat
fo'ced my hand. I had ter git him ter pertect my
own life. (*With cruel satisfaction.*) And I got him
right, you b'lieve me!

CEELY (*putting her hands over her face with a
low moan of terror*). May de good Lawd pardon
yo' wickedness! Oh Lawd! What yo' po' ole
Mammy gwine say if she hear tell – an' she never
knowin' how bad you's got.

DREAMY (*fiercely*). Hell! You ain't tole her, is
you?

CEELY. Think I want ter kill her on the instant?
An' I didn' know myse'f – what you done – till
you tells me. (*Frightenedly.*) Oh, Dreamy, what

you gwine do now? How you gwine git away? (*Almost wailing.*) Good Lawd, de perlice don' kotch you suah!

DREAMY (*savagely*). Shut yo' loud mouth, damn you! (*He stands tensely listening for some sound from the hall. After a moment he points to the bed.*) Is Mammy sleepin'?

CEELY (*tiptoes to the bed*). Seems like she is. (*She comes back to him.*) Dat's de way wid her — sleep fo' a few minutes, den she wake, den sleep again.

DREAMY (*scornfully*). Aw, dere ain't nothin' wrong wid her 'ceptin' she's ole. What yuh wanter send de word tellin' me she's croakin', and git me comin' here at de risk o' my life, and den find her sleepin'. (*Clenching his fist threateningly.*) I gotter mind ter smash yo' face for playin' de damn fool and makin' me de goat. (*He turns toward the door.*) Ain't no us'en me stayin' here when dey'll likely come lookin' for me. I'm gwine out where I gotta chance ter make my git-away. De boys is all fixin' it up for me. (*His hand on the doorknob.*) When Mammy wakes, you tell her I couldn't wait, you hear ?

CEELY (*hurrying to him and grabbing his arm — pleadingly*). Don' yo' go now, Dreamy — not jest yit. Fo' de good Lawd's sake, don' you go befo' you speaks wid her! If yo' knew how she's been a-callin' an' a-prayin' for yo' all de day —

DREAMY (*scornfully but a bit uncertainly*). Aw, she don' need none o' me. What good kin I do

16

watchin' her do a kip? It'd be dif'frunt if she was croakin' on de level.

CEELY (*in an anguished whisper*). She's gwine wake up in a secon' an' den she call: "Dreamy. Whar's Dreamy?" – an' what I gwine tell her den? An' yo' Mammy is dyin', Dreamy, sho's fate! Her min' been wanderin' an' she don' even recernize me no mo', an' de doctor say when dat come it ain't but a sho't time befo' de en'. Yo' gotter stay wid yo' Mammy long 'nuff ter speak wid her, Dreamy. Yo' jest gotter stay wid her in her las' secon's on dis yearth when she's callin' ter yo'. (*With conviction as he hesitates.*) Listen heah, yo' Dreamy! Yo' don' never git no bit er luck in dis worril ary agin, yo' leaves her now. De perlice gon' kotch yo' suah.

DREAMY (*with superstitious fear*). Ssshh! Can dat bull, Ceely! (*Then boastfully.*) I wasn't pinin' to beat it up here, git me? De boys was all per-suadin' me not ter take de chance. It's takin' my life in my hands, dat's what. But when I heerd it was ole Mammy croakin' and axin' ter see me, I says ter myse'f: "Dreamy, you gotter make good wid old Mammy no matter what come – or you don' never git a bit of luck in yo' life no mo'." And I was game and come, wasn't I? Nary body in dis worril kin say de Dreamy ain't game ter de core, n'matter what. (*With sudden decision walks to the foot of the bed and stands looking down at Mammy. A note of fear creeps into his voice.*) Gawd, she's quiet 'nuff. Maybe she done passed away in her sleep like de ole ones does. You go see, Ceely; an' if she's on'y sleepin', you wake her up. I wanter speak wid her quick — an' den I'll make a break outa here. You make it fast, Ceely Ann, I tells yo'.

CEELY (*bends down beside the bed*). Mammy! Mammy! Here's de Dreamy.

MAMMY (*opens her eyes — drowsily and vaguely, in a weak voice*). Dreamy?

DREAMY (*shuffling his feet and moving around the bed*). Here I is, Mammy.

MAMMY (*fastening her eyes on him with fascinated joy*). Dreamy! Hit's yo'! (*Then uncertainly.*) I ain't dreamin' nor seein' ha'nts, is I?

DREAMY (*coming forward and taking her hand*). 'Deed I ain't no ghost. Here I is, sho' 'nuff.

MAMMY (*clutching his hand tight and pulling it down on her breast — in an ecstasy of happiness*). Didn' I know you'd come! Didn' I say: "Dreamy ain't gwine let his ole Mammy die all lone by he'se'f an' him not dere wid her." I knows yo'd come. (*She starts to laugh joyously, but coughs and sinks back weakly.*)

DREAMY (*shudders in spite of himself as he realizes for the first time how far gone the old woman is — forcing a tone of joking reassurance*). What's dat foolishness I hears you talkin', Mammy? Wha' d' yuh mean pullin' dat bull 'bout croakin' on me? Shoo!

18

Tryin' ter kid me, ain't you? Shoo! You live ter plant de flowers on my grave, see if you don'.

MAMMY (*sadly and very weakly*). I knows! I knows! Hit ain't long now. (*Bursting into a sudden weak hysteria.*) Yo' stay heah, Dreamy! Yo' stay heah by me, yo' stay heah – till de good Lawd takes me home. Yo' promise me dat! Yo' do dat fo' po' ole Mammy, won't yo'?

DREAMY (*uneasily*). 'Deed I will, Mammy, 'deed I will.

MAMMY (*closing her eyes with a sigh of relief – calmly*). Bless de Lawd for dat. Den I ain't skeered no mo'. (*She settles herself comfortably in the bed as if preparing for sleep.*)

CEELY (*in a low voice*). I gotter go home fo' a minute, Dreamy. I ain't been dere all de day and Lawd knows what happen. I'll be back yere befo' ve'y long.

DREAMY (*his eyes fixed on Mammy*). Aw right, beat it if yuh wanter. (*Turning to her – in a fierce whisper.*) On'y don' be long. I can't stay here an' take dis risk, you hear?

CEELY (*frightenedly*). I knows, chile. I come back, I swar!

> (*She goes out quietly. Dreamy goes quickly to the window and cautiously searches the street below with his eyes.*)

MAMMY (*uneasily*). Dreamy. (*He hurries back*

*and takes her hand again.*) I got de mos' 'culiar
feelin' in my head. Seems like de years done all
roll away an' I'm back down home in de ole place
whar you was bo'n. (*After a short pause.*) Does yo'
'member yo' own mammy, chile?

DREAMY. No.

MAMMY. Yo' was too young, I s'pec'. Yo' was
on'y a baby w'en she tuck 'n' die. My Sal was a
mighty fine 'oman, if I does say hit m'se'f.

DREAMY (*fidgeting nervously*). Don' you talk,
Mammy. Better you'd close yo' eyes an' rest.

MAMMY (*with a trembling smile – weakly*). Shoo!
W'at is I done come ter wid my own gran' chile
bossin' me 'bout. I wants ter talk. You knows
you ain't give me much chance ter talk wid yo'
dese las' years.

DREAMY (*sullenly*). I ain't had de time, Mammy;
but you knows I was always game ter give you
anything I got. (*A note of appeal in his voice.*) You
knows dat, don' you, Mammy?

MAMMY. Sho'ly I does. Yo' been a good boy,
Dreamy; an' if dere's one thing more'n 'nother
makes me feel like I mighter done good in de
sight er de Lawd, hits dat I raised yo' fum a
baby.

DREAMY (*clearing his throat gruffly*). Don' you
talk so much, Mammy.

MAMMY (*querulously*). I gotter talk, chile. Come
times – w'cn I git thinkin' yere in de bed – w'at's

gwine ter come ter me a'mos' b'fore I knows hit —
like de thief in de night — en den I gits skeered.
But w'en I talks wid yo' I ain't skeered a bit.

DREAMY (*defiantly*). You ain't got nothin' to be
skeered of — not when de Dreamy's here.

MAMMY (*after a slight pause — faintly*). Dere's a
singin' in my ears all de time. (*Seized by a sudden
religious ecstasy.*) Maybe hit's de singin' hymns of
de blessed angels I done heah fum above. (*Wildly.*)
Bless Gawd! Bless Gawd! Pity dis po' ole sinner.

DREAMY (*with an uneasy glance at the door*).
Ssshh, Mammy! Don' shout so loud.

MAMMY. De pictures keep a whizzin' fo' my
eyes like de thread in a sewing machine. Seem 's if
all my life done fly back ter me all ter once.
(*With a flickering smile — weakly.*) Does you know
how yo' come by dat nickname dey alls call yo' —
de Dreamy? Is I ever tole yo' dat?

DREAMY (*evidently lying*). No, Mammy.

MAMMY. Hit was one mawnin' b'fo' we come
No'th. Me an' yo' mammy — yo' was des a baby
in arms den —

DREAMY (*hears a noise from the hall*). Ssshh,
Mammy! For God's sake, don't speak for a
minute. I hears somep'n. (*He stares at the door,
his face hardening savagely, and listens intently.*)

MAMMY (*in a frightened tone*). W'at's de matter,
chile?

DREAMY. Ssshh! Somebody comin'. (*A noise of*

*footsteps comes from the hall staircase. Dreamy springs to his feet.*) Leggo my hand, Mammy — jest for a secon'. I come right back to you.

> (*He pulls his hand from the old woman's grip. She falls back on the pillows moaning. Dreamy pulls a large automatic revolver from his coat pocket and tiptoes quickly to the door. As he does so there is a sharp rap. He stands listening at the crack for a moment, then noiselessly turns the key, unlocking the door. Then he crouches low down by the wall so that the door, when opened, will hide him from the sight of anyone entering. There is another and louder rap on the door.*)

MAMMY (*groaning*). W'at's dat, Dreamy? Whar is yo'?

DREAMY. Ssshh! (*Then muffling his voice he calls.*) Come in.

> (*He raises the revolver in his hand. The door is pushed open and Irene enters, her eyes peering wildly about the room. Her bosom is heaving as if she had been running and she is trembling all over with terrified excitement.*)

IRENE (*not seeing him calls out questioningly*). Dreamy?

# THE DREAMY KID

DREAMY (*lowering his revolver and rising to his feet roughly*). Close dat door!

IRENE (*whirling about with a startled cry*). Dreamy!

DREAMY (*shutting the door and locking it — aggressively*). Shut yo' big mouth, gal, or I'll bang it shut for you! You wanter let de whole block know where I is?

IRENE (*hysterical with joy — trying to put her arms around him*). Bless God, I foun' you at last!

DREAMY (*pushing her away roughly*). Leggo o' me! Why you come here follerin' me? Ain't yo' got 'nuff sense in yo' fool head ter know de bulls is liable ter shadow you when dey knows you's my gal? Is you pinin' ter git me kotched an' sent to de chair?

IRENE (*terrified*). No, no!

DREAMY (*savagely*). I gotter mind ter hand you one you won't ferget! (*He draws back his fist.*)

IRENE (*shrinking away*). Don' you hit me, Dreamy! Don' you beat me up now! Jest lemme 'xplain, dat's all.

MAMMY (*in a frightened whimper*). Dreamy! Come yere to me. Whar is yo'? I'se skeered!

DREAMY (*in a fierce whisper to Irene*). Can dat bull or I'll fix you. (*He hurries to the old woman and pats her hand.*) Here I is, Mammy.

MAMMY. Who dat yo's a-talkin' wid?

DREAMY. On'y a fren' o' Ceely Ann's, Mammy,

23

askin' where she is. I gotter talk wid her some mo' yit. You sleep, Mammy. (*He goes to Irene.*)

MAMMY (*feebly*). Don' yo' leave me, Dreamy.

DREAMY. I'se right here wid you. (*Fiercely, to Irene.*) You git the hell outa here, you Reeny, you heah — quick! Dis ain't no place for de likes o' you wid ole Mammy dyin'.

IRENE (*with a horrified glance at the bed*). Is she dyin' — honest?

DREAMY. Ssshh! She's croakin', I tells yo' — an' I gotter stay wid her fo' a while — an' I ain't got no time ter be pesterin' wid you. Beat it, now! Beat it outa here befo' I knocks yo' cold, git me?

IRENE. Jest wait a secon' for de love o' Gawd. I got somep'n ter tell you —

DREAMY. I don' wanter hear yo' fool talk. (*He gives her a push toward the door.*) Git outa dis, you hear me?

IRENE. I'll go. I'm going soon — soon's ever I've had my say. Lissen, Dreamy! It's about de coppers I come ter tell you.

DREAMY (*quickly*). Why don' you say dat befo'? What you know, gal?

IRENE. Just befo' I come here to find you de first time, de Madam sends me out to Murphy's ter git her a bottle o' gin. I goes in de side door but I ain't rung de bell yet. I hear yo' name spoken an' I stops ter lissen. Dey was three or four men in de back room. Dey don't hear me open de outside door, an' dey can't see me, 'course. It was Big Sullivan from de Central Office talkin'. He was talkin' 'bout de killin' you done last night and he tells dem odders he's heerd 'bout de ole woman gittin' so sick, and dat if dey don't fin' you none of de udder places dey's lookin', dey's goin' wait for you here. Dey s'pecs you come here say good-bye to Mammy befo' you make yo' git-away.

DREAMY. It's aw right den. Dey ain't come yit. Twister Smith done tole me de coast was clear befo' I come here.

IRENE. Dat was den. It ain't now.

DREAMY (*excitedly*). What you mean, gal?

IRENE. I was comin' in by de front way when I sees some pusson hidin' in de doorway 'cross de street. I gits a good peek at him and when I does — it's a copper, Dreamy, suah's yo' born, in his plain clo'se, and he's a watchin' de door o' dis house like a cat.

DREAMY (*goes to the window and stealthily crouching by the dark side peeps out. One glance is enough. He comes quickly back to Irene*). You got de right dope, gal. It's dat Mickey. I knows him even in de dark. Dey're waitin' — so dey ain't wise I'm here yit, dat's suah.

IRENE. But dey'll git wise befo' long.

DREAMY. He don' pipe you comin' in here?

IRENE. I skulked roun' and sneaked in by de

back way froo de yard. Dey ain't none o' dem dar yit. (*Raising her voice – excitedly.*) But dere will be soon. Dey're boun' to git wise to dat back door. You ain't got no time to lose, Dreamy. Come on wid me now. Git back where yo' safe. It's de cooler for you certain if you stays here. Dey'll git you like a rat in de trap. (*As Dreamy hesitates.*) For de love of Gawd, Dreamy, wake up to youse'f!

DREAMY (*uncertainly*). I can't beat it – wid Mammy here alone. My luck done turn bad all my life, if I does.

IRENE (*fiercely*). What good's you gittin' pinched and sent to de chair gwine do her? Is you crazy mad? Come away wid me, I tells you!

DREAMY (*half-persuaded – hesitatingly*). I gotter speak wid her. You wait a secon'.

IRENE (*wringing her hands*). Dis ain't no time now for fussin' wid her.

DREAMY (*gruffly*). Shut up! (*He makes a motion for her to remain where she is and goes over to the bed – in a low voice.*) Mammy.

MAMMY (*hazily*). Dat you, Dreamy? (*She tries to reach out her hand and touch him.*)

DREAMY. I'm gwine leave you – jest for a moment, Mammy. I'll send de word for Ceely Ann –

MAMMY (*wideawake in an instant – with intense alarm*). Don' yo' do dat! Don' yo' move one step out er yere or yo'll be sorry, Dreamy.

DREAMY (*apprehensively*). I gotter go, I tells you. I'll come back.

MAMMY (*with wild grief*). O good Lawd! W'en I's drawin' de las' bre'fs in dis po' ole body — (*Frenziedly.*) De Lawd have mercy! Good Lawd have mercy!

DREAMY (*fearfully*). Stop dat racket, Mammy! You bring all o' dem down on my head! (*He rushes over and crouches by the window again to peer out — in relieved tones.*) He ain't heerd nothin'. He's dar yit.

IRENE (*imploringly*). Come on, Dreamy! (*Mammy groans with pain.*)

DREAMY (*hurrying to the bed*). What's de matter, Mammy?

IRENE (*stamping her foot*). Dreamy! Fo' Gawd's sake!

MAMMY. Lawd have mercy! (*She groans.*) Gimme yo' han', chile. Yo' ain't gwine leave me now, Dreamy? Yo' ain't, is yo'? Yo' ole Mammy won't bodder yo' long. Yo' know w'at yo' promise me, Dreamy! Yo' promise yo' sacred word yo' stay wid me till de en'. (*With an air of sombre prophecy — slowly.*) If yo' leave me now, yo' ain't gwine git no bit er luck s'long's yo' live, I tells yo' dat!

DREAMY (*frightened — pleadingly*). Don' you say dat, Mammy!

IRENE. Come on, Dreamy!

DREAMY (*slowly*). I can't. (*In awed tones.*) Don' you hear de curse she puts on me if I does?

MAMMY (*her voice trembling with weak tears*). Don' go, chile!

DREAMY (*hastily*). I won't leave dis room, I swar ter you! (*Relieved by the finality in his tones, the old woman sighs and closes her eyes. Dreamy frees his hand from hers and goes to Irene. He speaks with a strange calm.*) De game's up, gal. You better beat it while de goin's good.

IRENE (*aghast*). You gwine stay?

DREAMY. I gotter, gal. I ain't gwine agin her dyin' curse. No, suh!

IRENE (*pitifully*). But dey'll git you suah!

DREAMY (*slapping the gun in his pocket significantly*). Dey'll have some gittin'. I git some o' dem fust. (*With gloomy determination.*) Dey don't git dis chicken alive! Lawd Jesus, no suh. Not de Dreamy!

IRENE (*helplessly*). Oh, Lawdy, Lawdy! (*She goes to the window — with a short cry.*) He's talkin' wid some one. Dere's two o' dem. (*Dreamy hurries to her side.*)

DREAMY. I knows him — de udder. It's Big Sullivan. (*Pulling her away roughly.*) Come out o' dat! Dey'll see you. (*He pushes her toward the door.*) Dey won't wait down dere much longer. Dey'll be comin' up here soon. (*Prayerfully, with a glance at the bed*.) I hopes she's croaked by den', fo' Christ I does!

IRENE (*as if she couldn't believe it*). Den you ain't gwine save youse'f while dere's time? (*Pleadingly*.) Oh, Dreamy, you can make it yit!

DREAMY. De game's up, I tole you. (*With gloomy fatalism*.) I s'pect it hatter be. Yes, suh. Dey'd git me in de long run anyway — and wid her curse de luck'd be agin me. (*With sudden anger*.) Git outa here, you Reeny! You ain't aimin' ter get shot up too, is you? Ain't no sense in dat.

IRENE (*fiercely*). I'se stayin' too, here wid you!

DREAMY. No you isn't! None o' dat bull! You ain't got no mix in dis jamb.

IRENE. Yes, I is! Ain't you my man?

DREAMY. Don' make no dif. I don't wanter git you in Dutch more'n you is. It's bad 'nuff fo' me. (*He pushes her toward the door*.) Blow while you kin, I tells you!

IRENE (*resisting him*). No, Dreamy! What I care if dey kills me? I'se gwine stick wid you.

DREAMY (*gives her another push*). No, you isn't, gal. (*Unlocking the door — relentlessly*.) Out wid you!

IRENE (*hysterically*). You can't turn me out. I'm gwine stay.

DREAMY (*gloomily*). On'y one thing fo' me ter do den. (*He hits her on the side of the face with all his might, knocking her back against the wall where*

29

*she sways as if about to fall. Then he opens the door and grabs her two arms from behind.*) Out wid you, gal!

IRENE (*moaning*). Dreamy! Dreamy! Lemme stay wid you! (*He pushes her into the passage and holds her there at arm's length.*) Fo' Gawd's sake, Dreamy!

MAMMY (*whimperingly*). Dreamy! I'se skeered!

IRENE (*from the hall*). I'se gwine stay right here at de door. You might s'well lemme in.

DREAMY (*frowning*). Don' do dat, Reeny. (*Then with a sudden idea.*) You run roun' and tell de gang what's up. Maybe dey git me outa dis, you hear?

IRENE (*with eager hope*). You think dey kin?

DREAMY. Never kin tell. You hurry — through de back yard, 'member — an' don' git pinched, now.

IRENE (*eagerly*). I'm gwine! I'll bring dem back!

DREAMY (*stands listening to her retreating footsteps — then shuts and locks the door — gloomily to himself*). Ain't no good. Dey dassent do nothin' — but I hatter git her outa dis somehow.

MAMMY (*groaning*). Dreamy!

DREAMY. Here I is. Jest a secon'. (*He goes to the window.*)

MAMMY (*weakly*). I feels — like — de en's comin'. Oh, Lawd, Lawd!

DREAMY (*absent-mindedly*). Yes, Mammy. (*Aloud to himself.*) Dey're sneakin' cross de street. Dere's anudder of 'em. Dat's tree.

> (*He glances around the room quickly – then hurries over and takes hold of the chest of drawers. As he does so the old woman commences to croon shrilly to herself.*)

DREAMY. Stop dat noise, Mammy! Stop dat noise!

MAMMY (*wanderingly*). Dat's how come yo' got dat – dat nickname – Dreamy.

DREAMY. Yes, Mammy.

> (*He puts the lamp on the floor to the rear of the door, turning it down low. Then he carries the chest of drawers over and places it against the door as a barricade.*)

MAMMY (*rambling as he does this – very feebly*). Does yo' know – I gives you dat name – w'en yo's des a baby – lyin' in my arms –

DREAMY. Yes, Mammy.

MAMMY. Down by de crik – under de ole willow – whar I uster take yo' – wid yo' big eyes a-chasin' – de sun flitterin' froo de grass – an' out on de water –

DREAMY (*takes the revolver from his pocket and puts it on top of the chest of drawers*). Dey don' git de Dreamy alive – not for de chair! Lawd Jesus, no suh!

MAMMY. An' yo' was always – a-lookin' – an' a-thinkin' ter yo'se'f – an' yo' big eyes jest a-dreamin' an' a-dreamin' – an' dat's w'en I gives yo' dat nickname – Dreamy – Dreamy –

DREAMY. Yes, Mammy. (*He listens at the crack of the door – in a tense whisper.*) I don' hear dem – but dey're comin' sneakin' up de stairs, I knows it.

MAMMY (*faintly*). Whar is yo', Dreamy? I can't – ha'dly – breathe – no mo'. Oh, Lawd have mercy!

DREAMY (*goes over to the bed*). Here I is, Mammy.

MAMMY (*speaking with difficulty*). Yo' – kneel down – chile – say a pray'r – Oh, Lawd!

DREAMY. Jest a secon', Mammy. (*He goes over and gets his revolver and comes back.*)

MAMMY. Gimme – yo' hand – chile. (*Dreamy gives her his left hand. The revolver is in his right. He stares nervously at the door.*) An' yo' kneel down – pray fo' me. (*Dreamy gets on one knee beside the bed. There is a sound from the passage as if some one had made a misstep on the stairs – then silence. Dreamy starts and half aims his gun in the direction of the door. Mammy groans weakly.*) I'm dyin', chile. Hit's de en'. You pray for me – out loud – so's I can heah. Oh, Lawd! (*She gasps to catch her breath.*)

# THE DREAMY KID

DREAMY (*abstractedly, not having heard a word she has said*). Yes, Mammy. (*Aloud to himself with an air of grim determination as if he were making a pledge.*) Dey don't git de Dreamy! Not while he's 'live! Lawd Jesus, no suh!

MAMMY (*falteringly*). Dat's right — yo' pray — Lawd Jesus — Lawd Jesus — (*There is another slight sound of movement from the hallway.*)


(*The Curtain Falls*)

# Before Breakfast

## A Play in One Act

# Before Breakfast

SCENE. *A small room serving both as kitchen and dining-room in a flat in Christopher Street, New York City. In the rear, to the right, a door leading to the outer hall. On the left of the doorway, a sink, and a two-burner gas stove. Over the stove, and extending to the left wall, a wooden cupboard for dishes, etc. On the left, two windows looking out on a fire-escape where several potted plants are dying of neglect. Before the windows, a table covered with oilcloth. Two cane-bottomed chairs are placed by the table. Another stands against the wall to the right of door in rear. In the right wall, rear, a doorway leading into a bedroom. Farther forward, different articles of a man's and a woman's clothing are hung on pegs. A clothes line is strung from the left corner, rear, to the right wall, forward.*

*It is about eight-thirty in the morning of a fine, sunshiny day in the early autumn.*

*Mrs. Rowland enters from the bedroom, yawning, her hands still busy putting the finishing touches on a slovenly toilet by sticking hairpins into her hair which is bunched up in a drab-coloured mass on top of her round head. She is of medium height and inclined to a shapeless stoutness, accentuated by her formless blue dress, shabby and worn. Her face is characterless,*

3

# BEFORE BREAKFAST

*with small regular features and eyes of a non-
descript blue. There is a pinched expression
about her eyes and nose and her weak, spiteful
mouth. She is in her early twenties but looks
much older.*

*She comes to the middle of the room and
yawns, stretching her arms to their full length.
Her drowsy eyes stare about the room with the
irritated look of one to whom a long sleep has not
been a long rest. She goes wearily to the clothes
hanging on the right and takes an apron from a
hook. She ties it about her waist, giving vent
to an exasperated "damn" when the knot fails to
obey her clumsy fingers. Finally gets it tied and
goes slowly to the gas stove and lights one burner.
She fills the coffee-pot at the sink and sets it over
the flame. Then slumps down into a chair by
the table and puts a hand over her forehead as
if she were suffering from headache. Suddenly
her face brightens as though she had remembered
something, and she casts a quick glance at the
dish cupboard; then looks sharply at the bedroom
door and listens intently for a moment or so.*

MRS. ROWLAND (*in a low voice*). Alfred! Alfred!
(*There is no answer from the next room and she continues suspiciously in a louder tone.*) You needn't
pretend you're asleep.

> (*There is no reply to this from the bedroom,
> and, reassured, she gets up from her
> chair and tiptoes cautiously to the dish*

4

*cupboard. She slowly opens one door, taking great care to make no noise, and slides out, from their hiding place behind the dishes, a bottle of Gordon gin and a glass. In doing so she disturbs the top dish, which rattles a little. At this sound she starts guiltily and looks with sulky defiance at the doorway to the next room.*)

(*Her voice trembling.*) Alfred!

(*After a pause, during which she listens for any sound, she takes the glass and pours out a large drink and gulps it down; then hastily returns the bottle and glass to their hiding-place. She closes the cupboard door with the same care as she had opened it, and, heaving a great sigh of relief, sinks down into her chair again. The large dose of alcohol she has taken has an almost immediate effect. Her features become more animated, she seems to gather energy, and she looks at the bedroom door with a hard, vindictive smile on her lips. Her eyes glance quickly about the room and are fixed on a man's coat and waistcoat which hang from a hook at right. She moves stealthily over to the open doorway and stands there, out of sight of anyone inside, listening for any movement.*)

5

# BEFORE BREAKFAST

(*Calling in a half-whisper.*) Alfred!

> (*Again there is no reply. With a swift movement she takes the coat and waistcoat from the hook and returns with them to her chair. She sits down and takes the various articles out of each pocket but quickly puts them back again. At last, in the inside pocket of the vest, she finds a letter.*)

(*Looking at the handwriting – slowly to herself.*) Hmm! I knew it.

> (*She opens the letter and reads it. At first her expression is one of hatred and rage, but as she goes on to the end it changes to one of triumphant malignity. She remains in deep thought for a moment, staring before her, the letter in her hands, a cruel smile on her lips. Then she puts the letter back in the pocket of the waistcoat, and still careful not to awaken the sleeper, hangs the clothes up again on the same hook, and goes to the bedroom door and looks in.*)

(*In a loud, shrill voice.*) Alfred! (*Still louder.*) Alfred! (*There is a muffled, yawning groan from the next room.*) Don't you think it's about time you got up? Do you want to stay in bed all day? (*Turning around and coming back to her chair.*) Not that I've got any doubts about your being lazy enough to stay in bed for ever. (*She sits down and*

6

*looks out of the window, irritably.*) Goodness knows what time it is. We haven't even got any way of telling the time since you pawned your watch like a fool. The last valuable thing we had, and you knew it. It's been nothing but pawn, pawn, pawn, with you — anything to put off getting a job, anything to get out of going to work like a man. (*She taps the floor with her foot nervously, biting her lips.*) (*After a short pause.*) Alfred! Get up, do you hear me? I want to make that bed before I go out. I'm sick of having this place in a continual mess on your account. (*With a certain vindictive satisfaction.*) Not that we'll be here long unless you manage to get some money somehow. Heaven knows I do my part — and more — going out to sew every day while you play the gentleman and loaf around bar rooms with that good-for-nothing lot of artists from the Square.

> (*A short pause during which she plays nervously with a cup and saucer on the table.*)

And where are you going to get money, I'd like to know? The rent's due this week and you know what the landlord is. He won't let us stay a minute over our time. You say you *can't* get a job. That's a lie and you know it. You never even look for one. All you do is moon around all day writing silly poetry and stories that no one will buy — and no wonder they won't. I notice I can always get a position, such as it is; and it's only that which keeps us from starving to death.

7

# BEFORE BREAKFAST

*(Gets up and goes over to the stove – looks
into the coffee-pot to see if the water is
boiling; then comes back and sits down
again.)*

You'll have to get money to-day somehow. I
can't do it all, and I won't do it all. You've got to
come to your senses. You've got to beg, borrow,
or steal it somewheres. *(With a contemptuous
laugh.)* But where, I'd like to know? You're too
proud to beg, and you've borrowed the limit, and
you haven't the nerve to steal.

*(After a pause – getting up angrily.)* Aren't you
up yet, for heaven's sake? It's just like you to go
to sleep again, or pretend to. *(She goes to the bedroom door and looks in.)* Oh, you are up. Well, it's
about time. You needn't look at me like that.
Your airs don't fool me a bit any more. I know
you too well – better than you think I do – you
and your goings-on. *(Turning away from the door –
meaningly.)* I know a lot of things, my dear.
Never mind what I know, now. I'll tell you before
I go, you needn't worry.

*(She comes to the middle of the room and
stands there, frowning.)*

*(Irritably.)* Hmm! I suppose I might as well
get breakfast ready – not that there's anything
much to get. *(Questioningly.)* Unless you have
some money? *(She pauses for an answer from the
next room which does not come.)* Foolish question!
*(She gives a short, hard laugh.)* I ought to know

8

you better than that by this time. When you left here in such a huff last night I knew what would happen. You can't be trusted for a second. A nice condition you came home in! The fight we had was only an excuse for you to make a beast of yourself. What was the use pawning your watch if all you wanted with the money was to waste it in buying drink?

*(Goes over to the dish cupboard and takes out plates, cups, etc., while she is talking.)*

Hurry up! It don't take long to get breakfast these days, thanks to you. All we got this morning is bread and butter and coffee; and you wouldn't even have that if it wasn't for me sewing my fingers off. *(She slams the loaf of bread on the table with a bang.)*

The bread's stale. I hope you'll like it. *You* don't deserve any better, but I don't see why *I* should suffer.

*(Going over to the stove.)* The coffee'll be ready in a minute, and you needn't expect me to wait for you.

*(Suddenly with great anger.)* What on earth are you doing all this time? *(She goes over to the door and looks in.)* Well, you're *almost* dressed at any rate. I expected to find you back in bed. That'd be just like you. How awful you look this morning! For heaven's sake, shave! You're disgusting! You look like a tramp. No wonder no one will give you a job. I don't blame them — when

you don't even look half-way decent. (*She goes to the stove.*) There's plenty of hot water right here. You've got no excuse. (*Gets a bowl and pours some of the water from the coffee-pot into it.*) Here.

> (*He stretches his hand into the room for it. It is a sensitive hand with slender fingers. It trembles and some of the water spills on the floor.*)

(*Tauntingly.*) Look at your hand tremble! You'd better give up drinking. You can't stand it. It's just your kind that get the D.T.'s. *That would be* the last straw! (*Looking down at the floor.*) Look at the mess you've made of this floor — cigarette ends and ashes all over the place. Why can't you put them on a plate? No, you wouldn't be considerate enough to do that. You never think of me. You don't have to sweep the room and that's all you care about.

> (*Takes the broom and commences to sweep viciously, raising a cloud of dust. From the inner room comes the sound of a razor being stropped.*)

(*Sweeping.*) Hurry up! It must be nearly time for me to go. If I'm late I'm liable to lose my position, and then I couldn't support you any longer. (*As an afterthought she adds sarcastically.*) And then you'd have to go to work or something dreadful like that. (*Sweeping under the table.*) What I want to know is whether you're going to look for a job to-day or not. You know your family won't help us any more. They've had enough of you, too. (*After a moment's silent sweeping.*) I'm about sick of all this life. I've a good notion to go home, if I wasn't too proud to let them know what a failure you've been – you, the millionaire Rowland's only son, the Harvard graduate, the poet, the catch of the town – Huh! (*With bitterness.*) There wouldn't be many of them now envy my catch if they knew the truth. What has our marriage been, I'd like to know? Even before your *millionaire* father died owing every one in the world money, you certainly never wasted any of your time on your wife. I suppose you thought I'd ought to be glad you were *honourable* enough to marry me – after getting me into trouble. You were ashamed of me with your fine friends because my father's only a grocer, that's what you were. At least he's honest, which is more than anyone could say about yours. (*She is sweeping steadily toward the door. Leans on her broom for a moment.*)

You hoped every one'd think you'd been forced to marry me, and pity you, didn't you? You didn't hesitate much about telling me you loved me, and making me believe your lies, before it happened, did you? You made me think you didn't want your father to buy me off as he tried to do. I know better now. I haven't lived with you all this time for nothing. (*Sombrely.*) It's lucky the poor thing was born dead, after all. What a father you'd have been!

*(Is silent, brooding moodily for a moment —
      then she continues with a sort of savage
      joy.)*

But I'm not the only one who's got you to thank
for being unhappy. There's one other, at least,
and *she* can't hope to marry you now. *(She puts
her head into the next room.)* How about Helen?
*(She starts back from the doorway, half frightened.)*

Don't look at me that way! Yes, I read her
letter. What about it? I got a right to. I'm your
wife. And I know all there is to know, so don't
lie. You needn't stare at me so. You can't bully
me with your superior airs any longer. Only for
me you'd be going without breakfast this very
morning. *(She sets the broom back in the corner —
whiningly.)* You never did have any gratitude for
what I've done. *(She comes to the stove and puts the
coffee into the pot.)* The coffee's ready. I'm not
going to wait for you. *(She sits down in her chair
again.)*

*(After a pause — puts her hand to her head — fret-
fully.)* My head aches so this morning. It's a
shame I've got to go to work in a stuffy room all
day in my condition. And I wouldn't if you were
half a man. By rights I ought to be lying on my
back instead of you. You know how sick I've been
this last year; and yet you object when I take a
little something to keep up my spirits. You even
didn't want me to take that tonic I got at the drug
store. *(With a hard laugh.)* I know you'd be glad
to have me dead and out of your way; then you'd

12

be free to run after all these silly girls that think you're such a wonderful, misunderstood person — this Helen and the others. (*There is a sharp exclamation of pain from the next room.*)

(*With satisfaction*). There! I knew you'd cut yourself. It'll be a lesson to you. You know you oughtn't to be running around nights drinking with your nerves in such an awful shape. (*She goes to the door and looks in.*)

What makes you so pale? What are you staring at yourself in the mirror that way for? For goodness' sake, wipe that blood off your face! (*With a shudder.*) It's horrible. (*In relieved tones.*) There, that's better. I never could stand the sight of blood. (*She shrinks back from the door a little.*) You better give up trying and go to a barber shop. Your hand shakes dreadfully. Why do you stare at me like that? (*She turns away from the door.*) Are you still mad at me about that letter? (*Defiantly.*) Well, I had a right to read it. I'm your wife. (*She comes to the chair and sits down again. After a pause.*)

I knew all the time you were running around with some one. Your lame excuses about spending the time at the library didn't fool me. Who is this Helen, anyway? One of those artists? Or does she write poetry, too? Her letter sounds that way. I'll bet she told you your things were the best ever, and you believed her, like a fool. Is she young and pretty? I was young and pretty, too, when you fooled me with your fine, poetic talk;

13

but life with you would soon wear anyone down.
What I've been through!

(*Goes over and takes the coffee off the stove.*)
Breakfast is ready. (*With a contemptuous glance.*)
Breakfast! (*Pours out a cup of coffee for herself and
puts the pot on the table.*) Your coffee'll be cold.
What are you doing – still shaving, for heaven's
sake? You'd better give it up. One of these morn-
ings you'll give yourself a serious cut. (*She cuts
off bread and butters it. During the following
speeches she eats and sips her coffee.*)

I'll have to run as soon as I've finished eating.
One of us has got to work. (*Angrily.*) Are you
going to look for a job to-day or aren't you? I
should think some of your fine friends would help
you, if they really think you're so much. But I
guess they just like to hear you talk. (*Sits in silence
for a moment.*)

I'm sorry for this Helen, whoever she is.
Haven't you got any feelings for other people?
What will her family say? I see she mentions
them in her letter. What is she going to do – have
the child – or go to one of those doctors? That's
a nice thing, I must say. Where can she get the
money? Is she rich? (*She waits for some answer
to this volley of questions.*)

Hmm! You won't tell me anything about her,
will you? Much I care. Come to think of it, I'm
not so sorry for her after all. She knew what she
was doing. She isn't any school-girl, like I was,
from the looks of her letter. Does she know you're

married? Of course, she must. All your friends know about your unhappy marriage. I know they pity you, but they don't know my side of it. They'd talk different if they did.

(*Too busy eating to go on for a second or so.*)

This Helen must be a fine one, if she knew you were married. What does she expect, then? That I'll divorce you and let her marry you? Does she think I'm crazy enough for that — after all you've made me go through? I guess not! And you can't get a divorce from me and you know it. No one can say *I've* ever done anything wrong. (*Drinks the last of her cup of coffee.*)

She deserves to suffer, that's all I can say. I'll tell you what I think; I think your Helen is no better than a common street-walker, that's what I think. (*There is a stifled groan of pain from the next room.*)

Did you cut yourself again? Serves you right. (*Gets up and takes off her apron.*) Well, I've got to run along. (*Peevishly.*) This is a fine life for me to be leading! I won't stand for your loafing any longer. (*Something catches her ear and she pauses and listens intently.*) There! You've overturned the water all over everything. Don't say you haven't. I can hear it dripping on the floor. (*A vague expression of fear comes over her face.*) Alfred! Why don't you answer me?

(*She moves slowly toward the room. There is the noise of a chair being overturned*

*and something crashes heavily to the
floor. She stands, trembling with fright.)*

Alfred! Alfred! Answer me! What is it you
knocked over? Are you still drunk? (*Unable to
stand the tension a second longer she rushes to the door
of the bedroom.*)
Alfred!

> (*She stands in the doorway looking down at
> the floor of the inner room, transfixed
> with horror. Then she shrieks wildly
> and runs to the other door, unlocks it and
> frenziedly pulls it open, and runs
> shrieking madly into the outer hall.*)

**(The Curtain Falls)**

# Lazarus Laughed
## and
# Dynamo

# Lazarus Laughed
## and
# Dynamo
Two Plays by
Eugene O'Neill

# Lazarus Laughed

## (1925-1926)

A Play for an Imaginative Theatre

Act One :

Scene One : Lazarus' home in Bethany—a short time after the miracle.

Scene Two : Months later. Outside the House of Laughter in Bethany. Late evening.

Act Two :

Scene One : A street in Athens. A night months later.

Scene Two : A temple immediately inside the walls of Rome. Midnight. Months later.

Act Three :

Scene One : Garden of Tiberius' palace. A night a few days later.

Scene Two : Inside the palace. Immediately after.

Act Four :

Scene One : The same. A while after.

Scene Two : Interior of a Roman theatre. Dawn of the same night.

# Characters

LAZARUS OF BETHANY
HIS FATHER
HIS MOTHER
MARTHA } *his sisters*
MARY
MIRIAM, *his wife*
SEVEN GUESTS, *neighbours of Lazarus*
CHORUS OF OLD MEN
AN ORTHODOX PRIEST
CHORUS OF LAZARUS' FOLLOWERS
A CENTURION
GAIUS CALIGULA
CRASSUS, *a Roman General*
CHORUS OF GREEKS
SEVEN CITIZENS OF ATHENS
CHORUS OF ROMAN SENATORS
SEVEN SENATORS
CHORUS OF LEGIONARIES
FLAVIUS, *a centurion*
MARCELLUS, *a patrician*
CHORUS OF THE GUARD
TIBERIUS CÆSAR
POMPEIA
CHORUS OF YOUTHS AND GIRLS
CHORUS OF THE ROMAN POPULACE
CROWDS

# ACT ONE

## SCENE ONE

SCENE. *Exterior and interior of Lazarus' home at Bethany. The main room at the front end of the house is shown—a long, low-ceilinged, sparely furnished chamber, with white walls grey in the fading daylight that enters from three small windows at the left. To the left of centre several long tables placed lengthwise to the width of the room, around which many chairs for guests have been placed. In the rear wall, right, a door leading into the rest of the house. On the left, a doorway opening on a road where a crowd of men has gathered. On the right, another doorway leading to the yard where there is a crowd of women.*

*Inside the house, on the men's side, seven male Guests are grouped by the door, watching Lazarus with frightened awe, talking hesitantly in low whispers. The Chorus of Old Men, seven in number, is drawn up in a crescent, in the far corner, right, facing Lazarus.*

*[All of these people are masked in accordance with the following scheme : There are seven periods of life shown : Boyhood (or Girlhood), Youth, Young Manhood (or Womanhood), Manhood (or Womanhood), Middle Age, Maturity, and Old Age ; and each of these periods is represented by seven different masks of general types of character as follows : The Simple, Ignorant ; the Happy, Eager ; the*

A*                              9

*Self-Tortured, Introspective ; the Proud, Self-Reliant ; the Servile, Hypocritical ; the Revengeful, Cruel ; the Sorrowful, Resigned. Thus in each crowd (this includes among the men the Seven Guests who are composed of one male of each period-type as period one—type one, period two—type two, and so on up to period seven—type seven) there are forty-nine different combinations of period and type. Each type has a distinct predominant colour for its costumes, which varies in kind according to its period. The masks of the Chorus of Old Men are double the size of the others. They are all seven in the Sorrowful, Resigned type of Old Age.]*

*On a raised platform at the middle of the one table placed lengthwise at centre sits Lazarus, his head haloed and his body illumined by a soft radiance as of tiny phosphorescent flames.*

*Lazarus, freed now from the fear of death, wears no mask.*

*In appearance Lazarus is tall and powerful, about fifty years of age, with a mass of grey-black hair and a heavy beard. His face recalls that of a statue of a divinity of Ancient Greece in its general structure, and particularly in its quality of detached serenity. It is dark-complected, ruddy and brown, the colour of rich earth upturned by the plough, calm but furrowed deep with the marks of former suffering endured with a grim fortitude that had never softened into resignation. His forehead is broad and noble, his eyes black and deep-set. Just now he is staring straight before him as if his vision were still fixed beyond life.*

*Kneeling beside him with bowed heads are his wife, Miriam; his sisters, Martha and Mary; and his Father and Mother.*

*Miriam is a slender, delicate woman of thirty-five, dressed in deep black, who holds one of his hands in both of hers, and keeps her lips pressed to it. The upper part of her face is covered by a mask which conceals her forehead, eyes and nose, but leaves her mouth revealed. The mask is the pure pallor of marble, the expression that of a statue of Woman, of her eternal acceptance of the compulsion of motherhood, the inevitable cycle of love into pain into joy, and new love into separation and pain again, and the loneliness of age. The eyes of the mask are almost closed. Their gaze turns within, oblivious to the life outside, as they dream down on the child forever in memory at her breast. The mouth of Miriam is sensitive and sad, tender with an eager, understanding smile of self-forgetful love, the lips still fresh and young. Her skin, in contrast to the mask, is sunburned and earth-coloured like that of Lazarus. Martha, Mary, and the two parents all wear full masks which broadly reproduce their own characters. Martha is a buxom middle-aged housewife, plain and pleasant. Mary is young and pretty, nervous and high-strung. The Father is a small, thin,*

*feeble old man of over eighty, meek and pious.
The Mother is tall and stout, over sixty-five, a
gentle, simple woman.*

*All the masks of these Jews of the first two
scenes of the play are pronouncedly Semitic.*

*A background of twilight sky. A dissolving
touch of sunset still lingers on the horizon.*

*It is some time after the miracle and Jesus
has gone away.*

CHORUS OF OLD MEN (*in a quavering rising and
falling chant—their arms outstretched toward
Lazarus*). Jesus wept !
Behold how he loved him !
He that liveth,
He that believeth,
Shall never die !

CROWD (*on either side of house, echo the chant*).
He that believeth
Shall never die !
Lazarus, come forth !

FIRST GUEST (*a Simple Boy—in a frightened
whisper after a pause of dead silence*). That
strange light seems to come from within him !
(*With awe.*) Think of it ! For four days he
lay in the tomb ! (*Turns away with a shudder.*)

SECOND GUEST (*a Happy Youth—with reassuring
conviction*). It is a holy light. It came from Jesus.

FIFTH GUEST (*an Envious, Middle-Aged Man*).
Maybe if the truth were known, our friend there
never really died at all !

FOURTH GUEST (*a Defiant Man, indignantly*). Do you doubt the miracle ? I tell you I was here in this house when Lazarus died !

SEVENTH GUEST (*an Aged, Sorrowful Man*). And I used to visit him every day. He knew himself his hour was near.

FOURTH GUEST. He wished for death ! He said to me one day : " I have known my fill of life and the sorrow of living. Soon I shall know peace." And he smiled. It was the first time I had seen him smile in years.

THIRD GUEST (*a Self-Tortured Man—gloomily*). Yes, of late years his life had been one long misfortune. One after another his children died——

SIXTH GUEST (*a Mature Man with a cruel face— with a harsh laugh*). They were all girls. Lazarus had no luck.

SEVENTH GUEST. The last was a boy, the one that died at birth. You are forgetting him.

THIRD GUEST. Lazarus could never forget. Not only did his son die, but Miriam could never bear him more children.

FIFTH GUEST (*practically*). But he could not blame bad luck for everything. Take the loss of his father's wealth since he took over the management. That was his own doing. He was a bad farmer, a poor breeder of sheep, and a bargainer so easy to cheat it hurt one's conscience to trade with him !

13

SIXTH GUEST (*with a sneer—maliciously*). You should know best about that !

(*A suppressed laugh from those around him.*)

FIRST GUEST (*who has been gazing at Lazarus—softly*). Ssssh ! Look at his face !

(*They all stare. A pause.*)

SECOND GUEST (*with wondering awe*). Do you remember him, neighbours, before he died ? He used to be pale even when he worked in the fields. Now he seems as brown as one who has laboured in the earth all day in a vineyard beneath the hot sun !

(*A pause.*)

FOURTH GUEST. The whole look of his face has changed. He is like a stranger from a far land. There is no longer any sorrow in his eyes. They must have forgotten sorrow in the grave.

FIFTH GUEST (*grumblingly*). I thought we were invited here to eat—and all we do is stand and gape at him !

FOURTH GUEST (*sternly*). Be silent ! We are waiting for him to speak.

THIRD GUEST (*impressively*). He did speak once. And he laughed !

ALL THE GUESTS (*amazed and incredulous*). Laughed ?

THIRD GUEST (*importantly*). Laughed ! I heard him ! It was a moment after the miracle——

MIRIAM (*her voice, rich with sorrow, exultant now*). Jesus cried, " Lazarus, come forth ! "

> (*She kisses his hand. He makes a slight movement, a stirring in his vision. The Guests stare. A frightened pause.*)

FIFTH GUEST (*nudging the Second—uneasily*). Go on with your story !

THIRD GUEST. Just as he appeared in the opening of the tomb, wrapped in his shroud——

SECOND GUEST (*excitedly—interrupting*). My heart stopped ! I fell on my face ! And all the women screamed ! (*Sceptically.*) You must have sharp ears to have heard him laugh in that uproar !

THIRD GUEST. I helped to pry away the stone, so I was right beside him. I found myself kneeling, but between my fingers I watched Jesus and Lazarus. Jesus looked into his face for what seemed a long time, and suddenly Lazarus said " Yes," as if he were answering a question in Jesus' eyes.

ALL THE GUESTS (*mystified*). Yes ? What could he mean by yes ?

THIRD GUEST. Then Jesus smiled sadly but with tenderness, as one who from a distance of years of sorrow remembers happiness. And then Lazarus knelt and kissed Jesus' feet and both of them smiled and Jesus blessed him and called him " My Brother " and went away ; and Lazarus, looking after Him, began to laugh softly like a man in love with God ! Such a laugh I never heard ! It made my ears drunk ! It was like wine ! And though I was half-dead with fright I found myself laughing, too !

MIRIAM (*with a beseeching summons*). Lazarus, come forth !

CHORUS (*chanting*). Lazarus ! Come forth !

CROWD (*on either side of the house—echoing the chant*). Come forth ! Come forth !

LAZARUS (*suddenly in a deep voice—with a wonderful exultant acceptance in it*). Yes !

> (*The Guests in the room, the Crowds outside, all cry out in fear and joy and fall on their knees.*)

CHORUS (*chanting exultantly*). The stone is taken away !
The spirit is loosed !
The soul let go !

LAZARUS (*rising and looking around him at everyone and everything—with an all-embracing love—gently*). Yes !

> (*His family and the Guests in the room now throng about Lazarus to embrace him. The Crowds of men and women on each side push into the room to stare at him. He is in the arms of his Mother and Miriam while his Sisters and Father kiss and press his hands. The five are half-hysterical with relief and joy, sobbing and laughing.*)

16

FATHER. My son is reborn to me !

CHORUS. Hosanna !

ALL (*with a great shout*). Hosanna !

FATHER. Let us rejoice ! Eat and drink ! Draw up your chairs, friends ! Music ! Bring wine !

> (*Music begins in the room off right rear—a festive dance tune. The company sit down in their places, the Father and Mother at Lazarus' right and left, Miriam next to the Mother, Martha and Mary beside the Father. But Lazarus remains standing. And the Chorus of Old Men remain in their formation at the rear. Wine is poured and all raise their goblets toward Lazarus— then suddenly they stop, the music dies out, and an awed and frightened stillness prevails, for Lazarus is a strange, majestic figure whose understanding smile seems terrible and enigmatic to them.*)

FATHER (*pathetically uneasy*). You frighten us, my son. You are strange—standing there—(*In the midst of a silence more awkward than before he rises to his feet, goblet in hand—forcing his voice, falteringly.*) A toast, neighbours !

CHORUS (*in a forced echo*). A toast !

ALL (*echoing them*). A toast !

FATHER. To my son, Lazarus; whom a blessed miracle has brought back from death !

LAZARUS (*suddenly laughing softly out of his vision, as if to himself, and speaking with a strange unearthly calm in a voice that is like a loving whisper of hope and confidence*). No! There is no death!

> (*A moment's pause. The people remain with goblets uplifted, staring at him. Then all repeat after him questioningly and frightenedly.*)

ALL. There—is—no—death?

SIXTH GUEST (*suddenly blurts out the question which is in the minds of all*). What did you find beyond there, Lazarus?

> (*A pause of silence.*)

LAZARUS (*smiles gently and speaks as if to a group of inquisitive children*). O Curious Greedy Ones, is not one world in which you know not how to live enough for you?

SIXTH GUEST (*emboldened*). Why did you say yes, Lazarus?

FOURTH GUEST. Why did you laugh?

ALL THE GUESTS (*with insistent curiosity but in low awed tones*). What is beyond there, Lazarus?

CHORUS (*in a low murmur*). What is beyond there? What is beyond?

CROWD (*carrying the question falteringly back into silence*). What is beyond?

LAZARUS (*suddenly again—now in a voice of loving exultation*). There is only life! I heard the

18

heart of Jesus laughing in my heart; " There is Eternal Life in No," it said, " and there is the same Eternal Life in Yes ! Death is the fear between ! " And my heart reborn to love of life cried " Yes ! " and I laughed in the laughter of God !

> (*He begins to laugh, softly at first—a laugh so full of a complete acceptance of life, a profound assertion of joy in living, so devoid of all self-consciousness or fear, that it is like a great bird song triumphant in depths of sky, proud and powerful, infectious with love, casting on the listener an enthralling spell. The crowd in the room are caught by it. Glancing sideways at one another, smiling foolishly and self-consciously, at first they hesitate, plainly holding themselves in for fear of what the next one will think.*)

CHORUS (*in a chanting murmur*). Lazarus laughs !
Our hearts grow happy !
Laughter like music !
The wind laughs !
The sea laughs !
Spring laughs from the earth !
Summer laughs in the air !
Lazarus laughs !

LAZARUS (*on a final note of compelling exultation*). Laugh ! Laugh with me ! Death is dead !

Fear is no more ! There is only life ! There
is only laughter !

CHORUS (*chanting exultingly now*). Laugh !
    Laugh !
Laugh with Lazarus !
Fear is no more !
There is no death !

> (*They laugh in a rhythmic cadence dominated
> by the laughter of Lazarus.*)

CROWD (*who, gradually, joining in by groups or one
    by one—including Lazarus' family with the
    exception of Miriam, who does not laugh but
    watches and listens to his laughter with a tender
    smile of being happy in his happiness—have now
    all begun to laugh in rhythm with the Chorus—
    in a great, full-throated pæan as the laughter of
    Lazarus rises higher and higher*). Laugh !
    Laugh !
Fear is no more !
There is no death !

CHORUS. Laugh ! Laugh !
There is only life !
There is only laughter !
Fear is no more !
Death is dead !

CROWD (*in a rhythmic echo*). Laugh ! Laugh !
Death is dead !
There is only laughter !

> (*The room rocks, the air outside throbs with
> the rhythmic beat of their liberated*

*laughter—still a bit uncertain of its freedom, harsh, discordant, frenzied, desperate and drunken, but dominated and inspired by the high, free, aspiring, exulting laughter of Lazarus.)*

CURTAIN

## SCENE TWO

SCENE. *Some months later. Exterior of Lazarus' home in Bethany, now known as the House of Laughter. It is a clear bright night, the sky sparkling with stars. At the extreme front is a road. Between this and the house is a small raised terrace. The house is low, of one story only, its walls white. Four windows are visible with a closed door in the middle of the wall. Steps lead up to this door, and to the left of door a flight of stairs goes up to the balustraded roof. The windows shine brilliantly with the flickering light of many candles which gives them a throbbing star-like effect. From within comes the sound of flutes and dance music. The dancers can be seen whirling swiftly by the windows. There is continually an overtone of singing laughter emphasizing the pulsing rhythm of the dance.*

*On the road in the foreground, at left and right, two separate groups of Jews are gathered. They are not divided according to sex as in the previous scene. Each is composed about equally*

21

*of men and women, forty-nine in each, masked and costumed as before. It is religious belief that now divides them. The adherents of Jesus, the Nazarenes, among whom may be noted Martha and Mary, are on the left; the Orthodox, among whom are Lazarus' Father and Mother and a Priest, are at right. Between the two hostile groups is the same Chorus of Old Men, in a formation like a spearhead, whose point is placed at the foot of the steps leading to the terrace. All these people are staring fascinatedly at the house, listening entranced, their feet moving, their bodies swaying to the music's beat, stiffly, constrainedly, compelled against their wills. Then the music suddenly stops and the chant of youthful voices is heard:*

FOLLOWERS OF LAZARUS (*from within the house*).
Laugh ! Laugh !
There is only life !
There is only laughter !

CHORUS OF OLD MEN (*as if they were subjects moved by hypnotic suggestion—miserably and discordantly*). Ha-ha-ha-ha !
There is only laughter !
Ha-ha——

CROWD (*in the same manner*). Ha-ha——

MARY. Ha—— (*Then frantically—half-weeping with indignant rage—to the Nazarenes.*) Stop !
Oh, how can we laugh ! We are betraying Jesus !
My brother Lazarus has become a devil !

22

THE ORTHODOX PRIEST (*his mask is that of a religious fanatic. He is sixty or so*). Ha—ha— (*Tearing his beard and stamping with rage.*) Stop it, you fools ! It is a foul sin in the sight of Jehovah ! Why do you come here every night to listen and watch their abominations ? The Lord God will punish you !

MARY (*echoing him—to her people*). Jesus will never forgive you !

THE PRIEST (*angrily*). Jesus ?

> (*He turns to look at the Nazarenes disdainfully and spits on the ground insultingly.*)

> (*The members of the two groups begin to glare at each other. The Chorus falls back, three on each side, leaving one neutral figure before the steps. The Priest goes on tauntingly.*)

Did you hear her, friends ? These renegade Nazarenes will soon deny they are Jews at all ! They will begin to worship in filthy idolatry the sun and stars and man's body—as Lazarus in there (*points to the house*), the disciple of their Jesus, has so well set them the example !

> (*This is followed by an outburst of insulting shouts of accusation and denial from both sides.*)

A NAZARENE (*the Fourth Guest of Scene One*). You lie ! Lazarus is no disciple ! He is a traitor to Jesus ! We scorn him !

PRIEST (*sneeringly*). But your pretended Messiah did not scorn him. According to your stupid lies, he raised him from the dead ! And answer me, has your Jesus ever denied Lazarus, or denounced his laughter ? No ! No doubt he is laughing, too, at all you credulous fools—for if Lazarus is not his disciple, in the matter of the false miracle he was his accomplice !

> (*This provokes a furious protest from the Nazarenes and insulting hoots and jeers from the Orthodox, penetrated by a piercing scream from Lazarus' Mother, who, crushed in the crowd, sinks fainting to the ground. The Father bends over her. The group of the Orthodox falls back from them. With frightened cries Martha and Mary run from the group of Nazarenes and kneel beside her.*)

FATHER (*pitifully*). Rachel ! Darling ! Speak to me !

MARTHA (*practically*). She has only fainted.

MARY. She is opening her eyes ! Mother, dear !

MOTHER (*weakly*). Did I fall ? (*Recognizing Martha and Mary.*) Martha—and Mary—my dear ones ! (*They embrace her, weeping.*) I have not kissed you since you left home to follow that Jesus—— Oh, if we were only at home again— and if, also, my poor boy, Lazarus—— (*She sobs.*)

FATHER (*gruffly*). You must not speak of him !

24

MARTHA. Do not worry your head about Lazarus. He is not worth it!

MARY (*with surprising vindictiveness*). He is accursed! He has betrayed our Lord!

PRIEST (*to those around him—mockingly*). Do you hear? They already call the Nazarene "Lord"! A Lord who is in the common prison at Jerusalem, I heard to-day! A fine Lord whom our High Priests have had arrested like a thief!

MARY (*with fanatic fervour*). He is a king! Whenever He chooses He will gather a great army and He will seize His kingdom and all who deny Him shall be crucified!

PRIEST (*tauntingly*). Now their jail-bird is a king, no less! Soon they will make him a god, as the Romans do their Cæsars!

MARY (*her eyes flashing*). He is the Messiah!

PRIEST (*furiously*). The Messiah! May Jehovah smite you in your lies! Step back among your kind! You defile us! (*As she stands defiantly he appeals to the Father.*) Have you no authority? She called him the Messiah —that common beggar, that tramp! Curse her!

FATHER (*confused, pitifully harried, collecting his forces*). Wait! Go back, Mary! You chose to follow that impostor——

MARY (*defiantly*). The Messiah!

MARTHA (*trying to calm her*). Ssssh! Remember he is our father!

MARY (*fanatically*). I deny him ! I deny all who deny Jesus !

MOTHER (*tearfully*). And me, darling ?

MARY. You must come to us, Mother ! You must believe in Jesus and leave all to follow Him !

FATHER (*enraged*). So ! You want to steal your mother away, to leave me lonely in my old age ! You are an unnatural daughter ! I disown you ! Go, before I curse——

MOTHER (*beseechingly*). Father !

MARTHA (*pulling Mary away*). Mary ! Jesus teaches to be kind.

MARY (*hysterically*). He teaches to give up all and follow Him ! I want to give Him everything ! I want my father to curse me !

FATHER (*frenziedly*). Then I do curse you ! No—not you—but the devil in you ! And the devil in Martha ! And the great mocking devil that dwells in Lazarus and laughs from his mouth ! I curse these devils and that Prince of Devils, that false prophet, Jesus ! It is he who has brought division to my home and many homes that were happy before. I curse him ! I curse the day he called my good son, Lazarus, from the grave to walk again with a devil inside him ! It was not my son who came back but a devil ! My son is dead ! And you, my daughters, are dead ! I am the father only of devils ! (*His voice has risen to a wailing lament.*) My children are dead !

LAZARUS (*his voice rings from within the house in exultant denial*). Death is dead ! There is only laughter ! (*He laughs.*)

> (*The voices of all his Followers echo his laughter. They pour in a laughing rout from the doorway on to the terrace. At the same moment the Chorus of Followers appears on the roof and forms along the balustrade, facing front.*)

> (*These Followers of Lazarus, forty-nine in number, composed about equally of both sexes, wear a mask that, while recognizably Jewish, is a Lazarus mask, resembling him in its expression of fearless faith in life, the mouth shaped by laughter. The Chorus of Followers, seven in number, all men, have identical masks of double size, as before. The Period of all these masks is anywhere between Youth and Manhood (or Womanhood).*)

> (*The music continues to come from within. Laughing, the Followers dance to it in weaving patterns on the terrace. They are dressed in bright-coloured diaphanous robes. Their chorused laughter, now high and clear, now dying to a humming murmur, stresses the rhythmic flow of the dance.*)

27

CHORUS OF FOLLOWERS. Laugh ! Laugh !
There is no death !
There is only laughter !

FOLLOWERS. There is only laughter !
Death is dead !
Laugh ! Laugh !

CROWD (*the two groups of Nazarenes and Orthodox, on the appearance of the Followers, immediately
forget their differences and form into one mob, led by
their Chorus of Old Men, whose jeering howls they
echo as one voice*). Yaah ! Yaah ! Yaah !

> (*But they cannot keep it up. The music and
> laughter rise above their hooting. They
> fall into silence. Then they again
> begin to feel impelled by the rhythm and
> laughter, their feet move, their bodies
> sway. Their lips quiver, their mouths
> open as if to laugh. Their Chorus of
> Old Men are the first to be affected.
> It is as if this reaction were transmitted
> through the Chorus to the Crowd.*)

PRIEST (*his mouth twitching—fighting against the
compulsion in him—stammers*). Brothers—listen
—we must unite—in one cause—to—stamp out
—this abomination !

> (*It is as if he can no longer control his speech.
> He presses his hand over his mouth
> convulsively.*)

AN AGED ORTHODOX JEW (*the Seventh Guest of
Scene One—starts to harangue the crowd. He*
28

*fights the spell but cannot control his jerking body nor his ghastly, spasmodic laughter).* Neighbours! Our young people are corrupted! They are leaving our farms—to dance and sing! To laugh! Ha—! Laugh at everything! Ha-ha——! *(He struggles desperately to control himself.)*

CHORUS OF OLD MEN *(a barking laugh forced from them).* Ha-ha——!

CROWD *(echoing this).* Ha-ha——!

THE AGED JEW. They have no respect for life! When I said in kindness, " You must go back to work," they laughed at me! Ha—! "We desire joy. We go to Lazarus," they said—and left my fields! I begged them to stay—with tears in my eyes! I even offered them more money! They laughed! " What is money? Can the heart eat gold? " They laughed at money! Ha-ha——! *(He chokes with exasperated rage.)*

CHORUS OF OLD MEN *(echoing him).* Ha-ha——!

CROWD *(echoing the Chorus).* Ha-ha!——

AGED JEW *(shaking his fist at Lazarus' Followers).* That loafer taught them that! They come to him and work for nothing! For nothing! And they are glad, these undutiful ones! While they sow, they dance! They sing to the earth when they are ploughing! They tend his flocks and laugh toward the sun! Ha-ha-ha——! *(He struggles again.)*

CHORUS OF OLD MEN (*as before*).   Ha-ha-ha——

CROWD (*as before*).   Ha-ha-ha——

AGED JEW.   How can we compete with labour for laughter !   We will have no harvest.   There will be no food !   Our children will starve !   Our race will perish !   And he will laugh !   Ha-ha-ha-ha !   (*He howls with furious, unconstrained laughter.*)

CHORUS OF OLD MEN (*echoing his tone*).   Our children will starve !
Our race will perish !
Lazarus laughs !
Ha-ha-ha-ha !   Ha-ha-ha-ha !

CROWD (*as before*).   Ha-ha-ha-ha! Ha-ha-ha-ha!

(*Their former distinctions of Nazarenes and Orthodox are now entirely forgotten. The members of Lazarus' family are grouped in the centre as if nothing had ever happened to separate them. The Chorus of Old Men is again joined in its spearhead formation at the stairs. Apparent first in this Chorus, a queer excitement begins to pervade this mob. They begin to weave in and out, clasping each other's hands now and then, moving mechanically in jerky steps to the music in a grotesque sort of marionettes' country dance. At first this is slow but it momentarily becomes more hectic and peculiar. They raise clenched fists or hands distended into threatening talons.*)

*Their voices sound thick and harsh and
animal-like with anger as they mutter
and growl, each one aloud to himself or
herself.)*

CHORUS OF OLD MEN (*threateningly, gradually
rising to hatred*).   Hear them laugh !
See them dance !
Shameless !   Wanton !
Dirty !   Evil !
Infamous !   Bestial !
Madness !   Blood !
Adultery !   Murder !
We burn !
We kill !
We crucify !
Death !   Death !
Beware, Lazarus !   (*This last in a wild frenzy.*)

CROWD (*frenziedly*).   Beware, Lazarus !
We burn !   We kill !
We crucify !
Death !   Death !

> (*They crowd toward the gateway, their arms
> stretched out as if demanding Lazarus
> for a sacrificial victim.   Meanwhile
> they never cease to hop up and down, to
> mill around, to twist their bodies toward
> and away from each other in bestial
> parody of the dance of the Followers.*)

> (*The tall figure of Lazarus, dressed in a
> white robe, suddenly appears on the roof
> of the house.   He stands at the balus-*

*trade in the middle of the Chorus.
Beside him, a little behind, Miriam
appears dressed in black, her face
upturned, her lips praying. She appears to have grown older, to be forty
now. Lazarus' body is softly illumined by its inner light. The change in
him is marked. He seems ten years
younger, at the prime of forty. His
body has become less angular and stiff.
His movements are graceful and pliant.
The change is even more noticeable in
his face, which has filled out, become
purer in outline, more distinctly Grecian.
His complexion is the red-brown of rich
earth, the grey in his black, curly beard
has almost disappeared.)*

*(He makes a sign and the music ceases. His
Followers remain fixed in their dancing
attitudes like figures in a frieze. Each
member of the mob remains frozen in a
distorted posture. He stares down at
the mob pityingly, his face calm.)*

LAZARUS *(speaks amid a profound silence. His
voice releases his own dancers and the mob from their
fixed attitudes. The music begins to play again
within the house, very soft and barely audible, swell-
ing up and down like the sound of an organ from a
distant church).* You laugh, but your laughter is
guilty ! It laughs a hyena laughter, spotted,
howling its hungry fear of life ! That day I

32

returned did I not tell you your fear was no more, that there is no death? You believed then— for a moment! You laughed—discordantly, hoarsely, but with a groping toward joy. What! Have you so soon forgotten, that now your laughter curses life again as of old? (*He pauses —then sadly*). That is your tragedy! You forget! You forget the God in you! You wish to forget! Remembrance would imply the high duty to live as a son of God—generously!—with love!—with pride!—with laughter! This is too glorious a victory for you, too terrible a loneliness! Easier to forget, to become only a man, the son of a woman, to hide from life against her breast, to whimper your fear to her resigned heart and be comforted by her resignation! To live by denying life! (*Then exhortingly.*) Why are your eyes always either fixed on the ground in weariness of thought, or watching one another with suspicion? Throw your gaze upward! To Eternal Life! To the fearless and deathless! The everlasting! To the stars! (*He stretches out his arms to the sky—then suddenly points.*) See! A new star has appeared! It is the one that shone over Bethlehem! (*His voice becomes a little bitter and mocking.*) The Master of Peace and Love has departed this earth. Let all stars be for you henceforth symbols of Saviours—Sons of God who appeared on worlds like ours to tell the saving truth to ears like yours, inexorably deaf! (*Then exaltedly*). But the greatness of Saviours is that they may not save! The greatness of

Man is that no god can save him—until he
becomes a god !

> (*He stares up at the stars, rapt in contempla-*
> *tion, oblivious to all around him now.*)

> (*Rapidly approaching from the left a man's*
> *voice jarring in high-pitched cruel*
> *laughter is heard. They all listen,*
> *huddled together like sheep.*)

MESSENGER (*the Third Guest of Scene One rushes*
*in breathlessly, shouting*). The Nazarene has been
crucified !

PRIEST (*with fierce triumph*). Jehovah is
avenged ! Hosanna !

ORTHODOX. Hosanna ! The false prophet is
dead ! The pretended Messiah is dead !

> (*They jump and dance, embracing one*
> *another. The Nazarenes stand para-*
> *lysed and stunned. The two groups*
> *mechanically separate to right and left*
> *again, the Chorus of Old Men dividing*
> *itself as before.*)

MARY (*in a frenzy of grief*). Do not believe
him ! Jesus could not die !

> (*But at this moment a Nazarene youth,*
> *exhausted by grief and tears, staggers*
> *in from the left.*)

MESSENGER (*Second Guest of Scene One*). Jesus
is dead ! Our Lord is murdered !

> (*He sinks on his knees sobbing. All the*

34

*Nazarenes do likewise, wailing, rending their garments, tearing their hair, some even beating their heads on the ground in the agony of their despair.)*

MARY (*insane with rage now*). They have murdered Him ! (*To her followers—savagely.*) An eye for an eye ! Avenge the Master !

(*Their frenzy of grief turned into rage, the Nazarenes leap to their feet threateningly. Concealed swords and knives are brought out by both sides.*)

MIRIAM (*leaning over the balustrade—in a voice of entreaty*). Mary ! Brothers !

(*But none heed her or seem to see her. Lazarus and his Followers remain oblivious to men, arms upstretched toward the stars, their heads thrown back.*)

MARY (*wildly*). Vengeance ! Death to His murderers !

PRIEST (*fiercely to his followers*). Death to the Nazarenes !

(*With cries of rage the two groups rush on one another. There is a confused tumult of yells, groans, curses, the shrieks of women, the sounds of blows as they meet in a pushing, whirling, struggling mass in which individual figures are indistinguishable. Knives and swords flash above the heads of the mass, hands in every tense attitude*

35

*of striking, clutching, tearing are seen
upraised. As the fight is at its height
a Roman Centurion and a squad of
eight Soldiers come tramping up at the
double-quick. They all are masked.
These Roman masks now and henceforth in the play are carried out according to the same formula of Seven
Periods, Seven Types, as those of the
Jews seen previously, except that the
basis of each face is Roman—heavy,
domineering, self-complacent, the face
of a confident dominant race. The
Centurion differs from his soldiers only
in being more individualized. He is
middle-aged, his soldiers belong to the
Period of Manhood. All are of the
Simple, Ignorant Type.)*

CENTURION (*shouts commandingly*). Disperse !
(*But no one hears him—with angry disgust to his
Soldiers.*) Charge ! Cut them down !

> (*The Soldiers form a wedge and charge with
> a shout. They soon find it necessary
> to use their swords, and strike down
> everyone in their way.*)

MIRIAM. Mercy, Romans ! (*As they pay no
attention to her, in desperation she embraces Lazarus
beseechingly, forcing his attention back to earth.*)
Lazarus ! Mercy !

LAZARUS (*looks down upon the struggling mass and
cries in a ringing voice*). Hold !

(*Each person stands transfixed, frozen in the
last movement, even the Roman Soldiers and the Centurion himself. Ten
dead and mortally wounded lie on the
ground, trampled by the feet of friend and
foe alike. Lazarus looks at the Crowd.
To each he seems to look at him or her
alone. His eyes are accusing and stern.
As one head, the heads of all are averted.
Even the Centurion stares at the ground
humbly, in spite of himself. Finally Lazarus speaks in a voice of infinite disdain.*)

Sometimes it is hard to laugh—even *at* men !

(*He turns his eyes from them, staring straight
before him. This seems to release
them from their fixed positions. The
Nazarenes and the Orthodox separate
and slink guiltily apart. The Chorus
of Old Men forms again, the apex at
the centre of the steps as before. A low
wail of lamentation arises from them.
The two crowds of Nazarenes and
Orthodox echo this.*)

CHORUS OF OLD MEN (*in a wailing chant*). Woe
unto Israel !
Woe unto thee, Jerusalem !
O divided house,
Thou shalt crumble to dust,
And swine shall root
Where thy Temple stood !
Woe unto us !

37

CROWD (*in a great echoing cry*).   Woe unto us !

CENTURION (*gruffly to hide his embarrassment at being awed by Lazarus*).   Here, you !   Drag your carcasses away !   (*From each side men and women come forward to identify and mourn their dead. The wail of lamentation rises and falls. The Centurion looks up at Lazarus—harshly.*)   You, there !   Are you he whom they call the Laugher ?

LAZARUS (*without looking at him—his voice seeming to come from some dream within him*).   I am Lazarus.

CENTURION.   Who was brought back from death by enchantment ?

LAZARUS (*looking down at him now—with a smile, simply*).   No.   There is no death !

CHORUS OF FOLLOWERS (*chanting joyously*).   There is no death !

FOLLOWERS (*echoing*).   There is no death !

AN ORTHODOX MAN (*bending beside the body of Lazarus' father*).   Here is your father, Lazarus. He is dead.

AN ORTHODOX WOMAN.   This is your mother, Lazarus.   She is dead.

A NAZARENE.   Here is your sister, Martha, Lazarus.   She is dead.

A NAZARENE WOMAN.   And this is Mary, Lazarus.   She is dead.

MIRIAM (*suddenly—with deep grief*).   And Jesus who was the Son of Man, who loved you and gave you life again, has died, Lazarus—has died !

LAZARUS (*in a great triumphant voice*). Yes !
Yes ! ! Yes ! ! ! Men die ! Even a Son of
Man must die to show men that Man may live !
But there is no death !

CENTURION (*at first in a tone of great awe—to his
Soldiers*). Is he a god ? (*Then gruffly, ashamed
of his question.*) Come down, Jew ! I have
orders to bring you to Rome to Cæsar !

LAZARUS (*as if he were answering not the Centurion
but the command of his fate from the sky*). Yes !
(*He walks down the narrow stairs and, Miriam
following him, comes down the path to the road. He
goes and kneels for a moment each beside the bodies of
his Father, Mother, and Sisters, and kisses each in turn
on the forehead. For a moment the struggle with his
grief can be seen in his face. Then he looks up to the
stars and, as if answering a question, again says
simply and acceptingly*). Yes ! (*Then exultantly.*)
Yes ! ! (*And begins to laugh from the depths of his
exalted spirit. The laughter of his Chorus and then
of his Followers echoes his. The music and dancing
begin again.*)

> (*The Centurion grins sheepishly. The Sol-
> diers chuckle. The Centurion laughs
> awkwardly. The Soldiers laugh. The
> music from the house and the laughter
> of the Followers grow louder. The
> infection spreads to the Chorus of Old
> Men whose swaying grief falls into the
> rhythm of the laughter and music as
> does that of the mourners.*)

LAZARUS' FOLLOWERS (*led by their Chorus*). Laugh ! Laugh !

CHORUS OF OLD MEN (*torn by the conflict— torturedly*). Ha-ha-ha— Woe to us, woe !

CROWD (*beside the bodies*). Woe to us, woe ! Ha-ha—— !

CENTURION (*laughingly*). You are brave, you Laugher ! Remember Tiberius never laughs ! And boast not to Cæsar there is no death, or he will invent a new one for you !

LAZARUS (*with a smile*). But all death is men's invention ! So laugh !

> (*He laughs, and the Centurion and Soldiers laugh with him, half dancing clumsily now to the beat of the music.*)

CHORUS OF LAZARUS' FOLLOWERS. Laugh ! Laugh !
Fear is no more !
There is no death !
There is only life !
There is only laughter !

FOLLOWERS (*dancing*). Laugh ! Laugh !
Fear is no more !
Death is dead !

CHORUS OF OLD MEN (*forgetting their grief—their eyes on Lazarus now, their arms outstretched to him as are those of the crowd grouped around the bodies but forgetting them*). Death is no more !

Death is dead !
Laugh !
    CROWD.  Laugh !  Laugh !
Death is no more !

    CENTURION (*laughing, to his laughing Soldiers*).
Forward !

> (*They tramp, dancing, off.*)

> (*Lazarus and Miriam start to follow.*)

    MIRIAM (*suddenly pointing to his Followers who
are dancing and laughing obliviously—pityingly*).
But your faithful ones who love you, Lazarus ?

    LAZARUS (*simply, with a trace of a sad sternness*).
This is their test.  Their love must remember—
or it must forget.  Come !

> (*With a last gesture back like a blessing
> on all he is leaving, he goes.  The
> laughter of the Soldiers recedes.  That
> of the Chorus of Old Men and of the
> Crowd falters and breaks into lamenting
> grief again, guilt-stricken because of its
> laughter.*)

    CHORUS OF OLD MEN.  Laugh !  Laugh !
Death is dead !
Laugh !—But woe !
There lie our dead !
Oh shame and guilt !
We forget our dead !

    CROWD (*with fierce remorseful grief*).  Woe to
        us, woe !
There lie our dead !

CHORUS OF LAZARUS' FOLLOWERS (*their voices and the music growing more and more hesitating and faint*).   Laugh !   Laugh !
There is only life !
There is only—
Laugh—   (*Their dance is faltering and slow now.*)
Fear is no—
Death is—
Laugh—

> (*The music and dancing and voices cease. The lights in the windows, which have been growing dim, go out.   There is a second of complete, death-like silence. The mourning folk in the foreground are frozen figures of grief.   Then a sudden swelling chorus of forlorn bewilderment, a cry of lost children, comes from the Chorus of Followers and the Followers themselves.   They huddle into groups on the roof and on the terrace.   They stretch their arms out in every direction supplicatingly.*)

CHORUS OF FOLLOWERS.   Oh, Lazarus, laugh !
Do not forsake us !
We forget !
Where is thy love fled ?
Give back thy laughter,
Thy fearless laughter !
We forget !

FOLLOWERS.   Give back thy laughter !
We forget !

CHORUS OF FOLLOWERS (*with dull, resigned terror now*).   Death slinks out
Of his grave in the heart !
Ghosts of fear
Creep back in the brain !
We remember fear !
We remember death !

FOLLOWERS.   Death in the heart !
Fear in the brain !
We remember fear !
We remember death !

CHORUS OF FOLLOWERS (*wailing hopelessly now*).
    Forgotten is laughter !
We remember
Only death !
Fear is God !
Forgotten is laughter !
Life is death !

FOLLOWERS.   Forgotten is laughter !
Life is death !

ALL (*the Chorus of Old Men and the Crowd joining in*).   Life is a fearing,
A long dying,
From birth to death !
God is a slayer !
Life is death !

CURTAIN

# ACT TWO

SCENE. *Some months later. A square in Athens about ten o'clock at night. In the rear, pure and beautiful in the light of a full moon, is the façade of a temple. An excited crowd of Greeks of both sexes is gathered in the square as if for some public festival. They are masked according to the scheme of Seven Periods in Seven Types of Character for each sex. Here, of course, the foundation of the mask is the Grecian type of face.*

*On the left, the Chorus of Greeks is grouped, seven in number, facing front, in the spearhead formation. As before, the Chorus wears masks double the life size of the Crowd masks. They are all of the Proud Self-Reliant type, in the period of Young Manhood.*

*These seven are clad in goat skins, their tanned bodies and masks daubed and stained with wine lees, in imitation of the old followers of Dionysus. Rumour has led them to hope and believe that Lazarus may be the reincarnation of this deity.*

*The people in the crowd are holding themselves in restraint with difficulty, they stir and push about restlessly with an eager curiosity and impatience. All eyes are fixed off left. A buzz of voices hums in the air.*

*Acting as police, a number of Roman legionaries (masked like the soldiers of Scene*

44

*Two) armed with staves, keep back the crowd from the line of the street that runs from left to right, front. They resent this duty, which has already kept them there a long time, and are surly and quick-tempered with the Greeks.*

*At front, pacing impatiently up and down, is a young Roman noble of twenty-one, clad richly, wearing beautifully wrought armour and helmet. This is Gaius, the heir of Tiberius Cæsar, nicknamed Caligula by the soldiers, in whose encampments he was born and where he spent his childhood. His body is bony and angular, almost malformed with wide, powerful shoulders and long arms and hands, and short, skinny, hairy legs like an ape's. He wears a half-mask of crimson, dark with a purplish tinge, that covers the upper part of his face to below the nose. This mask accentuates his bulging, prematurely wrinkled forehead, his hollow temples and his bulbous, sensual nose. His large troubled eyes, of a glazed greenish-blue, glare out with a shifty feverish suspicion at every one. Below his mask his own skin is of an anæmic transparent pallor. Above it, his hair is the curly blond hair of a child of six or seven. His mouth also is childish, the red lips soft and feminine in outline. Their expression is spoiled, petulant and self-obsessed, weak but domineering. In combination with the rest of the face there is an appalling morbid significance to his mouth. One feels that its boyish cruelty, encouraged as a manly attribute*

*in the coarse brutality of camps, has long ago
become naïvely insensitive to any human suffering but its own.*

   *Walking with Caligula is Cneius Crassus, a
Roman general—a squat, muscular man of sixty,
his mask that of a heavy battered face full of
coarse humour.*

CHORUS OF GREEKS (*intoning solemnly*).  Soon
   the God comes !
Redeemer and Saviour !
Dionysus, Son of Man and a God !

   GREEK CROWD (*echoing*).   Soon the God comes !
Redeemer and Saviour !
Dionysus !

   FIRST GREEK.  They say an unearthly flame
burns in this Lazarus !

   SECOND GREEK.  The sacred fire !  He must
be the Fire-born, the son of Zeus !

   THIRD GREEK.  Many who have seen him
swear he is Dionysus, re-arisen from Hades !

   FOURTH GREEK (*importantly*).   I saw Lazarus at
Antioch where the galley on which they were
taking him to Rome had been thrice blown back
by a storm.  Fear of this warning omen is why
they now march with him by land.

   FIRST GREEK.  Does he truly resemble a god ?

   FOURTH GREEK (*impressively*).   One look in his
eyes while his laughter sings in your ears and you
forget sorrow !  You dance !  You laugh !  It
is as if a heavy weight you had been carrying

46

all your life without knowing it suddenly were lifted. You are like a cloud, you can fly, your mind reels with laughter, you are drunk with joy ! (*Solemnly.*) Take my word for it, he is indeed a god. Everywhere the people have acclaimed him. He heals the sick, he raises the dead, by laughter.

SEVENTH GREEK. But I have heard that when he has gone people cannot remember his laughter, that the dead are dead again and the sick die, and the sad grow more sorrowful.

FIFTH GREEK. Well, we shall soon see with our own eyes. But why should the god return in the body of a Jew ?

SIXTH GREEK. What better disguise if he wishes to remain unknown ? The fools of Romans will never suspect him!

THIRD GREEK (*laughing*). Never ! They are beginning to claim he is a Roman !

FIFTH GREEK. So much the better ! He will be in their confidence !

FOURTH GREEK. He will lead us against Rome ! He will laugh our tyrants into the sea ! Ha !

> (*He turns toward the Romans and laughs sneeringly. This is taken up by the Crowd—unpleasant, resentful laughter. They push forward aggressively and almost sweep the Soldiers from their feet.*)

47

CRASSUS (*angrily*). Drive them back !

CALIGULA (*suddenly with a distorted warped smile*). Order them to use their swords, Cneius. Let the scum look at their dead and learn respect for us !

SOLDIERS (*shoving and whacking*). Back ! Step back ! Back there !

> (*The crowd push back to their former line. There are muttered curses, groans, protests, which subside into the former hum of expectancy.*)

CALIGULA (*with the same smile*). The sword, my old hyena ! Corpses are so educational !

CRASSUS (*surlily*). I would like to, I promise you ! When I see how they hate us——!

CALIGULA (*carelessly*). Let them hate—so long as they fear us ! We must keep death dangling (*he makes the gesture of doing so*) before their eyes ! (*He gives a soft, cruel laugh.*) Will you not sacrifice in my honour ? What are a few Greeks ? (*Queerly.*) I like to watch men die.

CRASSUS. I dare not, Caligula. Cæsar has forbidden bloodshed.

CALIGULA. Tiberius is a miser. He wants to hoard all of death for his own pleasure ! (*He laughs again.*)

CRASSUS (*with rough familiarity*). I wager no one will make that complaint against you when you are Cæsar ! (*He chuckles.*)

CALIGULA (*with the sudden grandiose posturing of a bad actor unintentionally burlesquing grandeur*). When I, Gaius Caligula, am Cæsar, I— (*Then superstitiously looking up at the sky with cringing foreboding*). But it brings bad luck to anticipate fate. (*He takes off his helmet and spits in it—then with a grim smile.*) The heirs of a Cæsar take sick so mysteriously ! Even with you who used to ride me on your knee, I do not eat nor drink until you have tasted first.

CRASSUS (*nodding approvingly*). You are sensible. I suppose I, too, have my price—if they were only clever enough to discover it ! (*He laughs hoarsely.*)

CALIGULA (*steps back from him with an uneasy shudder*). You are honest, at least—too honest, Cneius ! (*Grimly.*) If my father Germanicus had had you for his counsellor, he might have escaped their poison. (*Then gloomily.*) I must fear everyone. The world is my enemy.

CRASSUS. Kill it then ! (*He laughs again.*)

CHORUS (*stretching out their arms in the direction
     from which Lazarus is expected—supplicat-
     ingly*). Son of the Lightning !
Deadly thy vengeance !
Swift thy deliverance !
Beholding thy Mother,
Greece, our Mother,
Her beauty in bondage,
Her pride in chains !
Hasten, Redeemer !

49

CROWD (*as before—echoing the chant*).    Hasten,
    Redeemer !
Son of the Lightning !
Deadly thy vengeance !
Swift thy deliverance !

CALIGULA (*disdainfully*).    What clods !    Mob
is the same everywhere, eager to worship any new
charlatan !    They have already convinced themselves this Lazarus is a reincarnation of Dionysus !
A Jew become a god !    By the breasts of Venus
that *is* a miracle. !    (*He laughs.*)

CRASSUS (*seriously*).    But he must be expert in
magic.    He was buried four days and came out
unharmed.    Maybe he is not a Jew.    Some say
his father was really a legionary of our garrison
in Judea.    And he teaches people to laugh at
death.    That smacks of Roman blood !

CALIGULA (*ironically*).    Better still !    He tells
them there is no death at all !    Hence the
multitude of fools who have acclaimed him
everywhere since he left his own country—and
why Tiberius has begun to fear his influence.

CRASSUS (*sententiously*).    Whom Cæsar fears—
disappears !

CALIGULA.    Yes, the dupes who follow Lazarus
will be killed.    But Tiberius believes this
Lazarus may know a cure for death or for renew-
ing youth, and the old lecher hopes he can worm
the secret out of him—before he kills him.    (*He
laughs ironically, then disgustedly.*)    That is why

I must escort this Jew to Rome—as a special honour ! (*With fierce, haughty resentment.*) I, the heir of Cæsar ! (*Savagely.*) Oh, if I were Cæsar—— !

CRASSUS (*with a coarse, meaning smirk*). Patience. Tiberius is old.

CALIGULA (*suddenly becoming terribly uneasy at some thought*). Cneius ! What if this Lazarus has really discovered a cure for old age and should reveal it to Tiberius ! (*His lips tremble, his eyes are terrified, he shrinks against Crassus for protection —with boyish pleading.*) Oh, Cneius, what could I do then ?

CRASSUS (*matter-of-factly*). Kill him before Cæsar can talk to him.

CALIGULA (*almost in tears*). But if he knows a charm against death, how could he be slain, old fool ?

CRASSUS (*gruffly*). Bah ! (*Then with grim humour.*) Death in bed I suspect, but when men are killed I know they stay dead ! (*Disgustedly.*) A moment ago you were laughing at him ! (*Scornfully.*) Do you fear him now ?

CALIGULA (*rather shamefacedly pulls himself together—then broodingly*). I fear every one who lives. Even you. As you advised me. (*He turns away.*)

CRASSUS (*contemptuously*). Well, maybe he can teach you to laugh at fear. You would welcome him then, eh, cry baby ?

CALIGULA (*with sudden passionate intensity but only half aloud, as if to himself*). I would love him, Cneius ! As a father ! As a god !

> (*He stands staring before him strangely. There is a new stir from the crowd, who again push forward.*)

CRASSUS (*pointing off right*). Look ! I see a great crowd ! Your Lazarus must be coming at last !

> CHORUS (*chanting in a deep rhythmic monotone, like the rising and falling cadences of waves on a beach*). He comes, the Redeemer and Saviour !

Laughing along the mountains !
To give back our lost laughter,
To raise from the dead our freedom,
To free us from Rome !

CROWD (*echoing this chant*). Fire-born ! Redeemer ! Saviour !
Raise from the dead our freedom !
Give back our lost laughter !
Free us from Rome !

> (*They have been pushing forward, more and more fiercely and defiantly. The Roman Soldiers in spite of their efforts are pushed backward step by step.*)

SOLDIERS (*angrily*). Back ! Back !

> (*The Soldiers work with a will, dealing out blows with their staves at every one in reach. But now these blows seem only*)

*to infuriate the Crowd, which steadily
pushes them back into the street. At
the same time the distant sound of
exultant music, singing and laughter
becomes steadily louder. Both Soldiers
and Crowd are inspired to battle by
these strains without their knowing it.
Caligula is listening spell-bound, his
mouth open, his body swaying and
twitching. Even Crassus stares off at
the oncomers, forgetful of the growing
plight of his Soldiers.)*

CROWD (*led by their Chorus—angrily*). Cowards !
    Pigs !
Strike ! Hit !
Stones ! Knives !
Stab ! Kill !
Death to the Romans !
Death !

A SOLDIER (*alarmed, calls to Crassus*). General !
Let us use our swords !

SOLDIERS (*enraged—eagerly*). Yes ! Swords !

CROWD. Death !

CRASSUS (*turning—uneasy, but afraid to give any
drastic order*). Bah ! Staves are enough. Crack
their skulls !

CROWD (*led by the Chorus—defiantly*). Death to
    Crassus !
Drunkard ! Coward !
Death to him !

(*They continue to push forward, hooting and jeering.*)

CRASSUS (*exploding for a second*). By the gods— ! (*To the Soldiers.*) Draw your swords !

(*The troops do so eagerly. The Crowd sag back momentarily with exclamations of fear.*)

CALIGULA (*listening as in a trance to the music and what is going on behind him—in a queer whisper*). Kill, Cneius ! Let me dance ! Let me sing ! (*The music and crashing of cymbals and the ferment of passions around him cause him to lose all control over himself. He gives a crazy leap in the air and begins to dance grotesquely and chant in a thick voice.*) He is coming ! Death, the Deliverer ! Kill, soldiers ! I command you ! I, Caligula ! I will be Cæsar ! Death !

CROWD (*led by the Chorus—savage now*). Beast ! Cur !
Death to Caligula !

(*They crowd forward.*)

CALIGULA (*drawing his sword and flourishing it drunkenly—his eyes glazed*). Death !

CRASSUS (*drawing his own sword in a frenzy*). Strike ! Death !

(*His Soldiers raise their swords. The Crowd have raised whatever weapons they have found—knives, clubs, daggers, stones, bare fists.*)

CHORUS (*chanting fiercely*). Death !

ALL (*Romans and Greeks alike as one great voice*).
Death !

> (*The chorused word beats down all sound into
> a stricken silence. The wild joyous
> music ceases. The Romans and Greeks
> seem to lean back from one another and
> collect strength to leap forward. At
> this moment the voice of Larazus comes
> ringing through the air like a command
> from the sky.*)

LAZARUS.    There is no death !

> (*The Soldiers and Greeks remain frozen in
> their attitudes of murderous hate. Fol-
> lowing his words the laughter of
> Lazarus is heard, exultant and gaily
> mocking, filling them with the sheepish
> shame of children caught in mischief.
> Their hands hang, their arms sink to
> their sides. The music starts once more
> with a triumphant clash of cymbals,
> Lazarus' laughter is echoed from the
> throats of the multitude of his Followers
> who now come dancing into the square,
> preceded by a band of masked musicians
> and by their Chorus.*)

> (*This Chorus wears, in double size, the
> laughing mask of Lazarus' Followers
> in the same Period and Type as in the
> preceding scene, except that here the
> mask of each member of the Chorus has
> a different racial basis—Egyptian,*)

*Syrian, Cappadocian, Lydian, Phrygian, Cilician, Parthian. The Followers are costumed and masked as in the preceding scene, seven Types in seven Periods, except that, as in the Chorus, racially there are many nations represented. All have wreaths of ivy in their hair, and flowers in their hands which they scatter about. They whirl in between the Soldiers and Crowd, forcing them back from each other, teasing them, sifting into the Crowd, their Chorus in a half-circle, confronting the Chorus of Greeks.)*

CHORUS OF FOLLOWERS. Laugh ! Laugh !
There is no death !
There is only life !
There is only laughter !

FOLLOWERS (*echoing*). Laugh ! Laugh !
There is no death !

(*Caligula and Crassus are swept to one side, left. Then the cries and laughter of all become mingled into one exclamation :*)

ALL. Lazarus ! Lazarus !

(*The squad of Roman Soldiers led by the Centurion who had taken Lazarus prisoner, march in with dancers' steps, like a proud guard of honour now, laughing, pulling a chariot in which Lazarus stands dressed in a tunic of*

56

*white and gold, his bronzed face and
limbs radiant in the halo of his own
glowing light.)*

*(Lazarus now looks less than thirty-five.
His countenance now might well be
that of the positive masculine Dionysus,
closest to the soil of the Grecian gods,
a Son of Man, born of a mortal. Not
the coarse, drunken Dionysus, nor the
effeminate god, but Dionysus in his
middle period, more comprehensive in
his symbolism, the soul of the recurring
seasons, of living and dying as processes
in eternal growth, of the wine of life stirring forever in the sap and blood and
loam of things. Miriam is beside him,
dressed in black, smiling the same sad
tender smile, holding Lazarus' arm as if
for protection and in protection. She
appears older, a woman over forty-five.)*

CHORUS OF GREEKS *(rushing to Lazarus' car).*
   Hail, Dionysus !
Iacchus !
Lazarus !
Hail !

*(They surround him, throw over his shoulders
and head the finely dressed hide of a bull
with great gilded horns, force into his
right hand the mystic rod of Dionysus
with a pine cone on top, then prostrate
themselves.)*

Hail, Saviour !
Redeemer !
Conqueror of Death !

ALL (*in a repeated chorus which finally includes even the Roman Soldiers, raising their arms to him*). Hail, Lazarus !
Redeemer !
Hail !

> (*They are silent. Lazarus looks at them, seeming to see each and all at the same time, and his laughter, as if in answer to their greetings, is heard rising from his lips like a song.*)

CRASSUS (*awed*). Look ! He is more than man !

CALIGULA (*trembling, in a queer agitation*). I dare not look !

CRASSUS. Do you hear his laughter ?

CALIGULA (*chokingly—puts his hands over his ears*). I will not hear !

CRASSUS. But you must welcome him in Cæsar's name !

CALIGULA (*his teeth chattering*). I must kill him !

LAZARUS (*looking directly at him—gaily mocking*). Death is dead, Caligula ! (*He begins to laugh again softly.*)

CALIGULA (*with an hysterical cry of defiant terror*). You lie ! (*Sword in hand he whirls to confront*

*Lazarus, but at the first sight of his face he stops in
his tracks, trembling, held fascinated by Lazarus'
eyes, mumbling with a last pitiful remainder of
defiance.*) But you lie—whatever you are ! I
say there *must* be death ! (*The sword has fallen
to his side. He stares open-mouthed at Lazarus.
There is something of a shy, wondering child about
his attitude now. Lazarus looks at him, laughing
with gentle understanding. Caligula suddenly drops
his sword, and covering his face with his hands weeps
like a boy who has been hurt.*) You have murdered
my only friend, Lazarus ! Death would have
been my slave when I am Cæsar. He would have
been my jester and made me laugh at fear ! (*He
weeps bitterly.*)

LAZARUS (*gaily*). Be your own jester instead,
O Caligula ! Laugh at yourself, O Cæsar-
to-be !

> (*He laughs. The Crowd now all join in
> with him.*)

> (*Caligula suddenly uncovers his face, grins
> his warped grin, gives a harsh cackle
> which cracks through the other laughter
> with a splitting discord, cuts a hopping
> caper like some grotesque cripple which
> takes him to the side of Lazarus' chariot,
> where he squats on his hams and,
> stretching out his hand, fingers Lazarus'
> robe inquisitively and stares up into
> his face in the attitude of a chained
> monkey.*)

CALIGULA (*with a childish, mischievous curiosity*). Then if there is no death, O Teacher, tell me why I love to kill?

LAZARUS. Because you fear to die! (*Then gaily mocking.*) But what do you matter, O Deathly-Important One? Put yourself that question—as a jester! (*Exultantly.*) Are you a speck of dust danced in the wind? Then laugh, dancing! Laugh yes to your insignificance! Thereby will be born your new greatness! As Man, Petty Tyrant of Earth, you are a bubble pricked by death into a void and a mocking silence! But as dust, you are eternal change, and everlasting growth, and a high note of laughter soaring through chaos from the deep heart of God! Be proud, O Dust! Then you may love the stars as equals! (*Then mockingly again.*) And then perhaps you may be brave enough to love even your fellow-men without fear of their vengeance!

CALIGULA (*dully*). I cannot understand. I hate men. I am afraid of their poison and their swords and the cringing envy in their eyes that only yields to fear!

LAZARUS (*gaily mocking*). Tragic is the plight of the tragedian whose only audience is himself! Life is for each man a solitary cell whose walls are mirrors. Terrified is Caligula by the faces he makes! But I tell you to laugh in the mirror, that seeing your life gay, you may begin to live as a guest, and not as a condemned one! (*Raising his hands for silence—with a playful smile.*)

Listen ! In the dark peace of the grave the man called Lazarus rested. He was still weak, as one who recovers from a long illness—for, living, he had believed his life a sad one ! (*He laughs softly, and softly they all echo his laughter.*) He lay dreaming to the croon of silence, feeling as the flow of blood in his own veins the past re-enter the heart of God to be renewed by faith into the future. He thought : " Men call this death "— for he had been dead only a little while and he still remembered. Then, of a sudden, a strange gay laughter trembled from his heart as though his life, so long repressed in him by fear, had found at last its voice and a song for singing. " Men call this death," it sang. " Men call life death and fear it. They hide from it in horror. Their lives are spent in hiding. Their fear becomes their living. They worship life as death ! "

CHORUS OF FOLLOWERS (*in a chanting echo*).
  Men call life death and fear it.
They hide from it in horror.
Their lives are spent in hiding.
Their fear becomes their living.
They worship life as death !

LAZARUS. And here the song of Lazarus' life grew pitiful. " Men must learn to live," it mourned. " Before their fear invented death they knew, but now they have forgotten. They must be taught to laugh again ! " And Lazarus answered " Yes ! " (*He now addresses the crowd —especially Caligula, directly, laughingly.*) Thus sang his life to Lazarus while he lay dead ! **Man** must learn to live by laughter ! (*He laughs.*)

CHORUS OF FOLLOWERS. Laugh ! Laugh !
There is only life !
There is only laughter !
Fear is no more !
Death is dead !

CHORUS OF GREEKS. Laugh ! Laugh !
Hail, Dionysus !
Fear is no more !
Thou hast conquered death !

ALL (*laughing—in a great laughing chorus*).
Laugh ! Laugh !
Fear is no more !
Death is dead !

LAZARUS (*as to a crowd of children—laughingly*).
Out with you ! Out into the woods ! Upon the hills ! Cities are prisons wherein man locks himself from life. Out with you under the sky ! Are the stars too pure for your sick passions ? Is the warm earth smelling of night too desirous of love for your pale introspective lusts ? Out ! Let laughter be your new clean lust and sanity ! So far man has only learned to snicker meanly at his neighbour ! Let a laughing away of self be your new right to live for ever ! Cry in your pride, " I am Laughter, which is Life, which is the Child of God ! "

> (*He laughs, and again his voice leads and dominates the rhythmic chorus of theirs. The music and dancing begin again.*)

THE TWO CHORUSES (*chanting in unison*). Laugh !
Laugh !
There is only God !
We are His Laughter !

ALL (*echoing*). There is only God !
We are His Laughter !
Laugh ! Laugh !

> (*They take hold of his chariot traces, and as
> he had come, in the midst of a happy
> multitude, now augmented by all the
> Greeks, and the Roman Soldiers who
> had awaited him, dancing, playing,
> singing, laughing, he is escorted off.
> The noise of their passing recedes.
> Caligula and Crassus are left in the
> empty square, the former squatting on
> his hams, monkey-wise, and brooding
> sombrely.*)

CRASSUS (*is swaying and staggering, like a man in
a drunken stupor, in a bewildered, stubborn struggle
to control himself. He stammers after the Soldiers*).
Ha-ha-ha— Halt ! Halt, I say ! No use—
they are gone—mutiny—Halt ! (*He continues to
stumble toward left.*) Ha-ha— Stop it, curse
you ! Am I laughing ? Where am I going ?
After Lazarus ? Thirty years of discipline and
I— Halt, traitor ! Remember Cæsar ! Remember Rome ! Halt, traitor ! (*He faints with
the violence of his struggle and falls in a limp heap.*)

CALIGULA (*startled by his fall, terrified, hops to his
feet and snatches up his sword defensively, glancing*

*over his shoulder and whirling around as if he ex-
pected someone to stab him in the back. Then,
forcing a twisted grin of self-contempt—harshly).*
Coward ! What do I fear—if there is no death ?
(*As if he had to cut something, he snatches up a hand-
ful of flowers—desperately.*) You must laugh,
Caligula ! (*He starts to lop off the flowers from
their stems with a savage intentness.*) Laugh !
Laugh ! Laugh ! (*Finally, impatiently, he cuts
off all the remaining with one stroke.*) Laugh !
(*He grinds the petals under his feet and breaks out
into a terrible hysterical giggle.*) Ha-ha——

CURTAIN

SCENE TWO

SCENE. *A midnight, months later. Immediately
inside the walls of Rome. In the foreground is
the portico of a temple between whose massive
columns one looks across a street on a lower level
to the high wall of Rome at the extreme rear.
In the centre of the wall is a great metal gate.
The night is thick and oppressive. In the sky
overhead lightning flashes and thunder rumbles
and crashes but there is no rain.*

    *Within the portico on rows of chairs placed
on a series of wide steps which are on each side,
members of the Senate are seated in their white
robes. High hanging lamps cast a wan light
over their faces. They are all masked in the
Roman mask, refined in them by nobility of blood*

64

*but at the same time with strength degenerated, corrupted by tyranny and debauchery to an exhausted cynicism. The three periods of Middle Age, Maturity and Old Age are represented in the types of the Self-Tortured, Introspective ; Proud, Self-Reliant ; the Servile, Hypocritical ; the Cruel, Revengeful ; and the Resigned, Sorrowful. The Senators are divided into two groups on each side, thirty in each. Seated in the middle of the lower of the three high broad stairs that lead to the level from which the columns rise is the Chorus of Senators, seven in number, facing front, in double-sized masks of the Servile, Hypocritical type of Old Age.*

*Lazarus, in his robe of white and gold, the aura of light surrounding his body seeming to glow more brightly than ever, stands in the rear at the edge of the portico, centre, gazing upward into the pall of sky beyond the wall. His figure appears in its immobility to be the statue of the god of the temple. Near him, but to the rear and to the left of him, facing right, Miriam is kneeling in her black robes, swaying backward and forward, praying silently with moving lips like a nun who asks for mercy for the sins of the world. She has grown much older, her hair is grey, her shoulders are bowed.*

*On the other side, placed similarly in relation to Lazarus and facing Miriam, Caligula is squatting on his hams on a sort of throne-chair of ivory and gold. He is dressed with foppish richness in extreme bright colours, a victory wreath around his head. He stares blinkingly and inquisitively at Lazarus, then at Miriam. He is half-drunk. A large figured goblet of gold is in his hand. A slave with an amphora of wine crouches on the steps by his chair. The slave wears a black negroid mask.*

*At the opening of the scene there is heard the steady tramp of departing troops, whose masks, helmets and armoured shoulders can be seen as they pass through the street before Lazarus to the gate beyond. Finally with a metallic clash the gate is shut behind them and there is a heavy and oppressive silence in which only the murmured prayers of Miriam are heard.*

CHORUS OF THE SENATE (*intones wearily, as if under a boring compulsion*). The Roman Senate.

Is the Roman Senate
The Mighty Voice
Of the Roman People,
As long as Rome is Rome.

CALIGULA (*as if he hadn't heard—sings hoarsely an old camp song of the Punic Wars, pounding with his goblet*). A bold legionary am I !
March, oh march on !
A Roman eagle was my daddy,
My mother was a drunken drabby.
Oh, march on to the wars !

Since lived that lady Leda—
March, oh march on !
Women have loved high-fliers,

And we are eagles of Rome !
Oh march on to the wars !

Comrades, march to the wars !
There's pretty girls in Carthage,
And wine to swill in Carthage,
So we must capture Carthage
And fight for Mother Rome !

> (*Holds out his goblet to be refilled. There is
> silence again. He stares at Lazarus with
> a sombre intentness. He says thickly.*)

The legions have gone, Lazarus.

> (*Lazarus gives no evidence of having heard
> him. Caligula gulps at his wine.
> The Senators begin to talk to each other
> in low voices.*)

FIRST SENATOR. How does that Jew make that
light come from him, I wonder ? It is a well-
contrived bit of magic.

SECOND SENATOR. What are we waiting for ?
A messenger came to me with Cæsar's command
that the Senate meet here at midnight.

THIRD SENATOR (*bored*). Some new whim of
Tiberius, naturally—(*with a meaning titter*)—of
rather I should say, unnaturally !

FOURTH SENATOR. Perhaps Cæsar has decided
to abolish our august body by a massacre in mass !

THIRD SENATOR (*yawning*). There was a feast
at Cinna's last night that lasted until this evening.
I could welcome my own murder as an excuse for
sleeping !

FIFTH SENATOR (*pompously*). Tiberius would not dare harm the Senate. He may mistreat individual Senators, but the Roman Senate is the Roman Senate !

CHORUS OF THE SENATE (*as before—wearily as if under a boring compulsion—intones*). While Rome is Rome
The Senate is the Senate—
The Mighty Voice of the Roman People.

FIRST SENATOR (*with the ghost of a laugh—wearily*). The Senate is an empty name—a pack of degenerate cowards with no trace of their ancient nobility or courage remaining—that and no more !

THIRD SENATOR (*flippantly*). You are too severe with yourself, Lucius !

(*A titter of laughter.*)

FIRST SENATOR (*wearily*). A degenerate coward. I am, I confess it. So are you too, Sulpicius —a hundred fold !—whether you admit it or not.

(*Sulpicius laughs weakly, without taking offence.*)

SIXTH SENATOR (*after a pause—sighing*). In truth, the Senate is not what it used to be. I can remember——

FIRST SENATOR. Let us forget, if we can ! (*Then impatiently.*) What are we doing here ?

SECOND SENATOR. I imagine it has something to do with the followers of this Lazarus encamped outside the wall. Probably the legions are to butcher them in their sleep.

SEVENTH SENATOR. And what part do we play
—official witnesses ? But how can we witness at
night and through a wall ? (*With bored resignation.*) Ah well, the moods of Tiberius are strange,
to say the least. But Cæsar is Cæsar.

CHORUS (*again with bored weariness as before*).
   Hail !
Cæsar is Cæsar—
The August One,
Prince of the Senate,
Tribune over Tribunes,
Consul of Consuls,
Supreme Pontiff,
Emperor of Rome,
God among gods.
Hail !

FIRST SENATOR (*after a pause of silence—dryly*).
Cæsar is a beast—and a madman !

FIFTH SENATOR (*pompously*). Respect, sir !
More respect for Cæsar !

THIRD SENATOR (*mockingly*). Or caution, Lucius. One of us might repeat your opinion to him.

FIRST SENATOR. You would if it would pay
you. But all my money is squandered. My
death is worthless to Tiberius. He would not
reward you. Moreover, you would not be
revenged on me, for I long for death.

THIRD SENATOR (*dryly*). Your stomach must
be out of order.

FIRST SENATOR. The times are out of order.

But let us change the subject. Is it true Tiberius has fled to Capri ?

FOURTH SENATOR. Yes. He was terrified by the multitude of laughing idiots who appeared to-day with that charlatan. (*He points to Lazarus.*)

SECOND SENATOR. There are thousands of them outside the wall. Cæsar refused to let them enter the city. The story is, this Lazarus was dead four days and then restored himself to life by magic.

FIRST SENATOR. I have a mind to question him. (*Calls as to a slave.*) You, there ! Jew, turr .und ! In the name of the Senate !

> (*Lazarus seems not to hear him. Lucius remarks with a weary smile.*)

So much for our authority !

SIXTH SENATOR (*with injured dignity*). What insolence ! (*In a rage.*) Ho, barbarian cur, turn round ! The Senate commands you !

> (*Lazarus does not seem to hear, but Caligula turns on them fiercely.*)

CALIGULA. Silence ! Leave him alone ! (*With insulting scorn.*) I, Caligula, command you !

> (*The Senators seem to shrink back from him in fear, all but Lucius, who answers with a mocking servility.*)

FIRST SENATOR. At least, grant us the boon to see this corpse's face, O gracious Gaius !

CALIGULA (*fixing his cruel, burning eyes on him—softly*). I heard you wish for death, Lucius. When I am Cæsar you shall scream and pray for it !

FIRST SENATOR (*dryly and haughtily*). You were bred in camp, Gaius. You should have learned more courage there along with your coarseness. But accept my gratitude for your warning. I shall take care to die before you become Cæsar—and life becomes too idiotic !

CALIGULA (*his grin becoming ferocious with cruelty*). No. You are too weak to kill yourself. Look at me, Lucius ! I am imagining what I shall have done to you !

> (*The Senators are now trembling. Even Lucius cannot repress a shudder of horror at the face glaring at him. Suddenly Caligula throws the cup from him and springs to his feet.*)

What good is wine if it cannot kill thought ? Lazarus ! It is time. I must give the signal ! The legions are waiting. It is Cæsar's command that they spare none of your followers. (*He has walked toward Lazarus.*)

MIRIAM (*stretches out her hands to Caligula imploringly*). Mercy ! Spare them who are so full of life and joy !

CALIGULA (*harshly*). For their joy I will revenge myself upon them ! Mercy ? If there is no death, then death is a mercy ! Ask that man ! (*He points accusingly to Lazarus.*) And why should you plead for them, Jewess ?   There are few Jews among them.   They are mostly those whom your people call idolators and would gladly see murdered.

MIRIAM (*with deep grief*).   I am a mother of dead children.   I plead for the mothers of those about to die.

CALIGULA (*contemptuously*).   Pah !   (*He turns from her and puts his hand on Lazarus' shoulder.*) Lazarus !   Do you hear ?   I must signal to the legions !

LAZARUS (*turns.   He has grown more youthful. He seems no more than thirty.   His face is exalted and calm and beautiful.   His eyes shine with an unearthly glory.   The Senators lean forward in their seats, fascinated by his face.   A low murmur of admiration comes from them.   Lazarus speaks commandingly*).   Wait !   I will awaken my beloved ones that their passing may be a symbol to the world that there is no death !

> (*He turns, throwing back his head and stretching up his arms, and begins to laugh low and tenderly, like caressing music at first, but gradually gaining in volume, becoming more and more intense and insistent, finally ending up on a triumphant, blood-stirring call to that ultimate attainment in which all prepossession with self is lost in an ecstatic affirmation of Life.   The voices of his Followers from beyond the wall, at first one by one, then several at a time, then*

*multitudes, join in his laughter.  Even
the Senators are drawn into it.  Now
every one of these is standing up,
stretching out his arms toward Lazarus,
laughing harshly and discordantly and
awkwardly in his attempt to laugh.
Terrific flashes of lightning and crashes
of thunder seem a responsive accom-
paniment from the heavens to this
laughter of thousands which throbs in
beating waves of sound in the air.
Mingled with the laughing from beyond
the wall comes the sound of singing and
the music of flutes and cymbals.  Miriam
has crawled on her knees to the edge of
the portico where her black figure of
grief is outlined below and to the left
of Lazarus, her arms raised outward
like the arms of a cross.)*

FOLLOWERS OF LAZARUS (*in a great chanting
singing chorus*).  Laugh !   Laugh !
There is only God !
Life is His Laughter !
We are His Laughter !
Fear is no more !
Death is dead !

CHORUS OF SENATORS (*taking it up in a tone
between chanting and their old solemn intoning*).
Laugh !   Laugh !
Fear is no more !
Death is dead !

ALL (*the multitude beyond the wall, all the Senators, every one except the never-laughing Miriam and Caligula and the Men of the Legions*). Laugh! Laugh!
Death is dead!

CALIGULA (*in a queer state of mingled exaltation and fear—hopping restlessly about from foot to foot—shouting*). The signal! Shall I give the signal to kill, Lazarus?

MEN OF THE LEGIONS (*following a brazen trumpet call, are suddenly heard from beyond the wall beginning to laugh their hoarse, bass laughter, a deeper note than all the others*). Laugh! Laugh!

CALIGULA (*listening—with dismay*). I hear the legions, Lazarus! They are laughing with them! (*He cries with a strange pitifulness and beseeching.*) You are playing me false, Lazarus! You are trying to evade death! You are trying to spare your people! You are small and weak like other men when the test comes! You give way to pity! Your great laughter becomes pitiful! (*Working himself into a rage.*) You are a traitor, Lazarus! You betray Cæsar! Have you forgotten I will be Cæsar? You betray me, Lazarus! (*He rushes to the edge and, making a megaphone of his hands, bellows.*) You on the wall! Sentry! It is I, Caligula! Kill!

> (*The brazen trumpets of the Legions sound from beyond the wall. He springs near Lazarus again, in a fiendish ecstasy,*

*dancing a hopping grotesque sword dance
behind him, chanting as he does so.)*

Kill !   Kill  laughter !   Kill  those  who  deny
Cæsar !   I will be Cæsar !   Kill those who deny
Death !   I  will  be  Death !   My  face  will  be
bright with blood !   My laughing face, Lazarus !
Laughing  because  men  fear  me !   My  face  of
victorious Fear !   Look at me !   I am laughing,
Lazarus !   *My*  laughter !   Laughter  of  gods
and Cæsars !   Ha-ha-ha-ha !

> *(He laughs, his laughter fanatically cruel and
> savage, forced from his lips with a
> desperate, destroying abandon.   For a
> moment, above all the chorus of other
> sounds, his voice fights to overcome that
> of Lazarus, whose laughter seems now to
> have attained the most exultant heights of
> spiritual affirmation.   Then Caligula's
> breaks into a cry of fear and a sob, and,
> casting his sword aside, he hides his face
> in his hands and cries beseechingly.)*

Forgive me !   I love you, Lazarus !   Forgive me !

> *(At this second the blaring trumpets of the
> Legions  are  heard  approaching  and
> their  great  bass  chorus  of  marching
> tramping laughter.)*

MEN  OF  THE  LEGIONS  (*chanting*).   Laugh !
Laugh !   Laugh !
Fear, no more !
Death, no more !
Death is dead !

75

(*There is now no sound of the singing or the laughter or music of Lazarus' Followers. Miriam rocks to and fro and raises a low wail of lamentation. The Senators cheer and shout as at a triumph.*)

CHORUS OF SENATORS (*saluting Lazarus*). Hail, Victor !
Hail, Divine One !
Thou hast slain fear !
Thou hast slain death !
Hail ! Triumph !

SENATORS. Hail ! Hail !
Slayer of Fear !
Slayer of Death !

(*The gate in the wall is clanged open. The returning Legions burst through and gather in a dense mob in the street below Lazarus, who looks down upon them, silent but smiling gently now. They stare at him with admiration. Only a sea of their masks can be seen, their eyes shining exultantly. Crassus, their general, ascends the steps until he stands a little below Lazarus. Their Chorus of Legionaries in double-sized masks climb to the step below Crassus, forming behind him. They are in the Period of Manhood, of the Simple, Ignorant Type. No weapons can be seen—only their masks and helmets and armour gleaming in the lightning flashes and in the flicker-*)

*ing light of torches. Their laughter
seems to shake the walls and make the
pillars of the temple dance.*)

CHORUS OF THE LEGIONS. Fear, no more !
Death, no more !
Death is dead !

LEGIONARIES (*echoing*). Laugh ! Laugh !
Laugh !
Death is dead !

CRASSUS (*raising his hand*). Silence ! (*They
obey. He turns to Lazarus and bows his head, falling on one knee, raising his right arm.*) Hail !

LEGIONARIES (*as one man—raising their arms*).
Hail !

CALIGULA (*suddenly pushes forward impudently
and strikes a grandiose attitude*). I am here, my
brave ones !

(*There is a roar of mocking laughter from the
Legionaries.*)

CRASSUS (*not unkindly*). Not you, Little Killer !
We hail the Great Laugher !

CALIGULA (*harshly*). Have you killed all his
followers ?

CRASSUS. No. They died. They did not
wait for our attack. They charged upon us,
laughing ! They tore our swords away from
us, laughing, and we laughed with them ! They
stabbed themselves, dancing as though it were a
festival ! They died, laughing, in one another's

arms ! We laughed, too, with joy because it seemed it was not they who died but death itself they killed ! (*He stops uncertainly, bowing to Lazarus, awkwardly.*) I do not understand this. I am a soldier. But there is a god in it somewhere ! For I know they were drunk, and so were we, with a happiness no mortal ever felt on earth before ! And death was dead ! (*In a sudden outburst as if he were drunk with excitement, he takes off his helmet and waves it.*) Hail, Deliverer ! Death is dead ! We left our swords with them ! What virtue in killing when there is no death ? Your foe laughs. The joke is on you. What a fool's game, eh ? One can only laugh ! Now we want peace to laugh in—to laugh at war ! Let Cæsars fight—that is all they are good for—and not much good for that !

CALIGULA (*frenziedly*). Silence, impious traitor !

CRASSUS (*smiling drunkenly*). Shut up, yourself, camp-brat ! Though you were Cæsar this minute I would laugh at you ! Your death is dead ! We will make Lazarus Cæsar ! What say you ? (*He appeals to the Soldiers.*)

CALIGULA. No !

CHORUS OF THE LEGIONS (*with laughing intoxication*). Hail, Lazarus Cæsar ! Hail !

LEGIONARIES. Lazarus Cæsar, hail !

CRASSUS (*appealing to Senate*). And you, Senators !

CHORUS OF SENATORS (*with the same joyous in-*

*toxication as the Soldiers*). Hail, Lazarus Cæsar !
Hail !

SENATORS. Lazarus Cæsar, hail !

CALIGULA (*piteously*). No, Lazarus ! Say no
for my sake !

LAZARUS (*with gay mockery*). What is—Cæsar ?

> (*He begins to laugh with mockery. All ex-
> cept Caligula and Miriam join in this
> laughter.*)

CRASSUS. Ha-ha ! What is Cæsar ? You
are right ! You deserve better from us. A
god ? How is that ? We will build you a
temple, Lazarus, and make you a god !

LAZARUS (*laughingly*). When men make gods,
there is no God ! (*He laughs. They all laugh.*)

CRASSUS (*with puzzled good-nature*). I do not
understand. But there is a god in it somewhere
—a god of peace—a god of happiness ! Perhaps
you are already he, eh ? Are you ? Well, never
mind now, remember our offer. Give us your
answer to-morrow. Good night to you !

LAZARUS (*as the Soldiers start to march away
behind Crassus, and the Senators turn to retire, he
stops them all for a moment with a gesture—with a
deep earnestness*). Wait ! When you awake to-
morrow, try to remember ! Remember that
death is dead ! Remember to laugh !

ALL (*as if taking an oath with one voice*). We
will remember, Lazarus !

79

CRASSUS (*making a sign to the regimental musicians jovially*). And we will laugh ! Play there !

> (*The bands crash out. The Legions tramp away.*)

CHORUS OF THE LEGIONS (*chanting to the music*).
Laugh ! Laugh ! Laugh !
Cæsar, no more !
War, no more !
Wounds, no more !
Death is dead !
Dead ! Dead ! Dead !

LEGIONARIES. Laugh ! Laugh ! Laugh !
Death is dead !
Dead ! Dead ! Dead !

CHORUS OF SENATORS (*following them*). Cæsar,
no more !
Fear, no more !
Death, no more !
Laugh ! Laugh ! Laugh !

SENATE (*elated, excited as a crowd of schoolboys going on a vacation. Marching after them*).
Laugh ! Laugh ! Laugh !
Death is dead !

> (*Lazarus, Miriam and Caligula remain.*)

LAZARUS (*with a great yearning*). If men would remember ! If they could ! (*He stares after them compassionately.*)

CALIGULA (*crouching beside Lazarus. Plucks at his robe humbly*). You will not laugh at Cæsar,

80

Lazarus, will you—when I am Cæsar ?   You will not laugh at gods when they make me a god ?

*(Lazarus does not answer.   Caligula forces a cruel vindictive smile.)*

I swear you shall not laugh at death when I am Death !   Ha-ha—— *(He starts to laugh harshly —then suddenly, terrified, slinks away and sidles off at right.)*

MIRIAM *(from where she kneels bowed with grief— brokenly).*   Those who have just died were like your children, Lazarus.   They believed in you and loved you.

LAZARUS.   And I loved them !

MIRIAM.   Then how could you laugh when they were dying ?

LAZARUS *(exultingly).*   Did they not laugh ? That was their victory and glory !   *(With more and more of a passionate, proud exultation.)*   Eye to eye with the Fear of Death, did they not laugh with scorn ?   " Death to old Death," they laughed !   " Once as squirming specks we crept from the tides of the sea.   Now we return to the sea !   Once as quivering flecks of rhythm we beat down from the sun.   Now we re-enter the sun !   Cast aside is our pitiable pretence, our immortal ego-hood, the holy lantern behind which cringed our Fear of the Dark !   Flung off is that impudent insult to life's nobility which gibbers : ' I, this Jew, this Roman, this noble or this slave, must survive in my pettiness for ever ! '   Away

81

with such cowardice of spirit ! We will to die !
We will to change ! Laughing we lived with
our gift, now with laughter give we back that gift
to become again the Essence of the Giver ! Dying
we laugh with the Infinite ! We are the Giver
and the Gift ! Laughing, we will our own
annihilation ! Laughing, we give our lives for
Life's sake—! (*He laughs up to heaven ecstatic-
ally.*) This must Man will as his end and his new
beginning ! He must conceive and desire his
own passing as a mood of eternal laughter and cry
with pride, " Take back, O God, and accept in
turn a gift from me, my grateful blessing for
Your gift—and see, O God, now I am laughing
with You ! I am Your laughter—and You are
mine ! " (*He laughs again, his laughter dying linger-
ingly and tenderly on his lips like a strain of music
receding into the silence over still waters.*)

MIRIAM (*with a sigh—meekly*). I cannot understand, Lazarus. (*Sadly.*) They were like your
children—and they have died. Must you not
mourn for them ?

LAZARUS (*gently*). Mourn ? When they
laughed ?

MIRIAM (*sadly*). They are gone from us. And
their mothers weep.

LAZARUS (*puts his arm around her and raises her
to her feet—tenderly*). But God, their Father,
laughs ! (*He kisses her on the forehead.*)

CURTAIN

# ACT THREE

SCENE. *Some days later—exterior of Tiberius' villa-palace at Capri. It is about two in the morning of a clear, black night. In the rear, the walls of the villa, which is built entirely of marble on the brow of a cliff, loom up with a startling clarity against the sky. The rear foreground is a marble terrace at the middle of which is a triumphal arch. On each side, leading up to it, are massive marble columns standing like the mummies of legionaries at attention. In the exact centre of the arch itself a cross is set up on which a full-grown male lion has been crucified. A lamp reflecting downward has been fixed at the top of the cross to light up an inscription placed over the lion's head. Below the steps to the terrace, in a line facing front, on each side of the cross, is the Chorus of the Guard in their double masks and gorgeous uniforms and armour. Their masks are the same as the Legionary Chorus of the previous scene.*

*The windows of the palace glow crimson-purple with the reflection of many shaded lamps. The sound of music in a strained theme of that joyless abandon which is vice is heard above a confused drunken clamour of voices, punctuated by the high, staccato laughter of women and youths. A squad of the Guard in the same uniforms as the Chorus, masked as all the Roman*

*Soldiers previously, enter from the left, front,
climbing up from the beach below. They are
commanded by a Centurion, Flavius. His
mask is that of a typical young patrician officer.
They are followed by Lazarus and Miriam.
Caligula walks behind, his drawn sword in his
hand. He is in a state of queer conflicting
emotion, seeming to be filled with a nervous
dread and terror of everything about him, while
at the same time perversely excited and elated
by his own morbid tension. Lazarus, looking
no more than twenty-five, haloed in his own
mystic light, walks in a deep, detached serenity.*

*Miriam, in black, her hair almost white
now, her figure bowed and feeble, seems more
than ever a figure of a sad, resigned mother of
the dead. The soldiers form in line with the
columns.*

FLAVIUS (*saluting Caligula—with an awed glance
at Lazarus*). I will announce your coming—(*as
if in spite of himself he bows awkwardly to Lazarus*)
—and that of this man. Cæsar was not expecting you so soon, I think.

CALIGULA (*forcing a light tone*). Lazarus
laughed and the galley slaves forgot their fetters
and made their oars fly as if they were bound
for the Blessed Isles of Liberty ! (*Then with an
ironic smile.*) But you need not tell Tiberius that,
good Flavius. Say it was due to my extreme
zeal.

FLAVIUS (*smiles with respectful understanding.*
84

*Caligula nods in dismissal. Flavius turns to go—
apologetically).* You may have to wait. I dare
not speak before he questions me.

> (*Flavius salutes and hastens to the villa,
> walking under an arm of the cross un-
> concernedly without an upward glance.
> As they follow him with their eyes
> Caligula and Miriam see the lion for
> the first time. He steps back with a
> startled exclamation. She gives a cry
> of horror and covers her eyes with her
> hands to shut out the sight.*)

LAZARUS (*immediately puts his arms around her
protectingly*). What is it, Beloved ?

> (*She hides her face on his breast, pointing
> toward the lion with a trembling hand.*)

CALIGULA (*pointing—curiously now, but with entire callousness*). This lion they have crucified.
Are you frightened, Jewess ? (*With a cruel
laugh.*) My grandfather frequently plants whole
orchards of such trees, but usually they bear
human fruit !

MIRIAM (*with a shudder*). Monster !

CALIGULA (*with genuine surprise—turning to her*).
Who ? Why ? (*He approaches the cross and
stares at it moodily.*) But why did he have it
placed here where he knew you must pass ?
Tiberius does not go to such pains to frighten
women. (*His eyes fasten on the inscription above
the lion's head.*) Aha ! I see ! (*He reads.*)

"From the East, land of false gods and superstition, this lion was brought to Rome to amuse Cæsar." (*A silence. Caligula shrugs his shoulders, turning away—lightly.*) A lesson for you, Lazarus. An example for other lions—not to roar—or laugh—at Cæsar ! (*He gives a harsh laugh.*) Tiberius must be terribly afraid of you. (*Then sombrely.*) You should never have come here. I would have advised you not to—but what are you to me ? My duty, if I wish to become Cæsar, is to Cæsar. Besides, you are no fool. Evidently you must desire your own death. Last night *you* might have been Cæsar. The legions were yours.

LAZARUS (*smiling without bitterness—with a sad comprehension*). But this morning the legions had forgotten. They only remembered—to go out and pick up their swords ! They also pillaged the bodies a little, as their right, believing now that they had slain them ! (*This last a bit bitterly.*)

CALIGULA (*tauntingly*). The legions did slay them ! It was only by some magician's trick you made them think your followers killed themselves.

LAZARUS (*not answering him—ironically to himself*). It is too soon. Men still need their swords to slash at ghosts in the dark. Men, those haunted heroes ! (*He laughs softly.*)

CALIGULA (*irritably*). What are you laughing at ?

86

LAZARUS. At Lazarus when I find him feeling wronged because men are men ! (*He laughs again, softly and musically.*)

CALIGULA (*again taunting brutally*). You may be in his place soon ! (*He points to the lion.*) Will you laugh then ?

(*Miriam gives a cry of terror.*)

LAZARUS (*calmly*). Yes. (*Then humbly, bowing his head.*) I will laugh with the pride of a beggar set upon the throne of Man !

CALIGULA (*sneeringly*). You boast. (*Then as Lazarus does not answer, touching the lion with intentional provoking brutality.*) This one from Africa seems almost gone. They do not last as long as men.

LAZARUS (*walks up the steps to the cross and, stretching to his full height, gently pushes the lion's hair out of its eyes—tenderly*). Poor brother ! Cæsar avenges himself on you because of me. Forgive me your suffering !

CALIGULA (*with a start backward—with frightened awe*). Gods ! He licks your hand ! I could swear he smiles—with his last breath ! (*Then with relief.*) Now he is dead !

LAZARUS (*gently*). There is no death.

CALIGULA (*pointing to the lion*). What is that then ?

LAZARUS. Your fear of life.

CALIGULA (*impatiently*). Bah ! (*Then sombrely.*)

A little fear is useful even for lions—or teachers of laughter if they wish to laugh long ! (*Then with a sudden exasperation.*) Escape now, you fool, while there is still time !

LAZARUS (*laughing softly*). Escape—what ?

CALIGULA (*in a frenzy*). You know, you ass, you lunatic ! Escape death ! Death ! Death ! (*To Miriam.*) You, woman ! Talk to him ! Do you want him nailed up like that ?

MIRIAM (*with a pitiful cry*). Lazarus ! Come ! Caligula will help us !

CALIGULA (*harshly*). You presume, Jewess ! I have no wish to die ! (*Then with his wry smile.*) But I will turn my back—and shut my eyes—— (*He walks away to left.*)

MIRIAM (*beseechingly*). Lazarus ! I could no bear that aching hunger of my empty heart if you should die again !

LAZARUS (*coming to her—tenderly*). I will not leave you ! Believe in me ! (*He kisses her forehead tenderly.*)

MIRIAM (*after a pause—slowly and lamentingly*). I wish we were home, Lazarus. This Roman world is full of evil. These skies threaten. These hearts are heavy with hatred. There is a taint of blood in the air that poisons the breath of the sea. These columns and arches and thick walls seem waiting to fall, to crush these rotten men and then to crumble over the bones that raised them until both are dust. It is a world deadly to your joy, Lazarus. Its pleasure is a gorging of dirt, its fulfilled desire a snoring in a sty in the mud among swine. Its will is so sick that it must kill in order to be aware of life at all. I wish we were home, Lazarus. I begin to feel horror gnawing at my breast. I begin to know the torture of the fear of death, Lazarus—not of my death but of yours—not of the passing of your man's body but of the going away from me of your laughter which is to me as my son, my little boy !

LAZARUS (*soothing her*). Be comforted, Beloved. Your fear shall never be !

MIRIAM. On the hills near Bethany you might pray at noon and laugh your boy's laughter in the sun and there would be echoing laughter from the sky and up from the grass and distantly from the shining sea. We would adopt children whose parents the Romans had butchered, and their laughter would be around me in my home where I cooked and weaved and sang. And in the dawn at your going out, and in the evening on your return, I would hear in the hushed air the bleating of sheep and the tinkling of many little bells and your voice. And my heart would know peace.

LAZARUS (*tenderly*). Only a little longer ! There is God's laughter on the hills of space, and the happiness of children, and the soft healing of innumerable dawns and evenings, and the blessing of peace !

CALIGULA (*looks around at Lazarus impatiently. Then he makes a beckoning gesture to Miriam*). Ssstt !

*(Wonderingly she leaves Lazarus' side and follows him. Lazarus remains, his eyes fixed on the cross, directly in front of it. Caligula speaks gruffly to Miriam with a sneer.)*

Jewess, your Lazarus is mad, I begin to think. *(Then confusedly but helplessly inquisitive and confiding—bursting out.)* What is it troubles me about him ? What makes me dream of him ? Why should I—love him, Jewess ? Tell me ! You love him, too. I do not understand this. Why, wherever he goes, is there joy ? You heard even the galley slaves laugh and clank time with their chains ! *(Then with exasperation.)* And yet why can I not laugh, Jewess ?

MIRIAM *(in a tone of hushed grief)*. I may not laugh either. My heart remains a little dead with Lazarus in Bethany. The miracle could not revive all his old husband's life in my wife's heart.

CALIGULA *(disgustedly)*. What answer is that to me ? *(Then brusquely.)* But I called you to put you on your guard. *(He points.)* There is death in there—Tiberius' death, a kind from which no miracles can recall one ! *(He smiles his twisted smile.)* Since Lazarus will not help himself, you must protect him. I will not, for once in there I am *(mockingly)* the heir of Cæsar, and you are scum whom I will kill at his order as I would two beetles ! So keep watch ! Taste first of what he eats—even were I the one to give it to him !

LAZARUS (*suddenly laughs softly*).   Why do you delight in believing evil of yourself, Caligula ?

CALIGULA (*flying into a queer rage*).   You lie ! I am what I am !  (*With grandiose pride.*)  What could you know of a Cæsar ?

LAZARUS (*still laughing with an affectionate understanding.*)  What—I know !

> (*As he finishes speaking all the sound of music and voices from the house ceases abruptly and there is a heavy silence.*)

MIRIAM (*shaking her head and turning away sadly*).  This is too far, Lazarus.  Let us go home.

CALIGULA (*harshly*).  Sst !  Do you hear ? Flavius has told Cæsar.  (*Grimly forcing a harsh snicker.*)  Now we will soon know——

> (*There is the sudden blaring of a trumpet from within the palace.  A wide door is flung open and a stream of reddish light comes out against which the black figures of several men are outlined. The door is shut again quickly.  Several Slaves bearing lamps on poles escort the patrician, Marcellus, forward to the arch.  He passes under the crucified lion without a glance—then stands, cool and disdainful, to look about him.  He is a man of about thirty-five, wearing the type mask of a Roman patrician to which are added the dissipated courtier's*)

*characteristics of one who leans to evil
more through weakness than any in-
stinctive urge. He is dressed richly.
His smile is hypocritical and his eyes are
hard and cold, but when they come to
rest on Lazarus he gives a start of
genuine astonishment.)*

CALIGULA (*who has moved to Lazarus' side
defensively—in a quick whisper*). Beware of this
man, Lazarus ! (*Then advancing—with a con-
descending hauteur.*) Greeting, Marcellus !

MARCELLUS (*in an ingratiating tone*). Greeting,
Gaius. I have a message from Cæsar for the man
called Lazarus.

LAZARUS (*calmly*). I am Lazarus.

MARCELLUS (*makes a deep bow—flatteringly*). I
had surmised it, sir. Although I cannot pretend
to virtue in myself at least I may claim the merit
of recognizing it in others. (*He advances toward
Lazarus, smiling, with one hand kept hidden beneath
his cloak.*)

CALIGULA (*stepping between them—sharply*).
What is your message ?

MARCELLUS (*surprised—placatingly*). I am sorry,
Gaius, but it was Cæsar's command I speak to
Lazarus alone.

CALIGULA (*fiercely*). And then, Marcellus ?

(*Marcellus shrugs his shoulders and smiles
deprecatingly.*)

LAZARUS (*with a compelling dignity*). Let him speak. (*Inclining his head to Marcellus—strangely.*) Over here where it is dark you will not be seen— nor see yourself. (*He walks to the darkness at right.*)

CALIGULA (*turning his back on them, with angry boyish resentfulness that is close to tears*). Idiot ! Go and die, then !

MIRIAM (*with a terrified cry*). Lazarus ! (*She starts to go to him.*)

LAZARUS (*motioning her to remain where she is— gently*). Believe, Beloved ! (*He turns his back on them all and stands waiting.*)

MARCELLUS (*stares at Lazarus—then over his shoulder at Caligula—uncertainly*). What does he mean, Gaius ? (*Then suddenly putting on a brave front, he strides up behind Lazarus.*) Cæsar wished me to bid you welcome, to tell you how much regard he has for you, but he desired me to ask whether you propose to laugh here—in Cæsar's palace ? He has heard that you laugh at death— that you have caused others to laugh—even his legionaries. (*A pause, Marcellus remains behind Lazarus' back, the latter standing like a victim.*) Briefly, Cæsar requires your pledge that you will not laugh. Will you give it ? (*He frees his dagger from under his robe. A pause. Arrogantly.*) I am waiting ! Answer when Cæsar commands ! (*Then angrily, baffled.*) I will give you while I count three—or take your silence as a refusal ! One ! Two ! Three !

(*He raises his hand to stab Lazarus in the
back. Miriam stifles a scream. At
the same instant, Lazarus begins to
laugh, softly and affectionately. Marcellus stops, frozen in mid-action,
the dagger upraised. Caligula has
whirled around and stands staring, a
smile gradually coming to his face.
Lazarus turns, his laughter grown a
trifle louder, and faces Marcellus. The
latter steps back from him, staring open-
mouthed, fascinated. His arm sinks to
his side. The dagger falls from his
fingers. He smiles back at Lazarus—
the curious, sheepish, bashful smile of
one who has fallen in love and been
discovered.*)

LAZARUS (*going to him, puts both hands on his
shoulders and looks in his eyes, laughing affectionately—then quizzically.*) Here is another one who
believes in death ! But soon you will laugh with
life ! I see it in your eyes. Farewell, Marcellus !

(*He turns away from him and walks, laughing, toward the arch in rear. With
bowed head the black-robed figure of
Miriam follows him. Marcellus hides
his face in his hands, half-sobbing, and
half-laughing hysterically. Lazarus
pauses before the cross for a moment—
raises his hand as if blessing the dead
lion, then passes below it, moving*

*slowly on toward the palace in the rear.
His laughter rises with more and more
summoning power. The files of the
Guard, as he passes them, two by two
join in his laughter, saluting him as if
in spite of themselves.*)

CALIGULA (*sidling up to Marcellus, cruel and
mocking*). Are you weeping, Marcellus ? Laugh
at that blundering fool, yourself ! What will
Cæsar say ? Will he laugh when he has your
body broken one bone at a time with hammers ?
Why did you not kill ? For shame ! A patrician
exposed to laughter by a Jew ! Poor craven !
Why could you not strike ? There *must* be
death ! Coward ! Why did you not stab ?
(*Then in a queer awed whisper.*) I know ! Was
it not because of a sudden you loved him and
could not ?

MARCELLUS (*suddenly—eagerly*). Yes ! That
was it ! I loved him !

CALIGULA (*craftily and cruelly*). You were
about to murder him !

MARCELLUS (*tortured with remorse*). No ! No !
How could I ? What infamy ! (*Cries tearfully.*)
Forgive me, Lazarus !

CALIGULA (*with vindictive insistence*). Judge
yourself ! (*He takes up the dagger.*) Here is your
dagger ! Avenge him on yourself !

MARCELLUS (*trying to laugh*). Ha-ha— Yes !
(*He stabs himself and falls. Suddenly his laughter*

95

*is released.*)  I laugh !   You are a fool, Caligula !
There is no death !   (*He dies, laughing up at the
sky.*)

CALIGULA (*kicks his body with savage cruelty*).
You lie !  (*Then suddenly kneels and bends over it
imploringly.*)   Tell me you lie, Marcellus !   Do
me that mercy !—and when I am Cæsar, I——

> (*He begins to weep like a frightened boy, his
> head in his hands.   Meanwhile Laz-
> arus has arrived with Miriam at the
> steps  before  the  door  of  the  palace.
> As he starts to ascend these, the crimson-
> purple lights of the many windows of
> the palace go out one by one as if fleeing
> in terror from the laughter which now
> beats at the walls.*)

CHORUS OF THE GUARD.   Fear, no more !
Death, no more !
Laugh !   Laugh !   Laugh !
Death is dead !

ALL THE GUARDS (*now all in a great chorus, rais-
> ing their spears aloft and saluting Lazarus
> as if they were his own triumphal bodyguard*).
> Laugh !   Laugh !   Laugh !
Death is dead !

> (*Lazarus has ascended the steps.   He walks
> into the black archway of the darkened
> palace, his figure radiant and unearthly
> in his own light.   Miriam follows him.
> They disappear in the darkness.   There
> is a pause of dead silence.*)

CALIGULA (*raises his head uneasily, looks back toward the palace, jumps to his feet in a panic of terror, and runs toward the palace door, calling*). Lazarus! Wait! I will defend you! There is death inside there—death! Beware, Lazarus!

CHORUS OF THE GUARD (*as the laughter of Lazarus is heard again from the dark palace*). Laugh! Laugh! Laugh!
Death is dead!

ALL THE GUARDS. Dead! Dead! Dead!
Death is dead!

CURTAIN

SCENE TWO

SCENE. *The banquet hall in the palace of Tiberius— an immense high-ceilinged room. In the rear, centre, is a great arched doorway. Smaller arches in the middle of the side walls lead into other rooms. Long couches are placed along the walls at right and left, and along the rear wall on either side of the arch. Before these couches, a series of narrow tables is set. In the centre of the room on a high dais is the ivory and gold chair of Cæsar, a table in front of it, couches for him to recline on at either side. On this table, and on all the tables for his guests, gold lamps with shades of crimson-purple are placed.*

*Reclining on the couches on the right are*

D       97

*young women and girls, on the left, youths of an
equal number.*

*The masks are based on the Roman masks of
the periods of Boyhood (or Girlhood), Youth, and
Young Manhood (or Womanhood), and there
are seven individuals of each period and sex
in each of the three types of the Introspective,
Self-Tortured ; the Servile, Hypocritical ; and
the Cruel, Revengeful—a crowd of forty-two in
all. There is a distinctive character to the
masks of each sex, the stamp of an effeminate
corruption on all the male, while the female have
a bold, masculine expression. The male masks
are a blotched heliotrope in shade. These
youths wear female wigs of curled wire like
frizzed hair of a yellow gold. They are
dressed in women's robes of pale heliotrope,
they wear anklets and bracelets and necklaces.
The women are dressed as males in crimson or
deep purple. They also wear wire wigs but
of straight hair cut in short boyish mode, dyed
either deep purple or crimson. Those with
crimson hair are dressed in purple, and vice
versa. The female voices are harsh, strident,
mannish—those of the youths affected, lisping,
effeminate. The whole effect of these two
groups is of sex corrupted and warped, of invented lusts and artificial vices.*

*The Chorus in this scene and the next is com-
posed of three males and four females—the males
in the period of Youth, one in each of the types
represented, and three of the females in similar*

*type-period masks.   The fourth female is masked
in the period of Womanhood in the Proud,
Self-Reliant type.   They sit, facing front in
their double-sized masks, on the side steps of the
dais, four on right, three on left.*

*Pompeia, a Roman noblewoman, the favour-
ite mistress of Cæsar, sits at front, right.*

*She wears a half-mask on the upper part of
her face, olive-coloured with the red of blood
smouldering through, with great, dark, cruel
eyes—a dissipated mask of intense evil beauty,
of lust and perverted passion.   Beneath the
mask, her own complexion is pale, her gentle,
girlish mouth is set in an expression of agonized
self-loathing and weariness of spirit.   Her body
is strong and beautiful.   Her wig and dress are
purple.*

*Tiberius Cæsar stands on the dais, dressed in
deep purple, fringed and ornamented with
crimson and gold.   An old man of seventy-six,
tall, broad and corpulent but of great muscular
strength still despite his age, his shiny white
cranium rises like a polished shell above his
half-masked face.   This mask is a pallid purple
blotched with darker colour, as if the imperial
blood in his veins had been sickened by age and
debauchery.   The eyes are protuberant, leering,
cynical slits, the long nose, once finely modelled,
now gross and thickened, the forehead lowering
and grim.   Beneath the mask, his own mouth
looks as incongruous as Caligula's.   The lips
are thin and stern and self-contained—the lips*

*of an able soldier-statesman of rigid probity. His chin is forceful and severe. The complexion of his own skin is that of a healthy old campaigner.*

*As the curtain rises, slaves are hurriedly putting out the many lamps. From outside, the laughter of Lazarus rises on the deep ground swell of the Guard's laughter. The walls and massive columns seem to reverberate with the sound. In the banquet-room all are listening fascinatedly. Every reaction, from the extreme of panic fear or hypnotized ecstasy to a feigned cynical amusement or a pretended supercilious indifference, is represented in their frozen attitudes. Tiberius stands, shrinking back, staring at the doorway in the rear with superstitious dread. A squad of the Guard surround the dais, commanded by Flavius.*

TIBERIUS (*in a strained voice shaken by apprehension and awe*). Marcellus ! Strike him down ! Stab him !

SOLDIERS OF THE GUARD (*from without*). Laugh ! Laugh ! Laugh !
Death is dead !

TIBERIUS (*as he suddenly sees the shining figure of Lazarus appear at the end of the dark hall beyond the archway*). Gods ! Flavius, look ! (*He points with a shaking finger. Flavius has leaped up to his side.*)

FLAVIUS (*not without dread himself*). That is the man, Cæsar.

TIBERIUS. Man ? Say a dæmon ! (*To the slaves who are turning out the few remaining lamps.*) Quick ! Darkness ! (*He puts out the lamp on his table himself. Then as nothing is seen but the light from the approaching Lazarus.*) Flavius ! Stand here in my place ! It will think you are Cæsar ! (*He clumps heavily down the steps of the dais.*) Guards ! Here ! Cover me with your shields !

> (*He goes to the extreme right corner, front, and crouches there. His Guards follow him. They hold their shields so that they form a wall around him and half over him. Then Caligula's voice is heard screaming above the chorus of laughter as he enters the hall behind Lazarus.*)

CALIGULA. Beware of death ! I will defend you, Lazarus ! (*He is seen to rush past Lazarus, flourishing his sword and comes running into the room, shouting.*) Cæsar ! Dare not to murder Lazarus ! (*He leaps to the dais and up its steps in a frenzy.*) Dare not, I say ! (*He stabs Flavius with a savage cry.*) Ah ! (*Then as the body of Flavius falls heavily and rolls down the steps at right, he begins to laugh, at first a clear laughter of selfless joy, sounding startlingly incongruous from him.*) I have saved you, Lazarus—at the risk of my own life—and now, hear me, I can laugh !

> (*Lazarus appears in the archway, Miriam behind him. He stops laughing and*)

*immediately there is silence, except for
Caligula. Lazarus casts a luminous
glow over the whole room in which the
masked faces appear distorted and livid.
Caligula stands with upraised sword
by the chair of Cæsar. Suddenly his
laughter cracks, changes, becomes full of
his old fear and blood-lust.)*

CALIGULA. Ha-ha-ha ! See, Lazarus ! (*He
points to the body of Flavius with his sword.*) Welcome in the name of Cæsar, now Cæsar is slain
and I am Cæsar !

> *(He assumes the absurd grandiose posture of
> his imperial posing. No one looks at
> him or hears him. Their eyes are on
> Lazarus as he moves directly to where
> Tiberius crouches behind the shields of
> the Guards. Miriam follows him.
> Caligula turns and stares toward him,
> and then down at the body of Flavius
> and back, in a petrified, bewildered
> stupor. Lazarus steps up beside Tibe-
> rius. The Guards make way for him
> fearfully.)*

TIBERIUS (*feeling his nearness—straightening
himself with a certain dignity*). Strike ! I have
been a soldier. Thou canst not make me fear
death, Dæmon ! (*He draws his toga over his
face.*)

LAZARUS (*smiling gently*). Then fear not fear,
Tiberius !

(*He reaches out and pulls back the toga from his face. Tiberius looks into his eyes, at first shrinkingly, then with growing reassurance, his own masked face clearly revealed now in the light from Lazarus.*)

TIBERIUS (*at first falteringly*). So—thou art not evil? Thou art not come to contrive my murder? (*As Lazarus smilingly shakes his head, Tiberius frowns.*) Then why dost thou laugh against Cæsar? (*Then bitterly—with a twisted attempt at a smile.*) Yet I like thy laughter. It is young. Once I laughed somewhat like that— so I pardon thee. I will even laugh at thee in return. Ha-ha! (*His laughter is cold, cruel and merciless as the grin of a skeleton.*)

CALIGULA (*who has been staring in a bewildered stupor from Tiberius, whom he thought he had killed, to the body of Flavius—quaking with terror now as if this laugh was meant for him, drops to his knees, his sword clattering down the steps to the floor*). Mercy, Tiberius! I implore you forgive your Caligula!

TIBERIUS (*not understanding. Fixing his eyes on Caligula with a malevolent irony*). Come down from my throne, Caligula. (*Caligula slinks down warily.*) You are too impatient. But I must pardon you, too—for where could I find another heir so perfect for serving my spite upon mankind? (*He has walked toward the throne while he is speaking, Caligula backing away from him.*

*Lazarus remains where he is, Miriam beside
and to the rear of him. Tiberius, his eyes fixed on
Caligula, stumbles against the body of Flavius. He
gives a startled gasp and shrinks back, calling.*)
Lights ! A light here ! (*A crowd of masked
slaves obey his orders. One runs to him with a
lantern. He looks down at Flavius' corpse—half to
himself.*) I did wisely to stand him in my place.
(*To Caligula—with sinister emphasis.*) Too impatient, my loving grandchild ! Take care lest
I become impatient also—with your impatience !

> (*Caligula shudders and backs away to the
> extreme left corner, front, where he
> crouches on his haunches as incon-
> spicuously as possible. Tiberius sud-
> denly whirls around as if he felt a
> dagger at his back.*)

TIBERIUS.   Where—?   (*Seeing Lazarus where
he had been—with relief—staring at his face now
that the room is flooded with the purplish-crimson
glow from all the lamps.*) Ah, you are there.
More lights ! Darkness leads men into error.
My heir mistakes a man for Cæsar, and Cæsar, it
appears, has mistaken a man for a dæmon !
(*Scrutinizing him—with sinister finality.*) I can
deal with men.   I know them well.   Too well !
(*He laughs grimly.*) Therefore I hate them. (*He
mounts the steps of the dais and sits on the couch at
left of table—staring at Lazarus, wonderingly.*)
But you seem—something other than man !
That light ! (*Then he forces a harsh laugh.*) A

trick ! I had forgotten you are a magician.
(*Arrogantly.*) Stand there, Jew. I would question you about your magic. (*Smilingly Lazarus
ascends to where Tiberius points at the top of the dais.
Miriam remains standing at the foot. Tiberius
stares for a while with sombre intensity at Lazarus.*)
They say you died and have returned from death ?

LAZARUS (*smiling—as if he were correcting a
child*). There is no death, Cæsar.

TIBERIUS (*with a sneer of scepticism but with an
underlying eagerness*). I have heard you teach that
folly. (*Then threateningly.*) You shall be given
full opportunity to prove it ! (*A pause—then in
a low voice, bending down toward Lazarus.*) Do
you foretell the future ? (*Trembling but with a
pretence of carelessness.*) Must I die soon ?

LAZARUS (*simply*). Yes, Cæsar.

TIBERIUS (*jumping up with a shuddering start*).
Soon ? Soon ? (*Then his fear turning to rage.*)
What do you say ? Vile Jew, do you dare
threaten me with death ! (*Lazarus, looking into
his eyes, begins to laugh softly. Tiberius sinks back
on his couch, fighting to control himself—confusedly.*)
Laugh not, I ask you. I am old. It is not
seemly. (*Lazarus ceases his low laughter. A
pause. Tiberius broods—then suddenly.*) And
you were really dead ? (*He shudders.*) Come
nearer. I need to watch your face. I have
learned to read the lies in faces. A Cæsar gets
much practice—from childhood on—too much !

D*  105

(*With awe.*) Your eyes are dark with death. While I watch them, answer me, what cured thee of death ?

LAZARUS (*gently*). There is only life, Cæsar. (*Then gaily mocking but compellingly.*) And laughter ! Look ! Look well into my eyes, old Reader of Lies, and see if you can find aught in them that is not life—and laughter !

> (*He laughs softly. A ripple of soft laughter from the motionless figures about the room echoes his. Tiberius stares into his eyes. In the silence that ensues Pompeia gets up and walks over to the dais. She stops to stare for a moment with cruel contempt at Miriam, then stands and looks up at Lazarus, trying in vain to attract his or Cæsar's attention. Failing in this, she passes over and sits beside Caligula, whose attention is concentrated on Lazarus.*)

POMPEIA. I admire your strange magician, Caligula.

CALIGULA (*without looking at her*). He is no magician. He is something like a god.

POMPEIA (*longingly*). His laughter is like a god's. He is strong. I love him.

CALIGULA (*turning to her—coarsely*). Do not waste your lust. He is faithful to his wife, I warn you.

POMPEIA (*she points to Miriam*). Not that ugly slave ?

CALIGULA. Yes. And yet, on our journey, whole herds of women—and many as beautiful as you, Pompeia—threw themselves on him and begged for his love.

POMPEIA (*her voice hardening*). And he ?

CALIGULA. He laughed—and passed on. (*She starts. Caligula goes on wonderingly.*) But they seemed as happy as if his laughter had possessed them ! You are a woman. Tell me, how could that be ?

POMPEIA (*her voice cruel*). He shall not laugh at me !

CALIGULA (*tauntingly*). I will bet a string of pearls against your body for a night that he does.

POMPEIA (*defiantly*). Done ! (*Then she laughs —a low, cruel laugh—staring at Miriam.*) So he loves that woman ?

CALIGULA (*curiously*). What are you planning ?

POMPEIA. I shall offer her the fruit Cæsar preserves for those he fears.

CALIGULA (*with a careless shrug*). You will not win his love by killing her.

POMPEIA. I no longer want his love. I want to see him suffer, to hear his laughter choke in his throat with pain ! (*She speaks with more and more voluptuous satisfaction.*) Then *I* shall laugh ! (*She laughs softly and steps forward.*)

CALIGULA (*concernedly*). Stop. I am his protector. (*Then suddenly.*) But what is the Jewess to me ? (*With more and more of a spirit of perverse cruelty.*) Do it, Pompeia ! His laughter is too cruel to us ! We must save death from him !

POMPEIA (*walks to the dais which she ascends slowly until she stands by Cæsar's couch behind him, confronting Lazarus. But the two men remain unmindful of her presence. Tiberius continues to stare into Lazarus' eyes. His whole body is now relaxed, at rest, a dreamy smile softens his thin, compressed mouth. Pompeia leans over and takes a peach from the bowl of fruit on Cæsar's table and, taking Tiberius' hand in her other, she kisses it and calls insistently*). Cæsar. It is I, Pompeia.

> (*Lazarus does not look at her. She stares at him defiantly. Tiberius blinks his eyes in a daze.*)

TIBERIUS (*dreamily*). Yes ! A cloud came from a depth of sky—around me, softly, warmly, and the cloud dissolved into the sky, and the sky into peace ! (*Suddenly springing to his feet and staring about him in a confused rage—clutching Pompeia by the shoulder and forcing her to her knees.*) What are you doing here ?

POMPEIA. Forgive your loving slave ! I grew afraid this magician had put you under a spell. (*She stares at Lazarus, her words challenging him.*)

TIBERIUS (*confusedly, sinking back on his couch and releasing her*). A spell ? Could it be he laid a dream of death upon me, leading me to death ? (*He trembles timorously—appealing to Lazarus.*) Whatever magic thou didst to me, Dæmon, I beseech thee undo it !

LAZARUS (*smiling*). Do you fear peace ?

POMPEIA (*harshly and insolently*). Mock not at Cæsar, dog ! (*Lazarus continues to smile. His eyes remain on Cæsar. He seems absolutely unaware of Pompeia. This enrages her the more against him. She speaks tauntingly to Tiberius.*) Surely, Cæsar, this magician must have powerful charms, since he dares to mock Tiberius to his face !

TIBERIUS (*stung*). Be still ! (*Then in a low tone to her.*) Do you not know this Lazarus died and then by his magic rose from his tomb.

POMPEIA (*scornfully*). To believe that, I must have seen it, Cæsar !

TIBERIUS (*impatiently*). Do you think I would believe without good evidence ? I have had them take the statements of many witnesses. The miracle was done in conjunction with another Jew acting as this man's tool. This other Jew, the report states, could not possibly have possessed any magic power Himself, for Pilate crucified Him a short time after and He died in pain and weakness within a few hours. But this Lazarus laughs at death !

LAZARUS (*looks up, smiling with ironical bitterness*). Couldst Thou but hear, Jesus ! And men shall keep on in panic nailing Man's soul to the cross of their fear until in the end they do it to avenge Thee, for Thine Honour and Glory ! (*He sighs sadly—then after a struggle overcoming himself—with exultance.*) Yes ! (*His eyes fall again to Tiberius and he smiles.*) Yes ! Yes to the stupid as to the wise ! To what is understood and to what cannot be understood ! Known and unknown ! Over and over ! For ever and ever ! Yes ! (*He laughs softly to himself.*)

TIBERIUS (*with superstitious dread*). What dost thou mean, Dæmon ?

POMPEIA (*with indignant scorn*). Let him prove there is no death, Cæsar ! (*She appeals to the company, who straighten up on their couches with interest.*)

CHORUS (*chant demandingly*). Let him prove there is no death !
We are bored !

CROWD (*echoing*). Prove there is no death !
We are bored, Cæsar !

TIBERIUS (*waits to see what Lazarus will say— then as he says nothing, plucking up his courage—his cruelty aroused*). Do you hear, Lazarus ?

POMPEIA. Make him perform his miracle again !

CHORUS (*as before*). Let him perform a miracle !
We are bored, Cæsar !

CROWD (*they now stand up and coming from behind their tables, move forward toward the dais*). A miracle !
We are bored !

POMPEIA. Let him raise someone from the dead !

CHORUS (*chanting with a pettish insistence*). Raise the dead !
We are bored !

CROWD (*echoing—grouping in a big semicircle as of spectators in a theatre, around and to the sides of the dais, one sex on each side. Caligula moves in from the left in front of them. They form in three ranks, the first squatting on their hams like savages (as Caligula does), the second rank crouching over them, the third leaning over the second, all with a hectic, morbid interest*). We are bored !
Raise the dead !

POMPEIA (*with a cruel smile*). I have thought of a special test for him, Cæsar. (*She whispers in Cæsar's ear and points to Miriam and the fruit in her hand.*) And he must laugh !

TIBERIUS (*with a harsh, cruel chuckle*). Yes, I shall command him to laugh ! (*Then disgustedly.*) But she is sad and old. I will be only doing him a favour.

CALIGULA (*rocking back and forth on his haunches—looking at Lazarus with taunting cruelty*). No, Cæsar ! I know he loves her !

LAZARUS. Yes ! (*He steps down from the dais to Miriam's side and taking her head in both his hands, he kisses her on the lips.*)

TIBERIUS (*with a malignant grin*). Give her the fruit !

POMPEIA (*advances and offers the peach to Miriam —with a hard, cruel little laugh*). Cæsar invites you to eat !

MIRIAM (*to Lazarus—requesting meekly but longingly*). May I accept, Lazarus ? Is it time at last ? My love has followed you over long roads among strangers and each league we came from home my heart has grown older. Now it is too old for you, a heart too weary for your loving laughter. Ever your laughter has grown younger, Lazarus ! Upward it springs like a lark from a field, and sings ! Once I knew your laughter was my child, my son of Lazarus ; but then it grew younger and I felt at last it had returned to my womb—and ever younger and younger— until, to-night, when I spoke to you of home, I felt new birth-pains as your laughter, grown too young for me, flew back to the unborn—a birth so like a death ! (*She sobs and wipes her eyes with her sleeve—then humbly, reaching out for the fruit.*) May I accept it, Lazarus ? You should have new-born laughing hearts to love you. My old one labours with memories and its blood is sluggish with the past. Your home on the hills of space is too far away. My heart longs for the warmth of close walls of earth baked in the sun.

Our home in Bethany, Lazarus, where you and my children lived and died. Our tomb near our home, Lazarus, in which you and my children wait for me. Is it time at last?

LAZARUS (*deeply moved*). Poor lonely heart! It has been crueller for you than I remembered. Go in peace—to peace! (*His voice trembles in spite of himself.*) I shall be lonely, dear one. (*With a note of pleading.*) You have never laughed with my laughter. Will you call back— Yes!—when you know—to tell me you understand and laugh with me at last?

MIRIAM (*not answering him, to Pompeia, taking the peach and making a humble courtesy before her*). I thank you, pretty lady.

(*She raises the peach toward her mouth. Involuntarily one of Lazarus' hands half-reaches out as if to stop her.*)

POMPEIA (*with savage triumph, pointing*). See! He would stop her! He is afraid of death!

CHORUS (*pointing—jeeringly*). He is afraid of death! Ha-ha-ha-ha!

CROWD (*jeeringly*). Ha-ha-ha-ha!

MIRIAM (*bites into the peach and, chewing, begins, as if immediately affected, to talk like a garrulous old woman, her words coming quicker and quicker as her voice becomes fainter and fainter*). Say what you like, it is much better I should go home first, Lazarus. We have been away so long, there will

113

be so much to attend to about the house. And all the children will be waiting. You would be as helpless as a child, Lazarus. Between you and the children, things would soon be in a fine state ! (*More and more confused.*) No, no ! You cannot help me, dearest one. You are only in my way. No, I will make the fire. When you laid it the last time, we all had to run for our lives, choking, the smoke poured from the windows, the neighbours thought the house was burning ! (*She laughs—a queer, vague little inward laugh.*) You are so impractical. The neighbours all get the best of you. Money slips through your fingers. If it was not for me— (*She sighs—then brightly and lovingly.*) But, dearest husband, why do you take it so to heart ? Why do you feel guilty because you are not like other men ? That is why I love you so much. Is it a sin to be born a dreamer ? But God, He must be a dreamer, too, or how would we be on earth ? Do not keep saying to yourself so bitterly, you are a failure in life ! Do not sit brooding on the hilltop in the evening like a black figure of Job against the sky ! (*Her voice trembling.*) Even if God has taken our little ones—yes, in spite of sorrow—have you not a good home I make for you, and a wife who loves you ? (*She forces a chuckle.*) Be grateful, then— for me ! Smile, my sad one ! Laugh a little once in a while ! Come home, bringing me laughter of the wind from the hills ! (*Swaying, looking at the peach in her hand.*) What a mellow, sweet fruit ! Did you bring it home for me ?

*(She falls back into his arms. Gently he lets her body sink until it rests against the steps of the dais. Tiberius rises from his couch to bend over with cruel gloating. Pompeia steps nearer to Lazarus, staring at him mockingly. Caligula hops to her side, looking from Lazarus to Miriam. The half-circle of masked figures moves closer, straining forward and downward as if to overwhelm the two figures at the foot of the dais with their concentrated death wish.)*

TIBERIUS *(thickly)*. She is dead, and I do not hear you laugh !

LAZARUS *(bending down—supplicatingly)*. Miriam ! Call back to me ! Laugh ! *(He pauses. A second of dead silence. Then, with a sound that is very like a sob, he kisses her on the lips.)* I am lonely !

POMPEIA *(with savage malice—jeeringly)*. See ! He weeps, Cæsar ! *(She bursts into strident laughter.)* Ha-ha-ha-ha !

CHORUS *(echoing her laughter)*. Ha-ha-ha-ha ! There is fear ! There is death !

CROWD. There is death ! Ha-ha-ha-ha !

CALIGULA *(in a frenzy of despairing rage, hopping up and down)*. Liar ! Charlatan ! Weakling ! How you have cheated Caligula ! *(He suddenly slaps Lazarus viciously across the face.*) There is death ! Laugh, if you dare !

TIBERIUS (*standing—in a sinister cold rage, the crueller because his dream of a cure for death is baffled, yet feeling his power as Cæsar triumphant nevertheless*). And I thought you might be a dæmon. I thought you might have a magic cure— (*With revengeful fury.*) But death is, and death is mine ! I shall make you pray for death ! And I shall make Death laugh at you ! Ha-ha-ha-ha ! (*In a frenzy as Lazarus neither makes a sound nor looks up.*) Laugh, Lazarus ! Laugh at yourself ! Laugh with me ! (*Then to his soldiers.*) Scourge him ! Make him laugh !

CALIGULA (*running to soldiers—fiercely*). Give me a scourge !

POMPEIA (*running to the soldiers—hysterically*). Ha-ha-ha-ha ! Let me beat him, Cæsar !

> (*They group behind him. The rods and scourges are up-lifted over his back to strike, when in the dead expectant silence, Miriam's body is seen to rise in a writhing tortured last effort.*)

MIRIAM (*in a voice of unearthly sweetness*). Yes ! There is only life ! Lazarus, be not lonely ! (*She laughs and sinks back and is still.*)

> (*A shuddering murmur of superstitious fear comes from them as they shrink back swiftly from Lazarus, remaining huddled one against the other. Pompeia*

116

*runs to the feet of Tiberius and crouches
down on the steps below him, as if for
protection, her terrified eyes on Miriam.
Caligula runs to her and crouches beside
and beneath her.*)

LAZARUS (*kisses Miriam again and raises his head.
His face is radiant with new faith and joy. He
smiles with happiness and speaks to himself with a
mocking affection as if to an amusing child*). That
much remained hidden in me of the sad old
Lazarus who died of self-pity—his loneliness !
Lonely no more ! Man's loneliness is but his
fear of life ! Lonely no more ! Millions of
laughing stars there are around me ! And
laughing dust, born once of woman on this earth,
now freed to dance ! New stars are born of dust
eternally ! The old, grown mellow with God,
burst into flaming seed ! The fields of infinite
space are sown—and grass for sheep springs up
on the hills of earth ! But there is no death, nor
fear, nor loneliness ! There is only God's
Eternal Laughter ! His Laughter flows into the
lonely heart !

> (*He begins to laugh, his laughter clear and
> ringing—the laughter of a conqueror
> arrogant with happiness and the pride
> of a new triumph. He bends and
> picks up the body of Miriam in his arms
> and, his head thrown back, laughing,
> he ascends the dais and places her on
> the table as on a bier. He touches one*

*hand on her breast, as if he were taking
an oath to life on her heart, looks upward
and laughs, his voice ringing more and
more with a terrible unbearable power
and beauty that beats those in the room
into an abject submissive panic.)*

*(Tiberius grovels half under the table, his
hands covering his ears, his face on the
floor ; he is laughing with the agony
and terror of death. Pompeia lies face
down on the first step and beats it with
her fists ; she is laughing with horror
and self-loathing. Caligula, his hands
clutching his head, pounds it against
the edge of the steps ; he is laughing
with grief and remorse. The rest,
soldiers, slaves and the prostitutes of
both sexes, writhe and twist distractedly,
seeking to hide their heads against each
other, beating each other and the floor
with clenched hands. An agonized
moan of supplicating laughter comes
from them all.)*

ALL. Ha-ha-ha-ha ! Ha-ha-ha-ha !
Let us die, Lazarus !
Mercy, Laughing One !
Mercy of death !
Ha-ha-ha-ha ! Ha-ha-ha-ha !

> *(But the laughter of Lazarus is as remote
> now as the laughter of a god.)*

CURTAIN

118

# ACT FOUR

## SCENE ONE

SCENE. *The same as previous scene—the same night a short while later. All the lamps are out except the one on the table on the dais which, placed beside the head of Miriam, shines down upon the white mask of her face. In the half-darkness, the walls are lost in shadow, the room seems immense, the dais nearer.*

*Lazarus sits on the couch at the right on the dais. His face is strong and proud, although his eyes are fixed down on the face of Miriam. He seems more youthful still now, like a young son who keeps watch by the body of his mother, but at the same time retaining the aloof serenity of the statue of a god. His face expresses sorrow and a happiness that transcends sorrow.*

*On the other side of the table, at the end of the couch, Tiberius sits facing front, his elbows on his knees, his large hands with bloated veins hanging loosely. He keeps his gaze averted from the corpse. He talks to Lazarus half over his shoulder.*

*On the top step, Pompeia sits, facing right, her hands clasped about one knee, the other leg stretched down to the lower step. Her head is thrown back and she is gazing up into Lazarus' face.*

*On the step below her, Caligula squats on his haunches, his arms on his knees, his fists pressed to his temples. He is staring straight before him.*

*Only these four people are in the room now.*

119

TIBERIUS (*gloomily*). Was she dead, Dæmon, and was it thy power that recalled life to her body for that moment ? Or was she still living and her words only the last desire of her love to comfort you, Lazarus ? (*Lazarus does not reply.*) If thou dost not tell me, I must always doubt thee, Dæmon.

POMPEIA (*with a sigh of bewildered happiness, turns to Caligula*). I am glad he laughed, Caligula ! Did I say I loved him before ? Then it was only my body that wanted a slave. Now it is my heart that desires a master ! Now I know love for the first time in my life !

CALIGULA (*bitterly*). Fool ! What does he care for love ? (*Sombrely.*) He loves every one —but no one—not even me ! (*He broods frowningly.*)

POMPEIA (*following her own thoughts*). And now that hag is dead he will need a woman, young and beautiful, to protect and comfort him, to make him a home and bear his children ! (*She dreams, her eyes again fixed on Lazarus—then suddenly turning to Caligula.*) I am glad I lost our bet. But you must accept some other payment. Now I know love, I may not give myself to any man save him !

CALIGULA. I do not want you ! What are you but another animal ! Faugh ! (*With a grimace of disgust.*) Pleasure is dirty and joyless ! Or we who seek it are, which comes to the same thing. (*Then grimly.*) But our bet can rest.

This is not the end. There may still be a chance for you to laugh at him !

POMPEIA. No ! Now I could not ! I should weep for his defeat !

TIBERIUS (*gloomily arguing, half to himself*). His laughter triumphed over me, but he has not brought her back to life. I think he knows no cure for another's death, as I had hoped. And I must always doubt that it was not some trick— (*harshly*) until I have tested him with his own life ! He cannot cheat me then ! (*A pause— arguing to himself.*) But he was dead—that much has been proved—and before he died he was old and sad. What did he find beyond there ? (*Suddenly—turning to Lazarus now.*) What did you find beyond death, Lazarus ?

LAZARUS (*exaltedly*). Life ! God's Eternal Laughter !

TIBERIUS (*shaking his head*). I want hope— for me, Tiberius Cæsar.

LAZARUS. What is—you ? But there is hope for Man ! Love is Man's hope—love for his life on earth, a noble love above suspicion and distrust ! Hitherto Man has always suspected his life, and in revenge and self-torture his love has been faithless ! He has even betrayed Eternity, his mother, with his slave he calls Immortal Soul ! (*He laughs softly, gaily, mockingly—then to Tiberius directly.*) Hope for you, Tiberius Cæsar ? Then dare to love Eternity without your fear desiring to possess her ! Be brave enough to be possessed !

TIBERIUS (*strangely*). My mother was the wife of Cæsar. (*Then dully.*) I do not understand.

LAZARUS. Men are too cowardly to understand ! And so the worms of their little fears eat them and grow fat and terrible and become their jealous gods they must appease with lies !

TIBERIUS (*wearily*). Your words are meaningless, Lazarus. You are a fool. All laughter is malice, all gods are dead, and life is a sickness.

LAZARUS (*laughs pityingly*). So say the race of men, whose lives are long dyings ! They evade their fear of death by becoming so sick of life that by the time death comes they are too lifeless to fear it ! Their disease triumphs over death—a noble victory called resignation ! " We are sick," they say, " therefore there is no God in us, therefore there is no God ! " Oh, if men would but interpret that first cry of man fresh from the womb as the laughter of one who even then says to his heart, " It is my pride as God to become Man. Then let it be my pride as Man to recreate the God in me ! " (*He laughs softly but with exultant pride.*)

POMPEIA (*laughing with him—proudly*). He will create a god in me ! I shall be proud !

CALIGULA (*pounding his temples with his fists—tortured*). I am Caligula. I was born in a camp among soldiers. My father was Germanicus, a hero, as all men know. But I do not understand this—and though I burst with pride, I cannot laugh with joy !

TIBERIUS (*gloomily*). Obscurities ! I have found nothing in life that merits pride. I am not proud of being Cæsar—and what is a god but a Cæsar over Cæsars ? If fools kneel and worship me because they fear me, should I be proud ? But Cæsar is a fact, and Tiberius, a man, is one, and I cling to these certainties—and I do not wish to die ! If I were sure of eternal sleep beyond there, deep rest and forgetfulness of all I have ever seen or heard or hated or loved on earth, I would gladly die ! But surely, Lazarus, nothing is sure—peace the least sure of all—and I fear there is no rest beyond there, that one remembers there as here and cannot sleep, that the mind goes on eternally the same—a long insomnia of memories and regrets and the ghosts of dreams one has poisoned to death passing with white bodies spotted by the leprous fingers of one's lusts. (*Bitterly.*) I fear the long nights now in which I lie awake and listen to Death dancing round me in the darkness, prancing to the drum beat of my heart ! (*He shudders.*) And I am afraid, Lazarus— afraid that there is no sleep beyond there, either !

LAZARUS. There is peace !

> (*His words are like a benediction he pro-*
> *nounces upon them. Soothed in a*
> *mysterious, childlike way, they repeat*
> *the word after him, wonderingly.*)

POMPEIA. Peace ?

CALIGULA. Peace ?

TIBERIUS. Peace ? (*For a long moment there is complete silence. Then Tiberius sighs heavily, shaking his head.*) Peace ! Another word is blurred into a senseless sigh by men's longing ! A bubble of froth blown from the lips of the dying toward the stars ! No ! (*He grins bitterly—then looks at Lazarus—sombrely contemptuous and threatening.*) You are pleased to act the mysterious, Jew, but I shall solve you ! (*Then with a lawyer-like incisiveness.*) There is one certainty about you and I must know the cause—for there must be a cause and a rational explanation ! You were fifty when you died——

LAZARUS (*smiling mockingly*). Yes. When I died.

TIBERIUS (*unheeding*). And now your appearance is of one younger by a score. Not alone your appearance ! You *are* young. I see the fact, the effect. And I demand an explanation of the cause without mystic nonsense or evasion. (*Threateningly.*) And I warn you to answer directly in plain words—and not to laugh, you understand !—not to dare !—or I shall lose patience with you and—(*with a grim smile*) I can be terrible ! (*Lazarus smiles gently at him. He turns away with confused annoyance, then back to Lazarus, resuming his lawyer-like manner.*) What was it restored your youth ? How did you contrive that your body reversed the natural process

and grows younger ? Is it a charm by which
you invoke a supernatural force ? Or is it a pow-
der you dissolve in wine ? Or a liquid ? Or
an unguent you rub into the skin to revitalize
the old bones and tissues ? Or—what is it,
Lazarus ?

LAZARUS (*gently*). I know that age and time
are but timidities of thought.

TIBERIUS (*broodingly—as if he had not heard—
persuasively*). Perhaps you ask yourself, what
would Tiberius do with youth ? Then, because
you must have heard rumours of my depravity,
you will conclude the old lecher desires youth for
his lusts ! (*He laughs harshly.*) Ha ! Why,
do not my faithful subjects draw pictures of an
old buck goat upon the walls and write above
them, Cæsar ? And they are just. In self-contempt of Man I have made this man, myself, the
most swinish and contemptible of men ! Yes !
In all this empire there is no man so base a hog as
I ! (*He grins bitterly and ironically.*) My claim
to this excellence, at least, is not contested !
Every one admits therein Tiberius is by right their
Cæsar ! (*He laughs bitterly.*) Ha ! So who
would believe Tiberius if he said, I want youth
again because I loathe lust and long for purity !

LAZARUS (*gently*). I believe you, Cæsar.

TIBERIUS (*stares at him—deeply moved*). You
—believe— ? (*Then gruffly.*) You lie ! You
are not mad—and only a madman would believe

another man ! (*Then confidingly, leaning over toward Lazarus.*) I know it is folly to speak—but—one gets old, one becomes talkative, one wishes to confess, to say the thing one has always kept hidden, to reveal one's unique truth—and there is so little time left—and one is alone ! Therefore the old—like children—talk to themselves, for they have reached that hopeless wisdom of experience which knows that though one were to cry it in the streets to multitudes, or whisper it in the kiss to one's beloved, the only ears that can ever hear one's secret are one's own ! (*He laughs bitterly.*) And so I talk aloud, Lazarus ! I talk to my loneliness !

LAZARUS (*simply*). I hear, Tiberius.

TIBERIUS (*again moved and confused—forcing a mocking smile*). Liar ! Eavesdropper ! You merely—listen ! (*Then he turns away.*) My mother, Livia, that strong woman, giving birth to me, desired not a child, but a Cæsar—just as, married to Augustus, she loved him not but loved herself as Cæsar's wife. She made me feel, in the proud questioning of her scornful eyes, that to win her mother love I must become Cæsar. She poisoned Prince Marcellus and young Gaius and Lucius that the way might be clear for me. I used to see their blood dance in red specks before my eyes when I looked at the sky. Now—(*he brushes his hand before his eyes*)—it is all a red blot ! I cannot distinguish. There have been too many. My mother—her blood is in that blot, for I revenged myself on her. I did not kill her, it is true, but I deprived her of her power and she died, as I knew she must, that powerful woman who bore me as a weapon ! The murder was subtle and cruel—how cruel only that passionate, deep-breasted woman unslaked by eighty years of devoured desires could know ! Too cruel ! I did not go to her funeral. I was afraid her closed eyes might open and look at me ! (*Then with almost a cry.*) I want youth, Lazarus, that I may play again about her feet with the love I felt for her before I learned to read her eyes ! (*He half sobs, bowing his head. A pause.*)

CALIGULA (*nudging Pompeia—with a crafty whisper*). Do you hear ? The old lecher talks to himself. He is becoming senile. He will soon die. And I shall be Cæsar. Then I shall laugh !

POMPEIA (*staring up at Lazarus' face, hearing only Caligula's words without their meaning*). No. My Lazarus does not laugh now. See. His mouth is silent—and a little sad, I think.

LAZARUS (*gently and comfortingly*). I hear, Tiberius.

TIBERIUS (*harshly*). I hated that woman, my mother, and I still hate her ! Have you ever loved, Lazarus ? (*Then with a glance at Miriam's body and a shuddering away from it—vaguely.*) I was forgetting her. I killed your love, too, did I not ? Well, I must ! I envy those who are loved. Where I can, I kill love—for retribution's

sake—but much of it escapes me. (*Then harshly
again.*) I loved Agrippina. We were married.
A son was born to us. We were happy. Then
that proud woman, my mother, saw my happiness.
Was she jealous of my love ? Or did she know
no happy man would wish to be Cæsar ? Well,
she condemned my happiness to death. She
whispered to Augustus and he ordered me to
divorce Agrippina. I should have opened her
veins and mine, and died with her. But my
mother stayed by me, Agrippina was kept away,
my mother spoke to me and spoke to me and even
wept, that tall woman, strong as a great man, and
I consented that my love be murdered. Then my
mother married me to a whore. Why ? The
whore was Cæsar's daughter, true—but I feel
that was not all of it, that my mother wished to
keep me tortured that I might love her alone and
long to be Cæsar ! (*He laughs harshly.*) Ha !
In brief, I married the whore, she tortured me,
my mother's scheming prospered—that subtle
and crafty woman !—and many years passed in
being here and there, in doing this and that,
in growing full of hate and revengeful ambition
to be Cæsar. At last, Augustus died. I was
Cæsar. Then I killed that whore, my wife, and
I starved my mother's strength to death until she
died, and I began to take pleasure in vengeance
upon men, and pleasure in taking vengeance on
myself. (*He grins horribly.*) It is all very simple,
as you see ! (*He suddenly starts to his feet—with
harsh arrogance and pride, threateningly.*) Enough !

Why do I tell you these old tales ? Must I explain to you why I want youth ? It is my whim ! I am Cæsar ! And now I must lie down and try to sleep ! And it is my command that you reveal the secret of your youth to me when I awake, or else—(*with malignant cruelty*)—I will have to revenge the death of a hope on you—and a hope at my age demands a terrible expiation on its slayer ! (*He walks down and starts to go off, right —then turns and addresses Lazarus with grim irony.*) Good night to you, Lazarus. And remember there shall be death while I am Cæsar ! (*He turns to go.*)

LAZARUS (*smiling affectionately at him, shakes his head*). Cæsar must believe in death. But does the husband of Agrippina ?

TIBERIUS (*stops short and stares at Lazarus, confused and stuttering*). What—what—do you mean, Lazarus ?

LAZARUS. I have heard your loneliness.

TIBERIUS (*cruelly and grimly again*). So much the more reason why my pride should kill you ! Remember that ! (*He turns and strides off into the darkness at right.*)

CALIGULA (*peers after him until sure he is gone— then gets up and begins a grotesque, hopping dance, singing a verse of the legionary's song.*)
A bold legionary am I
March, oh march on !

A Roman eagle was my daddy,
My mother was a drunken drabby,
Oh, march on to the wars !

> (*He laughs gratingly, posturing and gesticulat-
> ing up at Lazarus.*)

Ha-ha-ha ! He is gone ! I can breathe ! His
breath in the same air suffocates me ! The gods
grant mine do the same for him ! But he is failing ! He talks to himself like a man in second
childhood. His words are a thick babble I could
not hear. They well from his lips like clots of
blood from a reopened wound. I kept listening
to the beating of his heart. It sounded slow,
slower than when I last heard it. Did you detect
that, Lazarus ? Once or twice I thought it
faltered— (*He draws in his breath with an
avid gasp—then laughs gratingly.*) Ha-ha-ha—
(*Grandiloquently.*) Tiberius, the old buck-goat,
will soon be gone, my friends, and in his place you
will be blessed with the beautiful young god, Caligula ! Hail to Caligula ! Hail ! Ha-ha-ha——

> (*His laughter suddenly breaks off into a
> whimper, and he stands staring around
> him in a panic of fear that he has been
> overheard. He slinks noiselessly up
> the steps of the dais and squats cower-
> ingly at Lazarus' feet, blinking up at
> his face in monkey-wise, clutching
> Lazarus' hand in both of his. His
> teeth can be heard chattering together
> in nervous fear.*)

(*Pompeia, whose gaze has remained fixed on Lazarus' throughout, has gradually moved closer to him until she, too, is at his feet, half-kneeling beneath the table on which Miriam lies, side by side with Caligula but as oblivious of him as he is of her.*)

(*Having grown calmer now, Caligula speaks again—mournful and bewildered.*)

CALIGULA.    Why should I love you, Lazarus ? Your laughter taunts me !   It insults Cæsar !   It denies Rome !   But I will warn you again. Escape !   To-night Tiberius' mood is to play sentimental, but to-morrow he will jeer while hyenas gnaw at your skull and lick your brain. And then—there is pain, Lazarus !   There is pain !

POMPEIA (*pressing her hand to her own heart—with a shudder*).    Yes, there is pain !

LAZARUS (*smiling down on them—gently*).    If you can answer Yes to pain, there is no pain !

POMPEIA (*passionately*).    Yes !   Yes !   I love Lazarus !

CALIGULA (*with a bitter grin*).    Do not take pain away from us !   It is our one truth.   Without pain there is nothing—a nothingness in which even your laughter, Lazarus, is swallowed at one gulp like a whining gnat by the cretin's silence of immensity !   Ha-ha !   No, we must keep pain ! Especially Cæsar must !   Pain must twinkle with

a mad mirth in a Cæsar's eyes—men's pain—or
they would become dissatisfied and disrespectful !
Ha-ha ! (*He stops his grating laughter abruptly and
continues mournfully.*) I am sick, Lazarus, sick of
cruelty and lust and human flesh and all the im-
becilities of pleasure—the unclean antics of half-
witted children ! (*With a mounting agony of longing.*) I would be clean ! If I could only laugh
your laughter, Lazarus ! That would purify my
heart. For I could wish to love all men, as you
love them—as I love you ! If only I did not fear
them and despise them ! If I could only believe
—believe in them—in life—in myself !—believe
that one man or woman in the world knew and
loved the real Caligula—then I might have faith
in Caligula myself—then I might laugh your
laughter !

LAZARUS (*suddenly, in a quiet but compelling voice*).
I, who know you, love you, Caligula. (*Gently
patting his head.*) I love Caligula.

CALIGULA (*staring up at him in pathetic confusion*). You ? You ? You, Lazarus ? (*He begins to tremble all over as if in a seizure—chokingly.*)
Beware ! It is not good—not just—to make fun
of me—to laugh at my misery—saying you
love— (*In a frenzy, he jumps to his feet threatening Lazarus.*) Are you trying to fool me,
hypocrite ? Do you think I have become so
abject that you dare—? Because I love you,
do you presume—? Do you think I am your
slave, dog of a Jew, that you can—insult—to my

face—the heir of Cæsar—— (*He stutters and stammers with rage, hopping up and down grotesquely, shaking his fist at Lazarus, who smiles at him affectionately as at a child in a tantrum.*)

LAZARUS (*catching his eyes and holding them with his glance—calmly*). Believe, Caligula !

CALIGULA (*again overcome—stuttering with strange terror*). Believe ? But I cannot ! I must not ! You cannot know me, if—— You are a holy man ! You are a god in a mortal body—you can laugh with joy to be alive—while I—— Oh, no, you cannot love me ! There is nothing in me at bottom but a despising and an evil eye ! You cannot ! You are only being kind ! (*Hysterically.*) I do not want your kindness ! I hate your pity ! I am too proud ! I am too strong ! (*He collapses weepingly, kneeling and clutching Lazarus' hand in both of his.*)

LAZARUS (*smiling*). You are so proud of being evil ! What if there is no evil ? What if there are only health and sickness ? Believe in the healthy god called Man in you ! Laugh at Caligula, the funny clown who beats the backside of his shadow with a bladder and thinks thereby he is Evil, the Enemy of God ! (*He suddenly lifts the face of Caligula and stares into his eyes.*) Believe ! What if you are a man and men are despicable ? Men are also unimportant ! Men pass ! Like rain into the sea ! The sea remains ! Man remains ! Man slowly arises from the past of the race of men that was his tomb of death ! For

Man death is not ! Man, Son of God's Laughter, *is* ! (*He begins to laugh triumphantly, staring deep into Caligula's eyes.*) *Is*, Caligula ! Believe in the laughing god within you !

CALIGULA (*bursting suddenly into choking, joyful laughter—like a visionary*). I believe ! I believe there is love even for Caligula ! I can laugh—now—Lazarus ! Free laughter ! Clean ! No sickness ! No lust for death ! My corpse no longer rots in my heart ! The tomb is full of sunlight ! I am alive ! I who love Man, I who can love and laugh ! Listen, Lazarus ! I dream ! When I am Cæsar, I will devote my power to your truth. I will decree that there must be kindness and love ! I will make the Empire one great Blessed Isle ! Rome shall know happiness, it shall believe in life, it shall learn to laugh your laughter, Lazarus, or I—— (*He raises his hand in an imperial autocratic gesture.*)

LAZARUS (*gaily mocking*). Or you will cut off its head ?

CALIGULA (*fiercely*). Yes ! I will—! (*Then meeting Lazarus' eyes, he beats his head with his fists crazily.*) Forgive me ! I forget ! I forget !

LAZARUS. Go out under the sky ! Let your heart climb on laughter to a star ! Then make it look down at earth, and watch Caligula commanding Life under pain of death to do his will ! (*He laughs.*)

CALIGULA (*laughing*). I will ! I do ! I laugh

at him ! Caligula is a trained ape, a humped cripple ! Now I take him out under the sky, where I can watch his monkey tricks, where there is space for laughter and where this new joy, your love of me, may dance !

(*Laughing clearly and exultantly, he runs out through the arched doorway at rear.*)

LAZARUS (*stops laughing—shaking his head, almost sadly*). They forget ! It is too soon for laughter ! (*Then grinning at himself.*) What, Lazarus ? Are you, too, thinking in terms of time, old fool so soon to re-enter infinity ? (*He laughs with joyous self-mockery.*)

POMPEIA (*who has crept to his feet, kisses his hand passionately*). I love you, Lazarus !

LAZARUS (*stops laughing, and looks down at her gently*). And I love you, woman.

POMPEIA (*with a gasp of delight*). You ? (*She stares up into his eyes doubtingly, raising her face toward his.*) Then—put your arms around me. (*He does so, smiling gently.*) And hold me to you. (*He presses her closer to him.*) And kiss me. (*He kisses her on the forehead.*) No, on the lips ! (*He kisses her. She flings her arms about his neck. passionately and kisses him again and again—then slowly draws away—remains looking into his eyes a long time, shrinking back from him with bewildered pain which speedily turns to rage and revengeful hatred.*) No ! No ! It is *my* love, not Love ! I want you to know *my* love, to give me back love

—for me—only for me—Pompeia—my body,
my heart—me, a woman—not Woman, women !
Do I love Man, men ? I hate men ! I love
you, Lazarus—a man—a lover—a father to
children ! I want love—as you loved that
woman there (*she points to Miriam*) that I poisoned
for love of you ! But did you love her—or just
Woman, wife and mother of men ? (*She stares—
then as if reading admission in his eyes, she springs to
her feet.*) Liar ! Cheat ! Hypocrite ! Thief !
(*Half hysterical with rage, pain and grief, she bends
over Miriam and smoothes the hair back from her
forehead.*) Poor wife ! Poor woman ! How
he must have tortured you ! Now I remember
the pity in your eyes when you looked at me !
Oh, how his soothing grey words must have
pecked at the wound in your heart like doves with
bloody beaks ! (*Then with sudden harshness.*)
But perhaps you were too dull to understand, too
poor and tired and ugly and old to care, too
slavish—! Pah ! (*She turns away with contempt and faces Lazarus with revengeful hatred.*)
Did you think I would take her place—become
your slave, wait upon you, give you love and
passion and beauty in exchange for phrases about
man and gods—you who are neither a man nor a
god but a dead thing without desire ! You
dared to hope I would give my body, my love, to
you ! (*She spits in his face and laughs harshly.*)
You insolent fool ! I shall punish you ! You
shall be tortured as you have tortured ! (*She
laughs wildly—then steps down from the dais and*

*goes off right, crying distractedly.*)  Cæsar !  This
man has made you a fool before all the world !
Torture him, Cæsar !  Now !  Let the people
witness !  Send heralds to wake them !  Torture
him, Cæsar, the man who laughs at you !  Ha-
ha-ha-ha !

> (*Her laughter is caught up by all the Girls
> and Youths of the palace, who, as she
> disappears, led by their Chorus, pour in
> from each side of the room and dance
> forward to group themselves around the
> dais as in the previous scene, staring at
> Lazarus, laughing cruelly, falsely,
> stridently.*)

CHORUS (*tauntingly*).  Ha-ha-ha-ha !
Laugh now, Lazarus !
Let us see you laugh !
Ha-ha-ha-ha !

CROWD (*echoing*).  Ha-ha-ha-ha !
Ha-ha-ha-ha !

LAZARUS (*moves, and immediately there is silence.
He bends down and kisses Miriam and picks her up in
his arms.  Talking down to her face—with a tender
smile*).  Farewell !  You are home !  And now
I will take your body home to earth !  Space is
too far away, you said !  Home in the Earth !
There will be so much for you to do there !
Home !  Earth !  (*His voice trembling a bit.*)
Farewell, body of Miriam.  My grief is a lonely
cry wailing in the home in my heart that you have
left for ever !  (*Then exultantly.*)  But what am

E*  137

I ? Now your love has become Eternal Love ! Now, since your life passed, I feel Eternal Life made nobler by your selflessness ! Love has grown purer ! The laughter of God is more profoundly tender ! (*He looks up in an ecstasy and descends the dais, carrying her.*) Yes, that is it ! That is it, my Miriam ! (*Laughing softly and tenderly, he walks around the dais and carries the body out through the doorway in rear.*)

> (*The Chorus and Youths and Girls make way for him in awed silence—then scurry around to right and left, forming an aisle through which he passes—then after he has gone out through the arch, they close into a semicircular group again, staring after him, and a whisper of strange, bewildered, tender laughter comes from them.*)

CHORUS (*in this whisper*). That is it !
Love is pure !
Laughter is tender !
Laugh !

CROWD (*echoing*). Laugh ! Laugh !
CURTAIN

### SCENE TWO

SCENE. *The arena of an amphitheatre. It is just before dawn of the same night. Cæsar's throne is on the left at the extreme front, facing right, turned a little toward front. It is lighted by*

138

*four immense lamps. In front of the throne is
a marble railing that tops the wall that encloses
the arena. In the rear the towering pile of the
circular amphitheatre is faintly outlined in
deeper black against the dark sky.*

*Tiberius sits on the throne, his eyes fixed on
the middle of the arena off right, where, bound
to a high stake after he had been tortured,
Lazarus is now being burnt alive over a huge
pile of faggots. The crackling of the flames is
heard. Their billowing rise and fall is reflected
on the masked faces of the multitude who sit on
the banked tiers of marble behind and to the rear
of the throne, with their Chorus, seven men
masked in Middle Age in the Servile, Hypocritical type, grouped on each side of the throne
of Cæsar on a lower tier.*

*Half-kneeling before Tiberius, her chin rest-
ing on her hands on top of the marble rail,
Pompeia also stares at Lazarus.*

*Before the curtain, the crackle of the flames
and an uproar of human voices from the multitude, jeering, hooting, laughing at Lazarus in
cruel mockery of his laughter. This sound has
risen to its greatest volume as the curtain rises.*

CHORUS (*chanting mockingly*). Ha-ha-ha-ha !
Burn and laugh !
Laugh now, Lazarus !
Ha-ha-ha-ha !

CROWD (*chanting with revengeful mockery*).
Ha-ha-ha-ha !

TIBERIUS. Who laughs now, Lazarus—thou or Cæsar? Ha-ha—! (*With awe.*) His flesh melts in the fire but his eyes shine with peace!

POMPEIA. How he looks at me! (*Averting her eyes with a shudder.*) Command them to put out his eyes, Cæsar!

TIBERIUS (*harshly*). No. I want to read his eyes when they see death! (*Then averting his face—guiltily.*) He is looking at me, not you. I should not have listened to your cries for his death.

POMPEIA (*turning to him again with a shudder of agony—beseechingly*). Have them put out his eyes, Cæsar! They call to me!

TIBERIUS (*as if not hearing her—to himself*). Why do I feel remorse? His laughter dies and is forgotten, and the hope it raised dies— (*With sudden excitement.*) And yet—he must know something—and if he would—even now he could tell— (*Suddenly rising to his feet he calls imploringly.*) Lazarus!

CHORUS (*chanting in a great imploring chorus now*). Lazarus!

CROWD (*echoing*). Lazarus!

SOLDIER'S VOICE (*calling from off beside the stake*). You had us gag him, Cæsar, so he might not laugh. Shall we cut away the gag?

POMPEIA (*in terror*). No, Cæsar! He will laugh! And I will go to him! (*Desperately.*)

He will laugh at you, Cæsar—and the mob will laugh with him !

TIBERIUS (*struggles with himself—then calls*). Lazarus ! If you hear let your eyes answer, and I will grant the mercy of death to end your agony ! Is there hope of love somewhere for men on earth ?

CHORUS (*intoning as before*).  Is there hope of love
For us on earth ?

CROWD.  Hope of love
For us on earth !

SOLDIER'S VOICE.  His eyes laugh, Cæsar !

TIBERIUS (*in a strange frenzy now*).  Hear me, thou Dæmon of Laughter ! Hear and answer, I beseech thee, who alone hath known joy ! (*More and more wildly.*) How must we live ? Wherein lies happiness ?

CHORUS.  Wherein lies happiness ?

CROWD.  Wherein, happiness ?

TIBERIUS.  Why are we born ? To what end must we die ?

CHORUS.  Why are we born to die ?

CROWD.  Why are we born ?

SOLDIER'S VOICE.  His eyes laugh, Cæsar ! He is dying ! He would speak !

CHORUS AND CROWD (*in one great cry*).  Cæsar ! Let Lazarus speak !

141

POMPEIA (*terrified*). No, Cæsar! He will laugh—and you will die—and I will go to him!

TIBERIUS (*torn—arguing with his fear*). But—he may know some hope— (*Then making his decision, with grim fatalism.*) Hope—or nothing! (*Calls to the Soldiers.*) Let him speak!

CHORUS AND CROWD (*cheering*). Hail, Cæsar!

LAZARUS (*his voice comes, recognizably the voice of Lazarus, yet with a strange, fresh, clear quality of boyhood, gaily mocking with life*). Hail, Cæsar!

CROWD (*frantic with hope*). Hail, Lazarus!

TIBERIUS. Pull away the fire from him! I see death in his eyes! (*The flaming reflections in the banked, masked faces dance madly as the Soldiers rake back the fire from the stake. With a forced, taunting mockery.*) What do you say now, Lazarus? You are dying!

CHORUS AND CROWD (*taking his tone—mockingly*). You are dying, Lazarus!

LAZARUS (*his voice a triumphant assertion of the victory of life over pain and death*). Yes!

TIBERIUS (*triumphant yet disappointed—with scorn and rage*). Ha! You admit it, do you, coward! Craven! Knave! Duper of fools! Clown! Liar! Die! I laugh at you! Ha-ha-ha-ha—— (*His voice breaks chokingly.*)

CROWD (*led by their Chorus—in the same frenzy of disappointment, with all sorts of grotesque and obscene gestures and noises, thumbing their fingers to*

142

*their noses, wagging them at their ears, sticking out their tongues, slapping their behinds, barking, crowing like roosters, howling, and hooting in every conceivable manner).* Yah! Yah! Yellow Gut! Bung-kisser! Muckheel! Scumwiper! Liar! Pig! Jackal! Die! We laugh at you! Ha-ha-ha—— *(Their voices, too, break.)*

POMPEIA *(rising to her feet like one in a trance, staring toward Lazarus).* They are tormenting him. I hear him crying to me! *(She moves to the top of the steps leading to the arena.)*

LAZARUS *(his voice thrilling with exultance).* O men, fear not life! You die—but there is no death for Man!

> *(He begins to laugh, and at the sound of his laughter, a great spell of silence settles upon all his hearers—then as his laughter rises, they begin to laugh with him.)*

POMPEIA *(descending the steps like a sleep-walker).* I hear his laughter calling. I must go to him.

TIBERIUS *(as if he realized something was happening that was against his will—trying feebly to be imperial).* I command you not to laugh! Cæsar commands—— *(Calling feebly to the Soldiers.)* Put back the gag! Stop his laughter!

> *(The laughter of Lazarus gaily and lovingly mocks back at him.)*

SOLDIER'S VOICE *(his voice gently remonstrating).* We may not, Cæsar. We love his laughter!

*(They laugh with him.)*

CHORUS AND CROWD *(in a soft, dreamy murmur).*
We love his laughter !
We laugh !

TIBERIUS *(dreamily).* Then—pile the fire back
around him. High and higher ! Let him blaze
to the stars ! I laugh with him !

SOLDIER'S VOICE *(gently and gravely).* That is
just, Cæsar. We love men flaming toward the
stars ! We laugh with him !

CHORUS AND CROWD *(as the flames, piled back and
fed anew by the Soldiers, flare upward and are
reflected on their masks in dancing waves of light).*
We love men flaming toward the stars !
We laugh !

POMPEIA *(in the arena).* The fire calls me.
My burning heart calls for the fire !

> *(She laughs softly and passes swiftly across
> the arena toward Lazarus.)*

TIBERIUS *(in a sort of childish complaint).* You
must pardon me, Lazarus. This is my Cæsar's
duty—to kill you ! You have no right to laugh
—before all these people—at Cæsar. It is not
kind. *(He sobs snuffingly—then begins to laugh at
himself.)*

> *(Suddenly the flames waver, die down, then
> shoot up again and Pompeia's laughter
> is heard for a moment, rising clear and
> passionately with that of Lazarus, then
> dying quickly out.)*

SOLDIER'S VOICE. A woman has thrown herself in the flames, Cæsar! She laughs with Lazarus!

TIBERIUS (*in a sudden panicky flurry—feverishly*). Quick, Lazarus! You will soon be silent! Speak!—in the name of man's solitude—his agony of farewell—what is beyond there, Lazarus? (*His voice has risen to a passionate entreaty.*)

CHORUS (*in a great pleading echo*). What is beyond there, Lazarus?

CROWD. What is beyond?

LAZARUS (*his voice speaking lovingly, with a surpassing clearness and exaltation*). Life! Eternity! Stars and dust! God's Eternal Laughter!

> (*His laughter bursts forth now in its highest pitch of ecstatic summons to the feast and sacrifice of Life, the Eternal.*)

> (*The crowds laugh with him in a frenzied rhythmic chorus. Led by the Chorus, they pour down from the banked walls of the amphitheatre and dance in the flaring reflection of the flames strange wild measures of liberated joy. Tiberius stands on the raised dais laughing great shouts of clear, fearless laughter.*)

CHORUS (*chanting as they dance*). Laugh!
Laugh!
We are stars!
We are dust!

We are gods !
We are laughter !

CROWD. We are dust !
We are gods !
Laugh ! Laugh !

CALIGULA (*enters from behind Tiberius. His aspect is wild, his hair dishevelled, his clothes torn, He is panting as if exhausted by running. He stares toward the flames stupidly—then screams despairingly above the chant*). Lazarus ! I come to save you ! Do you still live, Lazarus ?

TIBERIUS (*has been speaking. His words are now heard as the tumult momentarily dies down*). I have lived long enough ! I will die with Lazarus ! I no longer fear death ! I laugh ! I laugh at Cæsar ! I advise you, my brothers, fear not Cæsars ! Seek Man in the brotherhood of the dust ! Cæsar is your fear of Man ! I counsel you, laugh away your Cæsars !

CALIGULA (*with resentful jealousy and rage—in a voice rising to a scream*). What do I hear, Lazarus ? You laugh with your murderer ? You give him your laughter ? You have forgotten me—my love—you make him love you— you make him laugh at Cæsars—at me ! (*Suddenly springs on Tiberius in a fury and grabbing him by the throat chokes him, forcing him back on the throne—screaming.*) Die, traitor ! Die ! (*Tiberius' body relaxes in his hands, dead, and slips from the chair. Caligula rushes madly down the stairs into the midst of the oblivious, laughing, dancing crowd, screaming.*) You have betrayed me, dog of a Jew ! You have betrayed Cæsar ! (*Beginning to be caught by the contagion of the laughter.*) Ha-ah— No ! I will not laugh ! I will kill you ! Give me a spear ! (*He snatches a spear from a soldier and fights his way drunkenly toward the flames, like a man half overcome by a poisonous gas, shouting, half-laughing in spite of himself, half-weeping with rage.*) Ha-ha— The gods be with Cæsar Caligula ! O Immortal Gods, give thy brother strength ! You shall die, Lazarus—die— Ha-ha——! (*He disappears toward the flames, his spear held ready to stab.*)

CHORUS AND CROWD (*who have been entirely oblivious of him—chanting*). Laugh ! Laugh !

We are gods !
We are dust !

LAZARUS (*at his first word there is a profound silence in which each dancer remains frozen in the last movement*). Hail, Caligula Cæsar ! Men forget ! (*He laughs with gay mockery as at a child.*)

CHORUS AND CROWD (*starting to laugh*). Laugh! Laugh !

> (*Then there is a fierce cry of rage from Caligula and Lazarus' laughter ceases, and with it the laughter of the crowd turns to a wail of fear and lamentation.*)

147

CALIGULA (*dashes back among them waving his bloody spear and rushing up to the throne stands on it and strikes a grandiose pose*)   I have killed God ! I am Death !   Death is Cæsar !

CHORUS AND CROWD (*turning and scurrying away —huddled in fleeing groups, crouching close to the ground like a multitude of terrified rats, their voices squeaky now with fright*).   Hail, Cæsar !   Hail to Death !

(*They are gone.*)

CALIGULA (*keeping his absurd majestic pose, turns and addresses with rhetorical intoning, and flowing gestures, the body of Lazarus, high upon its stake, the flames below it now flickering fitfully*).   Hail, Caligula !   Hero of heroes, conqueror of the Dæmon, Lazarus, who taught the treason that fear and death were dead !   But I am Lord of Fear !   I am Cæsar of Death !   And you, Lazarus, are carrion !   (*Then in a more conversational tone, putting aside his grandiose airs, confidentially.*)   I had to kill you, Lazarus !   Surely your good sense tells you——   You heard what the old fool, Tiberius, told the mob.   A moment more and there would have been a revolution —no more Cæsars—and my dream—!   (*He stops—bewilderedly.*)   My dream ?   Did I kill laughter ?   I had just learned to laugh—with love !   (*More confusedly.*)   I must be a little mad, Lazarus.   It was one terror too many, to have been laughing your laughter in the night, to have been dreaming great yearning dreams of all the

good my love might do for men when I was Cæsar
—and then, to hear the old howling of mob lust,
and to run here—and there a high white flame
amidst the fire—you, Lazarus !—dying !—laughing with him—Tiberius—betraying me—who
loved you, Lazarus ! Yes, I became mad ! I
am mad ! And I can laugh my own mad laughter, Lazarus—my own ! Ha-ha-ha-ha ! (*He
laughs with a wild triumphant madness and again
rhetorically, with sweeping gestures and ferocious
capers.*) And all of men are vile and mad, and I
shall be their madmen's Cæsar ! (*He turns as if
addressing an amphitheatre full of his subjects.*) O
my good people, my faithful scum, my brother
swine, Lazarus is dead and we have murdered
great laughter, and it befits our madness to have
done so, and it is befitting above all to have Caligula for Cæsar ! (*Then savagely.*) Kneel down !
Abase yourselves ! I am your Cæsar and your
God ! Hail ! (*He stands saluting himself with a
crazy intensity that is not without grandeur. A
pause. Suddenly the silence seems to crush down
upon him ; he is aware that he is alone in the vast
arena ; he whirls about, looking around him as if he
felt an assassin at his back ; he lunges with his spear
at imaginary foes, jumping, dodging from side to side,
yelping.*) Ho, there ! Help ! Help ! Your
Cæsar calls you ! Help, my people ! To the
rescue ! (*Suddenly throwing his spear away and
sinking on his knees, his face toward Lazarus, supplicatingly.*) Lazarus ! Forgive me ! Help
me ! Fear kills me ! Save me from death !

(*He is grovelling in a paroxysm of terror, grinding his face in his fists as if to hide it.*)

LAZARUS (*his voice is heard in a gentle, expiring sigh of compassion, followed by a faint dying note of laughter that rises and is lost in the sky like the flight of his soul back into the womb of Infinity.*) Fear not, Caligula ! There is no death !

CALIGULA (*lifts his head at the first sound and rises with the laughter to his feet, until, as it is finally lost, he is on tip-toes, his arms straining upward to the sky, a tender, childish laughter of love on his lips*). I laugh, Lazarus ! I laugh with you ! (*Then grief-stricken.*) Lazarus ! (*He hides his face in his hands, weeping.*) No more ! (*Then beats his head with his fists.*) I will remember ! I will ! (*Then suddenly, with a return to grotesqueness—harshly.*) All the same, I killed him and I proved there is death ! (*Immediately overcome by remorse, grovelling and beating himself.*) Fool ! Madman ! Forgive me, Lazarus ! Men forget !

CURTAIN

# Dynamo

## Characters

REVEREND HUTCHINS LIGHT.

AMELIA, *his wife.*

REUBEN, *their son.*

RAMSAY FIFE, *superintendent of a hydro-electric plant.*

MAY, *his wife.*

ADA, *their daughter.*

JENNINGS, *an operator at the plant.*

# GENERAL SCENE

## Act One

The exterior of the homes of the Lights and the Fifes in a small town in Connecticut. These houses stand side by side, facing front, on the street. They are set close together, separated by narrow strips of lawn, with a lilac hedge at centre marking the boundary-line between the two properties, and a row of tall maples in the background behind the yards and the two houses. The Fife house, a small brownish-tinted modern stucco bungalow type, recently built, is at left; the Light home, a little old New England white frame cottage with green shutters, at right. Only the half-sections of the two houses are visible which are nearest to each other, the one containing the Fife sitting-room, with Ramsay's and May's bedroom directly above it, and the section of the Lights' home in which are their sitting-room and Reuben's bedroom on the floor above.

As the separate scenes of Part One require, the front walls of these rooms are removed to show the different interiors. All these rooms are small, the ones in the Light home particularly so.

It is the month of May of the present day. The lilacs are in bloom, the grass is a fresh green.

### SCENES

SCENE I.  The Light sitting-room and Reuben's bedroom above it.

3

# DYNAMO

SCENE 2. The Fife sitting-room with Ramsay's and May's bedroom on the floor above.

SCENE 3. The Light and Fife sitting-rooms.

SCENE 4. Reuben's bedroom.

*Act Two*

SCENE 1. Same as Act One.
Fifteen months later.
The Light sitting-room.

SCENE 2. Reuben's bedroom. Night of the same day.

SCENE 3. Exterior of the hydro-electric power plant near the town. Half an hour later.

*Act Three*

GENERAL SCENE. The Hydro-Electric Power Plant near the town.
Four months later.

*Scene One.* Exterior of the plant.

*Scene Two.* Interiors of the upper and lower switch galleries.

*Scene Three.* Interiors of the two switch galleries, the switchboard room, and the dynamo room.

4

# ACT ONE

SCENE. *It is evening. In the background between the two houses the outlines of the maples are black against a sky pale with the light of a quarter-moon. Now and then there is a faint flash of lightning from far off and a low mumble of thunder.*

*The Light sitting-room and Reuben's bedroom are revealed. Both are sparsely furnished with the bare necessities. Reuben's bedroom contains an old four-poster bed, front, facing left, a small table on which are stacked his textbooks, and a chair in left corner, front. In the left wall is a window. A washstand with bowl and pitcher is in the left corner, rear, and an old-fashioned bureau in the middle of the rear wall. To the right of this is the door of a clothes closet. The door to the hall and the stairs is at right, rear. There is a lighted kerosene lamp on the table.*

*In the sitting-room below there is a table at centre, front. The minister's arm-chair is beside this on the left. His wife's rocker is at the right of the table. Farther right is another chair. Three small hooked rugs are on the floor. Several framed prints of scenes from the Bible hang on the walls. The minister's small desk is placed against the left wall beside the window. On the table at centre are a cheap oil reading-lamp, a Bible, and some magazines.*

5

*There is a door to the hall in the right wall, rear.*

*The ceilings of both rooms are low, the wall-paper so faded that the ugliness of its colour and design has been toned down into a neutral blur. But everything in this home is spotlessly clean and in order, the old furniture and floors are oiled and polished.*

*The Reverend Hutchins Light is seated in his arm-chair, his wife in her rocker. He is a man in his early sixties, slightly under medium height, ponderously built. His face is square, ribbed with wrinkles, the forehead low, the nose heavy, the eyes small and grey blue, the reddish hair grizzled and bushy, the stubborn jaw weakened by a big indecisive mouth. His voice is the bullying one of a sermonizer who is the victim of an inner uncertainty that compensates itself by being boomingly over-assertive.*

*His wife, Amelia, is fifteen years his junior and appears even younger. Her stout figure is still firm and active, with large breasts and broad, round hips. She must have been pretty as a girl. Even now her dark-complexioned face, with its big brown eyes and wavy black hair, retains its attractiveness although it has grown fleshy. Her expression is one of virtuous resignation. Only her mouth is rebellious. It is a thin small mouth, determined and stubborn, sensual and selfish.*

*In the bedroom above, their son, Reuben, is sitting in his shirt-sleeves on the side of his bed.*

*He is seventeen, tall and thin. His eyes are large, shy and sensitive, of the same grey blue as his father's. His mouth is like his father's. His jaw is stubborn, his thick hair curly and reddish-blond. He speaks timidly and hesitatingly, as a much younger boy might. His natural voice has an almost feminine gentleness. In intercourse with the world, however, he instinctively imitates his father's tone, booming self-protectively.*

*Hutchins Light has a pad on which he has been trying to make notes for his next sermon, but his mind is abstracted. He stares before him with the resentful air of one brooding over a wrong done him and unsuccessfully plotting revenge. His wife is pretending to read, but her thoughts are actively elsewhere, and she glances inquisitively at her husband from under lowered lids.*

*In the bedroom above, Reuben's eyes are turned toward the window, his face eager with dreams.*

LIGHT (*arguing tormentedly within himself*). What did he mean about Reuben ? . . . that foul-mouthed scoundrel ! . . . " Better call in your son or some night I might mistake his odour of sanctity for a skunk's and fill his " . . . filthy word belching from his grinning mouth ! . . . " full of buckshot " . . . I heard the corner loafers laugh . . . and I had to slink by and pretend not to hear ! . . . If it weren't for my cloth I'd have beaten his face to a bloody pulp ! . . .

I'd . . . ! (*Suddenly horrified at himself.*) A murderer's thoughts ! . . . Lord God, forgive me ! . . .

MRS. LIGHT (*glances at him and speaks in a gentle tone that carries a challenging quality*). Hutchins, do you realize Reuben will graduate from school in less than a month ?

LIGHT (*oblivious*). But, Lord, Thou knowest what a thorn in the flesh that atheist, Fife, has been since the devil brought him next door ! . . . (*Protesting petulantly to his God.*) How long, O Lord ? . . . does not his foul ranting begin to try Thy patience ? . . . is not the time ripe to smite this blasphemer who defies Thee publicly to strike him dead ? . . . Lord God of Hosts, why dost Thou not strike him ? . . . If Thou didst, I would proclaim the awful warning of it over all America ! . . . I would convert multitudes, as it was once my dream to do ! . . .

MRS. LIGHT. Hutchins, please pay attention to what I'm saying. Don't you think we ought to decide definitely about Reuben's future ?

LIGHT (*turns to her with a frown*). I have decided. He shall follow in my footsteps—mine and those of my father before me, and his father before him. It is God's manifest will ! (*He presses his lips tightly together—an effort to appear implacable that gives his face the expression of a balky animal's.*)

MRS. LIGHT (*thinks scornfully*). He is always so sure of what God wills ! . . . but Reuben'll never be a minister if I can prevent it ! . . . I'd rather see him dead than go through the poverty and humiliation I've had to face ! . . . Reuben's got to go to college . . . then into business . . . marry a nice girl with money . . . he doesn't care anything about girls yet, thank goodness !

(*She speaks in a meek persuasive tone.*) Each of us must judge about Reuben according to the light vouchsafed by God. He doesn't feel any call to the ministry and I think it would be a great sin if——

LIGHT (*his voice booming*). And I tell you, Amelia, it is God's will !

REUBEN (*hearing his father's voice, jumps to his feet and stares down toward the room with an expression of boyish apprehension*). What's he shouting about ? . . . has he heard about Ada and me ? . . . he'll raise the roof ! . . . but Mother'll take my side against him . . . she's always sided with me . . . and she won't hate Ada when she knows I love her . . . (*Then resentfully.*) What do I care about him anyway ? . . . he hates Fife because he's scared of him . . . he's scared to take up Fife's challenge to debate about whether there's a God or not . . . when Fife took out his watch and said if there was a God let Him prove it by striking him dead in five minutes, why was it nothing happened ? . . . I should think if . . . (*He looks around uneasily, afraid of where his thoughts are leading him. A faint flash of lightning from the distant storm flickers through his window. He starts guiltily and hastily makes a reassuring declaration of faith.*) Of course there's a God ! . . . He wouldn't pay any attention to a fool like Fife, that's all ! . . .

LIGHT.   I believe that storm must be coming this way.   (*He gets to his feet—a bit shamefacedly.*) I think I'll close the shutters.

MRS. LIGHT.   But it'll make it so dreadfully close in here !   (*Then seeing his ashamed look, she smiles.*)   Oh, all right, close them if you're getting scared.

LIGHT (*his dignity ruffled, turns his back on her and goes to the window*).   Lightning gets on lots of people's nerves without their being afraid of it.

REUBEN.   Aw, what's the matter with me ? . . . that lightning had nothing to do with what I was thinking . . .   (*He goes to the window and looks over toward the Fife home.*)   She said she'd put a record on the Victrola as soon as she was free . . . then I was to meet her down by the lilacs . . .   (*He breathes in the spring.*)   Gee, those lilacs smell sweet ! . . .   I wish she'd hurry up ! . . .   I've got to get up my nerve and tell her I love her . . .

LIGHT (*stands by the window and sniffs the air*). Can you smell the perfume of the lilacs, Amelia ? Do you remember our first spring here ?

MRS. LIGHT.   Of course.   (*Then, after a pause, her voice turned bitter.*)   Twenty-three years !

It's a long time to live in this awful little house !
Hutchins, are you ever going to insist that they
instal electric lighting here ?   It's a shame the
way they deny you the ordinary comforts of life !

> LIGHT (*turns away and leans out of the window,
> staring into the night.*)   Comforts of life ! . . . she
> has always desired the comfortable path . . . where
> the spirit decays in the sinful sloth of the flesh . . .

(*From the open, curtained windows of the Fife
living-room a burst of laughter is heard— Fife's
voice, sardonic and malicious.   Light draws back into
the room, muttering viciously.*)   Scum of the earth !
(*Then turning on his wife.*)   Tell me, has Reuben
been having anything to do with that cursed pack
next door ?   That scoundrel called something at
me on the street to-day that made me think——

MRS. LIGHT (*impatiently*).   Don't you know that
man well enough by this time not to pay attention
to his trying to rile you ?

LIGHT.   Then answer me this : why has Reuben taken such a sudden notion to going out in the
evening lately ?

MRS. LIGHT.   Do you expect a boy of his age to
stay in like a poor stick-in-the-mud just because he
happens to be a minister's son—especially when
it's spring !

LIGHT.   I remembered that it's spring—and
I've just remembered that Fife has a daughter !

MRS. LIGHT. That painted flapper with her skirts hitched up over her knees ! Do you think for one moment that Reuben, who never looks at girls anyway—and knowing what her father is !— Really, Hutchins, you're getting just too stupid !

*(From the Fife house comes the sound of a Victrola starting a jazz record.)*

REUBEN *(starts from his dream by the window upstairs).* That's her signal ! . . . *(He hurriedly puts on his coat.)* I better sneak out the back . . . *(He blows out the light and makes his way carefully out the bedroom door in right, rear.)*

LIGHT *(listening to the Victrola, fixes his eyes on his wife combatively).* You may call me as stupid as you like, but I insist there was something back of what that Fife said about Reuben. He sneered that we'd better keep him home at night and insinuated he was hanging around their place. The thought of that girl of his never entered my head until a moment ago—but what else could he mean ? I'm going to face Reuben with it right now and we'll see what he has to say for himself !

MRS. LIGHT *(sharply).* Now don't you go preaching at him again ! You better let me talk to him first. He's never lied to me. *(She goes toward the door in rear, plainly worried now, but trying to make little of it.)* You're always so ready to believe the worst of him ! I know it's all nonsense ! *(She goes out.)*

12

LIGHT (*sits thinking gloomily*).  Never lied to her . . . she means he does to me . . . why ? . . . have I been too stern ? . . . but even when he was little I sensed in him his mother's rebellious spirit . . . and now . . . if it is Fife's daughter . . . what a feather in that blasphemer's cap to corrupt my son ! . . . how the gossips would sneer at me ! . . . (*This thought drives him frantic—he paces up and down trying vainly to calm himself.*)  No, no ! . . . Reuben could never be guilty of so base a treachery ! . . . (*He sits down by the table and, picking up his Bible, begins to read in a determined effort to get his mind off the subject.*)

MRS. LIGHT (*can be dimly made out entering the bedroom above just as Reuben, coming from the back door of the house, slinks stealthily around the rear corner across the patch of moonlit lawn to the shadow of the lilacs.  Keeping in this shadow he moves down until he comes to a small gap that is almost at the end of the hedge, front.  He stands by this, waiting nervously, peering through the gap at the Fife house.  Mrs. Light thinks worriedly*).  Gone to bed ? . . . so early ? . . . was he sick and didn't tell me ? . . . (*She has come to the bed—with sudden fear.*)  He's not here ! . . . he must have sneaked out ! . . . the first time he ever did such a thing ! . . . but how do I know it's the first ? . . . all the evenings I thought he was here studying ! . . . it can only mean one thing ! . . . a girl ! . . . not a good girl ! . . . it must be that Fife girl ! . . . but I simply can't believe ! . . . (*She goes to the window, peering out but keeping her head carefully inside—with fierce jealousy.*)  That dirty little . . . I'd like to see her try to catch my Reuben ! . . . (*There is a strong flash of distant lightning that suddenly reveals Reuben in his hiding-place by the hedge. She gives a gasp.*) Oh ! . . . there he is ! . . . watching their house ! . . . I've got to make sure ! . . . Oh, Reuben, I can't believe it, you've never noticed girls ! . . .

> *There is darkness for a moment—(as if the moon had passed behind a cloud)—to mark the end of* SCENE ONE. *No time elapses between* SCENES ONE *and* TWO.

### SCENE TWO

SCENE. *When it grows light again the outer walls of the two rooms in the Light home have been replaced, while the interiors of the Fife sitting-room and the couple's bedroom above it are now revealed. There is one small window on the top floor front of the Light home, two on the ground floor. Mrs. Light's head can be seen peering out of the side bedroom window at Reuben, crouched in the shadow of the lilacs. The two rooms in the Fife home, bright with all their electric lights on, are of a glaring newness. There is a table at centre, front, in the sitting-room, a Victrola in the rear corner, left, near the door in the left wall which leads to the hall. In the right wall are three windows looking out on the lawn toward the lilac hedge and the Light home. These windows are repeated in the same series in the bedroom above. The bed is at left, front, its head against the left wall. In the same wall to the rear of the bed, is the door. There is a dressing table with a big mirror against the rear wall, right, near the windows.*

*Ramsay Fife is seated at the left of the table, glancing through the pages of a technical book on Hydro-Electric Engineering. His wife is lying back in a chaise longue that she has pushed close to the windows on the right so she can stare up at the sky.*

*Fife is a small wiry man of fifty, of Scotch-Irish origin, with a sharp face and keen black eyes. His thin mouth is full of the malicious humour of the practical joker. He has a biting tongue, but at bottom is a good-natured man except where the religious bigotry of his atheism is concerned.*

*His wife is tall and stout, weighing well over two hundred. Her face must have once been one of those rosy-cheeked pretty doll-like faces, and in spite of its fat, it has kept its girlish naïveté and fresh complexion. Her figure is not formless nor flabby. It suggests, rather, an inert strength. A mass of heavy copper-coloured hair is piled without apparent design around her face. Her mouth is small, with full lips. Her eyes are round and dark blue. Their expression is blank and dreamy. Her voice is sentimental and wondering. She is about forty years old.*

*Their daughter, Ada, sixteen, who is upstairs in the bedroom putting on a heavy make-up of*

*rouge and mascara, resembles her father more
than her mother. She has his alert quality.
Her pretty face, with her mother's big blue eyes,
is alive and keen, her mouth has a touch of her
father's malicious humour. Her brown hair is
boyishly bobbed. Her manner is self-assertive
and consciously slangy. She is at the stage
where being a hardened flapper is her frank
ambition as her short skirts and obtrusive make-up
give evidence. Beneath her flip talk, however,
one senses a strong trace of her mother's senti-
mentality.*

MRS. FIFE (*dreaming sentimentally*). I hear Ada
upstairs . . . she's primping up before my mirror
. . . she's falling in love . . . it's nice to be in
love in May . . . I love May better than any
other month . . . May is when I first met Ramsay . . . it's warm to-night . . . I mustn't forget
to make Ramsay change to his summer underwear
this week . . . he always wears his heavies too
long and gets prickly heat and then he's terrible
cross . . .

FIFE (*reading—disgustedly*). " Hydro-Electric
engineering " . . . it's studying this stuff gives
those stuck-up engineers their diplomas . . .
" Frequency and number of phases " . . . " In-
herent Regulations " . . . " Parallel Working "
. . . " Wave Form " . . . diagrams and equa-
tions ! . . . " The kinetic energy of a rotor of
diameter D and axial length L, running at a speed
of rotation $n$, is theoretically proportional to $D4$
$Ln2$ " . . . arrh ! . . . the devil take their the-

ories ! . . . when anything goes wrong at the plant it's me who fixes it without any theory ! . . .

(*He tosses the book on the table and speaks to his wife.*) I wish Townsend wouldn't go forcing his books on me, telling me I owe it to myself to pass for engineer's papers. (*With a chuckle.*) Him arguing with me and at the same time admitting " Fife, you know a damn sight more about this game than I do."

MRS. FIFE (*mooning at him with adoring eyes— simply*). You know more than anyone, Ramsay.

FIFE (*pleased, but amused—teasing her as he would a big child*). Oho, I do, do I ? How the hell do you know ? (*Then complacently.*) Well, I do know more than most. There isn't a damn job in the game I haven't had a hand at some time or another.

(*He looks at her and sees she is not listening any more.*) Look at her ! . . . in a dope dream again . . . I might as well be married to a cow . . . (*Then amusedly.*) Well, she's a damn funny woman . . . I've never seen her equal any- where . . .

(*He sees the newspaper on the table and reaches for it. He glances at the head- lines and settles down to reading with a grunt of awakened interest.*)

MRS. FIFE (*has again fallen to dreaming senti- mentally of the past*). When I first met Ramsay he was a linesman . . . I loved him at first sight . . . he was so romantic looking with those steel climbing things on his legs . . . and he wore a coloured handkerchief round his neck just like a cowboy . . . Pa and Ma warned me linesmen were no good . . . they just ruined you and went their way . . . they were wrong about Ramsay . . . except he did ruin me . . . I said, why is it wrong when I love him ? . . . Pa yelled to get out, I'd disgraced the family . . . I never expected Ramsay'd marry me . . . he was the roving kind . . . but as soon as he knew he'd got me into trouble he spoke right up . . . " Oh, hell, then I guess I've got to marry you " . . . and I said yes, and I was awful happy . . . and five months after Ada was born and he was crazy about her from the first . . . and we've all been happy ever since . . . (*She sighs contentedly.*)

ADA (*in the bedroom above, finishes making up and inspects herself critically in the mirror—approvingly*). I got to hand it to you, baby, you're there ! . . . Gosh, how long is it since I put on that record ? . . . Rube'll be waiting . . . he's as bashful as a kid . . . but that's what I like about him . . . I'm sick of these fresh guys that think all they have to do is wink and you fall ! . . . Rube has got honest-to-God feelings . . . but of course, I'd never love him . . . he's too big a Mamma's boy for me . . . (*She goes to the door and puts her hand on the switch.*) Well, let's go . . . I'm dying to see if he'll have nerve enough to kiss me . . . (*She turns out the light.*)

REUBEN (*crouched by the hedge, gives a start as a flash of lightning flickers over the sky*). Gosh, I wish Ada'd hurry up . . . this isn't much fun . . . I'm losing all my nerve waiting . . .

MRS. LIGHT (*bending out of the window in Reuben's bedroom—in suspense between suspicion and hope*). She doesn't seem to be coming . . . maybe it's only some game he's playing . . . waiting to scare some friend of his . . .

FIFE (*looking up from his paper with a snort of rage and disgust just as Ada enters the room*). The bloody swinepot !

ADA (*comes and puts an arm around his shoulder teasingly*). What's the bad news, Pop ? Has another Fundamentalist been denying Darwin ?

FIFE (*boiling over with indignation, thrusting the paper on her, his finger pointing out the article*). Read this and you won't joke about it ! (*As Ada begins to read, he speaks to his wife.*) Of all the yellow tricks !

MRS. FIFE (*coming out of her dream with a start*). What, Ramsay ?

FIFE. This story in the paper ! There was a man in Ohio many years back killed another fellow in a fight about a girl. He got twenty years for it, but the girl helped him to escape and they both got clean away to the Coast, where he settled down under another name and they were married and had a daughter. He became one of the town's best citizens, and damned if his daughter didn't get engaged to the minister's son ! Then, just before the wedding, the old man feels he's honour bound to tell his future son-in-law the secret of his past ; so the damned idiot blathers the whole

story of his killing the man and breaking jail !
And what do you suppose that young skunk does ?
Breaks off with the girl and goes to the police with
the story, saying he's bound by his conscience to
squeal on him !

ADA (*who has finished reading the story*).   Phew !
Some louse, that boy !

FIFE.   Arrh !   They're all the same, the Bible-
punching breed !   (*Then with a touch of severity.*)
And mind you bear that in mind, young lady,
when you're fooling with that young ass next
door !

ADA.   Hey listen, Pop !   Honestly, I think
you've got a nerve to—— Why, it was you said
to start up an acquaintance with him, when I told
you I'd caught him staring at me, because you
knew how it'd get his old man's goat !

FIFE (*his sense of humour returning—with a
malicious grin*).   Aye, it will that !   I gave him a
strong hint on the street to-day that upset him.
Oh, if you'd only make a prize jackass of that
yellow Nancy son of his !

ADA.   Say, why have you got it in for Rube so ?
He's not to blame for his father.   (*Then hastily.*)
Not that it's anything in my young life.   I'm
simply having fun kidding him along.   (*Then
defensively again.*)   But Rube's a good scout—in
his way.   He isn't yellow.

MRS. FIFE (*suddenly—with a placid certainty*).
You're falling in love, Ada.

ADA (*confused*). Aw, Mom, where d'you get that stuff?

FIFE (*has glanced at her with suspicion*). So you don't believe that lad's yellow, don't you? What'll you bet he isn't? (*Then as she doesn't answer.*) I dare you to bring him in to-night, and let me talk to him and you listen, and if I don't show him up yellow then I'll buy you the best dress you can find in the town! (*As she hesitates—tauntingly.*) Are you afraid to take me up?

ADA (*with defensive flippancy, turns to go*). I'll think about it. There's a dress in Steele's I've had my eye on. (*She goes out the door on left.*)

FIFE (*looks after her—frowning*). She acts queer about him . . . it's time I took a hand in this . . . I've got to fix up a scheme on him quick . . . she'll bring him back if she has to drag him . . .

ADA (*has come out of the house by the front door, off left, and enters from the left, then hesitates for a moment, debating with herself*). Shall I make him come in? . . . he'll be scared stiff! . . . but Pop was only bluffing . . . well, I'll just call his bluff! . . . He can't get away with that stuff with me! . . . . (*She walks toward the gap in the hedge.*)

MRS. LIGHT (*has caught a glimpse of her from the window*). There she comes now! . . . .

ADA (*calling*). Rube.

REUBEN (*comes through the hedge to her—sheepishly*). Hello, Ada. (*Then, as he stands beside her, looking down into her face, a sudden thrill of desire almost overcomes his timidity.*) Gosh, Ada—you're pretty in the moonlight. I—I wish— (*His courage fails him—lamely.*) It's certainly grand to-night, isn't it ?

ADA. Yeah. It's great. (*She takes one of his hands.*) Come on in my house and meet Pop. I want you to see he isn't the devil out of hell your old man makes him out to be.

REUBEN (*immediately terrified*). I can't, Ada ! You know I can't ! Why don't we walk the same as——

ADA. I'm sick of walking. (*As he still holds back—tauntingly.*) Are you scared Pop will eat you ? You make me sick, Rube !

REUBEN. It's not because I'm scared of your father ; it's because——

ADA. Afraid your Mamma would spank you if she found out ? (*Then as he still hesitates.*) Oh, very well, you know what you can do, don't you ? (*She turns her back on him and walks away.*)

REUBEN. Ada ! Wait a minute ! Please don't get sore ! I'll come !

ADA. Good boy ! (*She suddenly raises herself on tiptoe and kisses him—with a little laugh.*) There ! That's to help keep your nerve up !

REUBEN (*a wave of passion coming over him, grabs her by the shoulders and bends his face close to hers*). Ada !

22

ADA. Ouch ! That hurts, Rube !

REUBEN. I don't care if it does ! I love you, Ada ! (*He tries to kiss her.*)

ADA (*struggling away from him*). Hey, cut it out ! What do you think I am ? (*Then, as, brought back to himself, he releases her in shamefaced confusion, she adds tartly, her confidence restored and her temper a bit ruffled.*) Listen here, Rube, just because I kissed you in fun, don't get too fresh !

REUBEN. I—I didn't mean nothing bad— honest I didn't !

ADA. All right, only don't get rough again. (*Taking his hand—in a bullying tone.*) Come on ! Let's go in !

(*Reuben follows her off left mechanically, a
look of growing dread on his face.*)

MRS. LIGHT. She kissed him ! . . . the brazen little harlot ! . . . where is she taking him ? . . . I've got to stop her ! . . .

(*She draws back quickly from the window.*)

FIFE (*irritably*). May the devil kill me if I can think up a good scheme . . .

(*He turns his exasperation on his wife.*) How can I think in the same room with you ? It's like trying to swim in glue ! For God's sake, get out of here !

MRS. FIFE (*raises herself to her feet placidly, with-*

*out a trace of resentment*). I'll go upstairs and read the paper.

FIFE (*starts to thrust the paper on her*). Here you are then ! (*But as he does so his eye lights on the same headline that had attracted his attention before and suddenly he has an inspiration and grins elatedly.*) By God, I've got it, May ! I'll try that on him ! All the pious folks in this town think I've a bad record behind me— (*He pushes the paper into her hands.*) Get out of here quick ! I don't want you around to give me away !

> (*She goes out. He waits, looking at the door, a grin of malicious expectancy on his face. At this moment Mrs. Light, who has come out by her kitchen door, appears around the corner of her house and slinks hurriedly across the patch of lawn to the shadow of the lilacs at the extreme edge of the hedge, front.*)

MRS. LIGHT (*peers stealthily around the corner of the hedge down the street—in an extreme state of agitation*). I can't see them . . . they're hiding somewhere . . . she'll be kissing him . . . oh, just wait till I tell her what I think of her ! . . . (*She starts out of the shadow of the lilacs as if to go down the street, but the brightness of the moonlight frightens her and she moves quickly back into the shadow.*) Supposing anyone should see me ! . . . oh, I don't know what to do ! . . . that nasty wicked boy ! . . . he'll be punished good for this ! . . .

# DYNAMO

(*There is darkness again for a moment, to mark the end of* SCENE TWO. *No time elapses between* SCENES TWO *and* THREE.)

## SCENE THREE

SCENE. *When the light comes on again, the wall of the Fife bedroom has been replaced. Their sitting-room is revealed as before with Fife still sitting looking expectantly at the door. And now the interior of the Light sitting-room is again shown with Light sitting as at the end of* SCENE ONE. *He holds the open Bible but he is staring moodily over it. Mrs. Light, as before, is hiding in the shadow of the lilac hedge, peering down the road, ashamed of her position and afraid she will be discovered.*

LIGHT (*thinking gloomily*). I must be honest with myself . . . who am I to cast the first stone at Reuben if he desires a woman ? . . . hasn't my love for Amelia been one long desire of the senses ? . . . I should understand Reuben's weakness and forgive him . . . (*Then his resentment smouldering up.*) But to betray me to Fife ! . . . that would go deeper ! . . . it would be treachery to God ! . . .

MRS. FIFE (*leans out of the front window of the bedroom upstairs*). I don't want to read the paper . . . I'd rather look at the moon . . . (*Mooning up at the moon.*) Ada loves that Light boy . . . he must be nice . . . he isn't to blame because his father believes in religion . . . maybe his father is nice too if you got to know him off the

25

job . . . Ramsay is always so cranky when he's at the plant . . . I love the plant . . . I love the dynamos . . . I could sit for ever and listen to them sing . . . they're always singing about everything in the world . . .

(*She hums to herself for a moment—an imitation of the metallic purr of a dynamo.*)

MRS. LIGHT (*hearing this noise, looks up around the corner of the hedge and sees her and immediately dissolves into abject shame and fright*). Oh, my God ! . . . did she see me ? . . . she'll tell the whole town I was spying ! . . . Oh, this is terrible ! . . . I ought to get Hutchins ! . . . but I can't move while she's watching ! . . .

FIFE (*standing up and looking at the door*). Ada's a long time bringing him . . . there's a lot of whispering in the hall . . . he's afraid, I'm thinking . . . about to enter the presence of Satan . . . I'll have to start in making him think that I'm the devil himself ! . . .

(*Ada comes in the doorway of the sitting-room, left, followed by Reuben, whose face wears an expression of mingled apprehension and bravado.*)

FIFE (*without waiting for an introduction, goes up and shakes Reuben's hand with an exaggerated cordiality*). So you're young Mr. Light, are you ? I'm damned glad to make your acquaintance. Sit down and make yourself at home.

(*All the time he is talking, he stares at Reuben's flustered face, keenly sizing*

26

*him up. He forces him to sit in the chair across the table from him. Ada sits down at right, watching her father with a challenging smile.*)

REUBEN (*stammers*). Pleased to meet you. Thank you. Thanks.

FIFE (*with a sudden change to severity*). I want a damned serious talk with you, young man ! That's why I had Ada invite you in ! (*As Reuben stares at him bewilderedly.*) But before we start that, let me ask you, is your reverend father ever going to take up my challenge to debate with me ?

REUBEN (*shamefacedly*). I—I don't think so.

FIFE (*jeeringly*). He's afraid I'd beat him.

REUBEN (*defensively*). No, he isn't ! He can answer all your arguments easy—with things right out of the Bible ! He's only scared that folks'd think he was wrong to argue with you ! (*Then raising his voice defiantly.*) But I'd argue with you if I was in his place !

MRS. LIGHT (*from her hiding-place by the hedge has caught Reuben's raised voice—with horrified stupefaction*). That was Reuben's voice ! . . . he's actually in there talking to that atheist ! . . . Oh, I wish I could get closer the window ! . . . but she'd see me ! . . .

(*But she comes around the end of the hedge as far as she can get and strains her ears.*)

FIFE (*smiling mockingly at Reuben*). Well, maybe after you're a minister you and me'll argue it out some time.

REUBEN (*glad to make a show of his independence before Fife*). I'm not going to be a minister ! Father wants me to, but Mother doesn't—and I don't want to be. Besides, I've never felt the call. You have to feel God calling you to His service.

FIFE (*with a leer*). And how does God call you, tell me ? I'm thinkin' He wouldn't use the telegraph or telephone or radio, for they're contraptions that belong to His arch-enemy, Lucifer, the God of Electricity.

> (*Reuben's face has flushed with mingled indignation and fear. He looks up at the ceiling apprehensively, then opens his mouth to make some retort to Fife when there is a vivid flash of lightning. He gives a start and half rises from his chair, controlling an impulse to run from the room. Fife's keen eyes are watching him and he grins with satisfaction.*)

REUBEN (*stammers*). You better not—talk like that, or—you better look out !

FIFE. What's the trouble, young fellow ? Are you afraid of a bit of lightning ? Don't worry about me. The devil looks after his own ! But a minister's son has reason to worry, maybe, when he's in a den of atheism, holding intimate converse with a damned man ! I'm thinking your Jehovah might aim a thunderbolt at me but Lucifer would deflect it on to you—and he's the better electrical expert of the two, being more modern in his methods than your God !

REUBEN (*in a turmoil of guilt and fright*).   I wish I'd never come here !  . . .   God may strike him !  . . .   He certainly ought to !  . . . if I was God, I'd kill him for blaspheming like that !  . . .

ADA (*observing Reuben—worriedly*).   Why did the poor boob let Pop get wise he was scared of lightning.  (*Then indignantly.*)   Pop has no right to pick on religion !  . . . that's hitting below the belt !  . . .

(*Protestingly.*)   Aw, Pop, lay off religion, can't you !

FIFE (*glances at her irritably—then with a calculating tone to Reuben*).   Ada's right, Mr. Light.   I didn't have you in to convert you to atheism. This is a free country and you're free to believe any God-forsaken lie you like—even the book of Genesis !  (*Then solemnly.*)   But here's what I did have you in for, and I'll come right to the point.   As a father, I want to know what your intentions are regarding my daughter !

(*Reuben stares at him in open-mouthed amazement.*)

ADA (*embarrassed but cannot help a giggle of amusement when she looks at Reuben*).   Aw, Pop, what——

FIFE.   Keep your tongue out of this !  (*Sternly, to Reuben.*)   I trust you mean honourably by her, young fellow, or it'll be the worse for you !   I'll have no young spark seducing my daughter— getting her with child, maybe, and then deserting her with no marriage lines to save her from disgrace !

*(Ada begins to see this as a huge joke, and she
has to bury her face in her hands to
choke back her laughter as she looks at
Reuben's face, on which is at first a
shocked look of stupefaction. But this
gives way to a fit of indignation that
anyone could think him so low.)*

REUBEN. What do you think I am? You
have no right to say that about me! I'm not
that kind of— *(Then his voice booming like his
father's with moral self-righteousness.)* I respect
Ada just as much as I do my mother! I'm going
to marry her!

ADA *(genuinely flustered—trying to laugh it off)*.
Gee, Rube, did I say you had no nerve? I take it
all back!

*(Reuben's nerve immediately deserts him.
He hangs his head in acute embarrassment, his eyes on the floor.)*

MRS. LIGHT *(by the end of the hedge)*. Marry
her! . . . I heard it clear as day! . . . respect
her like he does me! . . . damn her! . . .
Oh, I didn't mean to swear! . . . I don't know
what I'm doing! . . . *(Then weeping hysterically
and trying to stifle it.)* Oh, I'll get Hutchins to
beat him within an inch of his life! . . . *(She
sinks down on the ground, her hands over her face.)*
I've got to stop! . . . she'll hear me up there!
. . . she'll tell how I was crying! . . .

MRS. FIFE *(has noticed the noise of Mrs. Light's
movements and looks down vaguely)*. Some

animal's in the garden . . . maybe it's a skunk
. . . I'd love to have a skunk-skin coat next
winter . . . maybe Ramsay'll give me one for
Christmas . . . Ramsay calls the minister a
skunk . . . poor Mr. Light ! . . . Ramsay says
awful mean things sometimes . . . but it's only
because he loves to make jokes . . . he's the
kindest man in the world ! . . .

FIFE (*pretending to be sunk in thought, has been
staring calculatingly at Reuben—solemnly*). Young
man, I'll be honest with you. In view of your
honourable intentions I feel bound by my conscience to let you know the secret of the family
you're wanting to marry into. But you must give
me your word of honour, as man to man—I don't
ask you to swear on the Bible—that you'll never
repeat what I'm saying to anyone, no matter how
dreadful it seems to you ! Will you give me your
word ?

REUBEN (*made visibly uneasy, but forcing a manly
tone*). Sure. I wouldn't ever say anything.

ADA (*leaning forward in her chair and watching her father worriedly*). What's Pop going to
spring ? . . . Rube's looking pale behind the
gills, poor guy ! . . . aw, poor nothing ! . . . he
ought to have more guts ! . . .

FIFE (*with a tragic sigh*). There's not a living
soul knows it, barring my wife and Ada. It's
like putting my life in your hands. You know,
don't you, that no one knows what I done before I
came to this town, nor where I came from. I've
good reason for keeping it dark. Listen now.

Twenty years ago there was a man by the name of Andrew Clark lived in the town of Arming, Ohio— (*He pauses significantly, giving a quick side glance at Ada to see if she's caught the joke.*)

ADA (*a light breaking on her*). Gee, it's that newspaper story ! . . . he's going to pretend he's . . . (*Then indignantly.*) Does he think Rube'd ever do what that skunk did ? . . .

FIFE (*goes on with a guilty furtiveness—lowering his voice*). Now Clark was in love with a girl whose family had got her engaged to another fellow, but she loved Clark and used to meet him in the woods. But this fellow who was engaged to her got suspicious and one night he sneaked up on them lying in each other's arms—in sin, as you'd call it—and he rushed out with a knife at them both, but Clark picked up an axe and split his skull ! (*He finishes up with well-feigned savagery.*) And serve him right, the bloody sneak !

REUBEN (*stares at Fife with horror—stammers weakly*). You mean—Clark murdered him ?

FIFE (*with a great pretence of guilt-stricken protest*). Oh, don't say that ! Not murder ! He killed him in self-defence—when he was crazy with rage and love. Wouldn't you do the same if Ada was the girl and you was Clark ?

REUBEN. What is he asking ? . . . Ada ? . . . would I ? . . . (*Then his horror turning to a confused rage.*) I'd kill Ada if I caught her ! . . . but it was the other man who caught ! . . . and

they were engaged, too ! . . . she belonged to
him ! . . .

(*Harshly and condemningly—in his father's tone.*)
That other fellow should have killed them, that's
what I think ! That girl was engaged to the
other fellow ! She had no right to love Clark !
That wasn't love, it was lust ! She was an
adulteress ! It would have been only her just
punishment if that fellow had killed her ! I
would have !

FIFE. For the love of God, don't be so hard—
for what I was coming to tell you was that I was
Clark !

(*As if to punctuate this dramatic confession,
there is a flash of lightning, brighter
than any that has gone before.*)

REUBEN (*clutches the arms of his chair in superstitious terror, all the passion drained out of him
instantly, leaving him weak and penitent*). Oh,
God, please forgive me ! . . . I didn't mean
it ! . . . I wouldn't ever kill her ! . . . (*Then
glancing at Fife with fear.*) He's a murderer !
. . . he said himself he was damned . . .

FIFE (*eyeing Reuben keenly*). After I'd killed
him I gave myself up. The jury said it was
murder in the second degree and gave me twenty
years—but I fooled 'em with the help of the girl
and escaped and we both ran off to the far west
and settled down in Niclum, California, and I
married her under the name of Fife and we had a
daughter. That's Ada.

REUBEN (*keeping his eyes averted from Ada*). Then that's her mother ! . . . she's the daughter of an adulteress ! . . . and a murderer ! . . . how can I ever trust her ? . . . she's gone around with lots of fellows . . . how do I know she never— ? . . . (*Then torturedly.*) Oh, God, why did I ever come here to-night ? . . .

FIFE (*with a great pretence of uneasiness*). You don't say a word. Well, maybe I shouldn't have told you, because now I've made you an accessory in the murder, for you'll be shielding me unlawfully by keeping silence ! And the devil knows what sin you'll think it in the sight of God !

(*The clap of thunder from the preceding flash comes with a great rumble.*)

REUBEN (*filled with fear*). Accessory ! . . . the police can arrest me ! . . . (*Then summoning his manhood.*) But I won't tell them ! . . . ever ! . . . I gave my word ! . . . (*Then conscience-stricken.*) But God ! . . . I'll be guilty before God ! . . . but He knows I gave my word ! . . . but does that count with Him ? . . . when I didn't swear on the Bible ? . . . (*Then frantically.*) But He knows I love Ada ! . . . He wouldn't want me to tell on her father . . .

(*He suddenly jumps up and mumbles to Fife.*) I won't tell the police, you needn't worry.

ADA (*with a triumphant glance at her father*). Good for you, Rube !

REUBEN (*avoiding her eyes*). I've got to go home now.

FIFE (*searching Reuben's face—insistently*). I'm sorry to put such a load on your conscience, Mr. Light, but I felt it was only right of me.

REUBEN. Why does he rub it in? . . . God, I hate him! . . . I wish they'd hanged him! . . .

(*Angrily—his voice booming denouncingly like his father's.*) You needn't be afraid I'll tell—but you ought to go and tell yourself! You know you're guilty in the sight of God! Do you want to burn for ever in hell?

FIFE (*tauntingly*). Your hell and God mean no more to me than old women's nonsense when they're scared of the dark!

REUBEN (*threateningly*). Don't you dare talk like that! I won't stand for it—not now! If you don't stop your blaspheming, I'll—I mean, it'd serve you right if I— (*Hurrying toward the door as if in flight.*) I got to get home. (*He stops at the door and turns to Ada, but keeps his eyes averted.*) Good night, Ada. (*He goes out.*)

ADA. He was threatening Pop already he'd tell on him! . . . Gee, he is yellow all right! . . . (*Tears of mortification and genuine hurt come to her eyes—she brushes them back.*) Aw, what do I care about him? . . .

FIFE (*with a chuckle*). He'll be blabbin' my dreadful secret to his old man yet, wait and see!

35

ADA (*to his surprise, turns on him angrily*). It wasn't fair ! He never had a chance !

(*She flings herself on the chaise longue and begins to cry.*)

FIFE (*stares at her in astonishment*). Are you turning against me—for that lump ! (*Then he comes and pats her on the shoulder.*) I was only doing it for your sake, Ada. You ought to see him in his true colours so you'd not be thinking too much about him.

ADA (*forces back her tears and jumps up*). I didn't think anything ! Leave me alone about him, can't you ? (*With a great pretence of indifference she gets a book from the table and sits down again.*) I should worry about that poor fish ! I've got to study my algebra.

(*Her father stares at her puzzledly. There is a bright flash of lightning and Light, sitting as before in the sitting-room of the other house reading the Bible, jumps nervously to his feet.*)

LIGHT. I ought to conquer that silly fear in myself . . . the lightning is God's will . . . what on earth can Amelia be doing with Reuben all this time ? . . . (*He listens for a moment—uneasily.*) I'll go upstairs to them . . . she should be more considerate than to leave me alone when . . .

(*He walks toward the door on right.*)

(*There is a pause of darkness here to mark the end of* SCENE THREE. *In this darkness the clap of thunder from the preceding flash comes. No time elapses between Scenes Three and Four.*)

SCENE FOUR

SCENE. *When the light comes on again—but this time very dimly, as if the moon were behind clouds—the walls of the Fife and Light sitting-rooms have been replaced, while the interior of Reuben's bedroom is now revealed.*

*Mrs. Fife still leans out of her bedroom window and Mrs. Light sits crouching by the hedge.*

MRS. LIGHT (*suddenly jumping to her feet and peering up through the leaves at Mrs. Fife*). Oh God, isn't she ever going in ? . . . I'll scream in a minute ! . . .

MRS. FIFE. I love to watch lightning . . . the thunder clouds are getting nearer the moon . . . I'd like to be a cloud . . . it must be nice to float in the wind . . . but it must be getting bed-time . . .

(*She slowly backs herself into her room.*)

MRS. LIGHT (*as Mrs. Fife disappears*). Now I can get Hutchins . . .

(*She slinks back along the hedge and then quickly across the lawn around the corner of her house just as Reuben enters from the left by the Fife house.*)

37

REUBEN (*stands hesitating—uneasily*).   I thought
I'd walk around and think up some lie . . .
Mother'll guess something's wrong as soon as she
looks at me . . . but I'm not going to stay out in
the storm . . . (*He walks slowly over to where he
had stood with Ada—dully*.)   Here's where she
kissed me . . . why couldn't we have gone for a
walk ? . . . she'd have let me kiss her, . . .
I'd have had her in my arms . . . like her mother
was with Clark ? . . . no, I didn't mean that !
. . . I didn't mean sin ! . . . (*Then with desperate bravado*.)   Aw, what is sin, anyway ? . . .
maybe that's just old women's nonsense, like Fife
says ! . . . why should I have a guilty conscience ? . . . it's God's fault ! . . . why hasn't
He done something to Fife ? . . .   I should think
He'd have to punish adultery and murder . . . if
there is any God . . . (*There is a great flash of
lightning and he stands paralysed with superstitious
terror*.)   It comes every time ! . . . when I
deny ! . . . (*More and more obsessed by a feeling
of guilt, of being a condemned sinner alone in the
threatening night*.)   Fife's damned me with him !
. . . there's no use praying ! . . . it's getting
black ! . . . I'm afraid of God ! . . .

(*There is a crash of thunder. He cowers,
trembling—then cries like a frightened little boy*.)
Mother !   Mother !

> (*He runs off right, forgetting that he has
> sneaked out by the back, making for the
> front door.   At the same moment Light
> can be dimly made out as he enters
> Reuben's bedroom, and Fife sticks his*

*head out of his sitting-room window and looks toward the Light home.)*

FIFE. That was him I heard passing . . . I'll wait here and watch the fun . . . (*He chuckles to himself.*)

LIGHT (*pauses just inside the door in alarm at finding the room dark and empty—calls uneasily*). Amelia ! Reuben !

> (*He lights a match with trembling fingers and hurries over to the lamp and lights it. His wife's voice comes excitedly from the hall-way, calling.*)

MRS. LIGHT. Hutchins !

LIGHT (*hurries to the door, meeting her as she comes in*). Amelia ! Thank God !

MRS. LIGHT (*excitedly, her words pouring out*). Oh, Hutchins, something awful has happened— that Fife girl—I heard Reuben asking Fife if he could marry her !

> (*Light, completely stunned, stares at her blankly. There is the noise of the front door being slammed and Reuben's voice calling desperately.*)

REUBEN. Mother ! Where are you ?

MRS. LIGHT. Sshh ! Let him come up here. (*Pushing him toward the closet in rear.*) You hide in that closet and listen ! I'll make him acknowledge everything ! He'd only lie to you ! (*Vindictively.*) I promise I won't stand between him and punishment this time ! (*She gives him a final shove inside the door and closes it.*)

REUBEN (*his voice comes from the hall as he rushes upstairs*). Mother ! (*A second later he runs in and, too distracted to notice her expression, throws his arms around her.*) Mother ! (*He breaks down and sobs.*)

MRS. LIGHT (*alarmed by the state he is in, puts her arms around him, her immediate reaction one of maternal tenderness. She leads him front and sits on the side of the bed*). There, there ! It's all right, Reuben ! Mother's here ! (*Then indignantly.*) What have those awful people been doing to my boy to get him in such a state ? (*As he gives a start—sharply.*) Now don't deny you were there ! Don't make matters worse by lying ! What happened between you and that man ? Tell Mother !

REUBEN (*brokenly*). I can't ! I promised him I wouldn't. I can't tell anyone !

MRS. LIGHT (*changing to a tone of wheedling affection*). Yes, you can, Reuben. You can always tell Mother everything. You always have.

REUBEN (*clinging to her*). I love Mother better'n anything in the world . . . she always forgives me . . . I wish I could tell her . . . she'd know what was right . . .

(*There is a bright flash of lightning. He shrinks closer to her and blurts out.*) I'm scared, Mother ! I'm guilty ! I'm damned.

MRS. LIGHT (*startled*). Guilty ? . . . does he mean he ? . . . (*With sudden strong revulsion.*) And to think he's had those same arms hugging that little filthpot this very evening ! . . .

(*She pushes him away, but, holding his shoulders, stares down into his face.*) Do you mean to say you refuse to tell your own mother, just because you were forced into promising not to by that atheist ? Then all I can say is that my boy I thought I could trust has turned into a liar and a sneak, and I don't wonder you feel guilty in God's sight !

> (*As she finishes speaking, the roll of the thunder from the preceding flash comes crashing and rumbling. Reuben sinks down on his knees beside her, hiding his face in her lap.*)

REUBEN (*stammers*). I'll tell you, Mother—if you promise to keep it a secret—just between me and you—and never tell Father.

MRS. LIGHT. All right. I'll promise I won't tell your father.

REUBEN (*made uneasy by something in her tone—insistently*). You'll swear it on the Bible ?

MRS. LIGHT. Yes, I'll swear on the Bible I won't tell him.

REUBEN (*in a passion of eagerness to get the guilty tale off his conscience*). His name isn't even Fife, it's Clark ! He changed it because he'd murdered a man out in Ohio where he used to live. He got twenty years but he escaped and ran away to California ! Fife's a murderer, that's what he really is !

> (*While he has been telling this story, the closet door has opened and Light stands there, listening greedily. In his hand is a belt of Reuben's.*)

LIGHT (*thinking with a fierce, revengeful joy*). Lord God of Righteous Vengeance, I thank Thee ! . . . at last Thou strikest ! . . .

MRS. LIGHT (*dumbfounded, not knowing what to make of this strange tale—and disappointed that it is not a confession about Ada*). Wherever did you get hold of this story ?

REUBEN. He told me himself !

MRS. LIGHT. Do you expect me to believe Fife's such an idiot as to confess such things to you ?

REUBEN. He had a good reason to tell me ! I asked him if I could marry Ada and he thought he was honour bound to tell me ! He knew it'd be safe with me when I gave him my word——

> (*Then thinking with guilty shame.*) But I've told ! . . . I've just told ! . . . why did I ? . . . Oh, how Ada would hate me if she knew ! . . .

(*Pleadingly.*) Remember you swore on the Bible you'd never tell ! Remember, Mother !

MRS. LIGHT (*still gripping him, glaring into his face vindictively*). So you want to marry that little harlot, do you ?

REUBEN (*shakes her hands off his shoulders—shrinking back from her, still on his knees*). Don't you say that, Mother? I love Ada, Mother! I love her with all my heart!

MRS. LIGHT (*calls over her shoulder*). Do you hear that, Hutchins?

LIGHT (*grimly*). Yes, I hear. (*He takes a threatening step forward.*)

REUBEN. Father!

(*Then his eyes turn to his mother's vindictive face and he thinks in a tortured agony of spirit.*) He was hiding in the closet! . . . she knew it! . . . she cheated me! . . . when I trusted her! . . . when I loved her better than anyone in the world! . . .

(*He cries out in a passion of reproach.*) Oh Mother! Mother!

MRS. LIGHT (*misunderstanding this as a plea*). No, you needn't think I'm going to get you off this time! You punish him good, Hutchins! The very idea—kissing that dirty little ——!

REUBEN. Don't you say that!

LIGHT (*walks toward him*). Hold your tongue! How dare you address your mother——! (*Reuben cowers into the left corner front, his eyes fixed on the belt his father has in his hand.*) Get down on your knees!

REUBEN (*obeys mechanically, his thoughts whirling in his head*). Belt . . . Mother's face . . . she looks terrible . . . she wants him to beat me . . . she wants to hear me yell . . . (*Then with a defiant determination as if some hidden strength in him had suddenly been tapped.*) But I won't give her the satisfaction ! . . . no matter how it hurts ! . . .

LIGHT. Let this put back the fear of God into your sinful heart, Reuben !

> (*He brings the belt down heavily across Reuben's back. Reuben quivers, but not a sound comes from his lips. At the same moment there is a glaring flash of lightning and Light cringes back with a frightened exclamation.*)

MRS. LIGHT (*has winced when Reuben was hit —conscience-strickenly*). That must have hurt dreadfully ! . . . poor Reuben ! . . . (*Then with an exasperated sense of frustration, gazing at Reuben's set face.*) Why doesn't he cry ? . . . if he'd cry I'd stop Hutchins . . . that girl has changed him ! . . .

REUBEN (*expecting the next blow, thinking with a grim elation*). Come on ! . . . hit again ! . . . hit a million times ! . . . you can't make me show her you hurt me ! . . . (*Then stealing a glance up at his father's face.*) He looks scared ! . . . it was that lightning ! . . . I'll never be scared of lightning again ! . . . (*Then resolutely.*) I'll be damned if I'm going to let him beat me ! . . .

> (*He jumps to his feet and faces his father defiantly, with hatred in his eyes.*)

LIGHT (*guiltily*). I can't bear him looking at me like that ! . . . I really ought to feel grateful to him . . . his folly has delivered Fife into my hands . . .

(*He throws the belt on the bed—to his wife.*) Reuben's punishment can wait. I have my duty of denouncing that murderer to the proper authorities. (*Triumphantly.*) Haven't I always said, if the truth were known, that man was a criminal ! (*Turning toward the door.*) Keep Reuben here. He might warn Fife. I'll lock this door after me. (*Then hurriedly, as a crash of thunder comes.*) I must hurry. I want to get to the police station before the rain. (*He shuts the door behind him and locks it.*)

REUBEN (*staring after him with the same fixed look of hate—calls jeeringly*). Look out for the lightning ! (*Then he turns to his mother with a sneer—contemptuously.*) Picture my being scared of that boob all my life ! What did you ever see in him, to marry him ? He's yellow !

MRS. LIGHT (*frightened by the change in him, but attempting a bullying tone*). How dare you talk so disrespectfully——!

REUBEN. But you're yellow, too. And I'm yellow. How could I help being ? It's in my blood. (*Harshly.*) But I'll get him out of my blood, by God ! And I'll get you out, too !

MRS. LIGHT (*pitiably now*). What have I done, Reuben ?

REUBEN (*bitterly*). You knew he was in that closet ! You led me on to tell ! I thought you loved me better'n anyone, and you'd never squeal on me to him ! (*He starts to break down miserably.*)

MRS. LIGHT (*goes to him as if to take him in her arms*). I do love you better than anyone, Reuben ! I didn't mean——

REUBEN (*steps back from her—accusingly*). And you called Ada a harlot—after I told you I loved her with all my heart. (*Then a note of pleading in his voice.*) Do you mean you didn't mean that part of it—about her ?

MRS. LIGHT (*immediately furious again*). Yes, I did mean it about her ! I meant it and a lot more !

REUBEN. Then I'm through with you ! And as for him——!

(*He suddenly is reminded of something—thinking wildly.*) He went ! . . . police station ! . . . that'll finish me with Ada ! . . . (*There is the noise of the front door slamming.*) There's the front door ! . . . he's leaving ! . . .

(*He rushes to the door but finds it locked—pushes and pulls at it, trying to force it open.*)

MRS. LIGHT. I suppose you want to run over and warn your fine friends ! Fife'll be in a cell before long, please God, and if there was any real justice his girl'd be put in along with him, for she's no better than a street-walker !

46

REUBEN (*glares at her now*).   I'm glad you're talking like that !   It shows you up and I can hate you now !

MRS. LIGHT (*breaking down*).   Reuben !   For God's sake, don't say that—to your mother !

REUBEN.   You're not my mother any more ! I'll do without a mother rather than have your kind !

> (*He turns from her to the window and looks out.   As he does so, his father appears from right, coming from the front door. He is buttoned up to the neck in an old raincoat and carries an umbrella.*)

FIFE (*still leaning out of his sitting-room window, catches sight of Light—calls excitedly over his shoulder*).   Here's the old man now !   Come quick, Ada !   (*A moment later, just as Light comes up, she appears at the window next to her father. Her face is set in an ugly, sneering expression.   Fife calls to Light in a mocking tone.*)   Good evening, Your Holiness.

LIGHT (*stops short and stares at Fife with a rage that chokes him so that for a moment his lips move, forming words, but he can't utter them—finally finding his voice, he stammers*).   You—you murderer !

FIFE (*nudging Ada—with a great pretence of guilt*). Murderer ?   In the name of God, has your son ? —after he'd sworn his word of honour——!

LIGHT (*triumphantly*).   You thought you had him caught in your snares, did you ?—but God was simply using Reuben to bring retribution on your head. (*In a booming triumph.*) "Vengeance is mine, saith the Lord!"

REUBEN (*watching from his window*). He's talking to Fife! . . . he's telling! . . .

(*Then cursing his father aloud.*) God damn him! I'll show him! (*He drives back at the door with the weight of his whole body, and it crashes open and he stumbles over it and disappears in the hall.*)

MRS. LIGHT (*starts after him, calling frightenedly*). Reuben! Don't! Reuben!

FIFE (*enjoying himself hugely*). You wouldn't give me up to the police, would you?—a kind-hearted Shepherd of the Lord like you!

ADA (*suddenly flares up into a temper*). Aw, cut it out, Pop! This has gone far enough! (*To Light with sneering contempt.*) No wonder your son is a sap! Can't you see this is only a joke on you? Why, you poor fish, that murder story is in to-day's *Star*—the name Clark and everything! Pop simply copied that story—and if you go to the police you'll only be making a boob of yourself— but go ahead if you like!

(*As she speaks Reuben runs in from the right. He advances threateningly on his father, who is staring at Ada stupidly, overwhelmed by the conviction that what she has told him is true.*)

REUBEN. Did you tell—— ?

ADA. Look who's here! I was just telling your old man it was only a murder story out of the paper Pop told you to prove you were yellow! And you are, all right! Don't you ever dare speak to me again! You're a yellow rat! (*She breaks down, weeping, and rushes back into the room.*)

FIFE (*following her*). Ada! Don't waste crying over——

REUBEN. Ada! Listen! I didn't mean— I didn't know——!

(*He takes a few steps toward the window, then stops, thinking bitterly.*) So it was all a lie . . . a joke she played on me! . . . that's why she made me meet her old man! . . . so she could make a fool of me! . . .

(*He yells at the window.*) It's you who're the rat, Ada! You can go to hell!

MRS. LIGHT (*hurrying in from the right. She runs to him and tries to put her arms around him*). Reuben!

REUBEN (*pushing her away from him—furiously*). Leave me alone! You're to blame for this! You cheated me! I hate you!

MRS. LIGHT. For God's sake, Reuben!

LIGHT (*comes out of the state of humiliated stupefaction into which the knowledge of the joke has thrown him—bursting into a fatuous rage—to his wife*). As if I have not had enough to bear of humiliation! (*He points a shaking finger at Reuben.*)

This dunce—this stupid dolt—now I shall be the butt of all their sneers ! And to think I stayed my hand— ! But wait ! I'll show him what a real whipping is !

REUBEN (*fiercely*). You lie ! You'll never dare touch me again, you old fool ! I'm not scared of you any more !

> (*There is a blinding flash of lightning. Light, his nerves already at the breaking point, gives a gasp of superstitious fright and backs away from his son.*)

LIGHT. God have mercy !

REUBEN (*with a sneer*). What God ? Fife's God ? Electricity ? Are you praying to It for mercy ? It can't hear you ! It doesn't give a damn about you ! (*There is a tremendous crash of thunder. Reuben looks up and gives a wild laugh as though the thunder elated him. His mother and father shrink back from him in abject terror as he shouts up at the sky.*) Shoot away, Old Bozo ! I'm not scared of You !

MRS. LIGHT. Reuben ! You don't know what you're saying !

REUBEN (*with a hard mocking laugh—to his mother*). What's the matter ? Do you still believe in his fool God ? I'll show you. (*He jumps to his father's side and grabs his raincoat by the lapel—addressing the sky with insulting insolence.*) If there is his God let Him strike me dead this second ! I dare Him ! (*His father squeals with terror and tries to break away from his hold. His mother screams. He laughs triumphantly.*) There! Didn't I tell you ! (*Light finally tears his coat from Reuben's grip and runs panic-stricken off right, dragging his moaning wife by the arm. Reuben turns his back on his home determinedly and starts walking off left—with bitter defiance.*) There is no God ! No God but Electricity ! I'll never be scared again ! I'm through with the lot of you !

> (*As he disappears off left, the sound of wind and rain sweeping down on the town from the hills is heard.*)

CURTAIN

# ACT TWO

SCENE. *The same act as Act One. The interior of the Light sitting-room is revealed.*

*It is an early morning of a hot day in August. Fifteen months have elapsed.*

*Mrs. Fife is leaning out of one of the windows of their sitting-room, basking contentedly in the sun. She wears a faded blue wrapper.*

MRS. FIFE (*thinking with a sleepy content*). The sun is hot . . . I feel so dozy . . . I know why dogs love to lie in the sun . . . and cats and chickens . . . they forget to think they're living . . . they're just alive . . . (*She looks toward the Light house—with drowsy melancholy.*) Alive . . . poor Mrs. Light is dead . . . what is death like, I wonder ? . . . I suppose I'll have to die some time . . . I don't want to die before Ramsay . . . he wouldn't know how to take care of himself. . . .

> (*At a noise in the room behind her she half turns her head—then Ada leans out of the window next to her mother. Her face has a peaked look. Her manner is touchy and irritable and she has lost her former air of self-assured flippancy. There is no rouge on her face and she is dressed as if she had grown indifferent about her personal appearance.*)

52

ADA. For heaven's sake, what're you dope-dreaming about now, Mom?

MRS. FIFE. I was thinking of poor Mrs. Light——

ADA. Poor nothing! She hated us worse than poison! She'd have sung hymns of joy if any of us had cashed in! And why feel sorry for her, anyway? She's lucky, if you ask me! Life is the bunk!

MRS. FIFE (*looks at her worriedly—with a sigh*). I wish that Light boy would come back.

ADA (*immediately flying into a temper*). For God's sake, shut up! I've told you a million times how dumb that talk is and yet you keep on harping——!

MRS. FIFE. All right, Ada. I won't say anything.

ADA. What do I care about that poor fish! He can be dead for all I care! (*Then, as Fife's voice is heard calling from somewhere in the house.*) There's Pop howling his head off about something. You go in and smooth him down, Mom. I'm sick of his grouches.

MRS. FIFE (*as she turns to go*). I wish you'd make it up with your Pop, Ada. He feels so bad about it. You've kept a grudge against him ever since the night that Light boy——

ADA. There you go again! For Pete's sake, leave me alone!

(*Mrs. Fife disappears meekly without another word. Ada stares before her, thinking resentfully.*) I've got a good right to have a grudge against him . . . what he did that night wasn't on the level . . . it isn't a question of Rube . . . I don't give a darn about him . . . then why are you all the time thinking about him ? . . . I'm not ! . . . I liked him but that was all . . . and he was yellow, wasn't he ? . . . well, maybe you'd be worse if everything was framed against you the way Pop got him ! . . . poor Rube ! . . . what's he been doing all this time, I wonder ? . . . (*With a sad smile of scorn for herself.*) You poor boob ! . . . it must be love ! . . .

> (*In the sitting-room of the Light home, Hutchins Light enters from the rear, right. The grief over his wife's death has made him an old man. His hair has turned almost white, his mouth droops forlornly, his eyes are dull, his whole face is a mask of stricken loneliness. He comes and sits in his old chair and mechanically picks up his Bible from the table but lets it drop again and stares before him.*)

LIGHT (*thinking dully*). Another day . . . empty . . . all days are empty now . . . how long, O Lord ? . . . (*He sighs heavily.*) No sleep again last night except for a few minutes . . . and then nightmare . . . I dreamed Amelia was in my arms . . . and Reuben came and beckoned her and she went away with him . . . (*He shudders, flinging off the memory—then wonder-*

54

*ing bitterly*.) Does that dream mean Reuben is dead, too? . . . what does it matter? . . . ever since that night he has been dead for me . . . but he never gave Amelia a chance to forget him . . . a postal card every month or so . . . each with the same blasphemy . . . " We have electrocuted your God. Don't be a fool ! " . . . her last words ! . . . " don't be a fool," she kept saying to me . . . she couldn't have known what she was saying . . .

(*He breaks down, sobbing, and buries his head in his arms on the table.*)

MRS. FIFE (*reappears in the window beside Ada. She is smiling with a doting good-nature*). Your Pop told me to get out of the room and stop looking at him or he'd start breaking plates. My, but he's in a breakfast temper, though ! The men at the plant'll catch it—but they don't mind him. They know, like I do, that he's really the kindest man in the world.

ADA (*resentfully*). Oh, is he ? I suppose that's why he acted the way he did to Rube !

MRS. FIFE. He couldn't help being mean then. He'd be mean at first to any man he thought you cared for—especially a minister's son. But he'd get over it, you'd see. He'd like to see you happy, before everything. I'm sure he's been wishing for a long time that Light boy'd come home so he could make friends with him.

ADA. Aw, you're crazy, Mom ! (*Suddenly she leans over and kisses her mother affectionately.*) It's you who are the kindest in the world. (*Then*

55

*embarrassed—irritably.*) Gosh, this sun's hot !
I don't see how you stand it. (*She retreats into the
house.*)

MRS. FIFE (*blinking placidly in the sun*). It was
awful nice the way Ada kissed me . . . I wish
she'd get to kissing her Pop again that way . . .
she does it now as if she wished she was a mos-
quito with a stinger . . . the screen up in her
room has a hole rusted in it . . . I must remember to get it fixed or they'll be flying in keeping her
awake . . .

(*A pause—then Reuben Light comes slowly
in from the left and stands there, his eyes
fixed for a while on his home, taking in
every detail.    He does not for a moment
notice Mrs. Fife, nor she him.    A great
change has come over him ;  he is
hardly recognizable as the Reuben of
Act One.    Nearly nineteen now, his
body has filled out, his skin is tanned and
weather-beaten.    In contrast to his
diffident timid attitude of before, his
manner is now consciously hard-boiled.
The look on his face emphasizes the
change in him.    It is much older than
his years, and it is apparent that he
has not grown its defensive callousness
without a desperate struggle to kill the
shrinking boy in him.    But it is in his
eyes that the greatest change has come.
Their soft grey-blue has become chilled
and frozen, and yet they burn in their*

*depths with a queer devouring intensity. He is dressed roughly in battered shoes, dungaree trousers faded by many washings, a blue flannel shirt open at the neck, with a dirty coloured handkerchief knotted about his throat, and wears the coat of his old suit. Under his arm he carries six books, bound together with a strap.*)

REUBEN (*thinking jeeringly*). Home, Sweet Home! . . . the Prodigal returns! . . . what for? . . . I felt a sudden hunch I had to come . . . to have a talk with mother, anyway . . . well, I'll soon know what it's all about . . . and won't the old man be glad to see me! . . . yes! . . . he'll poison the fatted calf! . . .

(*He laughs aloud. Mrs. Fife turns and gives a startled exclamation as she recognizes him. He turns and looks at her for a moment—then with a swaggering impudence.*) Fine day, isn't it?

MRS. FIFE (*her eyes mooning at him, with a simple pleased smile*). I'm glad you've come home. Ada'll be glad. (*She stirs as if to go into the house.*) I'll tell her you're here.

REUBEN (*frowning*). No. I've got no time for her now. (*Then with a peculiar air of indifferent curiosity.*) Are you dead sure Ada'll be glad I'm back? I shouldn't think she would after what happened.

MRS. FIFE. That wasn't her doing. She's been sorry about it ever since.

REUBEN (*with the same detached interest*). She called me a yellow rat—and she had the right dope. I sure was dumb when it came to guessing what she really wanted or I would have—(*With a cold smile.*) Well, never mind what—but you can tell her I've changed. I've lived a lot and read a lot to find out for myself what's really what—and I've found out all right ! You can tell her I've read up on love in biology, and I know what it is now, and I've proved it with more than one female.

MRS. FIFE (*preoccupied with her own thoughts*). It was just one of Ramsay's jokes.

REUBEN .. He's a great little joker ! And I certainly fell for it. Well, there's no hard feelings. He did me a favour. He woke me up. (*With a laugh, a queer expression coming into his eyes.*) You can tell him I've joined his church. The only God I believe in now is electricity.

MRS. FIFE (*simply*). Ramsay'll be glad.

REUBEN (*indicating the books he carries*). I'm studying a lot of science. Sometimes I've gone without eating to buy books—and often I've read all night—books on astronomy and biology and physics and chemistry and evolution. It all comes down to electricity in the end. What the fool preachers call God is in electricity somewhere. (*He breaks off—then strangely.*) Did you ever watch dynamos ? What I mean is in them—somehow.

MRS. FIFE (*dreamily*). I love dynamos. I could watch them for ever. I love to hear them sing. They're singing all the time about everything in the world !

> (*She hums her imitation of a dynamo's metallic purr.*)

REUBEN (*startled—looks at her with growing interest*). " Singing all the time about everything in the world " . . . listen to her . . . she's caught the sound . . . she really makes you think of a dynamo, somehow . . . she's big and warm like . . . like what ? . . . damned if she doesn't remind me of mother the way she used to be . . . way back when I was a little kid and didn't know what she was really like . . . (*With a bitter grin.*) Wouldn't mother go wild if I told her that ! . . . maybe I will just to get her goat ! . . .

(*Abruptly he puts down his books and walks up to Mrs. Fife.*) Say, you're all right !

> (*He takes one of her hands in his clumsily— then lets go of it, grinning awkwardly.*)

MRS. FIFE (*sentimentally touched—beaming on him*). I always knew you must be a nice boy. (*With a coquettish, incongruously girlish air.*) But you save your holding hands for Ada ! (*Then she half turns around at some sound in the room behind her— in a hurried whisper to Reuben.*) She's coming ! You hide behind those bushes and we'll surprise her !

> (*Mechanically, reacting instinctively for a moment as the timid boy of formerly, he*)

*runs to the gap in the lilac bushes and
hides in the old place. Ada appears in
the window beside her mother. Her
face wears an expression of eager expec-
tation. Her eyes glance quickly on all
sides as if searching for some one.*)

ADA (*flusteredly*). I'm sure I heard some one
. . . it sounded like . . .

REUBEN (*almost as soon as he reaches his old
hiding-place is overcome by shame*). What'd I do
that for ? . . . hide ! . . . the old stuff ! . . .
(*Savagely.*) No, by God ! . . . her mother put
it in my head . . . but I'll soon show Ada ! . . .
She'll find out if I'm yellow now ! . . .

(*With a swagger and the cold smile of his
lips he walks through the gap just as
Mrs. Fife speaks to Ada.*)

MRS. FIFE (*with a teasing smile*). Ada, I've got
a big surprise for you. Guess—— (*But Ada
has already seen him.*)

ADA. Rube !

REUBEN (*walks toward her, the smile frozen on his
lips, his eyes fixed on hers*). Go right up and kiss
her ! . . . look at the way she's looking at you !
. . . she's easy now ! . . .

ADA (*staring at him, stammers his name again in a
tone in which there is now a note of panic*). Rube !

REUBEN (*pulls her head down and kisses her, keeping his lips on hers while she struggles instinctively for*

60

*a moment, until she gives up and returns his kiss—
then he pushes her a little away from him and laughs
quietly, his confidence in himself completely restored).*
Well, this prodigal gets the fatted kiss even if
"there ain't no calf." Hello, Ada! How's
every little thing?

MRS. FIFE (*sentimentally*). That's right. You
two kiss and make up. I'll leave you alone.
(*She goes back into the room.*)

ADA (*is staring at him with eyes that search his face
apprehensively*). Rube! You—you've changed.
I—I hardly know you! I shouldn't have kissed
you—like that. I don't know why I——

REUBEN. Well, I know. (*He takes her face
between his hands again and brings his close to it.*)
Because you love me. Isn't that right? (*As she
hesitates—insistently, giving her head a little shake.*)
Isn't it?

ADA (*helplessly*). I guess it is, Rube.

REUBEN. Guess, nothing! You loved me before I went away—even when you were bawling
me out for a yellow rat. That was what made
you so mad, wasn't it? You were ashamed of
loving me when I was so dumb and didn't get
what you wanted and was so damned scared to
touch you. (*He laughs—a self-assured insinuating
laugh that for her has something at once fascinating
and frightening about it.*) But you needn't worry
any more, Ada. I've learned a lot about love
since I left—and I get you now, all right! (*Then*

61

*with a sudden burst of threatening assertiveness.*)
You're damned right, I've changed ! I'm not
yellow about you or God or anything else !
Don't forget that, Ada ! (*Then as suddenly
changing to a passionate tone of desire.*) Gosh,
you're pretty ! I'd forgotten how pretty you
were ! You make all the girls I've been playing around with look like mistakes ! Your eyes
are grand—and your hair—and your mouth—!
(*He kisses them hungrily as he speaks—then controls
himself and breaks away from her, forcing a laugh.*)
Continued in our next ! Let's take a walk to-
night.

ADA (*staring at him helplessly*). Yes—no—I
don't think———

REUBEN. Sure you will. We'll walk out to
the top of Long Hill. That's where I was all
during the storm that night after I left here. I
made myself stand there and watch the lightning.
After that storm was over I'd changed, believe
me ! I knew nothing could ever scare me again
—and a whole lot of me was dead and a new lot
started living. And that's the right place for us
to love—on top of that hill—close to the sky—
driven to love by what makes the earth go round
—by what drives the stars through space ! Did
you ever think that all life comes down to electricity in the end, Ada ? Did you ever watch
dynamos ? (*She stares at him, frightened and
fascinated, and shakes her head.*) I've watched
them for hours. Sometimes I'd go in a plant and

get talking to the guys just to hang around, and I tried everywhere to get a job in a plant but never had any luck. But every job I've had—I never stuck to one long, I wanted to keep moving and see everything—every job was connected with electricity some way. I've worked for electricians, I've gone out helping linesmen, I shovelled sand on a big water-power job out West. (*Then with sudden eagerness.*) Say, Ada, I've just had a hunch ! I know now what drove me back here, all right ! You've got to get your old man to give me a job in his plant—any job, I don't care what !

ADA. Sure—I'll try, Rube.

REUBEN (*with a cold assurance*). You've got to, Ada. Because I can't stay on here without a job. I'm broke and I won't live home—even if the old gent would let me. And that reminds me, I better go and pay my little visit. I don't want to see him, but I want to have a talk with Mother. I've got over my hard feelings about her. She was so crazy jealous of you she didn't care what she did. I can make allowances for her—now. So I'll be friends again if she wants to—and then you watch me convert her over from that old God stuff of his ! (*He grins with resentful anticipation.*)

ADA (*has listened with blank astonishment—pityingly*). Then you don't— ? Why, I thought— Didn't they send for you ?

63

REUBEN (*unsuspectingly—with a grin*). Send for me to come home and be good ? I never gave them my address, kid. I didn't want them bothering me. I never wrote, except some postcards to mother I sent to get her goat—and his. (*Then picking up his books and turning toward his home.*) Guess I'll go round by the back. I don't want to run into him unless I have to. So long, Ada. Tell your old man I'd sure like that job !

> (*He walks to the hedge and then, stealthily, across the lawn and disappears behind the house.*)

ADA (*looking after him*). He doesn't know she's dead . . . ought I to have told him ? . . . oh, I couldn't ! . . . poor Rube ! . . . (*Then admiringly.*) How strong he's got ! . . . but it makes me afraid too . . . his eyes seemed to take all the clothes off me . . . and I didn't feel ashamed . . . I felt glad ! . . . (*Defiantly.*) I love him ! . . . I want him as much as he wants me ! . . . what of it ? . . . (*Then with a shudder she cannot repress.*) But his eyes are so queer . . . like lumps of ice with fire inside them . . . and he never said he loved me . . . aw, of course he does ! . . . he was nuts about me before he went away, wasn't he ? . . . (*Determinedly.*) I've got to make Pop give him that job or he might beat it again . . . he owes it to Rube to do something for him . . . I'll talk to him right now . . .

> (*She disappears inside the house just as Reuben slowly opens the door of the Light sitting-room. There is an ex-*

*pression of puzzled uneasiness on his face
as he peers around the half-opened door,
then slinks in as if he were a burglar.
Light is still sitting, his face hidden in
his arms on the table, in an attitude of
exhausted grief. Reuben does not at
first see him.)*

REUBEN. Something's all wrong here . . .
where the hell is every one ? . . . where's
mother ? . . . (*He has stepped on tiptoe into the
room and now suddenly he sees his father and a sneering smile immediately comes to his lips.*) There he
is, anyway . . . praying as usual . . . the poor
boob . . . there isn't a damn prayer ever got him
a thing . . . Mother used to make him pray for
electric lights in the house . . . (*Suddenly with a
pleased grin.*) That's a good hunch . . . I'll get
them put in the first money I save . . . it'll be
like bringing my gospel to the heathen . . . let
there be electric light ! . . . (*He chuckles, then
bends closer to look at his father.*) He must be
asleep . . . that's one on him to catch him . . .

(*He speaks with mocking geniality.*) Hello !
(*His father gives a frightened start, as if dodging a
blow, and stares at his son's face with stupefied
bewilderment.*) Sorry to disturb your little
snooze. (*His father continues to look at him, as if
he can't believe his eyes.*) Oh, this is me, all right.
(*Then the fact of his father's changed appearance
strikes him for the first time, and he blurts out in a
tone that is almost kindly.*) Say, you look all in.
What's the trouble ? Been sick ?

65

LIGHT (*thinking gropingly*). It's Reuben . . . Reuben . . . but he doesn't seem like Reuben . . .

REUBEN (*misunderstanding his father's silence as intentional, immediately becomes resentful*). What's the matter? Don't you want to talk to me? Well, I'm not here to talk to you either. I was just passing this way and thought I'd drop in to say hello to Mother. Where is she?

LIGHT (*thinking more clearly now—an unstrung fury rising within him*). Oh, yes, it's Reuben! . . . I recognize him now! . . . the same as that night . . . cruel and evil! . . . and now he's asking for the mother he . . . my poor Amelia! . . . he killed her! . . .

(*He lurches to his feet and leans against the back of his chair weakly, glaring at his son. Violently—in a voice that is like a croak.*) Murderer! You killed her!

REUBEN (*stares at him with a stunned look*). What the hell do you mean? (*Then harshly, taking a threatening step forward.*) Where's Mother, I'm asking you!

LIGHT (*his strength failing him—in a faltering tone hardly above a whisper*). She's dead—Reuben.

REUBEN (*terribly shaken*). You're a liar! You're just saying that to get my goat!

LIGHT (*going on as if he hadn't heard—in a tone of monotonous grief*). You can't see her—I can't— never—never see her again!

*(He breaks down abjectly, sinking on his chair
and sobbing, his face in his hands.)*

REUBEN (*stands looking at him stupidly, convinced
now of the truth and trying to make himself realize it
and accept it*).   Then it's straight goods . . . she
is dead . . . gone . . . no use making a fuss . . .
let him cry . . . why can't his religion buck him
up now ? . . . he ought to feel sure he's going to
see her again soon . . . in heaven . . . I'd like
to see her again . . . tell her I'm sorry for acting
so rough to her that night . . . (*He gulps and his
lips twitch.*)   I wish he'd stop crying . . .

*(He goes forward and pats his father on the back
gingerly.)*   Buck up.

(*His father doesn't seem to hear him.   He turns
and slumps into the chair at the far side of the table.*)
Why couldn't I have seen her just once again . . .
this is a rotten break . . .

*(He asks mechanically.)*   How long ago did she die ?

LIGHT (*mechanically in his turn—without lifting
his head*).   Two weeks ago yesterday.

REUBEN.   Two weeks . . . it was about then I
first felt that hunch to come home and see her
. . . that's damn queer ! . . . (*He stares at his
father—uneasily.*)   He said I killed her . . . what
the hell did he mean ? . . .

*(Forcing a casual tone.)*   What did she die of ?

LIGHT (*dully*).   Pneumonia.

REUBEN (*heaving a sigh of relief*).   Sure . . . I
knew he was only saying that to get my goat . . .

(*He speaks to his father in a defensive, accusing tone.*) Pneumonia, eh? Well, it's a damn wonder we didn't all die of it years ago, living in this dump! Ever since I can remember the cellar's leaked like a sieve. You never could afford to get it fixed right. Mother was always after you about it. And I can remember the ceiling in my room. Every storm the water'd begin to drip down and Mother'd put the wash basin on the floor to catch it. It was always damp in this house. Mother was always after you to make them put in a decent furnace instead of——

LIGHT (*has lifted his head and is glaring at his son*). Are you trying to say I killed her? It was you! She'd been pining away for almost a year. Her heart was broken because you'd gone! She hoped for a time you'd come back but finally she gave up hoping—and gave up wanting to live! And your horrible blasphemous postcards kept coming! She blamed herself for your ruin and she wrote long letters begging your forgiveness, and asking you to come home! But you'd never given her an address! She couldn't mail them, she knew you'd never read them, and that broke her heart most of all! You killed her as surely as if you'd given her poison, you unnatural accursed son!

REUBEN (*deeply disturbed but trying desperately to conceal it*). I never gave her my address because I thought she'd only write bawling me out.

(*Then harshly.*) Where are those letters she wrote ? They're mine !

LIGHT (*with a mean satisfaction*). I destroyed them ! I burnt them to the last scrap !

REUBEN (*starts for his father threateningly, his fists clenched*). You rotten son of a — (*He chokes it back—then helplessly, with a wounded look.*) Say, that was a dirty trick ! I'd like to have read——

(*Light averts his eyes and suddenly hides his face in his hands.*)

LIGHT (*remorsefully now*). He's right . . . I had no right . . . no right even to read them . . . how I wish I'd never read them ! . . .

(*Lifting his head.*) I destroyed them in a fit of anger. When I read them I realized that Amelia had been thinking of you all the time. And I felt betrayed ! I hated her and you ! I was insane with hatred ! God forgive me !

REUBEN (*after a pause—dully*). Did she ever talk about me ?

LIGHT (*immediately jealous again*). She never mentioned your name ! (*Then forcing himself to say it.*) I—I had forbidden her to.

REUBEN (*his face lights up with anger again, but he controls it*). Sure, you had to, didn't you ?—so what the hell ? (*Then insistently.*) But—didn't she ?—at the last ?—when she was dying ?—say anything ?

LIGHT (*fighting a furious battle with himself*). Have I got to tell him ? . . . that she'd even forgotten God ! . . . that her last words were his words ! . . . even her soul lost to me ! . . . must I tell this ? . . . (*Savagely.*) No ! . . . I don't owe him the truth ! . . . I must make him feel he is accursed ! . . .

(*He springs from his chair and leaning across the table, points his finger at Reuben denouncingly.*) Yes, with her last breath she cursed you for all the ruin and suffering you had brought on her—and on me ! (*Then as he sees Reuben shrinking back in his chair, a haunted look of horror on his face, the consciousness of the evil of the lie he is telling overwhelms him with guilty remorse. He stammers.*) No !— that's a lie, Reuben !—a terrible lie !—don't listen—don't believe me ! (*He stumbles hastily around the table to the dazed Reuben and with a pitiful gesture puts a trembling hand on his head— pleadingly.*) Forgive me, Reuben ! You are my son as well as hers, remember. I haven't the strength to resist evil. I wanted to punish you. She didn't curse you. Her last words were the very words you had written her. "Don't be a fool ! " she kept saying to me ! (*He shudders.*)

REUBEN (*springs from his chair in extreme agitation and grabbing his father by both shoulders, stares hungrily in his face*). What ? What's that ? Mother said that ?

LIGHT (*seeming to shrivel up in his son's grip—*

*trying unconvincingly to reassure himself*). She was delirious. She must have been delirious.

> REUBEN (*lets go of his father. The old man turns and stumbles back to his chair. Reuben stares before him, thinking excitedly*). " We have electrocuted your God. Don't be a fool " . . . that's what I kept writing her . . . her last words ! . . . then I'd converted her away from his God ! . . . the dying see things beyond . . . she saw I'd found the right path to the truth ! . . . (*His eyes shine with a new elation.*) By God, I'll go on now all right ! . . . (*He laughs aloud to himself exultantly.*)

LIGHT. For the love of God !

REUBEN (*immediately ashamed of himself*). I wasn't laughing at you, honest ! (*Then suddenly.*) Say, I think I'll go and visit Mother's grave. There's some things I'd like to get off my chest—even if she can't hear me. (*Turning to the door.*) Well, so long.

LIGHT (*dully*). Shall I have your room put in order for you ?

REUBEN (*frowning*). No. It isn't my room now. That me is dead.

> (*Then an idea comes to him—thinking.*) But maybe Mother'd want me to . . . maybe I'd get some message from her if I stayed here . . .

(*Then casually to his father.*) Oh, all right. I'll stay for a couple of days. After that I'm going to get a room out near the plant. Say, I might as well break the bad news to you. I'm getting a job in Fife's power house. (*Then quickly.*) I suppose you think I'm doing it to spite you, but I'm not.

LIGHT (*dully*). You have sold your soul to Satan, Reuben.

REUBEN (*immediately resentful—with his cold smile*). Your Satan is dead. We electrocuted him along with your God. Electricity is God now. And we've got to learn to know God, haven't we? Well, that's what I'm after! (*In a lighter tone—mockingly.*) Did you ever watch dynamos? Come down to the plant and I'll convert you! (*He cannot restrain a parting shot.*) I converted Mother, didn't I? Well, so long.

> (*He goes out and a moment later walks past the front of the house from the right. He is off guard and the callousness has gone from his face, which is now very like that of the boy of* ACT ONE.) I wish she hadn't died! . . . but she forgave me . . .

ADA (*sticks her head out of their sitting-room window as he passes the lilac hedge. Her face is flushed with excitement, happy and pretty now. She calls*). It's all right, Rube. Pop's got a job for you. A floor man is leaving Saturday.

REUBEN (*startled out of his thoughts, at first frowns then forces the cold smile to his lips*). That's great.

ADA (*coquettishly*). Well, don't I get anything?

REUBEN (*with his cold smile*). Sure!

> (*He goes to her and reaches up as if to kiss her— then checks himself, thinking remorsefully*). What

the hell am I doing? . . . I'm going out to Mother's grave . . . she hated her . . .

(*He steps back, frowning.*)  Wait till later, Ada. Well, so long.  See you to-night.  (*He turns his back on her abruptly and walks off left.*)

CURTAIN.

SCENE TWO

SCENE.  *The same except that Reuben's bedroom is now revealed while the wall of the sitting-room has been replaced.  It is about half-past eleven on the same night—a sultry, hazy sky with few stars visible.  There is no light in either house.*

*Reuben and Ada come in from the left.  She is hanging on his arm, pressing close to him as if she were afraid of his leaving her, glancing up into his face with a timid look of mingled happiness and apprehension.*

*Reuben's face shows that he also is struggling with conflicting emotions.  There is a fixed smile of triumph and gratified vanity on his lips, but his eyes are restless and there is a nervous uneasiness apparent in his whole manner.*

ADA.  You're sure you don't hate me now— because I let you—maybe I shouldn't have—but, oh, Rube, I do love you so much !  Say you love me just as much—that you always will !

REUBEN (*preoccupiedly*).  Sure I will.

ADA (*pleadingly*).  Put your arms around me

73

tight and kiss me again. Then I won't be scared
—or sorry.

REUBEN (*mechanically puts his arms around her
and kisses her at first perfunctorily, then with re-
awakening passion*). Gee, you're pretty, Ada!
You've certainly got me going!

ADA (*happily now*). Oh Rube, when you kiss
me like that nothing in the world matters but
you! Up on the hill when we—oh, I felt I was
just you, a part of you and you were part of me!
I forgot everything!

REUBEN (*suddenly moves away from her and stares
around him nervously—in a strange voice*). Sure.
You forget everything for a minute. You're
happy. Then something has to wake you up—
and start you thinking again.

ADA. What is it you're thinking about? Tell
me, and maybe I can help you forget it.

REUBEN (*shaking his head*). I can't forget.
(*Then determinedly.*) And I don't want to. I
want to face things. I won't ever be satisfied
now until I've found the truth about everything.

ADA (*trying to force a joking tone*). And where
do I come in?

REUBEN (*coldly*). You don't come in.

ADA. Rube! Don't say that—not after—
You scare me!

REUBEN (*irritably*). Cut out that talk of being
scared! What are you scared about? Scared

74

what we did was a sin ? You're the hell of an atheist ! (*Then jeeringly.*) And you're the one that used to be always kidding me about being a goody boy ! There's nothing to be scared about or sorry for. What we did was just plain sex— an act of nature—and that's all there is to it !

ADA (*pitifully—her voice trembling*). Is that all —it means to you ?

REUBEN. That's all it means to anyone ! What people call love is just sex—and there's no sin about it !

ADA. I wasn't saying there was, was I ? I've proved to you I don't—only— (*Then frightenedly.*) It's you, Rube. I can't get used to you, talking like that. You've changed so.

REUBEN (*with a coarse grin*). Well, you've got no kick coming. If I'd stayed the same poor boob I used to be you might have died an old maid.

ADA. But—you wanted to marry me then, Rube.

REUBEN (*roughly*). And a lot that got me, didn't it ?

ADA (*faintly*). Don't you want to—any more ?

REUBEN. Don't I what ? Talk sense, Ada ! We're married by Nature now. We don't need any old fool of a minister saying prayers over us ! (*Then after a moment's pause—with a forced laugh.*) Say, here's one on me, Ada—speaking of praying. It was out at Mother's grave. Before I thought,

I started to do a prayer act—and then suddenly it hit me that there was nothing to pray to. (*He forces another laugh.*) It just goes to show you what a hold that bunk gets on you when you've had it crammed down your throat from the time you were born! You can't pray to electricity unless you're foolish in the head, can you? (*Then strangely.*) But maybe you could, at that— if you knew how!

ADA. Is that where you went this afternoon— out to her grave?

REUBEN (*with affected indifference*). Sure. What of it?

ADA (*pityingly*). Poor Rube!

REUBEN (*frowning*). Poor nothing! She's dead, and that's all there is about it! You've got to face death as well as life.

ADA. I'm sorry she hated me so. I hope now she forgives us—for loving each other.

REUBEN (*with his cold smile*). You mean forgives us for what we did to-night? You don't know her! She never would! But what's the use of talking about it? Who gives a damn? Good night, Ada. I'm tired. I'm going to bed. See you to-morrow. (*He turns his back on her abruptly and walks off right toward the front door of his house.*)

ADA (*stands looking after him with bewildered hurt for a moment, then turns back toward her own front door and begins to cry softly, at the same time trying to reassure herself*). I mustn't . . . feel bad . . . he doesn't mean to hurt me . . . he's changed, that's all . . .

(*She disappears off left. A moment later, Reuben appears in his bedroom and lights the lamp. He sits down on the bed and stares before him.*)

REUBEN (*looking about the room now, thinking bitterly*). The last time I was here . . . there's the closet where she hid him . . . here's where she sat lying to me . . . watching him beat me . . . (*He springs to his feet—viciously.*) I'm glad she's dead ! . . . (*Then immediately remorseful.*) No . . . I don't mean that, Mother . . . I was thinking of how you acted that night . . . I wish I could have seen you after you'd changed . . . after you'd come back to my side . . . (*He goes to the window on the left and looks out.*) Here's where I was looking out, waiting for Ada to signal on the Victrola . . . gosh, that seems a million years ago ! . . . how scared I was of even kissing her ! . . . and to-night she was dead easy . . . like rolling off a log ! . . . (*He comes back to the bed and sits down.*) Mother said she was no better than a street-walker . . . she certainly didn't put up a fight . . . marry her ! . . . what does she think I am, a boob ? . . . she put one over on me and now I've put one over on her ! . . . we're square . . . and whatever's going to happen, will happen, but it won't be a wedding ! . . . (*Then with coarse sensuality.*) But it's grand to have her around handy whenever I want . . . the flesh, as the old man would call it ! . . . and she's all right

77

other ways, too . . . I like her . . . she got me
the job . . . she'll be useful . . . and I'll treat
her decent . . . maybe it's love . . . whatever
the hell love is ! . . . did Mother really love the
old man ? . . . she must have or how could she
stand him ? . . . and she made me with him . . .
act of Nature . . . like me and Ada . . . (*He
jumps to his feet distractedly*.) God, that seems
lousy somehow ! . . . I don't want to think of it !
. . . (*He paces up and down—then pauses and
appears to be listening for something*.) There's
something queer about this dump now ! . . . as
if no one was living here . . . I suppose that's
because Mother's gone . . . I'd like to reach her
somehow . . . no one knows what happens after
death . . . even science doesn't . . . there may
be some kind of hereafter . . . I used to kneel
down here and say my prayers . . . she taught
them to me . . . then she'd tuck me in, even after
I'd grown up . . . and kiss me good-night . . .
(*As if automatically he slips to his knees by the bed*.)
I'm sorry, Mother . . . sorry you're dead . . . I
wish I could talk to you . . . (*He scrambles to his
feet—angry at himself*.) You damn fool ! . . .
what's come over you anyway ? . . . what are
you praying to ? . . . when there's nothing . . .
(*Then strangely*.) Funny, that hunch I got when I
was talking to Ada . . . about praying to electricity, if you knew how . . . it was like a message . . . Mother believed what I believed when
she died . . . maybe it came from her . . .
(*Then suspicious of himself again*.) Aw, that's just
superstitious junk . . . but why is it ? . . . look
at how mysterious all this electrical wave stuff is
in radio and everything . . . that's scientific fact

78

. . . and why couldn't something like that that
no one understands yet ? . . . between the dead
and the living ? . . . (*He walks around nervously.*) No use trying to go to sleep . . . and
I want to keep on thinking . . . but not in here
. . . I'll go for a walk . . . why not go down to
the plant ? . . . take a look in at the dynamos
. . . watching them always helps me somehow
. . . sure, that's the stuff ! . . .

> (*He turns down the light and blows it out and
> can be seen going through the door in
> rear.*)

CURTAIN


SCENE THREE

SCENE.  *A half-hour later.  Exterior of the Light
and Power Company's hydro-electric plant about
two miles from the town.  The building is red
brick.  The section on the left, the dynamo room,
is much wider than the right section, but is a
story less in height.  An immense window and
a big sliding door are in the lower part of the
dynamo room wall, and there is a similar
window in the upper part of the section on right.
Through the window and the open door of the
dynamo room, which is brilliantly lighted by a
row of powerful bulbs in white globes set in
brackets along both walls, there is a clear view
of a dynamo, huge and black, with something
of a massive female idol about it, the exciter set
on the main structure like a head with blank
oblong eyes above a gross rounded torso.*

79

# DYNAMO

*Through the upper window of the right
section of the building, in the switch galleries,
by a dim light, one gets a glimpse of the mathe-
matically-ordered web of the disconnecting
switches, double busses, and other equipment
stretching up through the roof to the outgoing
feeders leading to the transmission towers.*

*The air is full of sound, a soft overtone of
rushing water from the dam and the river bed
below, penetrated dominatingly by the harsh,
throaty, metallic purr of the dynamo.*

*Reuben comes in from the right and approaches
until he is opposite the open doorway.  He
stands there staring at the dynamo and listening
to it.*

REUBEN (*after a pause—fascinatedly*).  It's so
mysterious . . . and grand . . . God, I love
dynamos ! . . . they make you feel things . . .
you don't need to think . . . you almost get the
secret . . . what electricity is . . . what life is
. . . what God is . . . it's all the same thing
. . . (*A pause—then he goes on in the same fascinated tone.*)  It's like a great dark idol . . . like
the old stone statues of gods people prayed to
. . . only it's living and they were dead . . . that
part on top is like a head . . . with eyes that
see you without seeing you . . . and below it is
like a body . . . not a man's . . . round like a
woman's . . . as if it had breasts . . . but not
like a girl . . . not like Ada . . . no, like a
woman . . . like her mother . . . or mine . . .
a great, dark mother ! . . . that's what the
dynamo is ! . . . that's what life is ! . . . (*He*

80

*stares at it raptly now*.) Listen to her singing
. . . that beats all organs in church . . . it's the
hymn of electricity . . . " always singing about
everything in the world " . . . if you could only
get back into that . . . know what it means . . .
then you'd know the real God ! . . . (*Then
longingly*.) There must be some way ! . . . there
must be something in her song that'd tell you if
you had ears to hear ! . . . some way that she'd
teach you to know . . . (*He begins to hum, swaying his body—then stops when he can't catch the
right tone*.) No, you can't get it ! . . . it's as far
off as the sky and yet it's all around you ! . . . in
you ! . . . (*Excitedly*.) I feel like praying now !
. . . I feel there is something in her to pray to !
. . . something that'll answer me ! . . . (*He
looks around him and moves to the right out of the
square of light from the open doorway*.) Supposing
anyone saw me . . . they'd think I was nutty
. . . that old prayer stuff . . . (*Then arguing
tormentedly with himself*.) But I feel it's right
. . . I feel Mother wants me to . . . it's the least
I can do for her . . . to say a prayer . . . (*He
gets down on his knees and prays aloud to the
dynamo*.) Oh Mother of Life, my mother is dead,
she has passed back into you, tell her to forgive
me, and to help me find your truth ! (*He pauses
on his knees for a moment, then gets slowly to his feet.
There is a look of calm and relief on his face now.
He thinks reverentially*.) Yes, that did it . . .
I feel I'm forgiven . . . Mother will help . . .
I can sleep . . . I'll go home . . . (*He walks
slowly off right*.)

CURTAIN

# ACT THREE

## SCENE ONE

SCENE. *Same as* ACT TWO, SCENE THREE—*Exterior of the power house four months later. It is a little after sunset and the equipment on the roof is outlined blackly against a darkening crimson sky.*

*The door of the dynamo room is shut but the interior is brilliantly lighted and the dynamo can be partly seen through the window. There is a dim light above in the switch galleries as in the previous scene. The overtone of rushing water from the dam sounds louder because of the closed door which muffles the noise of the dynamo to a minor strain.*

*Reuben enters from the left accompanied by Mrs. Fife. He has grown very thin, his dungarees sag about his angular frame. His face is gaunt and pale. His eyes are deeply sunken. He is talking with unnatural excitement as they come in. Mrs. Fife is unchanged. If anything, her moony dreaminess is more pronounced. She listens to Reuben with a fascinated far-away look, as if the sound of his voice hypnotized her rather than the meaning of the words.*

REUBEN (*insistently*) You understood all I explained to you up on the dam, didn't you ?—about how life first came out of the sea ?

MRS. FIFE (*nods dreamily*). Yes, Reuben. It sounds like poetry—" life out of the sea."

REUBEN. It is like poetry. Her song in there

82

—Dynamo's—isn't that the greatest poem of all— the poem of eternal life ? And listen to the water rushing over the dam ! Like music ! It's as if that sound was cool water washing over my hot body ! Like some one singing me to sleep—my mother—when I was a kid—calling me back to somewhere far off where I'd been once long ago and known peace ! (*He sighs with longing, his body suddenly gone limp and weary.*)

MRS. FIFE (*dreamily*). That's awful pretty, Reuben. (*She puts her arm around him—sentimentally.*) I'll be your mother—yours and Ada's. I've always wanted a boy.

REUBEN (*leans against her gratefully, his head almost on her shoulder, his eyes half closed*). Yes. You're like her—Dynamo—the Great Mother— big and warm— (*With a sudden renewal of his unnatural excitement, breaks away from her.*) But I've got to finish telling you all I've come to know about her—how all things end up in her ! Did I tell you that our blood-plasm is the same right now as the sea was when life came out of it ? We've got the sea in our blood still ! It's what makes our hearts live ! And it's the sea rising up in clouds, falling on the earth in rain, made that river that drives the turbines that drive Dynamo ! The sea makes her heart beat too !—but the sea is only hydrogen and oxygen and minerals, and they're only atoms, and atoms are only protons and electrons—even our blood and the sea are only electricity in the end ! And think of the

H*  83

stars ! Driving through space, round and round, just like the electrons in the atom ! But there must be a centre around which all this moves, mustn't there ? There is in everything else ! And that centre must be the Great Mother of Eternal Life, Electricity, and Dynamo is her Divine Image on earth ! Her power houses are the new churches ! She wants us to realize the secret dwells in her ! She wants some one man to love her purely and when she finds him worthy she will love him and tell him the secret of truth and he will become the new saviour who will bring happiness and peace to men ! And I'm going to be that saviour—the miracle will happen to-night —that's why I asked you to come—I want you to be a witness ! I know it will be to-night because I had a message from my mother last night. I woke up and saw her standing beside my bed— just as she used to when she came in to kiss me good-night—and she smiled and held out her arms to me. She came from the spirit of the Great Mother to tell me she had at last found me worthy of her love.

MRS. FIFE (*sentimentally*). Most people don't believe in ghosts. Ramsay doesn't. But I see them all the time. Sometimes I don't hardly know which are ghosts and which are real. Has she come many times, Reuben ?

REUBEN (*strangely*). Not lately—not since I gave up seeing Ada. Before that she used to come almost every night to warn me.

MRS. FIFE.  Warn you about what, Reuben?

REUBEN.  That I was living in sin—that Dynamo would never find me worthy of her secret until I'd given up the flesh and purified myself! (*Then proudly.*)  And I found the strength to do it.  It was hard!  I was beginning to really love Ada.

MRS. FIFE (*simply*).  Of course, you love Ada—and you shouldn't act so mean to her, Reuben. You haven't been around in a month or more. She's making herself sick worrying.

REUBEN (*intensely*).  I'd like to see her!  I'd love to!  But I can't!  Don't you understand I can't—that my finding the secret is more important than—but when I come back bringing peace and happiness to the world it will mean peace and happiness for Ada . and me too! Everything will be all right then!

(*Then thinking with sudden fear and doubt.*)  But supposing the miracle doesn't happen to-night? . . . have I got to go on and on like this? . . . Ada keeps coming to me every night in dreams . . . the temptation of her body . . . I've beaten myself with my belt till the pain drove it off . . . but I can't keep on much longer . . .

(*He sways dizzily on his feet, passing his hand over his eyes—then straightens himself and turns to Mrs. Fife.*)  I've got to go in.  They'll be missing me.  You'll stay around, won't you? (*He goes to the door.*)   You wait until your husband's gone home.   Then you come in.

MRS. FIFE.   All right, Reuben.

> (*Reuben slides back the dynamo room door and enters, closing it behind him. Mrs. Fife stares after him mooningly. A moment later the door from the dynamo room is opened again and Fife comes out, closing it behind him. He hasn't changed since his last appearance. He starts to walk hesitatingly off right—then stops without looking around him and does not notice his wife.*

FIFE (*thinking exasperatedly*).   That damned Rube !  . . . there's a queer look in those cold eyes of his lately !  . . . by God, I'd fire him to-night if Ada wouldn't make my life a hell for it !  . . . but he does his work good . . . too damned good !  . . . he's always pawing around a dynamo when he's no business . . .

MRS. FIFE.   Hello, Ramsay.   You better get home to supper.   I had mine early.   I had to go out.

FIFE (*turns on her with an irritated start*).   Oh, you did, did you ?   You're always having to go out these days, it seems !   (*Mrs. Fife stares at him as if she didn't hear him.   This drives Fife into a shrill scolding.*)   I won't have you gallivanting down here at all hours and staring at the dynamos

86

and humming like a half-wit ! What the hell's come over you anyway ? (*He finishes up lamely, the wind taken out of his sails by her indifference.*)

MRS. FIFE. Nothing's come over me, Ramsay. I was talking to Reuben. He took me up on the dam and told me about how we all used to live in the ocean once. (*Then in her tone of childish mooning.*) D'you suppose I ever was a fish, Ramsay ?

FIFE. Aye, a jellyfish, I'm thinking ! You've the brains for that ! (*Then angrily.*) You do too much gabbing with that Rube ! He'll addle the little sense you've left ! But if you've got to talk to him, make him talk turkey and say when is he planning to marry Ada ! Aren't you her mother, and don't you see she's worrying her heart out ? (*Lowering his voice.*) D'you think it's happened between them—you know what I mean ?

MRS. FIFE (*with naïve simplicity*). Yes, of course it has, Ramsay. She loves him the same as I did you when we——

FIFE. Don't be comparing him to me ! I was more of a decent man than he ever will be ! (*In a passion.*) I'll have a talk with that lad and if he don't do the decent thing by her, I'll beat decency into him ! (*He turns from her in a tantrum.*) To hell with you ! I'm hungry ! I'm going home! (*He goes off right.*)

*(Mrs. Fife looks after him with a placid smile—then she gives the big door a push that slides it open to its full width and steps inside and, as she sees Reuben, stops as she is about to pull the door closed again. He is kneeling just inside the doorway before the dynamo in the foreground, his arms stretched out to it supplicatingly.)*

REUBEN *(suddenly cries out with a note of despair).* Mother ! Don't you hear me ? Can't you give me some sign ? O Dynamo, who gives life to all things, hear my prayer ! Grant me the miracle of your love !

*(He waits, his body strained with suspense, listening as if he expected the dynamo to answer him. Ada comes from around the corner of the building at the left. Her manner is furtive as if she were doing something she is ashamed of. She looks worried and run down, although she has made a defiant effort with rouge and mascara to hide this.)*

ADA. He must be around some place . . . *(She moves cautiously to the window and peeks in, but cannot see him. Then with bitter self-contempt.)* Here I am chasing after him ! . . . but I couldn't stand it any more, waiting . . . oh, what a damn fool I was to give in so easy ! . . . no wonder he's sick of me ! . . . but he can't throw me over this way ! . . .

REUBEN (*his tense, supplicating attitude suddenly relaxing dejectedly*). She won't answer me . . . there must still be something I've got to do. (*Then guiltily.*) Maybe she feels I haven't killed all desire for Ada yet . . . that I ought to face her and conquer the flesh once for all . . .

(*He jumps to his feet and turns to Mrs. Fife pleadingly.*) Can't you tell me? You know what she means sometimes. (*He lowers his voice cautiously as if he didn't want the dynamo to overhear.*) Do you think it's something I've got to do about Ada?

MRS. FIFE (*simply*). Yes, you've got to do the right thing by Ada, Reuben.

REUBEN (*thinking with unnatural excitement*). Then that is it! . . . well, I'll go and face Ada right now!

(*Turning to Mrs. Fife.*) You stay here! I'll be back. (*He comes out, sliding the door closed after him.*)

ADA (*calls to him uncertainly*). Rube!

REUBEN (*whirls around and stands staring at her with strange fixity for a moment, his thoughts jumping at conclusions*). It's Ada! . . . Dynamo knew Ada was here! . . . she wanted me to come out and prove! . . .

ADA (*frightenedly*). What's the matter? Don't look at me like that, Rube!

REUBEN (*moved in spite of himself, instinctively takes a step toward her—in a queer detached tone*).

89

I didn't mean to scare you, Ada. You gave me a start, seeing you all of a sudden.

ADA (*looking at him hopefully*). You're not sore at me for coming, are you?

REUBEN. No. It's as if you'd been sent. Didn't you feel something driving you to come here right now?

ADA (*quickly*). Yes, I just had to come!

REUBEN (*strangely*). It was she who made you come.

ADA. She? Who's she?

REUBEN (*a lightning change comes over his face. He takes a threatening step toward her—denouncingly, his voice booming like his father's*). You blasphemous fool, you! Do you dare to deny her! "The fool saith in his heart—" (*He suddenly checks himself and forces a strange, shamefaced laugh.*) Say, did you get me quoting from the Bible, Ada? That's one on me! That comes from arguing with the old man lately. He's got some fool notion that Dynamo is the devil! (*Then his expression abruptly changing again—fiercely.*) But I'll make the old fool get down on his knees to her yet before I'm through with him! And I'll make you, too, Ada!

(*This puts a sudden idea into his head—thinking excitedly.*) What made me say that? . . . you, Mother? . . . make her pray to you? . . . not only conquer her flesh, but convert her? . . .

90

Listen to me, Ada ! To-night the miracle will happen !—and then there will be only the kingdom of happiness on earth—my kingdom !—for us, Ada ! (*Then suddenly grabbing her by the arm.*) Only you've got to help me !

ADA (*thinking frightenedly*). For God's sake, what's come over him ! . . . the damned dynamo ! . . . it's driving him crazy ! . . .

(*She puts her arms around him pityingly and tries to hug him to her.*) I'll do anything, Rube ! Don't you know how much I love you ?

REUBEN (*pushing her away from him—in a stammering panic*). Don't do that ! (*Then pleadingly.*) Why can't you understand ? You've got to believe in Dynamo, and bow down to her will ?

ADA (*soothingly*). All right, Rube.

REUBEN (*taking her hand—insistently*). Come with me ! I want to explain everything to you —all this plant means about her—you've got to believe, Ada ! (*She follows him off left, frightened but pitying and resolved to humour him. His voice is heard explaining excitedly as they climb the path to the dam. It recedes and then grows louder as they cross from the dam to the dynamo-room roof. A moment later he is seen there. He comes forward until he stands by the coping, front. He still has Ada by the hand. She follows him, holding back as much as she dares, a nervous look on her face. His unnatural excitement has increased, he looks around*)

91

*him with the rapt expression of one in a trance, his eyes burning feverishly.*) Oh, Ada, you simply can't help believing in her! You only have to listen to her! Her song is the hymn of eternal generation, the song of eternal life!

ADA (*uneasily*). Rube! I'm scared up here!

REUBEN (*turns and looks at her like a sleep-walker for a second—then with a sudden hungry passion*). You're so damned pretty! God, how I wish the miracle was over and we could—— !

ADA (*persuasively*). I'm scared on this roof, Rube. Let's go down!

REUBEN (*excitedly*). Yes, down to her! I was forgetting her! She's waiting for me!

> (*Then as she starts to go back the way they have come, he takes her hand again and pulls her through the door from the roof to the galleries.*)

ADA (*frightenedly*). Rube! I don't want to go——

> (*He slams the door behind them.*)

> (*There is a pause of darkness here to indicate the end of* SCENE ONE. *No time elapses between* SCENES ONE *and* TWO.)

# DYNAMO

## SCENE TWO

SCENE. *When the light comes on again the interiors of the upper and lower switch galleries are revealed. The lower gallery of the oil switches is a deep but narrow compartment with red brick walls. The oil switches, with their spindly steel legs, their square criss-crossed steel bodies (the containers inside looking like bellies), their six cupped arms stretching upward, remind one of Hindu idols tortured into scientific supplications. These switches extend in a straight row backward down the middle of the gallery, but in the dim light of one bulb in a bracket in the left wall only the front one in the foreground can be made out. Against the wall on the right is a stairway that extends backwards half-way up this wall, then turns and ascends diagonally upwards to the left to the upper gallery, and from thence up to the door to the roof of the dynamo room.*

*The upper gallery contains the disconnecting switches and the double busses. It is of double width and extends over the switchboard room also. This second gallery, dimly lighted like the one below, is a fretwork of wires, steel work, insulators, busses, switches, etc., stretching upward to the roof. Below the disconnecting switches is a raised platform.*

*Reuben and Ada are discovered by the dim light of this upper gallery standing just inside*

93

*the door to the dynamo-room roof at the top of the stairway.*

ADA (*looking around her frightenedly at the weird-shaped shadows of the equipment writhing upward in the dimly lighted gallery—shrinking close to Reuben, who is staring at all this with a rapt, questioning, listening look*). All this stuff scares me. I've only seen it in daylight before. It looks so weird—as if it was alive!

REUBEN (*strangely*). You're beginning to see, Ada! It is alive! Alive with the mighty spirit of her eternal life! (*Then with a start, he pushes her away from him roughly.*) What the hell are you doing? Don't press against me, I tell you! I'm wise to your dirty game—and I won't stand for it! Don't you realize we're in her temple now!

ADA (*pityfully*). Rube! Please don't talk like that—when you know how I love you!

REUBEN (*clutching her arm fiercely*). You mustn't say you love me in here, you fool, you! Don't you know all this is watching—listening—that she knows everything! Sssh! I want to hear if she's angry at me! (*He stands in a strained attitude of attention, listening to the dynamo's hum sounding from below—then evidently satisfied, turns to Ada with a relieved air.*) No, she isn't angry on account of you being here because she knows you're beginning to believe in her! It's all right for you to come close to me, Ada. (*He puts an arm around her and pulls her to him.*)

ADA (*persuasively*). Please let's go down, Rube.

REUBEN (*gently*). All right, Ada. (*They go down the first flight of steps. He stops as they get to the bottom and glances up and around him.*) You know, Ada, there used to be times when I was scared here too—when all these switches and busses and wires seemed like the arms of a devil fish—stretching out to suck me in—— (*He gives a shudder and presses her to him.*)

ADA (*soothingly*). You mustn't be afraid. I'm here with you.

REUBEN (*pleadingly—pointing to the platform beneath the disconnecting switches*). Listen, Ada! I want you to pray to her—up there where I pray sometimes—under her arms—with your arms like her arms, stretching out for me! (*He suddenly bends his face to her face, his eyes devouring it desirously.*) God, you're pretty! (*He controls himself with a violent effort and pushes her away from him, keeping his face averted from hers—in a voice that is almost supplicating.*) You must pray that she may find me worthy. You must pray for me, if you love me!

ADA (*soothingly—humouring him*). All right, Rube. (*She goes up the stairs to the platform and stands directly under the switches.*)

REUBEN (*remains standing below—thinking confusedly*). Mother would warn me if I was doing wrong . . . Dynamo means all this to happen to me . . . it's the great temptation . . . perhaps she wants me even to kiss Ada . . .

> (*He ascends to the platform and stands holding on to the rail, afraid to look at Ada.*)

ADA (*stretching her arms up, in the same position as the switch arms—tenderly and soothingly*). Why did you say a minute ago, if I loved you? Don't you know I do? Why have you stayed away from me so long, Rube? I've almost died, longing for you!

REUBEN (*without looking at her—dazedly*). You believe in her now, don't you? You wouldn't do anything to make me unworthy in her sight, would you?—when it means happiness for me—and for all mankind? You couldn't, could you?

ADA (*humouring him—gently*). Of course not.

REUBEN (*mechanically*). You swear to her?

ADA (*in the same tone*). Yes, I swear.

REUBEN (*mechanically*). Then I'm going to kiss you, Ada—just once—only kiss you—she wants me to—as a final test—to prove I'm purified— (*He looks up at her now and lurches forward with a groan of passion and takes her in his arms.*) Ada!

> (*He kisses her frantically, bending her backward and down toward the floor of the platform. She cries out frightenedly.*)

# DYNAMO

*(There is a pause of darkness to indicate
the end of* SCENE TWO. *A short time
is supposed to elapse between* SCENES
TWO *and* THREE.)*

## SCENE THREE

SCENE. *As the light slowly comes on again, Reuben
is heard sobbing brokenly from the gallery. The
interiors of the dynamo and switchboard rooms
are now also revealed.*

*The dynamo room is high and wide with red
brick walls and a row of great windows in the
left wall. The floor and an observation balcony
which projects into the dynamo room from the
switchboard room on the right (one story up), are
of concrete. The nearest dynamo, which we
have seen previously through the doorway,
occupies most of the floor space in the foreground.
A steel ladder runs up its side on the right to a
platform around the exciter.*

*The switchboard room is a small compartment
to the right of the dynamo room, one story up in
the other section of the building. In it are the
switchboard and a couple of chairs. It is
lighted by a shaded drop light over the desk.
Jennings, the operator on duty, a man of thirty
or so, is seated at the desk.*

*Mrs. Fife is sitting in the dynamo room just
under and to the left of the observation balcony.
She is staring dreamily at the front dynamo,*

97

*humming to herself, her big body relaxed as if she had given herself up completely to the spell of its hypnotic, metallic purr which flows insistently through the ears, numbing the brain, charging the nerves with electricity, making the heart strain with the desire to beat in its rhythm of unbroken, eternal continuity.*

*In the gallery, Ada and Reuben are still on the platform beneath the disconnecting switches. Reuben is on his knees, his back bowed, his face covered by his hands. Ada is standing before him, directly beneath the switches as before. She is bending over him in a tender attitude, one hand reaching down, the fingers touching his hair.*

REUBEN (*thinking torturedly*). Mother ! . . . I've betrayed you . . . you will never bless me with the miracle now ! . . . you have shut me from your heart for ever ! . . .

(*He groans and beats his head against the floor.*)

ADA (*puts her hand down and pats him on the back consolingly*). Poor Rube ! Why do you think about things so much ? I love you. Why don't you be happy ?

REUBEN (*shrinking away*). Don't touch me— ever again !

(*He springs to his feet, and shielding his face with one hand from the sight of her, runs down the stairs to the lower oil switch gallery. He stops there, look-*

98

*ing around him distractedly as if he didn't know
where to hide, his thoughts hounded by remorse.*)
Mother! . . . have mercy on me! . . . I hate her
now! . . . as much as you hate her! . . . give
me one more chance! . . . what can I do to get
you to forgive me? . . . tell me! . . . yes! . . .
I hear you, Mother! . . . and then you'll forgive
me? . . . and I can come to you? . . . (*A terrible look of murder comes on his face. He starts for
the stairs, his hands outstretched as if he were already
strangling her—then stops.*) No . . . not with
my hands . . . never touch her flesh again . . .
how? . . . I see . . . switchboard room . . .
in the desk. . . .

(*He dashes over into the switchboard room through
the door at left of the gallery. He has the startled
and terrified Jennings by the throat before the latter
knows it and flings him away from the desk, tears out
a drawer and gets the revolver and with it motions
him to the door to the office in the rear.*)   Get in
there!   Quick!

(*Jennings obeys hastily. Reuben turns the key in
the lock after him. In contrast to his furious haste of
a moment before, he now walks deliberately back
through the door to the oil switch gallery. His face
is as drained of all human feeling as a plaster mask.*)
I won't be a murderer . . . I'm your executioner,
Mother . . . that's why I'm so calm . . .

(*He glides stealthily across toward the foot of
the stairs.*)

ADA (*worried about him, has come down from the
platform and is beginning to descend the stairs to the*

99

*lower switch gallery—she calls uneasily).* Rube !
Where are you ?

REUBEN. Harlot ! . . . that's what Mother
called her !

(*He springs up the stairs, shouting fiercely.*) Harlot !

ADA (*she suddenly sees his face and the revolver
aimed at her breast as he stops directly beneath her—
in a terrified whisper*). Rube !

> (*Reuben fires, and she jerks back and pitches
> sideways on the stairs, dead.*)

REUBEN (*stares down at her body for a moment and
lets the gun fall from his hand and begins to tremble
all over. He calls pitifully*). Ada ! I didn't
mean to hurt you !

> (*Then thinking with an anguished appeal.*)
> Mother ! . . . where are you ? . . . I did it for
> your sake ! . . . why don't you call to me ? . . .
> don't leave me alone ! . . .

> (*He turns and runs headlong through the
> switchboard room, and down the stairs
> to the dynamo-room floor, where he
> lunges for the rungs on the dynamo's
> side and clambers-up frenziedly. Up
> on the platform, he stops for a moment,
> gasping for breath, stretching out his
> arms to the exciter-head of his Dynamo-
> Mother with its whirling metal brain
> and its blank oblong eyes.*)

MRS. FIFE (*dimly aware of him—dreamily*).

What was that noise up there, Reuben? It sounded like a shot.

REUBEN (*pleading like a little boy*). I don't want any miracle, Mother! I don't want to know the truth! I only want you to hide me, Mother! Never let me go from you again! Please, Mother!

> (*He throws his arms out over the exciter, his hands grasp the carbon brushes. There is a flash of bluish light about him and all the lights in the plant dim down until they are almost out and the noise of the dynamo dies until it is the faintest purring hum. Simultaneously Reuben's voice rises in a moan that is a mingling of pain and loving consummation, and this cry dies into a sound that is like the crooning of a baby and merges and is lost in the dynamo's hum. Then his body crumples to the steel platform and from there falls heavily to the floor. There is a startled cry from Mrs. Fife as she runs to the body. The dynamo's throaty metallic purr rises slowly in volume and the lights begin to come up again in the plant.*)

MRS. FIFE (*kneeling beside Reuben, one hand on the forehead of his upturned face*). Poor Reuben! She wouldn't tell you the secret after all, would she? (*She gets to her feet and stares with childish resentment and hurt at the dynamo.*) What are you

singing for ?   I should think you'd be ashamed !
And I thought you was nice and loved us !
(*The dynamo's purr has regained its accustomed pitch
now.   The lights in the plant are again at their full
brightness.   Everything is as before.   Mrs. Fife goes
over and pounds the steel body of the dynamo in a fit
of childish anger.*)   You hateful old thing, you !
(*Then she leaves off, having hurt her hands, and
begins to cry softly.*)

CURTAIN